Abortion after *Roe*

STUDIES IN SOCIAL MEDICINE
Allan M. Brandt, Larry R. Churchill, and
Jonathan Oberlander, editors

This series publishes books at the intersection of medicine, health, and
society that further our understanding of how medicine and society
shape one another historically, politically, and ethically. The series
is grounded in the convictions that medicine is a social science, that
medicine is humanistic and cultural as well as biological, and that it
should be studied as a social, political, ethical, and economic force.

Abortion
after *Roe*

JOHANNA SCHOEN

The University of North Carolina Press   Chapel Hill

*This volume was published with the assistance of the
Greensboro Women's Fund of the University of North Carolina Press.*
Founding Contributors: Linda Arnold Carlisle, Sally Schindel Cone,
Anne Faircloth, Bonnie McElveen Hunter, Linda Bullard Jennings,
Janice J. Kerley (in honor of Margaret Supplee Smith), Nancy Rouzer
May, and Betty Hughes Nichols.

Set in Miller by Tseng Information Systems, Inc.
Manufactured in the United States of America

The paper in this book meets the guidelines for permanence and
durability of the Committee on Production Guidelines for Book
Longevity of the Council on Library Resources. The University of
North Carolina Press has been a member of the Green Press
Initiative since 2003.

Jacket illustration: © Thinkstock.com/hi-studios hi-studios

Library of Congress Cataloging-in-Publication Data
Schoen, Johanna, author.
Abortion after Roe / Johanna Schoen.
pages cm. — (Studies in social medicine)
Includes bibliographical references and index.
ISBN 978-1-4696-2118-0 (cloth : alk. paper) —
ISBN 978-1-4696-2119-7 (ebook)
1. Abortion—Social aspects—United States. 2. Abortion—Political
aspects—United States. 3. Abortion—United States—Public opinion.
4. Abortion—Government policy—United States. 5. Abortion services—
United States. 6. Pro-life movement—United States. 7. Dilatation and
extraction abortion—United States. I. Title. II. Series: Studies in social
medicine.
HQ767.5.U5S36 2015
362.1988'80973—dc23
2015018009

To Alison, with all my love

The Potential for Human Life is enormous. Women are born with 80,000 eggs—can only use a few, men waste millions of sperm every time they ejaculate, and nature herself aborts 1 in every 5 pregnancies. For me the issue is not how to actualize all that life potential, but how to rid the world of ignorance and violence and poverty so that people born into it can lead productive and happy lives.

—TERRY BERESFORD

CONTENTS

ILLUSTRATIONS

ACKNOWLEDGMENTS

It is with great excitement that I finally turn to the part of the book where I can thank all of those who have helped me get to this point. It took more than a decade to research and write this book, and my debts are long-standing and wide-ranging.

Anyone researching and writing about abortion knows that it is almost impossible to secure funding for a project like this. Frequently, funding applications are either ignored or returned with comments indicating that reviewers find the topic too sensitive. Given this situation, I am extremely grateful for the funding that I did receive. In the early years of the project, the American Philosophical Society and the Iowa Arts and Humanities Initiative helped support several summers of research. The Sexuality Research Fellowship Program of the Social Science Research Council, with funds provided by the Ford Foundation, offered me a year off for research. The University of Iowa gave me a three-semester Faculty Scholar Award with leave time to finish the research and begin to write this book. After my move to Rutgers University in 2011, the Institute for Health, Health Care Policy, and Aging Research generously provided a teaching reduction for two semesters to facilitate the completion of this project. Without all of these, this book might never have seen the light of day.

My intellectual debts for this project go to Rosalind Petchesky and Carole Joffe, whose work on abortion stood as early models for me. Carole encouraged me to join the National Abortion Federation. The NAF community, initially puzzled by the presence of a historian, generously shared information. Members told me their stories, formally and informally. Stan Henshaw shared data from the Alan Guttmacher Institute and helped me figure out how to read it. Terry Beresford, Renee Chelian, Takey Crist, Chuck deProsse, Ron Fitzsimmons, Warren Hern, the late Susan Hill, Jerry Hulka, Claire Keyes, Frances Kissling, Uta Landy, Lynn Randall, Ann Rose, Charlotte Taft, Francine Thompson, Robert Thompson, Rosa Tilley, the late Morris Turner, Susan Wicklund, and Elinor Yeo agreed to be interviewed and were generous with their time and insights. Many also shared papers, pictures, and other mementos to help with my research. In addition, many others sat with me at panels, answered countless questions, and made me feel part of the organization. Thanks go especially to Curtis and Glenna Boyd, Marc Heller, Lisa Harris, Peg Johnston, Willie Parker, the late Robin Rothrock, Shelley Sella, and Tracy Weitz.

The wonderful group of medical historians who annually convene at the meetings of the American Association for the History of Medicine cheered me on and helped me figure out what I wanted to say about the topic. Special thanks go to Susan Reverby and Judy Houck, who read portions of the manuscript, providing support and encouragement. Leslie Reagan and Naomi Rogers read the entire manuscript and offered many useful suggestions. All of them helped to make this a better book.

A number of archivists helped with the research and facilitated the deposition of the records of abortion providers. At Duke University, Christina Favretto and Laura Micham from the Sally Bingham Center for Women's History and Culture were glad to give a home to the manuscript collections of abortion providers and supported this project from the very beginning. At the University of Iowa Women's Archive, Kären Mason and Janet Weaver guided me through the papers of the Emma Goldman Clinic, retrieved many boxes, and answered endless questions. Karen Kubby and Francine Thompson helped with research on the Emma Goldman Clinic collective and unearthed additional materials.

In Jacksonville, North Carolina, Marion Goodman and Mark Goodman offered me a home away from home during many weeks when I was processing and researching the papers of Takey Crist. Anne Joyner and Allan Parnell did the same in Mebane, North Carolina. To make me feel even more at home, they also offered me their pastures to mow—a very therapeutic experience after any ten-day stint processing manuscript collections—a hot tub, many walks, and food so delicious that I gave up being a vegetarian. Jackie Hall and Bob Korstadt were always ready for a glass of wine when I turned up on my research trips to North Carolina, and they offered a patient ear, helpful suggestions, and much support. During several Montana summers, Mary Murphy became a wonderful friend who offered many hours of conversation and whose love and support sustained me.

Several of my graduate students at the University of Iowa spent countless hours transcribing oral history interviews and helping with other research tasks. Thanks go to Jo Butterfield, Anna Flaming, Karissa Haugeberg, and Angela Keysor. Colleagues at Iowa offered support and invaluable feedback on the early stages of this project. Jennifer Glass, Linda Kerber, and Susan Lawrence heard, read, and commented on various drafts. Jennifer Sessions, Michaela Hoenicke Moore, Michael Moore, Glenn Penny, Jackie Blank, and Carl Claus offered friendship and many meals. David Kearns provided crucial support in helping me balance the personal and professional. At Rutgers University, James Reed read early versions of several chapters and told me to keep on writing. Cynthia Daniels read the manuscript and offered critical comments. Jesse Bayker and Amy Zanoni offered research help. Jennifer Jones, Jennifer Mittlestadt, and Marisa Fuentes provided me with writing accountability, support, and friendship. Carol Boyer, Barbara Cooper, Ann Fabian, Janet Golden, Jochen Hellbeck, Seth Koven, and Donna Murch also offered their friendship and support and quickly made Rutgers and the east coast feel like home. Doug Greenberg, Jim Masschaele, and Mark Wasserman offered encouragement and support. Olin and Sylvia Gentry and Courtney Doucette took me away from my work and offered friendship and entertainment during my Philadelphia years.

This book had many informal editors, all of whom were awesome. Kennie Lyman read the entire manuscript and made invaluable suggestions for organization and reorganization. Sian Hunter originally solicited this manuscript for UNC Press, and Kate Torrey shepherded it through the beginning stages. Joe Parsons, my editor at UNC Press, and his assistant, Allie Shay, went above and beyond when I struggled to finish during a family crisis. Nancy Raynor caught last mistakes and helped me fix my endnotes.

Lisa and Josh Heineman saw this book grow from an idea into a finished product. They sustained me—through easy and hard times. Over the last months, Josh and I joked who would be finished first: he with his animation or I with my book. Josh won! At the last minute, Alison Bernstein came along and offered loving support. She read the entire manuscript, made insightful comments at the very end stages, and cheered me on to the finish line.

ABBREVIATIONS AND ACRONYMS
USED IN THE TEXT

BCH	Boston City Hospital
CDC	Center for Disease Control (now the Centers for Disease Control and Prevention)
CPC	crisis pregnancy center
CRSH	Center for Reproductive and Sexual Health
D&C	dilation and curettage
D&E	dilation and evacuation
EGC	Emma Goldman Clinic
FACE	Freedom of Access to Clinic Entrances
FOCA	Freedom of Choice Act
FWHC	Feminist Women's Health Center
FWHO	Fargo Women's Health Organization
FWWHO	Fort Wayne Women's Health Organization
IUD	intrauterine device
LIFE	Life Is For Everyone Coalition
NAAF	National Association of Abortion Facilities
NAC	National Abortion Council
NAF	National Abortion Federation
NARAL	National Abortion Rights Action League
NCAP	National Coalition of Abortion Providers
NIH	National Institute of Health
NJWHO	New Jersey Women's Health Organization
NOW	National Organization for Women
NRLC	National Right to Life Committee
NWHO	National Women's Health Organization
ob-gyn	obstetrics and gynecology; obstetrician-gynecologist
OR	Operation Rescue
PPFA	Planned Parenthood Federation of America
UNC	University of North Carolina
WEBA	Women Exploited by Abortion

Introduction

In the early 1970s, Heather, an eighteen-year-old student at the University of North Carolina (UNC), went to see Takey Crist, an assistant professor of obstetrics and gynecology (ob-gyn), known on campus as "the sex man." Heather was pregnant and told Crist about her attempt earlier that year to get a prescription for the birth control pill at the student infirmary. The physician she saw told her that

> he didn't give contraceptives, and that the infirmary itself didn't give contraceptives out to unmarried people. And then he said, did I want to talk about it [her decision to become sexually active], or had I already made up my mind? And I said that I had pretty much made up my mind. And he said, "Well, you know, I like sex just as much as any other normal person." And then he said, "It's like a glass of wine, you don't guzzle it, in the same way you don't use sex to excess." And I just listened to him for a few more minutes, or rather, I didn't listen to him for a few more minutes. And then I left.[1]

Humiliated and frustrated, Heather gave up on her attempts to seek birth control. After several months of unprotected sex, she became pregnant and ended up in Takey Crist's office.

Young single women who sought contraceptive advice and sex education during the late 1960s and early 1970s tended to find all doors closed. Lacking training in this area, most physicians felt uncomfortable with issues of sexuality and considered prescribing contraceptives to single women immoral. A 1970 survey by the American College Health Association found that of 531 institutions of higher education, half prescribed contraceptives to their students but less than 10 percent did so for unmarried minors.[2] In many states, North Carolina included, the age of majority was 21. High school and college students who sought medical care thus needed parental consent even for their most intimate health care needs.[3] Most college-age women at UNC came from small North Carolina towns and had grown up steeped in religious values critical of premarital sex. As a result, they frequently felt they could not discuss their sexual activity with their parents. Susan Hill, who attended Meredith College in Raleigh, North Carolina, in the late 1960s, remembers that a lot of girls worried about their lack of access to birth control. "There weren't health clinics where you could walk in and get birth control. There was no Planned Parenthood in town. Your private doctors, you couldn't trust them. . . . You were afraid they would tell your parents. So we were aware of [birth control] and virtually unable to get it."[4]

In the late 1960s and early 1970s, young college students who discovered that they were pregnant worried about their parents' reaction and understood that an unwanted pregnancy could jeopardize their educational future. One young man described in an anguished letter to Crist how he and his pregnant girlfriend had approached his girlfriend's mother to ask for her consent to an abortion—by 1971, after a recent reform of the state's abortion laws, available to young women with parental consent.[5] But rather than help the couple obtain an abortion, the mother forced her daughter to return home and, after the young man tried repeatedly to reason with her, moved herself and her daughter without leaving a forwarding address. "I cannot even write to her anymore," he deplored, and concluded: "My girlfriend could still be in school today if we could have gotten an abortion."[6] Women students feared that parents would kick them out of the house or force them to return home before they could finish their college education. Many had witnessed the shocked reactions of parents when a sister or a brother's girlfriend got pregnant. "It was like hell in the family," one student recalled as she explained to Takey Crist why she could not tell her parents about her own unwanted pregnancy after her brother's girlfriend had gotten pregnant.[7] Children worried about the loss of financial or other support from their parents and concluded, as one girl noted, that their parents "would probably hate me for the rest of my life" if they found out about their unintended pregnancy.[8] Others feared their parents might become violent. After one father repeatedly told his daughter that if she ever got pregnant, she "wouldn't be able to marry the guy—because he would have killed him," the daughter was in despair when she did get pregnant. "My father is generally very levelheaded," she explained to Dr. Crist, "and it takes a lot to make him mad, but I know that would push him right past the limit."[9] Even students who did not fear their parents' scorn felt that knowledge of a pregnancy outside marriage would cause their parents unnecessary anguish and disappointment.[10] "The fear of telling our parents was worse than the fear of the abortionist," Hill remembered. "Being pregnant back then was worse."[11]

Young women who saw their friends kicked out of school as a result of an unwanted pregnancy often remembered the circumstances of their friends' expulsion for years after. Susan Hill recalled a Meredith College student who had gone to Cheraw, South Carolina, for an illegal abortion. She returned in the middle of the night with a severe infection. Her friends took the sick girl, who was barely able to walk, to the Meredith College infirmary from where she was quickly expelled. "We never saw her again," Susan Hill remembered. "They treated her and she left and we never saw her again. And for weeks, no one would tell us what had happened to her. Finally we heard she'd been packed up and sent home. . . . She just disappeared once they knew what she'd done. It's like she never existed."[12] It did not take many stories like these for women students to understand that an unwanted pregnancy during their college years posed a serious threat to their future.

Of course, unwanted pregnancy was not an experience limited to young college-age women. Women of all backgrounds experienced unwanted pregnancies, and many of them sought an abortion even when the procedure was illegal. In the mid-1950s, estimates of the number of illegal abortions ranged anywhere from 200,000 to 1.2 million a year. Among urban, white, educated women, Alfred Kinsey found in his 1958 study of women's sexual behavior that one-fifth to one-fourth of all pregnancies ended in abortion. The abortion rate climbed to 28 percent of all pregnancies among young wives between sixteen and twenty years old and to 79 percent among separated, divorced, and widowed women of all ages. Journalist Lawrence Lader noted in the mid-1960s that only about 8,000 abortions annually took place inside a hospital, constituting a fraction of the number of abortions performed each year.[13] Some women seeking illegal abortions were fortunate to find a skilled abortion provider. Across the country, physicians, nurses, and midwives, among others, practiced in secrecy, offering thousands of illegal abortions. In his 1966 book, *Abortion*, Lader lists twenty-nine states in which he was able to locate at least one skilled abortionist. Women also traveled abroad to seek abortions in Mexico, Puerto Rico, and England or as far away as Japan. But in most places the practice of skilled illegal providers was shrouded in secrecy, and not all women seeking illegal abortions were able to afford their fees, let alone travel to foreign locations.[14] Those without resources, poor white women as well as African American, Hispanic, and immigrant women, were forced to enter a world of underground abortions where care was frequently humiliating and the procedures dangerous. "Its practitioners," Lader cautioned, "preying mainly on poor and ignorant women, rarely have a medical degree. In an analysis of 111 consecutive convictions [of underground abortionists] in New York County, less than a third were physicians. The remaining two-thirds boasted such non-medical occupations as clerks, barbers, and salesmen."[15] Before the mid-1960s, the estimated mortality rate from illegal abortion stood at 1,000 to 8,000 deaths per year. Almost 80 percent of all abortion deaths occurred among non-white women.[16]

With eye-catching headlines and photos, often on the front page of newspapers, journalists described an underground world that connected illegal abortion to organized crime syndicates. Such press coverage not only thrilled the public, historian Leslie J. Reagan notes, but also threatened women, physicians, and others engaged in illegal abortion with arrest and exposure.[17] Other more serious investigations into illegal abortion drew attention to the devastating impact that criminal abortion laws had on women's health and lives and argued for reform. Lader charged that criminal abortion laws contributed to a system in which minority groups, the poor, and the unsuspecting were punished doubly. "No study," Lader noted, "could begin to measure the physical and psychological injury inflicted on women by quack abortionists, often virtual butchers. Nor could it encompass the damage women inflict on themselves in attempts at self-abortion."[18]

Despite these grim statistics, countless women concluded that seeking an illegal abortion was preferable to carrying an unwanted pregnancy to term. "The search for a skilled abortionist," Lader noted, "may be the most desperate period in a woman's life."[19] Women were often resourceful and asked around to locate an underground abortion provider. Many asked friends or any close medical contacts they might have or turned to their family physician or obstetrician for help. Susan Hill remembered that students at Meredith College had a map directing them to a doctor in Cheraw, South Carolina, who charged $600 cash for an illegal abortion.[20] Others, however, searched for weeks without success, losing valuable time, which made the abortion procedure more difficult—and thus riskier—as pregnancy progressed.

It Was Very Oppressive for Women: Sexism in Medicine

Women's frustration with the medical profession was not limited to worries about access to contraception and abortion. Women of all age groups found their physicians unresponsive to their health care needs and unwilling to address their concerns. Their frustration with the medical profession stood out most clearly in women's relationships with their ob-gyns, most of whom were male. Since they were the specialists responsible for women's most intimate health care needs, the personal demeanor and attitude of obstetricians and gynecologists toward women and sexuality were crucial to women's comfort. "A physician's personal outlook and even his sexual bias can change a routine pelvic examination from a mildly embarrassing or uncomfortable experience into one that is demeaning and humiliating," an article in *Modern Medicine* warned.[21] One prominent female ob-gyn noted about women patients' comments concerning their (mostly male) physicians: "One often sees such comments as: 'He doesn't explain anything to me.' 'He treats me like an ignorant and somewhat stupid child.' 'He can't seem to understand or relate to any of my emotional needs and problems.'"[22] Medical education contributed to this state of affairs. Into the 1970s, many ob-gyn textbooks taught medical students that most of women's complaints were the result of neuroses rather than symptoms of disease. Couched in a Freudian framework, the 1971 edition of *Obstetrics and Gynecology*, for instance, advised medical students that many symptoms of illness in pregnancy, such as excessive nausea or headache, are really a result of her "fear that the rewards [of pregnancy] will be denied because of past sins."[23]

Matters improved little once medical students left their textbooks behind and entered residency programs. Teaching practices frequently reinforced the notion that physicians need not listen to their patients. To teach residents at large teaching institutions how to conduct pelvic exams, for instance, instructors hid the woman's upper body behind a screen or curtain or put a bag over her head so that the resident did not have to learn a patient's identity or interact with her.[24] Indeed, medical students into the 1980s recalled learning how to perform pelvic exams at major university hospitals on patients who had been anesthetized for unrelated procedures.[25] As a result, many physicians were at best uncomfortable with their patients, at worst paternalistic and patriarchal. "It was very oppressive to women," a member of Iowa City's feminist health collective, the Emma Goldman Clinic (EGC), remembered.[26]

Starting in the late 1960s, women across the country began to challenge the patriarchal attitude of medical professionals. They complained to more sympathetic physicians about the demeaning behavior of their colleagues and came together to discuss their health care providers and search for answers to their medical questions. A group of women in Boston began to discuss childbirth, sexuality, and their doctors, whom they found "condescending, paternalistic, judgmental, and non-informative."[27] Group members researched and educated one another on a number of topics relating to women's health and in December of 1970 published the results under the title *Women and Their Bodies*, which three years later became better known as *Our Bodies, Ourselves*.[28] Women in Chicago formed Jane, an underground abortion referral service. Frustrated with the cost of abortion and their inability to ensure that women were not exploited by underground abortionists, Jane members quickly moved from counseling and referral to performing the abortions themselves. Between 1969 and 1973, almost 11,000 women received abortions through Jane. This, Jane members concluded, is how the procedure ought to be done: by women, for women, as acts of liberation and empowerment.[29] Women in San Francisco passed out a leaflet with the names of physicians in Mexico and Japan who performed abortions. As demand for the list soared, feminists in California established the Association to Repeal Abortion Laws and created mechanisms for regulating illegal abortion practices so as to ensure that they were sending women to safe practitioners.[30] In Los Angeles, Carol Downer, a housewife turned health activist, began to teach women how to perform cervical self-exams. In the fall of 1971, Downer and Lorraine Rothman, who had developed a menstrual extraction kit, the Del-Em, embarked on a twenty-three-city tour across the United States to demonstrate cervical self-exams and menstrual extraction and encourage women to start their own clinics.[31] They traveled to Iowa City, Iowa, for instance, where they taught a group of young feminists about cervical self-exams and discussed the establishment of women's health clinics. Cervical self-exams and the idea of starting a women's health clinic spread like wildfire. As one Iowa City activist recalls, "We were everywhere with self-help, educating women about their bodies. And I think that part of what we did, and countless other women in this country, *Our Bodies, Ourselves*, has helped young women to not feel as uptight about their bodies."[32]

Men, too, participated in the burgeoning reform movement surrounding sexual and reproductive health. After New York journalist Lawrence Lader found a number of reliable underground abortion providers when he researched *Abortion*, he shared the information with women who wrote to him asking for referrals.[33] Several prominent clergymen decided to establish a referral service to provide women with the names of trust-worthy abortion providers. Within a year, clergy across the country, led by Reverend Howard Moody of Judson Memorial Church in New York City's Greenwich Village, began to organize Clergy Consultation Service chapters across the country. Clergy members trained in "problem preg-nancy" counseling and, like California feminists, conducted extensive interviews and reviews of underground abortion providers to select those who were safe and trustworthy.[34] In the late 1960s, William R. Baird, a thirty-four-year-old medical school dropout and contraceptive salesman, emerged as a crusader for sexual and birth control information on col-lege campuses around the country. In the spring of 1967, students at Bos-ton University invited Baird to speak about sexuality and contraception. After Baird displayed various contraceptives before an audience of more than 2,500 people and gave an unmarried female student a can of Emko contraceptive foam, the Boston vice squad arrested him and charged him with crimes against chastity. Baird used his arrest to draw attention to the repressive attitudes that not only stifled people's intimate lives but also jeopardized women's health. Following his arrest and subsequent court battle, students across the country rallied in support of Baird, holding public demonstrations and demanding reproductive rights for women.[35] Male students offered lectures on birth control to classmates and wrote advice manuals on sexuality and reproduction. They relied on the assis-tance of physicians, psychologists, and educators who began to participate in the establishment of student health services that offered information about sexuality and contraception.[36]

They were joined by progressive physicians who worked to improve their patients' health care experiences. In the late 1960s and early 1970s, for instance, student health services at Brown, Stanford, Harvard, Yale, and the Universities of Illinois, Minnesota, Massachusetts, and Chicago began to offer contraceptive advice. Bolstered not only by growing de-mands from college students but also by increased funding for adoles-cent medicine under the War on Poverty, leaders in adolescent medicine lobbied for a change in state laws permitting minors to consent to treat-ment of sensitive health issues. By the late 1970s, adolescents had obtained the right to obtain contraceptives without parental consent.[37] UNC stood at the center of this change. After the North Carolina legislature passed an abortion reform bill in 1967 that legalized therapeutic abortion if a woman could obtain the support of three physicians, Takey Crist and the Depart-ment of Obstetrics and Gynecology at UNC's Memorial Hospital opened access to abortions and institutionalized sex and contraceptive education and health services on campus.[38] As word spread that physicians were increasingly willing to honor women's abortion requests, many physicians were confronted with patients who would have sought an underground abortion earlier. Students able to access these services expressed their immeasurable sense of relief. As one student wrote to Takey Crist after her abortion, "I have been given a beautiful chance at life again."[39]

By the end of 1972, students received more than contraceptive advice at Student Health. UNC freshmen learned about the availability of these services during freshman orientation. At the Student Stores, they could purchase a copy of the sex education booklet *Elephants and Butterflies*, written by three medical students under the direction of Takey Crist, which provided detailed information on sexuality, reproduction, and contraception and informed students where to turn for birth control and abortion. Students were able to write to the student newspaper, the *Daily Tar Heel*, which published a weekly column, "Questions to the Elephants and Butterflies," in which Crist and student Lana Starnes answered questions about sex. They could seek help from a peer counselor at the Human Sexuality Information and Counseling Service, which held daily office hours at the Student Union, offering advice on any sexual issue imaginable. For a more academic approach, students could enroll in HEED 33, an undergraduate course on human sexuality developed by Takey Crist, or invite Crist to present an evening education program at their dorm, sorority, or fraternity. Finally, they could seek contraceptive advice and therapeutic abortions at the Health Education Clinic established by Crist or call the Clergy Consultation Service (all phone numbers were listed in the back of *Elephants and Butterflies*) for a referral to abortion services in Washington, D.C., or New York State.[40]

This literal explosion of sex education services was part of a small but growing trend on campuses across the country. If, in the 1960s, state laws outlawing the distribution of contraceptives to unwed minors had significantly limited access to birth control information and devices, the 1972 Supreme Court decision *Eisenstadt v. Baird* greatly aided efforts to establish reproductive health services on college campuses. "If the right of privacy means anything," the decision read, "it is the right of the individual, married or single, to be free from unwarranted governmental intrusion into matters so fundamentally affecting a person as the decision whether to bear or beget a child."[41] In response to student interest, Planned Parenthood–World Population initiated a program of student community action to acquaint college students with the latest contraceptive techniques and devices and provide them with a vehicle for establishing contraceptive services on college campuses.[42] Whereas a 1966 survey conducted by the American College Health Association had found that physicians at only thirteen U.S. colleges and universities prescribed oral contraceptives to unmarried students, and most of these did so only for women over the age of twenty-one, by 1970 the association counted 118 institutions offering contraceptive services. Still, as historian Heather Prescott has pointed out, this was a small percentage of the more than 2,500 U.S. colleges and universities at the time.[43]

The Making of Roe v. Wade

A number of factors converged by the 1960s to set the stage for abortion reform. Responding to medical complaints about the lack of clear legal guidelines, the American Law Institute, made up of attorneys, judges, and law professors, proposed a model abortion law in 1959 that would clarify the legal exception for therapeutic abortion and enshrine it in law along more liberal lines. During the following decade, legal and medical organizations promoted the law institute's model in state legislatures and in the media. Women's rising labor force participation and college attendance contributed to falling birthrates and climbing abortion rates. Their growing need for access to safe abortion services became painfully evident to the medical professionals who were staffing the nation's emergency rooms and taking care of women who had obtained illegal abortions. The specter of women dying as a result of illegal abortions propelled activists who hoped to protect the lives of women by making therapeutic abortion more accessible.[44]

In 1962, the Sherri Finkbine case raised public awareness of the dangers of thalidomide, a tranquilizer that could cause fetal defects, and inaugurated a nationwide debate about the use of abortion to avoid birth defects. Finkbine, the host of a popular children's TV show, feared for her pregnancy after taking thalidomide and planned to have a therapeutic abortion performed by her physician. But her plan was thwarted when her situation became news and the hospital backed away. Finkbine, whose case became national and international news, subsequently traveled abroad for an abortion. Fears about the dangers of thalidomide were closely followed by a German measles epidemic that hit the United States in 1963. The ensuing debate not only altered national consciousness concerning abortion but also played a crucial role in emerging reform efforts.[45] In 1964 a group of prominent physicians, lawyers, clergy, and others established the Association for the Study of Abortion, which used the influence of its many experts to educate the public about abortion reform.[46] By the end of the decade, feminists began to organize to put pressure on the medical profession and state legislatures to repeal abortion laws.[47]

By the mid-1960s, state legislators across the country were debating abortion reform based on the American Law Institute's model law, and in 1967 Colorado, North Carolina, and California were the first states in the nation to pass reform legislation, closely followed by Alaska, Hawaii, and New York.[48] On April 11, 1970, New York governor Nelson Rockefeller signed a bill legalizing abortion in New York. The bill did not limit access to abortion to residents of New York, and on July 1, 1970, the day the law took effect, over 350 women called the Family Planning Information Service to ask for appointments. Although fewer than 100 of the 2,000 women who registered in New York that first day received legal abortions, over the coming 2 ½ years thousands of women traveled to New York for a legal abortion.[49] And New York was not the only state to legalize abortion. Two court decisions in the fall of 1969 led to abortion reform in California and Washington, D.C. On September 5, 1969, the California Supreme Court, in *People v. Belous*, declared California's abortion law unconstitutional and exonerated physician Dr. Leon Belous, who had been indicted for performing illegal abortions. Following this decision, California hospitals relaxed their abortion policies, and California's physicians increased the number of abortions they performed. By 1972, the state's abortion rate had climbed to 135,000 legal abortions per year, the second highest total behind New York. *People v. Belous* served as a precedent for a score of other challenges to similar state laws. When, two months later, Judge Arnold Gesell declared the District of Columbia abortion law unconstitutional in *United States v. Vuitch* and exonerated Dr. Milan Vuitch for performing illegal abortions, he cited the California decision. Following Gesell's decision, Vuitch established an outpatient abortion clinic a few blocks from the White House with four treatment rooms, a laboratory, and a recovery room. Soon, the clinic was taking 100 abortion cases a week. In 1971, Vuitch—with the help of the National Abortion Rights Action League (NARAL)—opened a model outpatient clinic called Preterm. Preterm was quickly followed by two other outpatient clinics in Washington, D.C., and by the end of 1971, 20,000 women had received legal abortions in Washington, D.C.[50] Developments in California, New York, and Washington, D.C., were followed by a repeal of abortion laws in Hawaii and Alaska shortly thereafter.[51]

On January 22, 1973, the U.S. Supreme Court legalized abortion with its *Roe v. Wade* and *Doe v. Bolton* decisions. The decisions overturned nearly all state abortion regulations existing at the time and expanded the fundamental right of privacy established in 1965 in *Griswold v. Connecticut*—a decision which held that intimate marital decisions around family planning were protected by a right of privacy—to include abortion.[52] Women, however, did not gain a right to legal abortion. Rather, *Roe v. Wade* permitted women, in consultation with their physicians, to decide in the privacy of a physician's office whether or not they wanted to end a pregnancy. Women's and physicians' ability to choose an abortion was not entirely unregulated. The decision set up a trimester framework during which a woman was free of state constraints on her decision if she was in the first twelve weeks of pregnancy. If she was in her second trimester, thirteen to twenty-four weeks, the state could restrict access to abortion only when necessary to protect the woman's health. The court established the twenty-fifth week of pregnancy as a threshold after which it considered the fetus viable and permitted the state to invoke an interest in protecting the fetus and to restrict abortion. However, a state could not restrict abortion when the procedure was deemed necessary to preserve a woman's life or health. In *Doe v. Bolton*, the Supreme Court further removed any requirements that women be a resident of the state in which they sought access to abortion and struck down requirements that abortions be performed in a hospital setting and that women obtain permission from a hospital abortion committee or that two other doctors endorse her physician's recommendation of an abortion.

Since women had no *right* to an abortion procedure, it was their own responsibility to find an abortion provider and pay for the procedure. As a result, women's actual access to abortion procedures emerged as a significant issue. Indeed, the *Roe v. Wade* decision signified the beginning, rather than the end, of a protracted political, legislative, and legal battle over access to abortion. As the antiabortion movement gained strength in the 1970s, antiabortion activists set out to overturn the *Roe v. Wade* decision by introducing a Human Life Amendment and eliminated public funding for any aspect of abortion care with passage of the 1976 Hyde Amendment. Still, throughout the 1970s and 1980s, the U.S. Supreme Court protected abortion as a private choice. The justices pondered two questions: First, what limitations on abortion are permissible under *Roe*? And second, did the right to an abortion require states to support access to the procedure for women who found it difficult to actually obtain an abortion? Initially, as states began to draft laws that would restrict women's access to abortion, the U.S. Supreme Court, in three key decisions, struck down attempts to limit access to abortion. In the first case, *Planned Parenthood of Central Missouri v. Danforth* (1976), the Supreme Court struck down a Missouri law requiring parental consent to a minor's abortion, a husband's written consent to his wife's abortion, a woman's written and informed consent, and a ban on second trimester saline procedures. Seven years later, in *Akron v. Akron Center for Reproductive Health, Inc.* (1983), the court struck down a twenty-four-hour waiting period, a hospitalization requirement for abortions after the first trimester, parental consent to abortions for girls aged fifteen or younger, a doctor-only counseling provision, a requirement that women receive specific information during the counseling session, and strict instructions about the disposal of fetal waste. In the 1986 *Thornburgh v. American College of Obstetricians and Gynecologists* decision—a case that challenged Pennsylvania's 1982 Abortion Control Act—the court rejected a state-mandated counseling script read by doctors to patients, a requirement that doctors attempt to save fetuses in postviability abortions, a requirement that two doctors attend postviability abortions, and a reporting requirement that allowed public access to abortion records.[53]

But because a central premise of the *Roe* ruling holds that a woman lacks a fundamental right to abortion per se, questions of public funding fared less well before the Supreme Court. In two cases, *Maher v. Roe* (1977) and *Harris v. McRae* (1980), the court determined that neither states nor the federal government was obligated to provide abortion funding for the poor. These decisions created an obvious class distinction. All women could choose abortion, but only those able to pay for the procedure could actually realize their choice and obtain an abortion. The cases also signaled the advent of a theory of negative rights that emboldened the pro-life movement. The majority of justices agreed that a woman's access to abortion could be denied through state omission—a lack of financial assistance to poor women—although not through active state-imposed hurdles. The state or federal government could thus legitimately assert its preference for birth over abortion by denying support for abortion.[54]

In 1989, the U.S. Supreme Court also began to shift away from its refusal to allow state-imposed restrictions to abortion. In its *Webster v. Reproductive Health Services* decision, the justices for the first time questioned the trimester framework that had established a protected zone for abortion and had limited states' ability to favor birth over abortion until the third trimester, when the *Roe* decision had considered the fetus to be viable. Now the court argued that, owing to the advancement of medical technology, viability changed over time and place. A fetus not considered viable in 1973 might, with advances in medical technology, be considered viable by the late 1980s. One not viable in a rural community hospital might be considered viable in a sophisticated neonatal unit in an urban hospital. Unwilling to leave the judgment over fetal viability in the hands of physicians, *Webster* asserted that states could express interest in fetal life prior to viability and could withhold state resources to assert this preference. In practice this meant that the state of Missouri was permitted to bar public facilities from offering abortion services. While *Roe* had protected abortion until viability, *Webster* embraced a new vision in which states could now express an interest in fetal life. The Supreme Court now allowed states to second-guess physicians by imposing specific directions and restrictions on abortion services. (*Webster*, for instance, upheld a Missouri provision that required physicians to perform viability tests before performing an abortion.)[55]

The shift away from physician authority to a stronger role of state legislatures in the performance of abortion was further strengthened in the 1992 decision in *Planned Parenthood of Southeastern Pennsylvania v. Casey*. Indeed, states wishing to impose abortion restrictions now simply had to demonstrate that the burden imposed on women's access to abortion was not "undue"—that is, placed no "substantial obstacle in the path of a woman seeking an abortion of a nonviable fetus."[56] This shift greatly undermined doctors' authority in abortion decisions, replacing the physician as gatekeeper to abortion with the state legislature, which could now set very precise terms under which abortions may take place. In *Casey*, the justices permitted abortion barriers that the Supreme Court had found unconstitutional in previous cases: a twenty-four-hour waiting period, state-mandated counseling, parental consent for minors, and a reporting requirement. The court also began to treat women as a group that needed to be protected from their own choices. Upholding state-mandated counseling language, for instance, suggested that women seeking abortions needed counseling, that physicians who counsel women before an abortion needed to be told how to counsel their patients, and that both parties were unreasonable and needed the state to step in.[57] Empowered by *Casey*, Supreme Court justices subsequently further expanded restrictions on abortion. Most significant, the 2007 *Gonzales v. Carhart* decision upheld the first ban on a particular abortion procedure—intact dilation and evacuation (D&E), or the so-called partial birth abortion procedure—without granting an exception to women's health or life. More broadly, for the past two decades states have drafted increasingly inventive legislation to impose all kinds of restrictions on abortion services, ranging from requiring particular building codes to the requirement that abortion providers have privileges at local hospitals to attempts to ban abortions after twenty weeks' gestation.[58] None of these restrictions increased the safety of abortion procedures, which were already the safest outpatient procedures available.[59] All of them made abortion services more difficult to access by placing obstacles in the way for women seeking abortion services or forcing abortion providers to raise their prices to meet burdensome and costly requirements.

Writing the History of Legal Abortion

The topic of abortion has captivated writers for decades. Given that it touches on questions of sex, life, death, and morality, this attention is not surprising. Scholars tracing the history of women's health activism have chronicled the history of feminist challenges to illegal abortion, the emergence of the women's health movement, and the establishment of feminist clinics which emerged as a result.[60] Others have traced the roots of anti-abortion activism, the escalation of violence, and the impact on the pro-choice movement.[61] A third group of scholars have analyzed the impact of policies limiting women's access to abortion. They have charted changes to abortion funding, tracked policies that regulate access to abortion, and analyzed the impact of legal decisions.[62] But despite the fact that policy approaches to abortion and the cultural climate surrounding abortion care underwent a fundamental shift over the past four decades, we lack a comprehensive study of the events that have changed the experiences of abortion care since 1973 and of the impact that these events have had on the abortion experience. For the pre-*Roe* period, the history of abortion is well documented.

Contrary to popular belief, abortion was not always illegal. Until the middle of the nineteenth century, abortion was largely unregulated. Historians have illustrated that anxieties about women's changing roles and declining birth rates, coupled with the desire of ob-gyns to establish themselves as the primary health care providers for women's reproductive needs, led to a public campaign that culminated in the criminalization of abortion by the late nineteenth century.[63] Although abortion remained criminalized until the early 1970s, women continued to seek the procedure. As the twentieth century progressed and law enforcement cracked down on illegal abortion, women obtained illegal abortions at increasingly higher risks to their life and health.[64]

Feminist scholars have noted that changes in medical technology, in particular the widespread dissemination of ultrasound images, significantly shaped the social meaning of pregnancy—and by extension the meaning and experience of pregnancy termination.[65] How abortion providers and their patients understood the provision of abortion care shifted as larger cultural understandings about pregnancy and the fetus changed. If many viewed abortion in the 1970s as central to women's emancipation and a right that women should have, this view began to change in the 1980s as the proliferation of fetal images began to contribute to a reshaping of the public understanding of the fetus. As fetal images gained in prominence, antiabortion activists began to articulate fetal interests and rights and to advance the notion that a fetus might have interests that stand in opposition to the interests of the woman carrying the fetus.[66] Much has been said about the rhetoric and stigma attached to abortion resulting from these changes. But we know little about the impact that this debate has had on the experience of those delivering and receiving abortion care: abortion providers and their patients.

Indeed, anyone researching the history of legal abortion will find the record curiously silent on positive depictions of the abortion experience. The silence surrounding the abortion experience—having one and performing them—has been "a productive taboo," reinforcing myths that abortion is never easy and positive but at best hard, at worst harmful to women.[67] Since the early days of legalization, writers discussing legal abortion have repeated pre-*Roe* tropes that characterized women seeking abortions as mentally deranged and physicians performing abortions as immoral and greedy. Legalization did not remove the shame that came with having an abortion. While women spoke and wrote more openly about their illegal abortions in the years after legalization, they were silent about their legal abortions. In addition, feminists, most likely to break the silence surrounding abortion, were also most critical of the male medical professionals who performed abortions. By the late 1980s, antiabortion writers had begun to dramatize the abortion experience from an antiabortion perspective, and accounts of abortion ranged from ambivalent to hostile. Gory descriptions of abortion procedures successfully pushed women and providers into the defensive, silencing an already taciturn community and leaving abortion providers and their supporters unprepared to defend the integrity and independence of medical practice as it relates to the performance of abortions particularly after the first trimester. Looking back at the rhetoric surrounding legal abortion, one observer noted in 2003 that conservatives, not liberals, had won the struggle around abortion rights.[68]

As the abortion conflict escalated, the increasingly hostile climate colored the experience of abortion providers and patients. The proliferation of negative visual images and the growing number of screaming protestors outside clinics colored the feelings that providers and patients might have about the medical procedure inside the clinic. Images and discourse outside became inevitably linked to and shaped experiences inside the clinic. The antiabortion discourse narrowed the interpretive framework for women and clinic personnel seeking to make sense of their experience and contributed further to the stigmatization of abortion care. In this context, it was, frankly, not acceptable to note that one felt good about one's abortion experience or liked working in an abortion clinic and performing abortion procedures. Indeed, the public reception of a YouTube video posted in spring 2014 by the young abortion counselor Emily Letts who had videotaped her own abortion confirms the taboo surrounding a positive discussion of abortion. Letts sought to dispel popular myths and fears about the abortion procedure and illustrate that having an abortion could be a positive experience. Her YouTube video raised a firestorm of objections, not only from those opposed to abortion but also from abortion rights advocates who felt the video inappropriate.[69]

Yet, despite their silence in public, in private women and abortion providers expressed positive sentiments about abortion. In evaluation forms at abortion clinics and in letters to their physicians, women noted over and over again that they appreciated legal abortion services, were relieved at their ability to end an unwanted pregnancy, and felt good about their abortion. Many abortion providers, in turn, enjoyed their work and were grateful for their ability to help women in a time of need. However, only in the late 1990s did abortion providers begin to express these sentiments publicly. Responding to a growing body of antiabortion propaganda that depicted abortion providers as greedy, immoral and unconcerned with women's health and safety and abortion procedures as painful and dangerous, abortion providers began to write about their work to correct the distortions and misperceptions.[70] And a handful of scholars began to analyze the marginalization of abortion providers pre- and post-*Roe* and to discuss the personal and professional toll that those who work in abortion care experience.[71] In response to the increasing stigmatization of abortion, pro-choice organizations, too, began to organize speak-outs and collect stories from women who had had abortions. Today, there are several websites where women post about their positive abortion experiences.[72]

Given these silences, finding accessible sources that might tell me about the provision of and experience with abortion care turned out to be challenging. My access to the world of abortion care came through so-called independent abortion providers, who, following legalization, started their own women's health and abortion clinics and sometimes expanded to a chain of clinics across several states. The papers of these independent providers were tucked away in filing cabinets in the back of their clinics or in storage units around the country. To learn more about their work, I needed to gain access to and legitimacy with this group of health care professionals. In the early 2000s, I joined the National Abortion Federation (NAF), a professional organization of abortion providers. At annual meetings, I approached members to ask about their papers. Over time, many of them agreed to donate their papers to the Duke University's Sally Bingham Center for Women's History and Culture. These collections are treasure troves. They contain often voluminous correspondence, newsletters, newspaper clippings, court documents, and rich materials from the anti-abortion movement. I also began to conduct oral history interviews with abortion providers, clinic owners, and others associated with the field of abortion care. This book is based on these materials.

While this source base has proven to be extraordinarily rich, there remain significant gaps. Data on the provision of abortion care, collected by the Centers for Disease Control and the Alan Guttmacher Institute, tends to be large and aggregate. We can learn about the numbers of abortions across the nation, broken down by community size, abortion procedure, gestational age, patient age, and a variety of other factors. The existence of such aggregate data is, however, coupled with a total absence of data that can be tied to any individual abortion clinic. And if historians want to learn any details about women seeking abortion services, they have to dig deep. No historical data exists that might offer more detailed social or demographic background information on abortion patients or reveal insights into women's thoughts about the abortion experience. Occasionally, clinics handed out patient questionnaires to assess women's satisfaction with the services provided. But even these are scattered over time and place and frequently raise more questions than they answer. Security concerns further compound the problems of researching the history of legal abortion. If statistical information about women seeking abortion is almost nonexistent, statistical information about abortion providers is completely unavailable. We do not even know how many of them there are. Only a fraction of physicians providing abortion care, for instance, are members of NAF, and its membership lists are, for security reasons, confidential. Nor do we know what kind of abortion services abortion providers perform. Although there is aggregate data on the number of procedures performed across the country, for instance, there is no data that might tell us who performs these procedures—or where they are performed. Proceedings at the annual meetings of NAF and information collected by the organization are confidential and cannot be disclosed outside the organization. Sources about the two main participants in the abortion experience, then, are mainly anecdotal in nature, gleaned from correspondence, personal recollections and testimonies, and oral history interviews.

The limitations in sources also obscure the impact of race on the abortion experience. This is in stark contrast to my first book, *Choice and Coercion*, which traced the history of public health birth control programs, eugenic sterilization, and abortion prior to legalization between the 1920s and the 1970s. Since questions of race and class drove policy approaches regarding women's reproductive control, race was very visible in the historical record. Historical subjects in *Choice and Coercion* were frequently identified by race, which allowed me to tell a story about race. As I turned my attention to the history of abortion after legalization, I found race largely invisible in the historical record. Aggregate data offers insights on the racial background of abortion patients, but until the late 1980s, statistics differentiated only between "white" and "nonwhite" patients. Starting in the late 1980s, demographers added categories for "black" and "Hispanic" patients. Yet this data existed only on the state level and offers no information beyond the number of women of different racial backgrounds having legal abortions. Letters and testimonials chronicling the patient experience frequently offer no information about the race of the author, making the experience of African American or Hispanic women, for instance, almost invisible. The record becomes even murkier if one is to write about the impact of race on abortion providers and clinic staff. Often only personal knowledge meant that I knew the race of a provider or staff member, although occasionally the context of a story identified the race of a subject. Yet, it is clear that race shapes the experience of abortion patients, providers, and clinic staff. Protestors targeted African American patients, for instance, with charges of racial genocide, and African American patients and providers drew on a civil rights tradition when they faced crowds of screaming protestors. This book, then, tells an incomplete story about abortion after legalization—but an important story nonetheless. Much more research is needed to help us understand how race shaped the experience of abortion care, including the collection of oral history interviews with abortion providers and clinic staff from a wide diversity of backgrounds.

Given the sensitive nature of this topic, where and how I collected material shaped my personal editorial decisions and determined whether or not I could write about the information I found. While I decided not to shy away from sensitive topics inside the abortion provider community, I was careful—when addressing sensitive issues—to use only information from public records accessible to anybody. Although research in archival records and oral history interviews with abortion providers generally yielded material I could actually draw on, attendance at the annual meetings of NAF or research at its offices could only inform my understanding of events and experiences. And because my interest in the experience of abortion care is both politically sensitive and very personal to those narrating their experiences, it is by nature anecdotal and individual. Still, writing about the experience of abortion care and the impact that the abortion conflict has had on women and abortion providers is a pressing theme. It exposes how all abortion is marshaled into the single groove of morality, successfully excluding any consideration that places women's control over their lives at the center of the debate.

Abortion is—and always has been—a key arena for contesting power relations between women and men. Feminists argued with male medical professionals about who should be in charge of performing abortions and how abortions should best be performed. In addition, the belief that women are incapable of acting as moral agents and cannot be trusted with the decision whether or not to end a pregnancy remains pervasive after forty years of legal abortion. Women's ability to control their own lives and bodies, however, depends on their ability to control the most private and personal aspects of their lives: whether and when to bear children. As this book will illustrate, while the legalization of abortion made abortion accessible to most women, abortion became highly politicized and stigmatized as antiabortion activists and legislators challenged women's ability and right to decide on abortion.

ALTHOUGH THIS IS NOT a legal history, two legal cases stand as bookends to this work: a 1974 case, *Edelin v. the Commonwealth of Massachusetts*, and the 2007 Supreme Court decision *Gonzales v. Carhart*. In 1974, Boston prosecutors charged Kenneth Edelin, a young African American ob-gyn resident at Boston City Hospital (BCH) with manslaughter after he performed a legal abortion. City prosecutors sought to challenge the newly legalized procedure by attacking a particular abortion procedure, hysterotomy, and charging Edelin with killing the fetus—"a baby boy"—in the course of the procedure. Unsuccessful in the 1970s—Edelin was found guilty in 1975, but the verdict was overturned a year later—antiabortion activists finally succeeded in banning an abortion procedure—intact

D&E—with the 2007 *Gonzales v. Carhart* decision. Indeed, *Gonzales v. Carhart* provides the logical culmination of more than three decades of antiabortion activism in which abortion opponents sought to redefine the fetus as a baby and pregnancy termination as murder. The 2007 case brings together a number of intellectual antiabortion strands whose emergence and development I trace in the body of the book and which, in the 1990s, provided the intellectual foundation for the attack on intact D&E.

Following the legalization of abortion, physicians across the country established a network of abortion clinics to provide abortion services to women. Even though the vast majority of abortions today are performed in Planned Parenthood clinics, only a handful of Planned Parenthood clinics participated in the early establishment of abortion services. The 1979 NAF directory lists only one Planned Parenthood clinic. While ten more had joined by the early 1980s, they still made up only 5 percent of all member clinics in the mainland United States.[73] The vast majority of clinics that opened their doors in the 1970s were established by independent providers, physicians, and businessmen and were only informally connected. While some investors created several clinics under the same ownership, most of the clinics were unaffiliated. Owners and physicians of these early clinics communicated with one another, offered one another support, and established professional organizations and guidelines to guide their work. In the 1970s and 1980s, this group of nonaffiliated abortion providers carved out the framework for abortion services and, in response to the damages inflicted by antiabortion activism, in the 1990s led the abortion provider community through innovative changes in abortion care. When Planned Parenthood did begin to offer abortion services, it tended to do so in well-established markets after independent clinics had established a presence for abortion providers. Moreover, Planned Parenthood had access to donations and government funding unavailable to smaller clinics and was frequently seen as the Walmart of abortion services that pushed smaller independent clinics out of the market. Independent clinics, on the other hand, were not beholden to a larger organization and had the flexibility to try new approaches in abortion care. I will trace the emergence of this network of independent clinics, discuss the services they established, and analyze how the emergence of the antiabortion movement influenced the shape of abortion services over time. It is up to future historians to write the surely rich history of Planned Parenthood's approach to abortion care.

Since my interest in abortion care is driven in part by an interest in the history and development of medical procedures, my analysis will focus on the development of pregnancy termination procedures and the ways in which the antiabortion movement influenced the procedures performed in the surgery room. From the very beginning, antiabortion activists described abortion procedures in gory detail and illustrated their description with graphic images and photos. Moreover, although more than 90 percent of abortions take place in the first trimester, antiabortion activists focused on the small percentage of abortions taking place after the twelfth week of pregnancy—and on the even smaller percentage of abortions performed after twenty weeks' gestation. Focusing on abortions after the first trimester was supposed to suggest that all abortions are performed late in pregnancy. To understand the impact of this debate, I will discuss surgical procedures performed after the first trimester, although they constitute only a small percentage of all abortions performed. Some readers might consider these discussions tasteless and unpleasant. Others might object that such discussion is politically too sensitive. Yet a consideration of these procedures is essential if we are to understand the fight over abortion care and its impact on abortion services.

This book does not discuss medical abortion—the abortion pill Mifepristone. Approved by the FDA in 2000, medication abortions quickly increased from 6 percent in 2001 to 23 percent in 2011 (36 percent of all abortions before nine weeks' gestation).[74] However, the story of medical abortion, while interesting, is really different from surgical abortion. Its recent adoption made me decide to exclude it from consideration in this book.

Finally, a note on language: How people talk about abortion changed significantly over time as decades of antiabortion activism stigmatized abortion and publicly silenced those who felt good about receiving and providing abortions. Because individuals create narratives to make sense of the world and their place in it, how they talk about abortion reflects their own subjectivity and influences the understanding of those around them. While narratives reflect subjective experiences, they express a reality for the narrator. Indeed, the narratives create subjectivity—a position in the world and an understanding of the narrator as part of the world and society. In the context of abortion, narratives were most important in situating a person vis-à-vis abortion: as participant and actor or victim and object. As the abortion debate unfolded in the course of the 1970s, bodies and acts that were once apolitical gained political meaning. This is particularly true for fetal bodies, which became highly politicized. And it extended to activities of individuals on both sides of the abortion debate.

Language used in the abortion debate frequently contributes to misinformation. In this book, I refer to those opposed to abortion as anti-abortion rather than pro-life, since I disagree with the implication that those not identified as pro-life are against life. Abortion is the removal of a fetus or embryo from the uterus prior to viability, the point at which independent life outside the uterus becomes possible—at the earliest around twenty-three to twenty-four weeks of gestation. Any termination of pregnancy after viability is not an abortion but a labor induction, a hysterotomy (a mini-cesarean delivery) or a pregnancy termination. The usage "late-term abortion" is a misnomer, used by antiabortion activists to give the impression that all abortions performed after the first trimester take place late in pregnancy, that is, in the third trimester. The same is true for the term "partial birth abortion," coined by antiabortion activists to describe an abortion procedure, intact D&E, sometimes used during the second trimester. "Partial birth abortion" is a political term designed to raise the impression that the procedure is performed moments before term delivery. Finally, the occupant in the uterus—referred to by antiabortion activists incorrectly as a baby, a child, an infant, or a preborn child, among others—is first an embryo, then a fetus.[75]

This book explores the connections between personal experiences, local histories, and larger political developments. Susan Wicklund, who spent much of her life providing abortion care to women in the Midwest and in Montana, was for years harassed by the militant antiabortion group Lambs of Christ. Antiabortion harassment against her culminated in the 1990s during the so-called partial birth abortion debate, when antiabortion propaganda depicted all abortions as taking place at term, "inches before birth." Wicklund, caught up in worries over her daughter's safety and fears for her own life, had no time to follow the national debate. She did not even connect her own experience with the procedure—after all, she provided only first trimester abortions. Nevertheless, the debate and propaganda profoundly affected her. Trying to live with the Lambs of Christ, she became politicized, went public with her work and about the harassment she endured, and forged her political beliefs and medical practice out of this experience. Wicklund's personal story—and her local history—give meaning to the lived experience of abortion care—a story that we usually trace in big politics: legal changes, legislative decisions, federal and state policies concerning women's reproductive rights. This book is grounded in personal stories and local histories to illustrate the lived consequences of the politics of reproductive rights.

1

Living through Some Giant Change

The Establishment of Abortion Services

On January 22, 1973, the United States Supreme Court legalized abortion in its decision *Roe v. Wade*. Minutes after the news was broadcast, Susan Hill, then a twenty-four-year-old social worker in Miami, Florida, received a call from physician Sam Barr. Would she like to join him in opening an abortion clinic, Barr inquired. Two weeks later, the new clinic opened its doors to hundreds of women seeking legal abortions from all across the southeastern United States. Across the country, a group of feminists in Iowa City, Iowa, who had previously referred women to underground abortion providers, picked up the phone to call local physicians and ask when they were going to start offering abortion services and how much an abortion would cost. "They virtually hung up on us," one of them remembered. "I mean they were just incensed that we had called because they had no intention of changing what it was they were doing."[1] Frustrated with the response of Iowa City physicians and inspired by the court victory and the growing women's self-help movement, they decided to form a feminist collective and open their own clinic. And in Highland Park, Michigan, twenty-one-year-old office assistant Renee Chelian began to schedule abortion patients for Dr. Gilbert Higuera. Prior to the *Roe v. Wade* decision, Chelian and Higuera had flown every weekend to Buffalo, New York, where abortion had been legal since 1970. There, they had provided abortion services out of a small office. Now Higuera closed his Buffalo clinic and moved all its equipment into his regular ob-gyn office outside Detroit. "For me, everything changed," Chelian remembered. "All of a sudden, I had a dream about what I thought things should be like."[2]

With the legalization of abortion and the simultaneous introduction of medical equipment to perform first trimester abortions with vacuum aspiration machines, a previously clandestine and dangerous procedure became safe, quick, and inexpensive almost overnight. As Americans witnessed the emergence of a growing network of abortion clinics, abortions that had previously been invisible, performed secretly by underground providers or behind the curtains of private physicians' offices, became visible. The number of legal abortions climbed from 744,610 in 1973 to over a million in 1975, while the estimated number of illegal abortions declined. This development had a dramatic impact on abortion mortality. While the mortality rate due to abortion hovered between 60 and 80 deaths per 100,000 cases in the decades prior to legalization, it sank to 1.3 by 1976–77. Legal abortions before sixteen weeks' gestation, the authors of a study on morbidity and mortality of abortion concluded, had become safer than any other alternative available to the pregnant woman, including continued pregnancy and childbirth.[3]

Physicians and women came to the field of abortion care with disturbing memories of illegal abortions. Many physicians interested in providing abortions had cared for women suffering from the complications of illegal abortion and had seen their patients die. Now they hoped to establish services that offered safe and affordable abortions to all women. And many of the women who found their way into the emerging field of legal abortion care in the early 1970s had themselves experienced an illegal abortion, participated in underground abortion services while abortion was illegal, referred others to those services, or had friends or relatives with such experiences. Inspired by the emerging women's movement and frustrated with traditional medical care, which they viewed as patriarchal and paternalistic, they looked to the field of abortion care as an opportunity to shape a more feminist future in medicine. Both groups came together in the early 1970s to establish a new system of abortion care. At times uneasy allies—male physicians found young feminist women challenging and demanding while young women found male physicians patronizing and dismissive of their concerns—they nevertheless negotiated over different aspects of abortion care and established a broad network of abortion clinics which influence abortion services to this very day.[4]

Their efforts were also influenced and moderated by other interests, however. The high demand for and scarcity of abortion providers meant that the establishment of abortion services promised to be extremely lucrative. While the establishment of feminist health services could mean good business, a focus on profits could also drive prices up and the quality of services down. Tugged on the one side by a demand for profits and on the other by feminist critiques of the commodification of abortion services and calls to put women's experience at the center of care, abortion providers established a broad range of services from clinics founded as profit-making endeavors to feminist health collectives. Where the clinics fell along this spectrum depended, however, less on the attitude toward profits and more on the influence of individuals associated with the emerging abortion clinics.

But the provision of abortion care met resistance from early on. Most physicians were not interested in providing legal abortions. Hospitals imposed limits on the number of legal abortions physicians could perform. Cities and townships turned to local ordinances, building codes and zoning restrictions to prevent the opening of abortion clinics. The successful establishment of abortion services required complicated negotiations with physicians, hospital administrators, public health officials, and local politicians. The ability to overcome legal and institutional obstacles varied by time and place and contributed to the uneven distribution of abortion services for years to come.

A Simple Mechanical Procedure: The Development of Pregnancy Termination Procedures

The legalization of abortion opened what had been a covert surgical procedure to the scrutiny of medical professionals and the lay public alike. If the illegal or only quasi-legal nature of abortion had previously stifled research on the topic, legalization opened the procedure to scientific inquiry and debate. Virtually overnight, abortion became one of the most studied procedures in the United States. Some physicians and journalists had spoken and written about abortion long before the procedure became legal, discussing methods, estimating morbidity and mortality rates, and arguing for legalization.[5] But now they began to systematically collect data on pregnancy termination procedures and to publish the results in medical journals across the country. The ability to collect and compare data in turn fostered the development and introduction of new procedures and quickly contributed to the refinement of physicians' techniques. While the systematic persecution of illegal abortionists in the 1950s and 1960s had driven abortion underground and turned it into a risky or even deadly procedure for most women, legalization made abortion into the safest and most widely performed surgical procedure in the United States.[6]

Physicians' perception of abortion procedures was shaped powerfully by their experience with illegal abortion. As historian Leslie J. Reagan's research has shown, in the decades just prior to *Roe v. Wade*, abortion providers were increasingly prosecuted, and fewer physicians were willing to perform abortions than in the 1930s and 1940s. While physicians in larger hospital settings might occasionally terminate a pregnancy, such procedures required complicated approval by hospital abortion committees. Some women might qualify for a so-called therapeutic abortion if a physician found that pregnancy and delivery seriously impaired a woman's health or endangered her life. But such approvals were rare. A 1944 article presenting a table showing the incidence of therapeutic abortion compared with the number of deliveries at seven hospitals noted that Johns Hopkins University topped the list, with a therapeutic abortion to delivery ratio of 1:35, whereas Margaret Hague Hospital in New Jersey had the lowest ratio of 1:16,750.[7] As a result, more women were forced to turn to underground abortion providers, leading to an increase in the number of women who entered hospital emergency rooms with complications from illegal abortions.

For a whole generation of physicians who entered medical school and internships in the postwar era, the experience of abortion was tied to memories of caring for women with abortion complications. Those memories were frequently frightening. Physicians recall their despair trying to save women's lives before they bled to death or died of overwhelming infections. "We had a ward of patients who we admitted during the weekend," one physician remembers of his time as an ob-gyn intern and resident. "You'd go up there and it would smell. They'd have a tomato soup discharge. I remember one patient and as fast as we'd put the blood in, it would run and fill up your shoes."[8] In addition, many physicians had been frustrated with a system in which women with money and connections could obtain a dilation and curettage (D&C) abortion—in which the cervix is dilated and the contents of the uterus scraped with a curette—from their private physicians, while women without such resources ended up in the emergency room with complications from illegal procedures. "The poor pulled the innards out or got soap shot up inside them," a St. Louis physician commented.[9] In some urban public hospitals, entire wards were reserved to care for patients admitted after illegal abortions had gone bad. On any given afternoon during the 1950s and early 1960s, for instance, Los Angeles County Hospital cared for 50 to 100 women who had obtained illegal abortions.[10] Every one of these hospital wards was staffed by residents and physicians who were profoundly influenced by their experiences with these patients. Their concern with women's health and safety drove the discussion and development of pregnancy termination procedures.

The very ease and speed with which patients gained access to abortions after legalization is tied to the invention of a procedure called vacuum aspiration. Prior to the introduction of this procedure, physicians seeking to terminate a pregnancy performed a D&C, which was relatively unpleasant to perform. As one physician recalls: "Doing an abortion by routine D&C was . . . a very bloody procedure. Frighteningly so, sometimes. . . . I don't think that without the advent of suction abortion that abortion would ever have been as accepted by the medical practice as it was . . . and not because you were interrupting a normal pregnancy, that wasn't it. . . . It was strictly the risks."[11] The risks included perforation of the uterus, hemorrhage, and infection. Vacuum aspiration, in which, as the name suggests, the contents of the uterus are sucked out by a vacuum aspiration machine, not only was quicker than performing a traditional D&C but also was safer, was more likely to result in the complete removal of all tissue, led to less blood loss and fewer major complications, and was more adaptable to local anesthesia.[12]

The development of vacuum aspiration was an international endeavor, taking place simultaneously in several places across the globe. Its early history dates back to 1860, when Sir James Young Simpson of Edinburgh pioneered the use of syringe suction inside the uterine cavity. In 1927, S. G. Bykov of Russia used a syringe to bring on menstruation. The modern development of suction curettage can be traced to three Chinese physicians who, in 1958, reported on vacuum aspiration in the *Chinese Journal of Obstetrics and Gynecology*. In 1960, Dr. E. Melks, a Soviet physician in collaboration with a Soviet engineer, designed an apparatus that they called the vacuum excochleator. The machine featured metal curettes with an opening at the tip which drew in the fetal material and a mechanical crusher driven by an electric motor to crush larger fetal parts. In 1963, at the 11th All Union Congress of Gynecologists in Moscow, Dr. E. Melks reported performing a large number of vacuum aspiration cases, and shortly thereafter, vacuum aspiration spread to Eastern Europe and Japan.[13]

The first two articles on the subject in the American literature appeared in the July 1967 issue of *Obstetrics and Gynecology* in which Drs. M. Vojta and Dorothea Kerslake discussed therapeutic abortion by vacuum aspiration in Czechoslovakia and England, respectively.[14] American physicians took note, and in 1968 the Association for the Study of Abortion, one of the first medical abortion rights groups, organized a conference on abortion in Hot Springs, Virginia, featuring a presentation by the Yugoslav Franc Novak in which he introduced American physicians to vacuum aspiration. Novak marveled at the ease of vacuum aspiration. "When the gynecologist who knows only the conventional D and C first sees the apparatus in action, he is impressed by the cleanness, apparent bloodlessness, speed, and simplicity of the operation. While a D and C gives the impression of a rude artisan's work, an abortion performed with suction gives the impression of a simple mechanical procedure."[15]

Immediately after the reform of North Carolina's abortion law in 1967, Jaroslav Hulka, an associate professor at the UNC School of Public Health and the Department of Obstetrics and Gynecology, traveled to Newcastle upon Tyne to observe Dr. Kerslake's procedure. Hulka had already seen a motion picture about the procedure that Kerslake had made. "I went and visited her to see if I could learn anything more. So, I bought the equipment that she had and that was the first equipment being used."[16] Together with his colleague Dr. Takey Crist, Hulka started performing vacuum aspirations at North Carolina Memorial Hospital. While their unfamiliarity with the equipment initially led to a high complication rate, they quickly learned how to use the machine properly, and their success convinced colleagues to adopt the new technique as well. "And, of course, he [Takey Crist] got into trouble and I got into trouble—I mean medical trouble, complications. We were doing abortions and we didn't really know how to do them and it was difficult at first. But then eventually it got ironed out and as they [their colleagues] saw that these two cowboys were actually doing this procedure, gradually more and more people wanted to learn how to do it. So, people learned eventually, went out and did it."[17]

The first suction machines were crude instruments (see ill. 1.1) that were noisy and even dangerous. It was impossible to measure the vacuum pressure, and some of the earliest equipment simply utilized the wall suction in the operating room. But by the late 1960s, California engineer William Murr—in cooperation with Dr. Alan Margolis, a gynecology professor at the University of California—had developed a vacuum aspiration machine (see ill. 1.2). Murr began to market the machine through his medical supply company, Berkeley Bio-Engineering.[18] When New York legalized abortion in 1970, women from all over the country traveled to the East Coast to obtain a legal abortion. New York physicians quickly placed orders for the new vacuum aspiration machines, and vacuum aspiration spread rapidly in the United States. Between July 1, 1970, and June 31, 1971, suction curettage accounted for 93 percent of all first trimester abortions performed, quickly replacing the traditional D&C.[19]

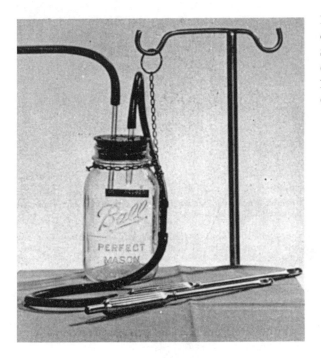

Ill. 1.1. First aspiration equipment used in Saint Paul, Minnesota (1970). Courtesy of Nancy Q. Burke and Gretchen Q. Banks.

Other companies joined the effort to develop new and better equipment, including quieter suction machines. One of these innovations, the plastic Karman cannula, allowed the physician to see the suctioned material as it passed from the uterus into the tubing. Plastic cannulas soon displaced older metal ones, making perforation of the uterus far less likely and allowing for early suction abortions with local or no anesthesia. This, along with the development of the paracervical block, which provided a form of local anesthesia, allowed abortions to be provided as outpatient services in the early 1970s.[20]

While revolutionary, these developments were not without controversy. Harvey Karman, a trained psychologist who had been involved in abortion prior to legalization and invented the Karman cannula, marketed both his cannula and a syringe, which he had developed for easy menstrual extraction. Advertised to women as a way to remove all their menstrual blood at one time at the beginning of their menstrual periods, menstrual extraction was often a euphemism for early abortion. With the help of population control organizations, he promoted his methods in developing countries where abortion was often illegal. Activists from the Feminist Women's Health Center (FWHC) in Los Angeles argued that their Del-Em Kit for menstrual extraction, developed by feminist health activist Lorraine Roth-

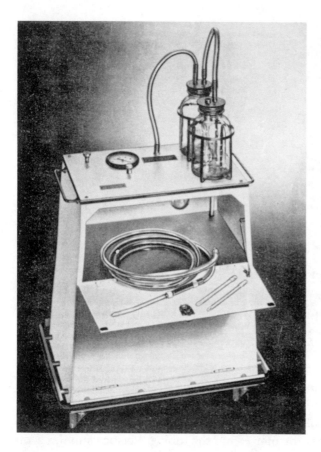

Ill. 1.2. Vacuum aspiration unit courtesy Berkeley Bio-Engineering. Courtesy of Nancy Q. Burke and Gretchen Q. Banks.

man, was better than Karman's syringe and charged Karman with subjecting women to untested and dangerous devices and consistently providing substandard care to his patients. Karman is "an international experimenter on women, supported and honored by population control forces, from the left and the right," one report from the FWHC noted.[21] But at the same time as some women's health activists dismissed Karman, others continued to work closely with him, among them Merle Goldberg (later Hoffman) who opened Choices Women's Medical Center on Long Island.[22]

While physicians described vacuum aspiration as a "relatively simple, innocuous procedure" during the first ten weeks of pregnancy, after the twelfth week complications of perforation and hemorrhage were thought too common to justify its use, and most doctors did not feel comfortable using it.[23] The most widely used method of terminating second trimester abortions in the early 1970s was saline instillation in which the physician withdrew amniotic fluid and replaced it with a concentrated salt solution, leading to miscarriage within twenty-four to thirty-six hours. Saline abortions had been around for decades. Here too, however, a "lack of experimental and theoretical support in research settings" prevented American physicians from using this method until the 1960s.[24] First described in 1939 by the Romanian surgeon and obstetrician Eugen Aburel, saline abortions were widely used by physicians in Japan in the late 1940s and early 1950s. By the mid-1950s, however, high complication and mortality rates discouraged Japanese physicians, and the method fell into disrepute.[25]

In 1960, Dr. Arpad I. Csapo, a well-known research physician at the St. Louis Washington University School of Medicine with a special interest in reproductive physiology, and his nephew Dr. Thomas Kerenyi, a Hungarian-born ob-gyn, established the effectiveness and relative safety of saline abortions and popularized the procedure in the United States.[26] Csapo and Kerenyi had been experimenting with rabbits to investigate techniques to stop premature labor. To do so, they first had to induce labor in the rabbits and found that injecting a concentrated salt-and-water solution into the animals' uterine cavities brought on contractions that eventually expelled the rabbits' litters. Kerenyi, who was at that point finishing his hospital internship in New York, realized the potential this technique held for inducing an abortion in women whose pregnancies were too far along for a traditional D&C. In the 1960s, the traditional technique for terminating a pregnancy that could no longer be ended with a D&C was to perform a hysterotomy, a procedure similar to a cesarean section in which the fetus was removed through an incision in the abdominal wall. But a hysterotomy left patients with a permanent scar and a permanently weakened uterus. And because hysterotomy required major abdominal surgery, the morbidity and mortality rates were roughly equivalent to those of cesarean sections.[27] When the abortion committee at his hospital approved the abortion of a seventeen-year-old girl who was twenty weeks pregnant, Kerenyi—appalled at the idea that a hysterotomy would leave the young woman an "obstetrical cripple"—convinced his colleagues to let him try his new procedure. The saline procedure was successful, and by 1970 the Kerenyi-model saline abortion had become the second trimester method of choice.[28] However, saline abortions could be performed only after the sixteenth week of pregnancy when the uterine cavity contained enough amniotic fluid to allow for this procedure. In the 1970s, this left a window of four weeks during which women were usually unable to terminate unwanted pregnancies.

In 1974, physicians began to add prostaglandin, unsaturated fatty acids that regulate uterine activity, to their toolbag of techniques for second trimester abortions. The fact that prostaglandins stimulate childbirth was first described in the medical literature in the 1960s when physicians noted high levels of prostaglandins in the amniotic fluid during spontaneous abortion and during miscarriage. By the late 1960s, researchers had established trials using prostaglandin for induction of labor, and in 1974 the FDA approved the drug for second trimester pregnancy terminations. Medical descriptions of saline instillations warned of possible hypernatremia—extreme dehydration that could lead to seizures and coma, renal and cardiac problems, and fluid overload.[29] Prostaglandins, physicians hoped, would be safer than either saline instillation or hysterotomy. Although women were more likely to experience nausea, vomiting, or diarrhea, they seemed less likely to suffer from serious complications as a result of the procedure.[30]

Following the 1970 legalization of abortion in New York, the Joint Program for the Study of Abortion, an initiative of the Center for Disease Control (CDC; now the Centers for Disease Control and Prevention) and the largest multicenter study of abortion complications, began to collect and compare data on the different pregnancy termination procedures.[31] With collection of this data, pregnancy termination procedures assumed a hierarchy that spoke to the safety and convenience of the procedures. Complication rates were lowest for suction abortion, followed by traditional D&C, saline instillation, hysterotomy, and hysterectomy. Of 72,988 abortions performed between July 1970 and June 1971 in the 66 participating institutions, 72.6 percent were performed by vacuum aspiration, followed by saline induction (20.1 percent), traditional D&C (4.5 percent), hysterotomy (1.3 percent), and hysterectomy (1.1 percent).[32] Physicians quickly realized that legally induced abortion was a "remarkably safe surgical procedure."[33] Indeed, a routine tonsillectomy carried a risk of death twice as high as that of legal abortion, and an appendectomy was approximately 100 times more dangerous. Despite its safety, physicians cautioned that complications from the procedure increased with advancing gestational age. Indeed, aside from the physician's technical skills, gestational age was the most important factor in rising complication rates. Nevertheless, pregnancy termination before sixteen weeks' gestation was safer than its alternative: pregnancy and childbirth.[34]

The Butcher Shops Closed: Early Days of Legal Abortion

Even before the 1970 passage of the New York reform bill, Charles de-Prosse and his colleagues purchased a vacuum aspiration machine for their

Ithaca, New York, group practice in anticipation of legal reform. "Even before we started doing them," deProsse remembers, "we had ordered a machine and all of the equipment that we needed to perform abortions using the suction procedure."[35] DeProsse and his colleagues had performed therapeutic abortions prior to 1970. Now they were poised to integrate legal abortions as one component in a whole range of obstetric and gynecological services. DeProsse's practice was the only one in the college town of Ithaca willing to provide legal abortions, and the number of abortion patients increased drastically and included patients referred by colleagues and friends from out of state. Nevertheless, deProsse found that he and his colleagues were able to integrate the new patients into their regular ob-gyn practice.[36] The largest abortion clinic in early 1970s New York was the Center for Reproductive and Sexual Health (CRSH), established by Howard Moody from the Clergy Consultation Service. Clinics founded by male physicians, however, were more typical. Child psychiatrist Harry Levin and obstetrician-gynecologist Moshe Hachamovitch from Einstein Medical Center founded the Pelham Medical Group. Norwegian psychiatrist Karl Fossum started the Eastern Women's Medical Center, and even out-of-state physicians established offices to provide legal abortions in New York. Detroit physician Gilbert Higuera, for instance, who in the late 1960s had sent his patients to London for legal abortions, established an office in Buffalo, New York, as soon as New York legalized abortion.

Pelham Medical Group in Westchester, New York, was typical of early freestanding abortion clinics. The clinic was located in a two-story brick building with four procedure rooms, exam rooms, and a recovery area on the bottom floor and a larger waiting room and counseling room upstairs. The space was attractive, modern, and middle-class looking.[37] Pelham was open six days a week and offered abortions up to twenty-four weeks of pregnancy—until the twelfth week of pregnancy at the Westchester site and for patients between the sixteenth and twenty-fourth weeks at Park Chester Hospital in the Bronx where Pelham's doctors had privileges. The clinic was busy, serving up to 100 women on any given Saturday. Even larger in scale was the CRSH, which served 60,000 women in the first two years alone. It employed fifty counselors and nurses and fifteen physicians to perform the abortions. In contrast, Higuera's Buffalo office was a tiny bare-bones operation, staffed by Higuera, Chelian, and a pilot who flew them from Detroit to Buffalo, New York, every weekend. Higuera served from 75 to 100 women from up to six different states on any given weekend day. He and his helpers worked from seven or eight in the morning until late in the night, with Higuera performing the abortions while Chelian aided in the procedures and sterilized the instruments and the pilot collected the fees.[38]

Clinic owners tended to adhere to standards set by referring agencies outside the state—frequently Planned Parenthood and the Clergy Consultation Service. Representatives from referral agencies visited the new outpatient clinics to decide where to send women seeking a referral. If you wanted to get those referrals, Frances Kissling, the former director at Pelham, noted, you had to follow their standards. Referral agencies insisted that clinics offer pre-abortion counseling, imposed price controls, and frequently demanded that for every ten paying patients the clinic perform one free abortion.[39] Counselors at Pelham, most of whom were young, college-educated feminists, provided group counseling sessions for eight to ten patients at a time. After the counseling session, they accompanied the patients into the procedure rooms where physicians performed the abortions in an assembly line process. Despite the routinized setup, staff treated patients well, and services were appropriate to the needs of most women. The relationship between counselors and physicians was "congenial," remembers Uta Landy, who in the early years worked as a counselor at Pelham, and the group counseling process was helpful, empowering, and destigmatizing to patients. "It felt good to have groups. Women came from everywhere and there was a sense of community."[40] The counselors cared deeply about issues of reproductive control and alerted Frances Kissling, then Pelham Medical Group director, if individual patients needed more attention or if any of the physicians were disrespectful.[41]

Within the first year of legalization in New York, 55,347 residents and 83,975 nonresidents sought legal abortions in New York City alone.[42] Especially in New York City, competition for patients was fierce. "Women were flying into LaGuardia," remembered Kissling. "You had all of the sort of Wild West elements of a newly legalized procedure. Women were coming from states where it was illegal. As far as they were concerned, it was illegal. The mentality was still clandestine even though it was legal. Taxi drivers would kidnap your patients and take them to other clinics that paid them money for bringing in a patient. Clinics would hire vans and limousines to pick up their patients at the airport so they wouldn't get stolen."[43] Enterprising entrepreneurs established abortion referral services to direct women to particular abortion providers. Initially, Higuera partnered with a couple who ran a cab company in Buffalo to schedule patients, pick them up, and deliver them on time to his Buffalo clinic. Eventually, he found a business partner who established a referral agency that advertised abortion services on billboards and provided counseling for women before sending them on to Higuera's office.[44] Some physicians found they were so overwhelmed with abortion patients that attention to their regular patients suffered. "As the referrals started coming in," one physician noted, "I was soon doing five abortions a week, then 10, and suddenly it was 20. I realized that in no time at all it would be 50. I felt that filling up that many beds—mostly with out-of-state patients—was not doing my community, my practice, or my hospital any good. I cut back to five a week."[45]

To be sure, the legalization of abortion in California, New York, and Washington, D.C., did not mean that all women had access to legal abortions. Many lacked the funds to travel and continued to rely on illegal abortions. Others never even learned about the existence of legal abortion services. White women were more likely to gain access to legal abortion services than nonwhite women. Byllye Avery, who in 1971 started referring women from Gainesville, Florida, to abortion services in New York, remembers the first time she tried to refer an African American woman for a legal abortion to New York after having successfully referred white women: "A black woman called, and we tried to give her the phone number [of the Clergy Consultation Service] and she said she didn't need no telephone number in New York. She didn't know nobody in New York. She didn't have no way to get to New York. She didn't have no money for New York, and all. And that woman died from a self-induced abortion."[46] Still, data from the CDC indicates that the establishment of legal abortion services prior to *Roe v. Wade* did increase African American women's access to legal abortions. Although only 7 percent (354) of therapeutic abortions performed in New York City between 1951 and 1962 were performed on nonwhite women, in 1971 that ratio had climbed to 20.8 percent, and the following year it rose to 24.3 percent.[47]

To be sure, providing legal abortion services was a good investment in the early 1970s. Hoping to convince physicians to start performing abortions, businessmen promised profits. Some set up clinic space where any physician could perform abortions at any price he cared to set, as long as the physician paid $100 for the use of the space. "One businessman wanted me to participate in the take-over of a bankrupt hospital for about $1,500,000," Richard Hausknecht, a New York City ob-gyn and medical adviser to NARAL reported. "A syndicate invited me to be its medical director for 'up to $250,000 a year.' They didn't plan to buy an entire hospital, just lease two or three floors. And I've had calls from real-estate people on everything from buying a brownstone near an abortion-minded proprietary hospital to taking over a vacant medical suite in a rundown apartment house in Queens for an abortion clinic."[48]

For-profit hospitals approached ob-gyn residents with offers that they moonlight for extra cash by performing abortions. Anticipating profits, abortion referral agencies purchased interests in for-profit hospitals to which they then directed abortion patients. The promise of profits was large enough to reach Wall Street, where two companies traded stocks with estimated abortion revenues. As a writer in *Health Economics* complained only six months after the legalization of abortion in New York, "Presumably the law was not designed to make numerous OBG men wealthy, turn fiscal red ink at some faltering proprietary hospitals to glossy black, or drop pots of gold into the laps of hastily created abortion referral agencies. But it seems to be doing all this, too."[49]

From the moment of legalization, the specter of abortion care as a business raised deep suspicions. The promise of profits had attracted many individuals to illegal abortion. While some abortionists who had performed illegal procedures had provided medically safe abortions, others had performed abortions under conditions that left women sick or even dying. The association of abortion with organized crime further reinforced the negative association between abortion and profits.[50] With the legalization of abortion, suspicions that the business of abortion meant expensive and dangerous procedures continued, discrediting those willing to establish legal abortion services. "They assumed you did it for the money, you didn't have the qualifications to be a real doctor. . . . You were either a drug addict, an alcoholic, a ne'er-do-well, you couldn't maintain a practice or you were owned by the Mafia," one physician commented.[51]

A focus on profits could indeed lead to practices detrimental to good medical care. Because clinics and most physicians were paid by the procedure, there was always a temptation to schedule as many patients per hour as possible. One physician recalled his experience during the early years of legal abortion: "They would put up these clinics and then they would bring in doctors, and the game was, how many can you do in an afternoon? There was a lot of pressure and a lot of anxiety and none of us liked the way we had to practice."[52] Such practices could lead to cursory pre-abortion counseling—or no counseling at all—and to physicians who rushed through the abortion procedures. Occasionally, it could result in practices that jeopardized women's health. Bernard Nathanson recalled his experience when he became medical director at the CRSH. Since clinics did not have ultrasound machines to help physicians determine how far along in her pregnancy a woman was, senior doctors had to confirm the gestational estimate of their younger colleagues. Some senior doctors intentionally underestimated the gestational age of fetuses. Bill Walden, one of the clinic's physicians, told Nathanson that when he was new at the clinic, he had estimated one patient to be sixteen weeks—too late for the clinic, which did not perform abortions past twelve weeks' gestation. Nathanson reports,

> [Walden] called in a "senior" with a solid reputation outside the clinic who told him, "She's only ten weeks. You can do her." Walden started to work and soon was in the middle of a treacherous sixteen-week abortion that took him an hour and a half. . . . Meanwhile, the "senior" doctor was running through three women and earning three times the pay while he [Walden] was tied up. . . . The old hands pulled this on a lot of the new boys, to tangle them in impossible cases and reduce the competition for fees. On the side, of course, there was the trifling matter that they were putting the women patients in unnecessary danger.[53]

While Nathanson's narrative is to be taken with some skepticism—he became a major spokesperson for the antiabortion movement a few years later—we cannot dismiss his memories as those of a pro-life crank. The structural problems to which he points were present in many abortion clinics. How much they influenced abortion care depended on the leadership of the particular clinic. Nathanson points out that he stopped such practices at the center when he took over as medical director.

Complaints about profiteering pointed to larger fears that legal abortion might lead to an "abortion bonanza."[54] Some worried that physicians would be lured by money rather than motivated by a sense of professional responsibility. "To be sure," an author in *Medical Economics* noted, "there are a number of high-principled physicians and institutions providing abortions out of a sense of duty. For some doctors, however, it's not duty but cash that calls."[55] Hospitals, too, restricted the number of abortions that individual doctors could perform or put abortion patients on the bottom of the waiting list.[56] As one ob-gyn remembered the response of the East Coast medical school where he tried to establish abortion services: "They wanted to make it very clear that I wouldn't make the hospital into an abortion mill."[57] Indeed, most ob-gyns were not interested in providing abortions. They shied away from the stigma of abortion care, faced institutional obstacles and hostile colleagues, or found that their practices were already too busy and they just lacked the time.[58] In practice, of course, such responses contributed to a shortage of abortion providers and made access to reasonably priced abortions performed in a respectful environment more difficult.

Finally, many of the critics continued to distrust women seeking abortion services. The fear of an "abortion bonanza" suggested that it was not only abortion providers who needed to control their greed, but also women who might be unrestrained in their demands for abortion. As the medical director of New York City Planned Parenthood commented in 1970: "The ultimate restraint must be women themselves. It's a good law that allows a woman to remedy a 'mistake.' But doctors must stress that abortion is not a substitute for good contraception."[59] Restricting services, then, would discipline physicians' greed and women's excessive demands.

To be sure, the hostility toward profiteering abortion providers stemmed in part from the fear that even after legalization abortions would remain too expensive for poor women to afford. Feminists, in particular, argued that women had a right to control their reproduction and thus needed to be able to afford abortion services. As a result, they pushed abortion providers to lower their rates and negotiated with physicians and clinics to perform a certain number of abortions for free. They were aided in 1970 by Planned Parenthood and the Clergy Consultation Service, which successfully pressured for-profit hospitals to cut their costs of abortions from $400-$500 to $200-$300.[60]

Despite all these fears, the legalization of abortion brought with it a drastic reduction of price and complication rates. Services may not have been perfect, but women were no longer getting sick or dying from botched abortions. In 1969, prior to the legalization of abortion in New York, statistics from New York City show that 6,500 women were admitted to municipal hospitals with incomplete abortions. After legalization, abortion became one of the safest outpatient surgical procedures, with a mortality rate of approximately one death per 100,000 abortions.[61] After only half a year of legal abortion in New York, Dr. M. Leon Tancer, professor of ob-gyn at New York University's medical school, reported: "We see damned few incomplete or septic abortions around our hospitals anymore. The answer is that the butcher shops are closed."[62]

A Confrontation All the Way Around: Abortion Clinics after Roe

What had begun on a somewhat experimental basis in New York, Washington, D.C., and California in the early 1970s took hold across the country after the *Roe v. Wade* decision. According to statistics from the Alan

Guttmacher Institute, the research arm of the Planned Parenthood Federation (PPFA), the number of physicians performing legal abortions after nationwide legalization climbed by 76 percent, from 1,550 in 1973 to 2,734 in 1979.[63] Abortion services were initially tied to hospitals. This was particularly true for public and municipal hospitals, which considered it an obligation to make abortion services available to women unable to obtain the procedure from a private physician, and for university hospitals, many of which were at the forefront of abortion research and medical reform. In Iowa City, Charles deProsse, who had left Ithaca, New York, in 1971 and joined the Department of Obstetrics and Gynecology at the University of Iowa Hospital, established abortion services during the immediate months after *Roe v. Wade*. By May 1973, abortion services at the University of Iowa Hospital offered vacuum aspirations and saline abortions to women from across the state. The department allowed deProsse to hire his own staff to ensure that all staff members supported the new program. Initially, the abortions were performed in the hospital—vacuum aspiration procedures in a minor surgical operating room and saline abortions in the gynecology ward. While staff in both programs were supportive of abortion, the location of the new saline service was unfortunate. In 1973, the gynecology ward consisted of a big room with 20 beds divided by curtains. This placed a sixteen-year-old patient with a saline abortion next to a seventy-eight-year-old patient dying from cervical cancer, making the experience uncomfortable for both patients. By the second year, however, deProsse was able to move the abortion services into a freestanding building separate from the hospital.[64]

But many parts of the country lacked hospital administrators and ob-gyn staff willing to establish abortion services. And even when hospitals established such services, they were frequently limited because only one or two physicians were willing to perform abortions.[65] Occasionally, physicians took up the slack and established saline programs in small proprietary hospitals instead. Dr. Ed Portman, an Atlanta physician with experience in abortion procedures after the first trimester, purchased a defunct ear, nose, and throat hospital called Midtown and established a nineteen-bed saline service there.[66] And Chelian took advantage of Detroit hospitals facing hard economic times and offered to fill empty hospital beds with saline patients. She hired a number of counselors as additional staff, providing physicians in the Detroit area with space and support staff to offer saline abortions. Physicians who had done their residency prior to 1973 and who had tended to women with complications from illegal abortion now came out of the woodwork to work in the newly established saline unit.[67]

But it was the proliferation of outpatient clinics which provided abortions in a nonhospital location that shaped the setting of abortion care for decades to come. In 1973, 81 percent of abortion providers were tied to a hospital; by 1979, that number had dropped to 56 percent.[68] Physicians all over the country opened freestanding clinics to establish first trimester abortion services. Physician Sam Barr opened his clinic EPOC in Winter Park, Florida, just outside Orlando.[69] Modeling his clinic after the Preterm clinic in Washington, D.C., Barr hired two other physicians and several counselors and began to provide abortion services to women from Florida, Georgia, South Carolina, Alabama, Louisiana, and Mississippi.[70] The clinic was part of an emerging network of women's health services in Florida. To the south, in Miami, Dr. Barkus offered abortions until the twentieth week of pregnancy. Just north of Miami, there was a new clinic in Fort Lauderdale. In Tallahassee, a feminist clinic was preparing to open, and Tampa had a feminist health center which offered education and referred women needing abortions to other clinics. These clinics closely followed each other's progress and referred patients to each other. EPOC sent patients whose pregnancies were beyond twelve weeks to Dr. Barkus in Miami, for instance. And the feminist clinics in Tallahassee and Tampa frequently sent patients to EPOC.[71]

Whether a physician was most likely to perform an abortion in a hospital setting, a physician's office, or a freestanding abortion clinic depended significantly on the physician's geographic location. In urban areas, almost three quarters of all women received their abortions in freestanding clinics. In rural areas, only half of all women sought abortions in freestanding clinics, the other half were evenly divided between hospitals and physicians' offices.[72] Physicians who had performed therapeutic abortions prior to *Roe* were quickest to integrate abortion services into their regular practices after the decision. Two weeks after *Roe v. Wade*, Takey Crist, who had already performed abortions while working as an assistant professor of ob-gyn at UNC, opened his own clinic, the Crist Clinic for Women in Jacksonville, North Carolina, to offer comprehensive health care services, including abortion care.[73]

In Pittsburgh, Pennsylvania, too, abortion services expanded from the hospital—Magee Women's Hospital, later associated with the University of Pittsburgh Medical Center—to freestanding clinics. Prior to *Roe*, physicians at Magee had performed the occasional therapeutic abortion and residents learned how to perform vacuum aspirations at Magee. Only weeks after the *Roe* decision, Pittsburgh social worker Leah Sayles opened the first freestanding abortion clinic, Women's Health Services, in Pittsburgh. In the early 1970s, staff at Pittsburgh's Free Clinic had provided many referrals to abortion services in New York and Washington, D.C., in the early 1970s. Now Sayles hired the young women who had offered problem pregnancy counseling at the Free Clinic prior to *Roe* to work as abortion counselors at Women's Health Services. Residents at Magee began to moonlight at the clinic. Among them were Robert Thompson and Morris Turner, both trained in ob-gyn. They joined their mentor Robert Garland Kisner in performing abortion services at Magee and Women's Health Services. "I learned to do the vacuum aspiration procedure at the hospital under general anesthesia, under sedation," Morris Turner remembered, "and it's a totally different process as an ambulatory site. So those of us who were interested in doing it, we'd have to moonlight. . . . There [at Women's Health Services] we'd do it under local anesthetic. That's pretty much where we learned how to do them."[74] All three were African American and knew what it meant to be locked into a life of poverty with the complication of unwanted pregnancies. Turner, who grew up as the son of Georgia sharecroppers, remembered a young woman with an unwanted pregnancy in 1966–67 Atlanta. "She had gone someplace, some house . . . and eventually was taken to Grady Hospital where she died of overwhelming sepsis, infection. And I remember even my mother back in the day when some young family member who had gotten pregnant, and you could buy quinine over the counter. . . . They knew if you took enough of this you could sometimes institute an abortion."[75] Experiences like these convinced the three to provide legal abortions as part of their work.

Indeed, the model of the freestanding abortion clinic appealed not only to physicians. It also offered feminists seeking an alternative to traditional medical care the opportunity to open an abortion clinic and put their vision of woman-centered health care into practice. Inspired by the court victory and the growing self-help movement, a group of young women in Iowa City, Iowa, decided to form a feminist collective and open their own clinic. Prior to the legalization of abortion, they had been active in an abortion referral service and had conducted a series of self-help classes for women interested in learning about their bodies. Between January and June 1973, they met on a weekly basis to discuss the possibility of opening a women's health clinic. "We would meet and we would debate endlessly about politics," Deb Nye recalled.[76] By the early summer, they had found a house and begun the arduous process of renovations. On September 1, 1973, the Emma Goldman Clinic for Women opened its doors to the public. The collective hired Dick Winter, a local physician, to perform abortions on

Tuesdays and Thursdays and staffed the clinic with collective members, all lay health workers, who received on-the-job training. During the first month of operation, Dick Winter performed 75 vacuum aspirations.[77] In addition to abortion, the clinic offered birth control counseling, psychotherapy, childbirth preparation classes, massage services, and legal advice.

The EGC was part of a nationwide movement of women who opened women's health clinics—many of which did not provide abortion services. To some feminists, however, the integration of abortion services was a logical extension of their commitment to feminist health care. Many saw women's access to affordable abortions as central to women's self-determination and realized that abortion services provided clinics with a steady income, allowing them to support a range of other services not as easily reimbursable. Carol Downer, a California housewife turned women's health activist, established a group of clinics, the Feminist Women's Health Centers. Intrigued by Downer's vision, feminists in Michigan, New Hampshire, Florida, and Georgia opened clinics affiliated with FWHC in Detroit, Concord, Tallahassee, and Atlanta, respectively. In Vermont and Massachusetts, feminists followed suit with clinics that, like the EGC, were not affiliated with FWHC.[78]

As the field of legal abortion care emerged, however, deceptive and even criminal business practices continued to tarnish the image of the abortion provider as profiteer. Susan Hill remembers a field dominated by sleazy business investors whose clinics quickly acquired a poor reputation. It was "all about money," she commented. "That was the whole field at that point."[79] Frequently, investors opened not one but a number of clinics across several states. To maximize their investments, some businessmen combined a variety of outpatient services. The Lipton brothers, for instance, owned Summit Clinics, an umbrella group of clinics in Atlanta, New York City, and Connecticut. In the mid-1970s, they sought Hill's advice for opening a clinic in Miami and took her to tour the proposed clinic building. The building was supposed to be an abortion clinic three days a week and an acupuncture clinic the other three days. "They had literally a sign that said 'Acupuncture,'" she recalled, "and they flipped it over and it said 'Abortion' on the front of the thing."[80]

Of course, business interests and good medical care were not necessarily incompatible with each other. The profits which the establishment of abortion clinics promised could lead to the establishment of outstanding services. In the mid-1970s, Susan Hill received an offer to establish abortion clinics for Joseph and Stuart Yacknowitz. The father and son owned the largest kosher catering service in the Northeast and invested their money in abortion clinics. "It's a good business," Joe Yacknowitz explained to Hill.[81] Starting in 1976, Hill managed the Yacknowitzs' group of four clinics. Together, they formed the National Women's Health Organization (NWHO) and opened an additional six clinics in the next four years. Hill was given free rein to implement her philosophy toward patient care—the establishment of safe and pleasant places where patients could receive abortions with dignity and respect. While the ultimate authority lay with the Yacknowitzs, both trusted her suggestions as they related to the establishment of abortion services.[82]

Yet, the legalization of abortion did not translate into a climate in which it was easy to open even freestanding abortion clinics. To be sure, some parts of the country, states such as New York, Florida, and California, for instance, saw the establishment of a range of outpatient abortion services in a very brief time period. But a New Jersey lawsuit in the mid-1970s illustrates how unequally *Roe v. Wade* was applied even in neighboring states. Abortion services in New Jersey were few and far between. Three out of four New Jersey residents, approximately 30,544 women, had to leave the state to obtain an abortion. In the summer of 1973, South Jersey resident Jane Doe and her husband had sought an abortion because they felt unable to provide for a fifth child. Jane Doe's physician was willing to perform the procedure, but hospitals in South Jersey still banned non-therapeutic abortions, and none would permit him to perform the procedure. The Rutgers Women's Litigation Clinic and the American Civil Liberties Union finally filed suit against three private South Jersey hospitals that refused to perform abortions, and in November 1976 the New Jersey Supreme Court agreed that Jane Doe had been illegally denied access to abortion. But the decision came too late for her. Unable to travel out of state for an abortion, she had since given birth to her fifth child.[83]

In the mid-1970s, Hill and the NWHO set out to open clinics in underserved areas of the country. Hill firmly believed that abortion services should come to the patient rather than the other way around. Women should be able to have abortions in their hometowns, she explained to Joe Yacknowitz. And Yacknowitz was happy to follow her suggestion. Opening in towns not yet served by other clinics also meant that there would be no competition for services. Such a plan made financial sense.

But opening abortion clinics in small-town America met significant local opposition. "It became a confrontation all the way around," Hill remembered.[84] Between 1976 and 1980, Hill and the NWHO opened clinics in Wayne, New Jersey; Wilmington, Delaware; White Plains, New York; Fort Wayne, Indiana; Raleigh, North Carolina; and Fargo, North Dakota.

In almost every case, local authorities met NWHO efforts with a range of procedural obstacles. In Wayne, a heavily Catholic area outside New York, the township's health officer, Oscar Acquino, argued that the clinic was an ambulatory care facility and thus needed a certificate of need to open. Certificates of need, which regulate the construction of hospital facilities, are intended to prevent construction of too many clinics in any given location. Such certificates are expensive, difficult to get, and not intended for physicians' offices, including freestanding abortion clinics. Hill objected, arguing that requiring a certificate of need violated *Roe v. Wade*, which declared that any restriction on abortion performed during the first three months of pregnancy was illegal. "It was clearly so unconstitutional," she recalled. "That was our first encounter with the fact that state and city officials don't care about the Constitution. They care about getting elected."[85] State health officials finally relented only after the NWHO threatened to sue the township of Wayne, and on September 16, 1976, the New Jersey Women's Health Organization (NJWHO) opened its doors to the public. But the victory did not mean an end to the opposition. It only moved the opposition from the state to the municipal level. Led by councilman James Duggan, an Irish-American, Catholic, conservative Republican and member of the Knights of Columbus, demonstrators began to picket the clinic and the medical director's private home. In addition, Duggan introduced a resolution to the Wayne Township Council asking that the county prosecutor's office investigate whether NJWHO was a clinic after all. If the office determined that NJWHO was a clinic, it would require not only a certificate of need but also a zoning variance and a sprinkler system. Duggan and his supporters hoped his efforts would shut the clinic down. While NJWHO remained open, the procedural challenges involved the clinic into a lengthy battle with local authorities.[86]

In other cities too, state and local officials looked to regulations, building codes, and zoning laws to block the opening of abortion clinics. When Hill tried to open the Delaware Women's Health Organization in 1977, she found that Delaware had never repealed its criminal abortion law. Despite *Roe v. Wade*, abortion was still a criminal act in Delaware, and the NWHO had to go to federal court to ask for a stipulation that Delaware's criminal abortion law was no longer valid.[87] In Fort Wayne, Indiana, opposition was particularly vehement. "Women in Fort Wayne do not need abortions," its mayor announced from the steps of City Hall as soon as news of the planned clinic reached him. "This clinic will never open."[88] The city blocked the clinic's renovation with building and zoning regulations and, once the building was ready, repeatedly sent unsympathetic inspectors who delayed the opening. Hill spent months traveling between Fort Wayne and the NWHO in New York City to argue with City Hall about the required permissions. The Fort Wayne Women's Health Organization (FWWHO) finally sued the City of Fort Wayne for damages of $1 million resulting from the endless delays. "The constant conflict with state or municipal officials exacts a daily toll on providers," abortion attorney Lynn Miller commented about such regulations. "Many times the experience takes on a distinct Kafkaesque air."[89] While city officials were eventually forced to permit the clinic to open, the opening was delayed by at least six months, and the fight seemed like the opening salvo of things to come in Fort Wayne.

Despite such hurdles, however, during the 1970s the number of abortion providers rose steadily across the country. As a result, abortion became generally more accessible throughout the decade. While 25 percent of all women who had obtained a legal abortion in 1973 reported that they had traveled outside their state of residency to obtain the service, by 1980 that number had fallen to six percent. Because of the rapid spread of vacuum aspiration, the fastest growing categories of abortion providers were freestanding clinics or physicians' offices. In 1980, 16.5 percent of all abortion facilities performed three-quarters of all abortions.[90] One in ten obstetrician-gynecologists performed abortions in their private offices. In contrast, the percentage of hospital-based abortion services fell from 81 percent of all providers in 1973 to 56 percent of all providers in 1979.[91]

The Thing Is That a Woman Could Choose:
Medical versus Feminist Model

What kind of abortion services women were to receive and how they experienced legal abortion depended not only on the kind of abortion provider a woman visited but also on the philosophical orientation and organizational structures which shaped abortion services inside the clinic walls. Abortion clinics established in the 1970s tended to follow either a medical or a feminist model. Physicians emphasized the delivery of high-quality medical services, contrasting their clinics with the back-alley abortion services which had sent so many women to hospital emergency rooms prior to legalization. Integrating abortion services into existing medical practices, physicians argued, would ensure the safety of the procedure. Feminists, in contrast, hoped that the legalization of abortion would mean that abortion would not only be performed in medical offices but also change medical practice. When Chelian thought of the early legal abortions Dr.

Higuera performed on weekends in the tiny Buffalo clinic, she thought of them as an act of compassion. After *Roe*, she hoped that Higuera would improve the conditions under which he offered legal abortions. Indeed, across the country, feminists tried to influence the establishment of abortion services. While physicians, most of them male, sought to keep tight control over the medical aspects of abortion care, they employed women as nurses, counselors, office assistants, and clinic administrators. These women brought their ideas about women-friendly health care services into the newly established abortion clinics.

Education and the dissemination of information were at the top of feminists' list. Feminist clinics embedded abortion services into a comprehensive program of health education, geared at transforming patient consciousness. Steeped in the women's health movement, activists sought to reclaim "the mystery that had surrounded so much of women's health" by educating patients about their bodies and encouraging them to make their own choices.[92] Offering free information over the phone was part of a democratization process geared at empowering patients. "People were calling us all day long to ask the simplest questions," Chelian remembered. "How do you put on a condom? And how do you know if you have crabs or lice? . . . It was basic information that they had never been able to get from anybody else or get anywhere else."[93] Feminist clinics also sought to offer written educational materials, complete with images that did not depict all female bodies as pregnant. But finding a drawing of a cervix or of an empty uterus was a challenging task for those lacking the artistic confidence to draw their own. Chelian finally located a booklet with appropriate images from the Montreal Health Press that she began to hand out to patients. Others set out to write their own educational materials, ranging from short pamphlets to educational treatises that included in-depth discussions of a number of health issues.[94]

Clinics also began to offer free pregnancy testing and free samples of birth control pills. For poor women, in particular, this was a drastic change. Prior to the introduction of over-the-counter pregnancy tests, getting a pregnancy confirmed meant making—and paying for—an appointment with a physician. After leaving a urine sample at the doctor's office, women had to wait several days for the lab results. Once the physician received the results, he might inform a patient over the phone—or make her come in and pay for another appointment. Women with limited financial resources often chose to wait. "If you were pregnant, you just waited long enough. If you didn't have a miscarriage and you didn't have your period, you were going to have a baby. So, by the time you missed your third period, you went in for maternity care, but not before in case you weren't pregnant," Chelian remembered.[95] The introduction of free pregnancy testing was radical—and not well received by the rest of the medical community, which well understood that patients would be unwilling to pay for pregnancy testing if they could get it free at an abortion clinic. Together with the offer of free birth control pill samples that many clinics handed out to their abortion patients, it proved revolutionary for women's ability to control their reproduction. "We all felt we were living through some giant change," Chelian commented. "We were seeing women who were experiencing for the first time in their lives the opportunity to have control over their reproductive lives."[96]

Information and the offer of a range of options, then, were crucial to feminist clinics. They allowed for the empowerment of women patients who could now make their own informed choices regarding reproductive health care. The staff at the Iowa City EGC offered extensive education, talked women through the abortion procedures, and encouraged women's participation by offering them choices.[97] No detail was too minute. Whether women wanted their legs in stirrups or just out became a significant political issue. As one collective member commented, "When you get right down to it, that is what the revolution is all about, deciding whether a woman is gonna have a choice to have her legs just out or have them in the stirrup. . . . The thing is that a woman could choose. We were concerned about that. That's what makes us feminist."[98]

Essential to fostering a feminist consciousness was the demonstration of cervical self-exams. Teaching cervical self-exam, women's health activists believed, was crucial since it illustrated the accessibility of a part of the female body heretofore presumed hidden and carried with it the appropriation of male medical tools for feminist purposes. Indeed, within the women's health movement, cervical self-examination served almost as a recruiting tool, motivating those who observed it to join the movement. As Carol Downer remarked in 1971 when she first started demonstrations, "The energy that is unleashed by doing self-examination was a moving force in everything we did."[99]

But what the women of the EGC hoped would foster transformation, followers of the medical model found inappropriate. "I had no objection to women looking at their cervix with a speculum," one EGC physician explained. "I think that that's very appropriate. . . . But to make a fetish of it is to me what sort of goes beyond the pale. . . . I keep thinking, how many women take a tongue blade and look at their tonsils when they're sixteen years old . . . like they are supposed to do with their vaginal pathways. . . . There was a disconnect there that I just didn't get."[100]

Indeed, some health activists doubted that cervical self-examinations would lead to the kind of structural change in health care that activists wanted to see. Although she sympathized with the goals of the women's health movement, author Elizabeth Fishel feared in 1973 that the practice would appeal more to middle-class women than to poor women and wondered whether cervical self-examination would lead to real change in health care policy and delivery.[101] Others found the practice intimidating. As Susan Hill remembered: "Any time you went to a feminist meeting you were invited to look at your cervix at the same time. . . . It was incredible. No matter how many other times you had done it. And it was almost, I remember feeling almost intimidated because if you didn't want to do it, that you weren't acceptable. . . . I did it once or twice. I can't remember where, at which meeting. And then I just sort of said, 'I've already seen it. I don't need to look at it.'"[102] Women, Hill concluded, should not be asked to "pass a test to get an abortion." "I thought there was a place for looking at your own cervix and all those things, self-help and all that. . . . I didn't think that the place for it was right before you had surgery. . . . I guess my theory was women didn't come to an abortion clinic wanting to be a feminist. They came wanting surgery. . . . I guess I just didn't think women needed to be taught anything to get an abortion. . . . And I thought the feminists kind of wanted to teach."[103]

Equally important to feminist clinics was the delivery of services by women rather than men. One collective member from the EGC explained: "We felt that if we, as women, we could provide those services, it would be better yet, than a male physician perhaps that was out to make a profit."[104] Indeed, collective members discovered that drawing blood, assisting in deliveries or abortions, or performing menstrual extractions was "a tremendously empowering experience."[105] Experiencing feminist services, they hoped, would trigger a similar sense of empowerment for patients and ideally lead patients themselves to question traditional gender relations. At times, the hope for a transformation in patient consciousness became an expectation that patients change. Every woman, the assumption was, should challenge traditional gender norms and become a little more feminist. "Women who went to the clinic were kind of asked to change a little bit," one collective member explained. "Like, if you went because you needed an abortion or you went for whatever reason, you were given information and then you were kind of expected, like 'take this and learn from it and change yourself a little bit.' . . . That was also an important thing for us all at that time. . . . It was this idea that women needed to change. We need to kind of break out of the ways we've been brought up, to defer and not to make our own choices, and to just come out and say: 'All this is available. We can do it.'"[106]

But although members of the EGC felt that all services at the clinic should be provided by women, they also quickly realized that the small number of women physicians meant they had to rely on male medical professionals if they wanted to offer abortions. Collective members worried about the effect this might have on the clinic as a woman's space.[107] Of similar concern was the question whether the collective was willing to train men or whether training should be limited to women. Collective members feared, for instance, that training male gynecologists how to fit cervical caps might give even more power to men in gynecology and thus mean a "loss of feminism."[108]

Within the parameters of a feminist clinic, women could debate these issues and, since they retained ultimate control over the clinic, determine how to structure patient services. But feminists who sought to change physicians' medical clinics to become more woman-friendly tended to meet resistance. Physicians' adherence to a medical model and their desire to maintain authority over the clinic further limited feminist influence. Chelian recalls arguing with Dr. Higuera about answering patient questions over the phone. "You don't get paid to sit on the phone," he told her. "If people want to ask questions, they need to make an appointment for an office visit and they can come in and pay for the doctor's time because that's what patients do. And I'll answer their questions."[109] In Florida, EPOC staff members were in communication with feminist clinics in Tallahassee and Tampa. Both referred clients to EPOC, and the director of Tampa's clinic worked as a counselor at EPOC for several months. But when they tried to get EPOC to adopt a feminist model, Barr was not interested. Hill recalls, "They wanted a feminist model, even in our clinic. He wasn't about to let that happen because it was his and he was a doctor and he wanted it as a doctor's office."[110] The integration of abortion into ob-gyn services itself, feminists realized, would not lead to change in the hierarchical relationship between physicians as the arbiters of basic information about sexual health and patients in need of health education. "There wasn't gonna be any evolution and any changing with him," Chelian concluded about her work with Higuera.[111]

The Price You Paid: The Clinic as Workplace

Thrown together within the confines of the abortion clinic, feminists and physicians grappled with the personal and political implications of their collaboration. In feminist clinics, the reversal of hierarchies–the feminist collective as employer, the physicians as employees–limited the amount of influence physicians had over clinic details. To ensure that clinic services would be feminist in nature even if abortions were performed by men, members of the EGC closely observed their male providers as they delivered services. Patients were always accompanied by a woman advocate, and other women assisted in the pregnancy termination procedure. At the end of procedure days, collective members would meet with the male providers to offer their criticism. "It might be how I said something to a patient while I was doing a procedure," Chuck deProsse, one of the clinic's abortion providers, recalls. "It might be what I didn't do when I was examining a patient with respect to explaining every detail of what I was doing."[112]

Physicians working at the EGC struggled with the nontraditional atmosphere of the clinic. This was probably further aggravated by the fact that the women employers were considerably younger and less educated than the doctors and had a predisposition to criticize. Physician Ric Sloan found street clothes and bare feet inappropriate for a clinic setting and in a moment of heightened frustration called the clinic a "backyard still."[113] DeProsse conceded that sometimes the women made important points in their critique. At other times, however, they seemed rigid in their expectations and their criticism was the result of their hostility toward traditional medicine rather than grounded in real complaints. "I sort of felt that I was the focus of some minor degree of animosity towards traditional medical care as I sat there with four or five or six women, all sort of picking things apart. . . . At times, maybe, it was not appropriate. . . . They were just doing something to sort of needle others [rather] than have good complaints."[114] The women, Ric Sloan complained, "were running him," while deProsse summarized his feelings with the comment: "I was reduced to being a technician."[115]

Remarkably, while some physicians left or threatened to leave as a result of these tensions, physician support for the clinic grew steadily, and most of Emma's providers decided to stick with it.[116] "I was always accommodating," Chuck deProsse remembered. "This was their clinic and I was perfectly happy doing that as long as it was within professional bounds."[117] A shared sense of disillusionment with traditional health care and a joint commitment to alternative care provided the common ground on which feminists and male abortion providers continued to meet. Most of the physicians who worked at EGC understood their work as an extension of their political activism. Several had previously worked at Iowa City's Free Medical Clinic or migrant clinics and considered themselves part of a larger movement of health activism that attracted health professionals in the 1960s and 1970s.[118] All supported the clinic's mission to involve women more closely in their own health care decisions, and most concluded that the personal gains outweighed the drawbacks at the clinic. As deProsse remembers conversations about the difficulties with his colleagues: "We'd sort of talk with each other about it and generally it ended up that one or the other of us would say, 'Oh, you know, that's the way it is.'"[119]

If, in feminist clinics, it was the physicians who had to figure out whether they were willing to "stick with it," in the more traditional medical settings it was often the women who weighed the advantages and disadvantages of staying on. Abortion clinics that ran on the medical model could provide important professional avenues for young women seeking a job in the women's health arena. During her two years at EPOC with Sam Barr, for instance, Susan Hill honed her skills as an administrator and director of counseling and gained significant knowledge in the field of medicine. Barr, she remembers, would take her along to surgery, allowing her to observe hysterectomies and other procedures she otherwise never would have seen. "He was a wonderful gynecologist," she remembered. "I learned so much, I loved what I did."[120]

But opportunity came at a price. During her two years at the clinic, Sam Barr also sexually harassed her. "He would talk to me about what we were going to do and plans—we wanted to do a women's hospital. And then he would stick his tongue down my throat. It was very bizarre behavior and at the time I really wasn't equipped to really understand what to do," she recalled. "The price you paid was that I cringed when I had to be alone with him. . . . It was just horrible at that point."[121] Eventually, she decided to leave and become a consultant for businessmen who ran abortion clinics as commercial ventures. But here, too, work often seemed to come with unwanted sexual advances. Hill remembers most of these businessmen as extremely sleazy. While crucial to the quick expansion of abortion services around the country, their treatment of female employees frequently mirrored that of Barr.

Sexual harassment, of course, was not the only problem that young women faced. Like male physicians in feminist clinics, many women in medical settings were frustrated by the lack of influence they had over service delivery. Many physicians refused to take criticism or were not interested in improving the experience of their women patients. If feminists expected that the legalization of abortion would result in more than safe abortion services, their expectations remained largely unfulfilled.

Nevertheless, physicians and businessmen provided important financial and institutional backing for an emerging network of abortion clinics and in the best cases could offer women such as Susan Hill and Renee Chelian the opportunity to help shape women's health services. "I got to do what I wanted to do," Hill recalled of her employment running clinics for the Yacknowitzs. "And I got to use their money to do it. . . . It was the perfect choice."[122] The opportunities provided by these clinics offered a generation of women an avenue into the medical field not only as medical staff but also as counselors, health administrators, and clinic directors. Once in those positions, feminists could participate in the shaping of more feminist and woman-centered clinics.

The legalization of abortion and the opening of abortion clinics had a profound impact on women seeking to control their reproduction, many of whom had had experiences with illegal abortion. Patients were grateful to have access to legal and safe abortion services. When EPOC opened in Winter Park, Florida, the clinic was immediately swamped with patients. Barr charged $200 for an abortion for pregnancies between eight and twelve weeks. Barr and his staff expected about twenty patients to come during the first day, but fifty showed up. Patients just walked in without an appointment, and the staff stayed until 1:00 A.M. to make sure everybody received service. With no existing clinics in the surrounding states, the clinic was overwhelmed seven days a week, with patients coming all the way from South Carolina, Georgia, Mississippi, or Alabama.[123]

The importance of legal abortion services to solve complex problems in patients' lives became immediately evident. After almost four decades, Susan Hill still remembered her third patient on the day EPOC opened its doors: a poor African American mother who had brought her young teenage daughter. The daughter, pregnant after being raped by a family member, suffered from cerebral palsy and mental retardation and could not respond to Hill's questions. Hill counseled the mother. But when Sam Barr examined the daughter, he found that she was eighteen to twenty weeks pregnant, too far along for an abortion at EPOC. The mother, who had driven five hours from Tallahassee, Florida, broke into tears. Hill felt utterly helpless. After considerable effort, Barr arranged for mother and daughter to see Dr. Barkus in Miami, who performed second trimester abortions. Staff found money so that mother and daughter could make the four-hour drive, and Barkus agreed to do the abortion for free. With the opening of clinics, staff realized the complexity of patients' personal problems that they would be expected to solve. Such cases left a lasting impression on staff, reminding them of the urgency of abortion care for years to come.[124]

Since clinic staff lacked a clear model for counseling and abortion care, the responses of patients were crucial in shaping abortion services in the early days. At EPOC, Sam Barr hired Susan Hill and several other young women to help him establish and run the clinic. While Barr drew up the protocols for the surgical procedures, Hill and her colleagues consulted with members of several underground abortion services, such as Clergy Consultation, on the development of a counseling component. Ultimately, Hill remembers, they "made it up. . . . I always say I was lucky because you couldn't be wrong because no one had ever done it really before."[125] For the first year, staff met every night after the clinic closed to talk about the cases they had seen and discuss what had been successful, what unsuccessful. As a result, patient reaction played a big role in the development of services. "We were really sort of getting it from the women that we saw, what they were asking, what they needed."[126] The willingness of staff to listen and respond to their patients proved crucial to the establishment of services and success of clinics. "The more we worked together, that part was great. . . . It was a good clinic, a sort of soothing clinic. And it ended up with a great reputation in the first year."[127]

Patient responses to abortion services were overwhelmingly positive. In a 1978 survey of patients at the EGC, 81 percent responded that they felt "very positive" about the clinic. They complimented the staff and the clinic atmosphere and praised the patient advocates. While the vast majority of patients indicated that they felt having an abortion was the right decision to make, many reported being sad and finding the experience very emotional. At the same time, they were glad to have had the choice of a legal abortion and reported feeling relieved after the procedure.[128] The fact that a patient advocate accompanied each patient through the entire process drew particular praise. As one patient commented, "The advocate I had that day saved my sanity. Because of their understanding and concern I can now put the whole thing behind me. I almost backed out (which would have been a mistake) simply because of fear. They saw me through the whole thing and never once let me down. I appreciate that they spoke to my boyfriend who was waiting, and offered to explain the procedure to him."[129] Patients also remarked on the clinic's positive reputation with Iowa City's medical community. "The general feeling regarding your clinic seems to be good," another patient wrote. "When discussing my experience with a physician friend who is fairly new to the Iowa City area, he has been given the impression from his profession [*sic*] peers that EGC has a good reputation and is a good place to send referrals. He indicated that I should feel very confident about the services you provide, and I do."[130]

But not all patients felt comfortable with the casual atmosphere of the EGC or confident that the feminist clinic really provided medical services on par with a more traditional physician's office. One woman complained about the music, noting that she did not want to listen to rock and roll songs with "lyrics about getting screwed, fucked over, sexist, patriarchal attitudes" during her abortion.[131] Others felt the clinic was giving too little pain medication and suggested staff either provide better medication or prepare patients adequately for the fact that they might experience pain.[132]

In more traditional clinic settings, it was most frequently physicians and insensitive staff that drew patient criticism. Indeed, while legalization meant that abortions were now medically safe, it did not guarantee that patients received respectful treatment. Following the legalization of abortion in New York, the Reverend Howard Moody's Clergy and Lay Advocates for Hospital Abortion received more than 1,000 complaints. One young woman objected that her pre-abortion counseling consisted of the explanation that "we stick a long needle in your belly to kill the baby."[133] Another patient, who had expressed surprise when the abortion provider she sought out told her the procedure would cost $700, protested his insensitive response: "You keep on playing games," he reportedly told her, "and you'll be beyond the 12 week limit and *then* see what it costs you."[134] And one woman, who wrote about her abortion experience in the *National Observer*, criticized the impersonal demeanor of the "faceless doctor" who performed her abortion. She described lying there and talking to Jean, the patient advocate,

> while never taking my eyes off the wordless robot trespassing down there on private property. Next he inserted the plastic tube, which Jean warned would hurt a bit. He turned on the suction pump and the room was filled with what sounded like a jackhammer and then like a dentist's drill once I got used to the sound. The accompanying pain was exactly like a severe menstrual cramp—a shrill persistent clamoring in the abdomen that bites the lower back and thighs as well. . . . The infernal machine finally stopped. It probably took all of an eternal 120 seconds. Next he scraped the cervical walls, and that hurt like blue blazes. . . . Then I erupted into tears. Here I thought I had been utterly com-

posed. I supposed the days of suppressed anxiety, the guilt, the remote possibility of death, combined with the sound of my innards changing from solid to liquid and that villain languidly watching my blood and tissue scurry through a tube must have come to my conscious realization. And during all this, here I was discussing Jean's educational history as though we were sitting over coffee and pound cake in Stouffer's. And still that brute never looked at me.[135]

Clearly, it took more than a patient advocate and a legal, presumably medically safe abortion procedure to make women feel good about the process. The attitude and demeanor of the abortion provider and the level of anxiety a patient felt were also crucial to the abortion experience.

BETWEEN 1973 AND 1980, the number of legal abortions performed more than doubled, from 744,610 in 1973 to 1,553,890 in 1980. Mortality and complication rates plummeted as more and more women gained access to legal abortion services and as abortion providers refined their techniques and honed their skills. By 1982, the Alan Guttmacher Institute counted 2,908 abortion providers, an increase of 88 percent from 1,550 in 1973.[136] Already in 1973, more than half of all abortion procedures were performed in outpatient clinics.[137] As services spread across the country, the proliferation of outpatient clinics that provided abortion services in a nonhospital location shaped the setting of abortion care.

Clinic owners found that the demand for services resulted in an explosive growth of their clinics. By 1980, many clinics had grown from new offices with a small staff to large clinics that offered a wide variety of services and served an increasing number of patients. After resigning from his teaching post at the UNC in late 1972, Takey Crist had borrowed $30,000 to open his practice in Jacksonville, North Carolina. Within the first two weeks of 1973, he saw his first patient. His new practice grew so quickly that Crist was able to repay his loans within four months. By 1975 the clinic had not only outgrown its location but Crist also needed the help of another physician.

Crist purchased a lot across the street from the new Onslow Memorial Hospital on Memorial Drive and enlisted the help of a friend to draw up plans for a new clinic. "At night, after we saw the last patients, we were on the floor of the waiting room at Johnson Boulevard [Crist's original clinic] and we were designing the clinic together. And I'd tell him about what I wanted, how many nurses I thought I might need, how I wanted the operating rooms designed, and that we needed an extra room for counseling."

By 1975, Crist had hired his first partner, Paul Williams, and moved into the new building. Patient demand quickly necessitated specialized staff in other areas. Patients came not only with medical complaints but also with questions about marriage and sexuality at a time when counseling services in such matters were nonexistent in eastern North Carolina. Crist began to teach sex education and family planning to teenagers and offered courses on human sexuality at Onslow Memorial Hospital. For a fee of $10, participants learned about human anatomy, family planning, abortion, and homosexuality and the full range of sexual experiences. Through these courses, Crist was also able to reach health and social work professionals in eastern North Carolina. In addition, he hired a professional marriage counselor for the clinic. In the late 1970s, the clinic developed the first services for battered women and rape victims in eastern North Carolina. With the help of grant funding, Crist trained nurses and counselors to identify and help women in abusive relationships and coordinated these services with the health and social services departments in Onslow County.[138] By 1980, the clinic offered a wide range of services from abortion to prenatal care, deliveries, complete physical exams, gynecological surgeries, and marriage and birth control counseling.

The EGC in Iowa City, Iowa, experienced a similar growth spurt. In the early summer of 1973, several Emma Goldman women had located a house on 715 North Dodge Street that seemed perfect for a women's health clinic. Five of EGC's founding members scraped together funds for a down payment, medical supplies, and equipment, drawing on their personal savings and loans, and on a small gift from the Clergy Council.[139] Over the summer of 1973, the women readied the building, sanding floors, painting, and laying tiles. When the clinic opened on September 1, 1973, staff consisted of four full-time and eight part-time employees, all members of the collective.

The clinic started on a modest scale. Staff planned on six abortions for the first day and the appointments filled immediately. Paula Klein remembers scheduling the first abortion. "I was sitting on my living room floor. I couldn't believe it. I felt that this was a very historic moment."[140] Staff received on-the-job-training, with collective members teaching one another the necessary skills. One member was a medical technician, a second was getting her degree in accounting, a third was a registered nurse. All staff members learned to sterilize instruments, draw blood, perform basic gynecological exams, and educate clients about their bodies. "In the original group we taught ourselves," Roxie Tullis remembered. "We learned fast and we learned from our mistakes."[141] Collective members also rotated jobs, so that all performed every aspect of the services. By the end of 1974, the clinic offered not only abortions but also gynecological and obstetrical care, positive pregnancy and well-child clinics, medical and legal advice, a twenty-four-hour medical crisis hotline, a health consumer complaint line, massages, and feminist psychotherapy. Especially on abortion days, staff members frequently put in ten-hour days. "They were a lot of fun," an early collective member recalled. "We'd have Linda Ronstadt on tape and we'd be taking women's medical histories while listening to 'I've got bad dreams.'"[142] The clinic quickly outgrew the space, and within the first year, the house was bursting at its seams. Working conditions were difficult, with desks crammed into every conceivable space, including the cold and damp basement.

By 1975, tensions between Dick Winter and the collective resulted in Winter's decision to take a leave of absence. Suddenly without an abortion provider, collective members turned for help to the University of Iowa Hospitals and Clinics and began to hire medical residents to provide abortion services. The crisis also resulted in a period of restructuring and a move away from a system of strict job rotation toward one that allowed for specialization in specific areas. Finally, the collective bought a second house on 707 North Dodge Street, next door to the original clinic. These developments helped members of the EGC to enter a period of tremendous productivity. By the end of the decade, the number of women served had increased from 3,000 to 11,500 women per year, and the clinic's annual operating budget, primarily derived from abortion services, had increased from $80,000 to $300,000.[143]

A variety of factors influenced how women experienced their pregnancy terminations. The details of service provision, whether a clinic was following the medical or feminist model, significantly shaped the character of clinics and influenced clinic services. Central to the medical model was the provision of quality medical care. Abortion was a form of surgery, rather than a transformative experience. Feminist clinics, in contrast, saw their mission in women's health as a political one. As one collective member recalls, "Emma was more than an abortion clinic. Abortion was the catalyst. It was the excuse that the clinic got started. The real issue was women's health care."[144]

But while clinics showed distinct characteristics, the professional collaboration between physicians and feminists also meant that both groups influenced each other. Feminist clinics were at the forefront of pushing health professionals to include more education and information. They emphasized the importance of patient participation and passed this information on to male medical professionals, transforming the teaching of medical skills to become more woman-friendly. Physicians and businessmen, in turn, provided important financial and institutional backing for an emerging network of abortion clinics and presented women with the opportunity to help shape women's health services. The opportunities provided by these clinics offered a generation of women an avenue into the medical field, not only as medical staff but also as counselors, health administrators, and clinic directors. Once in those positions, feminists participated in the shaping of more feminist and woman-centered clinics.

Aside from the character of a clinic and the interaction with clinic staff, patient experience was also shaped by more personal factors. Women's expectations of the procedure, the amount of anxiety they felt, and whether or not they experienced guilt further influenced women's perception of legal abortion services. A safe abortion during which a woman was accompanied by a helpful patient advocate was not always enough for a glowing review. Clinic staff could try to ameliorate women's apprehension. But political and cultural changes surrounding abortion care played an important role. Indeed, despite all the advances toward women's access to legal abortion in the 1970s, the decade also saw the emergence of a powerful opposition to legal abortion. This movement slowed the establishment of clinics and meant that not all women benefited equally from the growing network of abortion clinics.

By the end of the decade, women outside metropolitan areas continued to find access to abortion services difficult. In 1979, 80 percent of the nation's providers were located in metropolitan areas, but 59 of the nation's 305 metropolitan areas had no abortion provider and an additional 25 reported performing fewer than 50 abortions in 1980. In some states, the abortion occurrence rate was so low as to suggest that abortion services were virtually unavailable to women. In 1980, half the residents of South Dakota, West Virginia, and Wyoming who had an abortion traveled out of state for the procedure, while a quarter of women from Idaho, Indiana, Kentucky, Maryland, Mississippi, and Missouri did so. With the exception of Maryland, residents in these states had abortion rates well below the national average, leading experts from the Alan Guttmacher Institute to conclude that some women in these states were unable to obtain abortions because local services were not available.[145]

The backlash against *Roe v. Wade* that began in the 1970s shaped abortion care for decades to come. By the mid-1970s, legislators across the country were mounting financial and procedural challenges to again restrict women's access to abortion services. Antiabortion activists cast a wide net as they tried to reverse the gains made following the *Roe v. Wade* decision, from barring federal funding for abortions via the Hyde Amendment to state laws (first introduced in Missouri) prohibiting saline abortions and requiring wives to have their husband's consent and minors to have parental consent if they sought an abortion. Based on the belief that abortion was murder, antiabortion activists constructed an intellectual framework for their opposition that affected the establishment and delivery of abortion care from the very beginning. In 1974, the indictment of Kenneth Edelin, an African American resident in the Department of Obstetrics and Gynecology at Boston City Hospital, for manslaughter drew national attention as Boston city prosecutors started a frontal assault on legal abortion. The trial and its aftermath provided a first insight into the impact that the fight against abortion would have on the emerging field of abortion care.

2

Medicine at the Edges of Life
Abortion and Fetal Research

On February 15, 1975, Boston ob-gyn Kenneth Edelin was convicted of manslaughter for performing a hysterotomy, a second trimester abortion procedure akin to a cesarean section. Edelin had performed the procedure at BCH in October 1973, a time when abortion in Massachusetts was legal and restricted only by the willingness of physicians and hospitals to provide abortion services. After making his first incision, he swept his fingers through the uterine cavity, carefully detaching the anterior placenta from the uterine wall. Then he began to peel the amniotic sac away from the placenta, hoping to extract the intact sac through the incision. When the sac ruptured, Edelin changed course and began the process of removing the fetus. He took hold of the lower extremities of the fetus to pull it through the incision, leaving it physically inside the uterine cavity but detached from the placenta and removed from the sac. After feeling with his fingers for a heartbeat or other sign of life and finding none, he pulled the fetus out of the uterine cavity, placed it in a stainless steel bin, and completed the surgical procedure on Alice Roe. The fetus went to the pathology lab. There, second-year resident pathologist Dr. Frank Fallico looked at and weighed the fetus. He then placed the fetus in a two-quart plastic container with a solution of formaldehyde and set it aside for his supervisor's inspection. Two days later, the fetus was transferred to the morgue, where officials discovered it in early 1974 as they investigated fetal research practices at BCH. In April 1974, fifteen months after the legalization of abortion, Assistant District Attorney Newman Flanagan charged Edelin with manslaughter under an 1814 Grave-Robbing Statute.[1]

The trial, which ran from January 10 to February 15, 1975, juxtaposed two very different narratives of abortion. The prosecution charged that Edelin's action had killed a live baby. "The action of the defendant," Flanagan explained, "is that he allowed an independent human being, on its own systems, to remain in that particular environment [in Alice's uterus, after he had separated the placenta] for at least three minutes. These actions caused the death of a viable, independent human being—either born or in the process of being born."[2] Edelin's defense attorney, William Homans, contended that Edelin "engaged in a procedure which, in his best judgment as a physician, was sanctioned not only by good medical practice, but also by the law."[3]

Jurors and witnesses grappled with the fact that abortion inevitably implied the death of the fetus. "I said it often in there," one juror noted about the deliberation, "that he [Edelin] was doing an operation, that it was a hard fact but this [the death of the fetus] was involved in the operation. This was completely unpersuasive to the jury."[4] Witnesses debated when and how the fetus had died and what Edelin's responsibility toward the fetus had been. The status of the fetus was central to the meaning of the death. Was it a fetus, a male child, or a baby boy?[5] In the end, images of the fetus swayed jurors to conclude that the fetus was a baby and that Edelin was thus guilty of manslaughter. For those opposed to abortion and fetal research, the image of a fetus offered a powerful symbol supporting the belief that personhood began long before birth. When the prosecution introduced photographs of the fetus, defense attorney William Homans objected. Homans rightly anticipated that the introduction of fetal photographs as evidence in the trial would have an enormous emotional impact on the jurors and prove prejudicial to the case. And so it did. In his closing statement, prosecutor Flanagan urged the jurors to study the photograph as they tried to determine the status of the fetus. "Is this a subject? Is this just a specimen? Look at the picture, who is it to anybody? What would you tell you it was? Use your common sense when you go to your jury deliberation room and humanize that. Are you speaking about a blob, a big bunch of mucus, or what are we talking about here? I respectfully submit that we're talking about an independent human being that the Commonwealth of Massachusetts must protect as well as anybody in the courtroom, including the defendant."[6] The jurors agreed. Indeed, they were shaken by the photograph and concluded that the fetus looked well enough developed to live. "It looked like a baby," one juror told reporters. "It definitely had an effect on me."[7] And another commented that "the picture helped people draw their own conclusions. Everyone in the room made up their minds that the fetus was a person."[8] Since the fetus looked like a baby, it must have been a baby, the jury concluded, and they found Edelin guilty.

Edelin's conviction sent shock waves through the medical community. The fact that a jury could find that a twenty- to twenty-four-week-old fetus removed as a result of abortion was a born person painfully illustrated how issues surrounding the meaning of fetal life and death had become questions of bitter dispute. As the country transitioned from the pre- to the post-*Roe* era, both supporters and opponents of legal abortion focused on the fetus and the implications that the legalization of abortion had on the ways the general public might imagine the fetus.

The Edelin case is significant in several ways. First, the trial illustrates the convergence of two issues that came together immediately after the 1973 legalization of abortion: debates over the nature of pregnancy termination procedures and the growing debate over fetal research. Abortion, opponents charged, produced "hundreds of thousands of abortuses within the premises of bona fide medical centers [that] led directly to considerations of possible research uses for the unwanted fetuses, as well as research on the living fetus in anticipation of legal abortion."[9] Tapping into larger discussions about the protection of human subjects, antiabortionists treated the fetus as a vulnerable subject threatened by conscienceless physicians and legal abortion as a convenient avenue for physicians to gain access to research subjects.

Second, the trial became a forum to explore the status of the fetus. Was it an unborn person or fetal tissue? While the prosecution framed the event as a morality tale—the surgical procedure Kenneth Edelin had performed had resulted in a live baby which subsequently died as a result of Edelin's actions—the defense framed the event as a modern witch hunt: Edelin had been indicted for manslaughter after performing a legal medical procedure. Seeking to establish the fetus as a person, antiabortion activists constructed narratives that described the fetal experience of abortion and fetal death. With the emergence of the antiabortion movement in the late 1960s and early 1970s, such narratives took center stage in the unfolding debate. As they drew the attention from the mother to the fetus, these fetal stories held significant emotional power, and abortion opponents hoped that they might convince women not to terminate their pregnancies. In addition, these narratives helped to mobilize a grassroots campaign on behalf of the fetal subject, convincing abortion opponents to act in defense of the fetus.

Third, *Commonwealth v. Edelin* vividly demonstrates the threat to physicians who performed abortions near viability. Indeed, the question whether or not the fetus had been alive after Edelin had severed its connection to the mother and what Edelin's responsibilities in that case might have been stood at the center of the trial. Although defense attorneys argued that the fetus showed no heartbeat or other sign of life—in fact, Edelin suspected it had been dead for many hours—and that the hysterotomy Edelin had performed was a legal procedure, the prosecution charged that the fetus was, in effect, born at the moment Edelin severed its connection with its mother's uterus and claimed that the procedure constituted manslaughter.[10]

Although the guilty verdict was later overturned, the Edelin case had a chilling effect on abortion providers. It contributed to the establishment of live birth as a recognized complication of abortion procedures and ultimately factored into physicians' attempts to avoid procedures that carried the risk of live birth. By doing so, the case illustrates the remarkable influence that the antiabortion movement was going to have on the performance of abortion procedures around the country. Previously, access to technology and considerations of maternal health and mortality had determined the development of abortion procedures. Now, with the introduction of live birth as a complication, abortion providers had to consider the potential of legal charges by hostile prosecutors when deciding what procedures to use.[11]

"It Is Not Possible to Make This Fetus into a Child":
The Fetal Research Debate Pre- and Post-Roe

In 1971, when Edelin first arrived in Boston, many Boston women seeking an abortion went to New York where abortions had just been legalized. As a public hospital, BCH served a largely poor and urban population, the majority of whom lacked the funds to travel to New York and pay for a legal abortion. Instead, they came to BCH. Prior to *Roe v. Wade*, doctors at BCH had performed a small number of medically indicated therapeutic abortions—two to four per week. After the *Roe* decision, the numbers rose tenfold.[12] Many BCH nurses were Catholic and upset at this increase. And most BCH doctors took advantage of the hospital's "conscience clause," which allowed them to refuse to perform abortions. Indeed, in 1973, only two BCH doctors were willing to perform abortions—one of them was Kenneth Edelin.[13]

For Edelin, issues of women's reproductive health and social justice were inextricably linked. The youngest of four children, Edelin had grown up African American in segregated Washington, D.C., during the 1940s.

When he was twelve, his mother died of breast cancer. Devastated by her suffering, the young Edelin became determined to become a physician and save women's lives. Following his mother's death, Edelin was shuttled from relative to relative until he won a scholarship to Stockridge School, a progressive integrated boarding school in western Massachusetts. After graduation, he attended Columbia College in New York City, then Meharry Medical College in Tennessee. There he learned about the close connection between racism, poverty, and poor health and witnessed the death of a seventeen-year-old girl from an illegal abortion. These experiences—as well as his own experience seeking an illegal abortion for a girlfriend— further fostered his commitment to women's health, including abortion care.[14]

Not only did BCH physicians perform abortions prior to *Roe v. Wade*, but researchers at BCH also conducted fetal research. In the early 1970s, four researchers—Swedish scientist Agneta Philipson at Harvard on a visiting appointment; Leon Sabath, associate professor of medicine at Harvard Medical School; BCH physician David Charles; and BCH pathologist Leonard Berman—collaborated on a study of antibiotics. Philipson had conceived of the study when she was pregnant with her fourth child and contracted bronchitis. She began to take antibiotics and realized that her pregnancy altered her ability to metabolize the drug. During her year at Harvard, she discussed her observation with Sabath, and the two researchers decided to investigate how much two common antibiotics taken by pregnant women crossed the placenta and entered the blood stream of the fetus. While there was no reason to think that antibiotics would harm the fetus, the safest course of action was to conduct the study with women who were about to have an abortion. Philipson and Sabath asked David Charles, who performed abortions at BCH, and Leonard Berman, who was in a position to help investigators obtain tissue for the study, to participate.[15]

Indeed, the use of tissue from aborted fetuses and nonviable fetuses for medical research dates back to the early twentieth century. Anthropologist Lynn Morgan describes the work of neuroanatomist Davenport Hooker, one of the earliest and most influential researchers to use nonviable fetuses, who, between 1932 and 1958, performed neurological tests on 149 fetuses at the University of Pittsburgh. Local doctors notified Hooker when they expected a premature delivery or planned a therapeutic abortion. Hooker quickly moved the fetuses gained from these procedures to his laboratory, where they were immersed in a saline solution warmed to ninety degrees Fahrenheit. During the brief time span in which the fetuses were still alive—between seven and twenty minutes, depending on gestational age—Hooker performed neurological tests. He recorded the neurological responses using motion picture film. In 1952, he assembled his footage into a silent educational film called *Early Fetal Human Activity*, which featured six fetuses ranging from eight and a half to fourteen weeks and showed their "characteristic reactive behavior (muscle activity)."[16] Hooker was not alone. Into the 1960s, many others used nonviable but still living fetuses for research and to prepare superior specimen. They did so in a cultural context in which fetuses did not carry the same meaning they do in the early twenty-first century. "It is not that Hooker, his colleagues, or his audience *de*-humanized the fetus or hardened themselves against its charms," Morgan notes. "They had no charming fetuses in their repertoire; they had never humanized fetuses to begin with."[17] Not until much later, Morgan concludes, would it become possible to imagine fetuses as anything else but specimen.

In the course of the twentieth century, such research on dying fetuses and on tissue cultured from fetal cells led to important discoveries, such as our knowledge about fetal development and the 1954 development of the polio vaccine. In the early 1960s, researchers formalized the procedures for procuring and distributing fetal tissue. In 1961, the University of Washington established the Laboratory for the Study of Human Embryos and Fetuses which institutionalized the process of obtaining human fetal tissue for research purposes. At the same time, popular writers began to disseminate the scientific findings, and images of fetuses appeared in general publications. Several of Hooker's images, for instance, were published in 1962 in an early pregnancy guidebook by Geraldine Lux Flanagan, *The First Nine Months of Life*. Flanagan drew attention away from the details of the research that had led to the creation of the fetal images in the first place. While she noted that Hooker and his colleagues had "compiled thousands of feet of motion-picture film" which recorded the activities of "babies born very early," she did not mention therapeutic abortion, fetal remains, or the fact that the embryos and fetuses were filmed in their final minutes of life.[18] The dissemination of these images helped to transform the public's understanding of the fetus and undermined the conditions that allowed for the creation of the images in the first place. After the 1960s, encounters with the dead fetus were regarded as distasteful and macabre, and researchers rarely publicized the fact that fetal images came from dead or dying specimen.[19]

If discoveries about fetal development and the polio vaccine symbolized the success of modern medicine, then thalidomide babies warned of its failures. Thalidomide, developed in Germany in the 1950s to treat chronic insomnia, quickly became popular with pregnant women throughout Europe. Although the FDA never approved thalidomide for the American market, it found its way to the United States. By the early 1960s, after the birth of more than 16,000 babies with flipper-like stumps instead of arms and hands, physicians realized that thalidomide led to severe birth defects. A nationwide rubella epidemic in the early 1960s heightened the urgency to protect developing fetuses because the disease, if contracted by women in their first three months of pregnancy, could cause serious birth defects. In response, scientists across the country intensified studies to understand the cause and transmission of congenital malformations. Throughout the 1960s, faith in the power of American science and pharmaceuticals and the state's commitment to protecting the health of mothers and children through science led to an explosion of research.[20]

In 1975, the National Commission for the Protection of Human Subjects of Biomedical and Behavioral Research conducted a review of the scientific literature from the 1960s and early 1970s to ascertain the nature, extent, and purpose of research on the fetus. The commission found this research involved the fetus inside and outside the uterus and was intended to address a wide range of questions: knowledge of normal fetal growth and development, fetal disease or abnormality, fetal pharmacology and the effects of chemical and other agents on the fetus in order to develop fetal therapy, and the development of techniques to save the lives of ever smaller premature infants. Fetal research, the report noted, "may be as innocuous as observation, or involve mild manipulation such as weighing or measuring, or more extensive manipulation such as altering the environment, administering a drug or agent, or noninvasive monitoring. Diagnostic studies may involve sampling amniotic fluid, urine, blood, or spinal fluid, or performing biopsies. The most extensive and invasive procedures include perfusion studies and other attempts to maintain [fetal] function."[21] By 1969, tissue from an infected aborted fetus from the Washington Laboratory allowed investigators to develop a rubella vaccine. Other researchers used fetal tissue to develop tests for Rh incompatibility and amniocentesis screenings for other genetic anomalies.[22] BCH researchers followed this tradition and were able to conclude in the early 1970s that the antibiotics they had tested were a good alternative to penicillin for treating pregnant women.[23]

When, in June 1973, the four BCH scientists published their research results in the *New England Journal of Medicine*, antiabortion forces took note. Already upset at the rising numbers of abortions performed at BCH, abortion opponents sent several outraged letters about abortion and fetal experimentation to the Boston City Council. In September 1973, City Councilor Dapper O'Neil, chairman of the Health and Hospital Committee of the Boston City Council and himself strongly opposed to abortion, decided to call public hearings on the issue. He invited right-to-life activists familiar to him, and on September 18, 1973, several hundred people gathered in the council chambers to discuss abortions and fetal research at BCH.

Prior to the legalization of abortion, fetal research had evoked little public concern. Investigators had quietly planned, funded, completed, and published fetal research without drawing public attention. With *Roe v. Wade*, antiabortion activists recognized that putting a spotlight on fetal research could serve their broader political strategies and goals. In particular, activists focused on research involving nonviable fetuses outside the uterus. Such research was extremely rare—Dr. Maurice J. Mahoney, associate director of human genetics and pediatrics at Yale University, estimated in the 1970s that it pertained to well below 1 percent of all fetal research—and most of it was conducted outside the United States.[24] Notwithstanding, discussion of such studies was most likely to evoke disturbing images. Abortion opponents built their case against fetal research by focusing on research to develop life support systems for fetuses (artificial placentas) and studies of fetal metabolism.

Research on artificial placentas dated back to the 1960s when investigators in the United States, Scandinavia, and England had sought to develop an environment that could simulate the role of the mother's placenta by supplying oxygen to the immature fetus. One such study, conducted in the United States, involved eight living fetuses obtained after hysterotomy and weighing between 300 and 980 grams. The researchers had constructed an elaborate circulation system which, they hoped, would supply oxygen to the fetus. The fetuses were placed in tanks filled with warm saline solution, to mimic amniotic fluid, and small cannulas were inserted in the umbilical arteries and veins for pumping in and removing oxygenated blood. Ultimately, the experimental systems failed. The fetus to survive the longest lived for twenty-two hours. Some fetuses died in the course of the experiment, others died after researchers disconnected them from the artificial placenta.[25] Investigators observed about one fetus: "For the whole 5 hours of life, fetus did not respire, irregular gasping movements, twice a minute, occurred in the middle of the experiment but there was no proper respiration. Once the profusion [that is, the pumping in of oxygenated blood] was stopped, however, the gasping respiratory efforts increased to 8 to 10 per minute. . . . After stopping the circuit, the heart slowed, became irregular, and eventually stopped. . . . The fetus was quiet, making occasional stretching limb movements very like the ones reported in other human work. . . . The fetus died 21 minutes after leaving the circuit."[26]

Other studies of fetal physiology examined fetal brain metabolism. Conducted in Sweden, Finland, England, and Scotland, these studies examined whether the fetal body could metabolize glucose and fats. Given a state of fetal emergency, for instance, if a diabetic mother was failing to provide adequate glucose for the fetus, was it possible for the fetal brain to survive on body-stored fats? One such study, conducted in Finland with the involvement of an American researcher, included twelve fetuses between twelve and twenty-one weeks' gestation. All had died soon after delivery. Once the fetal heartbeat had ceased, researchers inserted a catheter into the major artery leading to the brain. Then they surgically "isolated" the head of the fetus—by cutting off the fetal heads—and perfused the fetal brains with glucose and D-β-OH butyrate as an alternative to the glucose. By measuring the rate at which the cerebral tissues took up the substances, investigators were able to demonstrate that the fetal brain could metabolize body fat as an energy source.[27]

The legalization of abortion immediately politicized the fetal bodies and made them highly contested. Were they gasping fetuses floating in a tank or fetal tissue that, if used in research, could help achieve scientific breakthroughs to the benefit of society? Were they alive or were they dead? Had they been born? What was their status?

New developments in medical research contributed to a growing unease about the role of medicine at the edges of life. The development of life-sustaining technologies such as the respirator in the 1950s meant that now machines confounded the definition of death. By the 1960s, some European transplant surgeons, for instance, had begun to remove organs from persons in *coma dépassé*, literally a state "beyond coma" defined by the loss of all reflexes and all brain activity in patients whose heart and lung functions could now be maintained by machines but whose consciousness never returned. The medical profession itself was unsure of the precise meaning of death. At conferences throughout the 1960s, surgeons discussed questions about the determination of death, and the medical literature manifested uncertainty over the appropriate point of removing organs for transplantation. As bioethicist Albert R. Jonsen notes, "persons who were the sources of organs were described as 'dead' or 'immanently dead' or 'irreversibly dying.' Problematic legal cases had already arisen. In

England, for example, organs were taken from a Mr. Potter who, to the transplanter, was 'virtually dead,' and to the coroner, was still alive. In the U.S., Clarence Nicks was beaten 'to death' by an assailant but, after being placed on a respirator, his heart continued to beat until it was transplanted into John Stuckwish."[28]

Popular culture reflected growing public anxiety over discussions of transplantation and the border between life and death. Fear of organ stealing was a main topic both in the tabloid press and in the low-budget movie industry in the 1950s and 1960s. As historian Martin Pernick notes, a wave of horror movies about Frankenstein, mummies, and zombies exploited the moral dangers of blurring the line between the dead and the undead.[29]

The line between life and death became even more confusing when it involved fetuses. Increasing sophistication of neonatal care in the 1960s led by the end of the decade to the very first fetal therapies. Indeed, the 1960s were a watershed decade in fetal diagnosis and treatment, resulting in the development of the Rh vaccine RhoGAM, of intrauterine transfusion technology, and of the first open fetal surgeries. With each new fetal treatment, the fetus moved further from the premodern conception of a tabula rasa and closer to a visible unborn patient.[30] And as an unborn patient, the fetus could now be rescued by technology prior to being born and saved from women seeking abortions and doctors conducting fetal experiments.[31]

While scientific research intensified in the post–World War II era and federal support for such work increased, both medical researchers and the federal government paid little attention to the rights and welfare of human research subjects. However, guidelines did exist. In response to medical experiments performed by Nazi doctors, the prosecuting team at the International Military Tribunal trial established the Nuremberg Code of 1947. Further revised by the World Medical Association into the 1964 Declaration of Helsinki, these codes expressed a set of ethical principles that should underlie the conduct of medical research with human subjects.[32] The United States endorsed both sets of guidelines. But without mechanisms of enforcement, the principles remained abstract ideals rather than concrete practices. Indeed, the general understanding was that the Nuremberg Code was "a good code for barbarians but an unnecessary code for ordinary physicians."[33]

Medical researchers were wary when, in the spring of 1968, Minnesota senator Walter Mondale opened hearings to discuss the effects of scientific advances in medicine. Mondale was hoping to stimulate a national dialogue on the implications of medical advances. Recent developments, he noted, raised grave and fundamental ethical and legal questions for society: "Who shall live and who shall die? How long shall life be preserved and how should it be altered? Who will make decisions? How shall society be prepared?"[34] But when he proposed the establishment of the President's Commission on Health Science and Society to study organ transplantation, genetic engineering, behavior control, human experimentation, and research funding, medical researchers were dismayed. Most admitted at the hearings that scientific advances held some troubling aspects, but they suggested that those aspects were exaggerated. And they vehemently opposed any interference with the progress of science. Indeed, the hearings provide an early example of both the growing public discomfort with the unregulated power of scientists and physicians and the resistance of scientists and physicians to any external oversight of their work.[35]

In the 1960s, a spate of troubling stories about unethical research using human subjects transformed the public discomfort with medical research into active resistance. In 1966, Henry Beecher, a professor of anesthesiology at Harvard Medical School, published an exposé of abuses in clinical research which drew attention to the exploitation of servicemen, prisoners, and such vulnerable populations as the institutionalized elderly and mentally disabled. The report was closely followed by other similar revelations, including news about the notorious Tuskegee Study in which African American men were for decades left untreated for syphilis to study the progression of the disease and a study in which children institutionalized at the Willowbrook State School for the Retarded were injected with live hepatitis viruses.[36]

At the same time, the emerging civil rights and women's rights movements gave voice to a new group of activists fighting for equal access to medical care and respectful treatment by medical professionals. By the mid-1960s, African American health care professionals challenged their discrimination by white colleagues and their exclusion from mainstream medical professional organizations such as the American Medical Association, medical schools, and staff positions at hospitals. Most African American patients, these activists pointed out, received substandard care, if they were able to receive health care services at all. Women, too, began to protest their disrespectful treatment by male medical professionals. By the late 1960s, women's health activists accused the pharmaceutical industry and physicians of persistently ignoring warning signs about the dangers of the newly approved birth control pill and, in the early 1970s, the Dalkon Shield intrauterine device (IUD). Both the birth control pill and the Dalkon Shield had, by 1974, led to the deaths of several women and serious complications for many more. By the mid-1970s, women's health activists were establishing a women's health network that stretched from Boston to Los Angeles and addressed issues from the involuntary sterilization of poor and nonwhite women to abortion rights and women's control over childbirth.[37] Trust in physicians plummeted. A Harris Poll revealed that between 1962 and 1972, public confidence in the medical establishment dropped from 73 to 42 percent.[38]

The antiabortion campaign against fetal research emerged in the context of these protests and took advantage of the growing public mistrust of the medical profession. While only 1 percent of research conducted in the United States by the late 1960s included the nonviable fetus ex utero, antiabortion activists collapsed the distinction between live and dead fetal bodies, lumping all fetal research into one category, which they described as barbaric and labeled as torture. As early as 1972, the *Handbook on Abortion*, an early foundational work of the antiabortion movement written by the Cincinnati couple Jack and Barbara Wilke, alleged that medical researchers used aborted fetuses for research purposes. The Wilkes, a physician and a nurse, came from the movement against sex education, where they had preached against contraception, pornography, and homosexuality. In the fall of 1970, they were recruited to the fledging antiabortion movement by Father Paul Marx from Minnesota, who had spoken against abortion since the early 1960s.

From the very beginning, antiabortion literature focused on the aesthetic characteristics of abortion and fetal research, describing both in grisly terms. The early editions of the *Handbook on Abortion* described four abortion procedures performed in the early 1970s: D&C, vacuum aspiration, saline instillation, and hysterotomy. In brief synopses, the authors explained what these procedures entailed. A surgeon performing a D&C "cuts the placenta and baby into pieces and scrapes them out into a basin." Vacuum aspiration "tears the baby and placenta into small pieces which are then sucked out of the uterus and into a bottle." Saline abortions poisoned "the baby," which "breathes and swallows" the salt solution, "struggles, sometimes convulses, and in about one hour dies." In a hysterotomy, finally, "the mother's abdomen is surgically opened, as is her uterus. The baby is then lifted out, and, with the placenta, discarded." "One hundred percent of all babies aborted by hysterotomy," the *Handbook* concluded, "are born alive. They must either be then killed or left to die from lack of attention."[39]

Accompanying these descriptions were photographs of aborted fetuses,

Ill. 2.1. The caption in *Handbook on Abortion* reads, "Abortion by suction at 10 weeks." Courtesy of J. C. Wilke.

which lend antiabortion publications of the early 1970s a gruesome character (see ills. 2.1 and 2.2).[40] Antiabortion activists began to employ visual images in the early 1970s. First introduced into the public discourse by the Wilkes, the now-so-familiar images of aborted fetuses seemed to provide the key to defeating the pro-choice side. Soon after joining the antiabortion movement, the Wilkes began collecting pictures of aborted fetuses from physicians and pathologists across the United States and Canada. These images of mutilated fetal bodies were intended to both fascinate and repel the viewer. At a Right to Life booth at the 1971 Ohio State Fair, Barbara Wilke discovered the emotional power of these photos. Volunteers had set up literature, bumper stickers, and copies of the *Handbook*. When nobody stopped by to look, the volunteers opened a couple of the *Handbooks* to the pictures. "And all of a sudden they had people ten feet deep. They were just mobbing the booth," Barbara Wilke recalled.[41] The pictures allowed antiabortion activists to create a discourse of pregnancy termination that powerfully shaped the perception of pregnancy and pregnancy termination procedures.[42] Scholars have noted that fetal images were photographed both to emphasize the fetus's Caucasian roots and to remind viewers of the iconography of the Christ child. Although some of

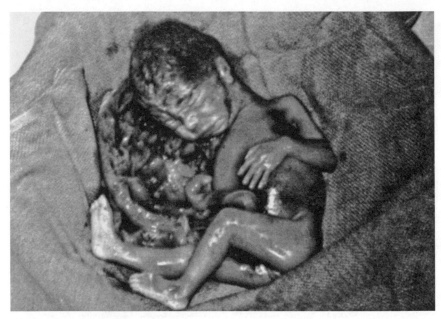

Ill. 2.2. The caption in *Handbook on Abortion* reads, "Abortion by salt poisoning at 19 weeks." Courtesy of J. C. Wilke.

the early imagery included pictures suggesting that babies of all colors and races fell victim to abortion, the lighting and sequencing of antiabortion images, feminist scholar Carol Mason has argued, positioned the white child alone as the victim of abortion.[43]

And from the very beginning, charges that abortion cut babies into pieces, tore fetal bodies apart, or burned them in utero were combined with allegations that medical researchers used aborted fetuses for research purposes. Human experimentation, the Wilkes claimed, was already common practice in England and the United States. Physicians had taken fetal brains and kept them alive as long as five months, had developed a new polio vaccine from cell cultures from human fetuses, and had done liver and other experiments on live tiny humans. A photograph of a medical researcher manipulating wires connected to an embryo illustrated the fate that seemed to await aborted fetuses (see ill. 2.3).

A caption described the photo as "the last hours of an aborted Baby" and explained that the researcher, Dr. Lawrence Lawn of Cambridge University's Department of Experimental Medicine in England, regularly experimented on living, legally aborted human fetuses that he obtained from the local abortion clinic. Medical researchers and those aiding them were cast as mad scientists, lacking in humanity and moral framework. The

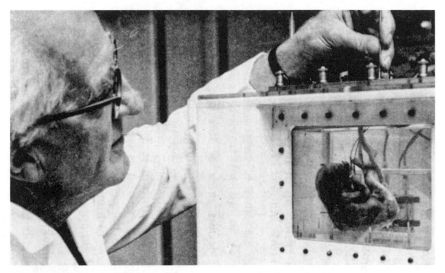

Ill. 2.3. Medical researcher with fetus. From *Handbook on Abortion*,
courtesy of J. C. Wilke.

Wilkes quoted Lawn and a spokesperson for the abortion clinic, Philip
Stanley, depicting them as cynical, even cruel. "The position is quite clear,"
Stanley was quoted as saying. "A fetus has to be 28 weeks to become legally
viable. Earlier than that it is so much garbage."[44] Insinuating that all fetal
research included fetuses that were still alive at the time of the experiments, the Wilkes concluded with a grim warning about the fate of the
fetuses: "Reports are piling up of liver and other experiments on live tiny
humans. All donors are then killed."[45]

The first public debate regarding the acceptability of fetal research
emerged in Great Britain in 1970, when British parliamentarians became
aware of rumors that British scientists were buying human fetuses from
abortion clinics for experimental purposes. The British secretary for social services quickly established an advisory commission to study fetal research and its moral and scientific implications. The recommendations
of this commission, presented in the so-called Peel Report, proposed
that fetal research be limited to fetuses of up to twenty weeks' gestation
and weighing less than 300 grams.[46] News of the developments in Britain quickly spread to the United States. Hoping the United States could
avoid similar controversies, officials at the Department of Health, Education, and Welfare requested that the National Institute of Health (NIH)
consider the implications of fetal research and propose a set of guidelines similar to those outlined in the Peel Report. The NIH charged two

advisory groups to come up with regulatory proposals. Both suggested restricting research on the live fetus and establishing local review boards to approve research proposals and provide research oversight. But the two groups differed in their understanding of the fetus. One group treated the fetus-scheduled-for-abortion differently from the fetus-to-be-carried-to-term, categorizing the former—but not the latter—as an organ or tissue procured for research and thus easing the use of fetuses for medical research. The other study group proposed that all fetuses be treated as helpless subjects, entitled to the same protections as minors and prisoners, regardless of whether or not the particular fetal subject was to be aborted.[47]

In April 1973, the quiet deliberation process inside the walls of the NIH was shattered when a reporter from the medical newsletter *Ob-Gyn News* tape-recorded one of the meetings where the two proposals were being considered. Even before *Ob-Gyn News* was able to publish portions of the draft proposals, reporters from the *Washington Post* learned about the story and decided to publish their own. "Live-Fetus Research Debated," published in the *Washington Post* on April 10, 1973, introduced the topic of fetal research to the American public. There was no question about the newspaper's position on the debate. "Such tiny infants if delivered intact," *Washington Post* reporter Victor Cohn noted, "may often live for an hour or so with beating heart after abortion. They cannot live longer without aid, primarily because their lungs are still unexpanded. But artificial aid—fresh blood and fresh oxygen—might keep them alive for three or four hours."[48] Statements from the government scientists debating the issue reflected the lingering scientific view of the fetus as specimen rather than charming infant-to-be and thus seemed even more alarming. One geneticist was quoted as explaining to Cohn that fetal research was not unethical. "It is not possible to make this fetus into a child, [and] therefore we can consider it as nothing more than a piece of tissue."[49] And a professor of obstetrics, who cautioned the advisory groups not to justify fetal research on the grounds that the fetus is going to be aborted anyway, was quoted as warning that such a rationalization would be "the German approach." The researcher, Cohn explained, was referring to "Nazi experiments on doomed concentration camp inmates during World War II."[50] Fetuses scheduled for abortion, his explanation insinuated, were like inmates of Nazi concentration camps—ready material for medical experimentation.

Opponents of fetal research were careful to describe fetal experiments in graphic terms, evoking a new narrative framework in which fetal specimens were really fragile infants who were subjected to horrendous medical experiments while they were still alive. Over the following days, Cohn elaborated on the experiments:

> An intense scientist named Dr. Gerald Gaull in periodic trips to Finland injects a radioactive chemical into the fragile umbilical cords of fetuses freshly removed from their mothers' wombs in abortions. The fetus in each case is too young to survive, but in the brief period that its heart is still beating, Gaull—chief of pediatrics research at the New York State Institute for Basic Research in Mental Retardation on Staten Island— then operates to remove its brain, lung, liver, and kidneys for study. ... Dr. Robert Schwartz, chief of pediatrics at Cleveland Metropolitan General Hospital, goes to Finland for a similar purpose. After a fetus is delivered, while it is still linked to its mother by the umbilical cord, he takes a blood sample. Then, after the cord is severed, he "as quickly as possible," he states, operates on this aborted being to remove other tissues and organs. The fetuses in these cases are so small and undeveloped that their lungs are not fully formed. They cannot breathe, and their brains undoubtedly die within a matter of minutes, though their hearts beat much longer.[51]

Cohn pointed out that the subjects not only were defenseless but also became victims of precisely those medical professionals who were supposed to protect them: pediatricians. Evoking images of organ harvesting, these narratives led to charges that physicians "no longer acknowledge their responsibility to preserve life, but fully acknowledge their authority to destroy life."[52]

The details of the article were clearly intended to shock, and public response was immediate and strong. In a single week, fetal research was catapulted into the public domain, and federal science policymakers turned from publicly acknowledging that the NIH was assessing the merits of fetal research to publicly denouncing such research. Many Americans concluded that NIH policy in fact permitted research on live aborted fetuses. The day after the *Washington Post* story, NIH officials were confronted by a group of Catholic high school students protesting on the grounds of the NIH campus. "If there is a more unspeakable crime than abortion itself," John Cardinal Krol of Philadelphia was quoted as saying three days later, "it is using victims of abortion as living human guinea pigs." Now on the defensive, NIH deputy director Robert Berliner insisted that "there are no circumstances at present or in the foreseeable future which would justify NIH support of research on live aborted human fetuses."[53]

At a congressional hearing two months later, Republican representative Angelo D. Roncallo, seeking to restrict National Science Foundation support for fetal research, spun a tale of horror that echoed age-old fears about the power of medicine over life and death.[54] Targeting the work of physician Peter A. J. Adam from Case Western Reserve University, Roncallo alleged:

> Supported by NIH funds, he and three Finnish researchers performed some of the most abominable experiments on live human fetuses that I have ever heard of. Let me quote to you the description printed in *Medical World News*: "To produce these data, the investigators severed the heads of 12 previable fetuses obtained by abdominal hysterotomy at 12 to 20 weeks of gestation. The heads were then perfused through the internal carotid arteries." Can you believe this, Mr. Chairman? It is the making of a new Frankenstein. These people cut the heads off living human fetuses while they still had a heartbeat and stuck them up on tubes. All this to find out if some sugar substitute called BOHB could serve as a human energy source.[55]

Roncallo's criticism picked up on an element of researchers' actions likely to strike many as distasteful. His example also illustrates the pervasiveness of distortion and the trivialization of research purpose that characterized abortion opponents' critique of fetal research. Although he described them as live human fetuses, all fetuses in this research had died and no longer had a heartbeat prior to onset of the research. And when referring back to the experiment nine months later, Roncallo quipped that he would stick to saccharine as a sugar substitute rather than condone vivisection of live human fetuses to understand whether the fetus could process the sugar substitute BOHB.[56] His gibe implied that rather than trying to understand the impact of complications from maternal diabetes on fetal development, the researchers had sought to solve trivial dietary questions regarding coffee sweeteners. In the larger critique of fetal research, the distasteful exception came to stand for all medical research. Medical researchers, one defender of fetal research complained, were turned into "fiends in lab coats who derived sadistic pleasure from experimenting on and torturing helpless 'infants.'"[57]

It was against this backdrop that Boston city councilor Dapper O'Neil called his public hearings in September 1973. Charges at O'Neil's hearings that BCH researchers conducted fetal research echoed the detailed fetal research narratives now so familiar to the public through the *Washington Post*. Boston antiabortion activists could now employ these narratives on their home turf. The hearings offered them a public forum in which to establish the link between abortion and fetal research at BCH. Witness after witness charged BCH researchers with conducting fetal experimentation—"inhumane procedures"—on live-born fetuses. Abortion at BCH, Monsignor Paul Harrington claimed, would lead the hospital and expectant mothers to declare some "unborn babies" of no value. These "unborn babies" would then, by "violent and destructive methods" be "snuffed out, destroyed, extinguished, annihilated, and exterminated." "We object to research and experimentation on live human aborted babies," he declared.[58] Although both the acting chairman of the Boston Board of Health and Hospitals and a representative of BCH nurses assured the audience that the hospital did not perform abortions for the purpose of fetal experimentation nor experiment on live fetuses, the majority of witnesses maintained that a link existed between abortion and fetal research. Indeed, several witnesses alleged that the research conducted by the four BCH researchers must have involved live fetuses. Echoing the *Washington Post* descriptions of Dr. Robert Schwartz taking fetal blood samples while the fetus was still linked to its mother by the umbilical cord, Boston physician and Massachusetts Citizens for Life member Dr. Joseph R. Stanton declared erroneously that it would have been impossible to get useful blood samples from the fetuses unless their hearts were beating.[59] The hearings wound down with the emotional testimony of Rosetta Harrington, who had worked as a nurse at BCH from 1963 to 1971. She had left, she stated, "because of all the abortions they were doing at that time." Harrington described saline abortions performed during the late 1960s that in her eyes had resulted in live fetuses—although BCH pediatricians at the time seemed to disagree. "I have taken live aborted babies to the nurseries during this time," Rosetta Harrington recalled, "and have gotten a lot of harassment from those people down there: 'Why are you bringing us these specimens? Because now we have to do them up, to get rid of them.'"[60] Clearly, what constituted meaningful signs of life and whether or not a fetus deserved the attention of pediatricians were contested issues.

It Looked Like a Baby: The Edelin Trial

On October 3, 1973, a little more than two weeks after the O'Neil hearings, Kenneth Edelin performed the hysterotomy on Alice Roe. Toward the end of 1973, Assistant District Attorney Newman Flanagan's office received a number of calls from people claiming that the Boston city morgue held "two big babies in bottles."[61] Flanagan asked Dr. George Curtis, the Suffolk County coroner, to visit the morgue. When Curtis confirmed the presence of the specimen, Flanagan asked him to perform an autopsy on the bodies to determine their cause of death. "We were most interested in the Roe baby [the fetus Edelin had removed from Alice], since that was the biggest one and had been delivered by hysterotomy," Flanagan remembered. And, following the suggestion of the Wilkes' *Handbook on Abortion* that fetuses removed by hysterotomy were alive, he explained: "I wondered if possibly that baby had been alive at the time it was taken from the mother."[62] After receiving the autopsy report, Flanagan decided to convene a grand jury to explore the question how the fetus had died. On February, 14, 1974, he subpoenaed Edelin to testify. Flanagan asked Edelin whether the fetus was still alive when he started the hysterotomy, whether it was alive when Edelin removed it from the uterus, and whether Edelin had filed a death certificate for the fetus. Edelin responded that he thought the fetus was dead when he started the hysterotomy, that it was certainly dead when he removed it from the uterus, and that he did not need to file a death certificate because he was performing an abortion.[63] As Edelin recalls, "For the first time, I felt fear. I had thought that this was a hearing to investigate the fetal experimentation, but the longer I stayed at the courthouse, the more I became convinced that it was an investigation into abortions."[64]

While Edelin testified that the fetus had been dead when he removed it from the uterus, others disagreed. Indeed, it was the testimony of three physicians, Enrique Giminez-Jimeno, Charles L. Sullivan, and George Curtis that led to the eventual indictment of Edelin for manslaughter. Giminez, a second-year BCH resident who refused to perform abortions under the conscience clause but had been present to observe the hysterotomy testified that Edelin had first separated the placenta from the uterus but had only removed the placenta and fetus after waiting a few minutes—a time during which the fetus was no longer connected to the mother's circulation since the placenta was now unattached.[65] Newman Flanagan, convinced that the fetus had been alive and that the manner in which Edelin had performed the procedure had led to its death, put the question of how the fetal life had been terminated front and center. In gory detail, he narrated an imagined course of events to witness Dr. Charles L. Sullivan:

> Doctor, there has twice been a saline injection for the purpose of terminating the fetus' life and assuming both times it was unsuccessful and subsequent to that a hysterotomy is performed and assuming further, Doctor, that after the woman is opened up the placenta is first removed rather than the fetus. Ripped from the mother and taken out. . . . As-

suming that the doctor stands there in the o.r., operating room, and by the clock waits five minutes before he removes the fetus and when the fetus is removed after that period it is dead, do you have any opinion as to what would cause the death?[66]

Sullivan, an obstetrician-gynecologist, opined that "the baby would suffocate."[67] Suffolk County coroner Dr. Curtis concurred. The fetus, he testified, was viable when Edelin initiated the hysterotomy and died when Edelin removed the placenta and "the oxygen is cut off from the mother. . . . It is a form of asphyxia. Same type of thing if you cut off the air of the lungs, you cut off oxygen and that is what keeps you going. If you remove a placenta and leave a baby in utero so it can't breathe, that is a form of anoxia or asphyxia . . . death by suffocation."[68] On April 11, 1974, Newman Flanagan called Edelin to inform him of his indictment for manslaughter. In addition, Flanagan also filed indictments for the four BCH-affiliated medical researchers who had conducted the fetal research on the transmission of antibiotics. "I felt sick," Edelin remembered.[69]

From the very beginning, critics charged that the Edelin trial was both an attempt by the Boston Catholic community to undo the gains made under *Roe v. Wade* and that the trial was racially motivated. The Boston medical community, Richard Knox wrote in the *Boston Globe*, "generally views the indictments as a politically motivated attempt to set up a test case against both abortion and fetal experiments."[70] Knox also noted that Edelin was the first black chief resident of obstetrics and gynecology in the history of BCH, which served a largely black clientele.[71] The impression that the trial was about race and that Edelin was being set up hardened as the trial opened in January 1975 and Edelin faced a white jury. "The members of the jury are Dr. Edelin's peers only in the legal sense," the *Boston Globe* reported on January 13, 1975. "None is black, none is a doctor."[72] Abortion providers across the country took an interest in the trial. Morris Turner, then one of several African American physicians at the Department of Obstetrics and Gynecology at the University of Pittsburgh's Magee Women's Hospital, recalls that all his colleagues followed the trial closely. "The outcome was going to affect pretty much any program that was doing it [abortions]," he noted.[73] But Boston racial politics seemed remote from Pittsburgh. Turner's colleague Robert Thompson, also African American, remembers: "We thought of Boston as Mississippi North." To them, the Edelin case was memorable not because it targeted an African American resident but because Edelin himself had impressive credentials. "This was an African American," Turner recalls, "who was at Harvard [and] who was the chief resident. That made much more of an impression to me than what he was being charged with."[74]

Over the following month, the trial revisited all the issues central to the debate about the status of the fetus. Because the prosecution relied heavily on expert witnesses who were either members of or held positions in antiabortion organizations, the trial pitched an antiabortion interpretation of the events against those defending Edelin's actions as legal and best medical practice. Basic definitions were contested. Witnesses argued over the definition of birth. Was the fetus born once it was detached from the placenta but still inside Alice's body, as prosecuting witness Dr. Mildred Jefferson, a general surgeon on the staff of Boston University Medical Center and vice president of Massachusetts Concerned for Life, testified?[75] Or does "born" mean disconnected from and outside the mother's body, as defense witnesses claimed? And what was the definition of abortion? Was it the termination of pregnancy prior to twenty weeks' gestation, as prosecuting witness Dr. Demos Cavanagh of St. Louis University claimed?[76] Or was abortion the termination of pregnancy before viability, as Edelin argued the prominent textbook *Williams' Obstetrics* defined it?[77]

Basic facts, such as the precise gestational age of the fetus, were also disputed, with estimates ranging from twenty to twenty-eight weeks. Four different people had examined Alice prior to her hysterotomy, estimated her gestational age, and testified at the trial about their findings. While Edelin and witness for the defense Dr. Hugh Holtrap, chief of the ob-gyn clinic at BCH, who had performed the initial exam on Alice, testified that Alice's fetus was of twenty or twenty-one weeks' gestation, witnesses for the prosecution, third-year Boston University medical student Alan Silberman and second-year resident Dr. Enrique Giminez-Jimeno, testified that the fetus was twenty-four weeks old. (Silberman noted that he lacked experience and felt unsure about his estimate.) Further witnesses for the prosecution offered additional estimates of twenty-four to twenty-eight weeks' gestation, based on their reading of the medical records.[78]

Disagreements continued as witnesses pondered whether or not the fetus had been alive when Edelin removed it from its mother. "The subject did breathe outside the uterus," two prosecuting witnesses, the medical examiner for Suffolk County and a pathologist from Pittsburgh, testified based on their reading of the lung tissue.[79] "The fetus did not respire air after removal from the uterus," perinatal pathologist Kurt Benirschke disagreed.[80] Witnesses also debated whether the fetus was viable. Prosecuting witness Dr. Joe Kennedy, a neonatologist and director of Newborn

Nursery at St. Margaret's Hospital, testified that he believed the fetus was still alive after Edelin separated the placenta and would still be alive had Edelin immediately removed the fetus from the uterus. Defense witnesses, on the other hand, did not believe the fetus to be viable.[81] A number of witnesses argued that the fetal lungs were not developed enough to sustain independent life, that the fetal birth weight was too low for a viable fetus, and that the fetus would have died shortly after delivery had it been born alive.[82] The argument about whether or not the fetus was viable was further complicated by conflicting testimony regarding the fetus's gestational age and disagreements over the fetus's weight. Did it weigh 600 grams, as pathology resident Frank Fallico recorded when he first received and weighed the specimen? Or did it weigh upward of 700 grams, as prosecuting witness Dr. John Ward, an assistant clinical pathologist at the University of Pittsburgh Medical School, claimed?[83] Did formaldehyde increase or decrease fetal weight? Experts could not agree. But even Dr. Kennedy admitted under prolonged questioning by the defense attorney that in all his years of practice he had never seen a fetus this young survive. Chances of survival, he conceded, were "very small."[84]

Edelin's actions were subject to disagreement too. What had he done? While Flanagan and Giminez-Jimeno claimed that Edelin had caused the death of the fetus when he detached the placenta and left the fetus inside the uterus while watching a clock on the wall for three minutes, a medical student and two nurses who had been present at the procedure denied that Edelin had left his hand in the uterus. Indeed, one nurse argued that there had been no clock in the operating room, as it had been removed for repair.[85] And what was Edelin's responsibility toward the fetus? The prosecution charged that Edelin had neglected his responsibilities. The defense countered that Edelin had followed standard medical procedure and that the death of the fetus was implicit in an abortion. Edelin testified that he had felt for a fetal heartbeat and, finding none, had been content that the fetus was dead and had turned his attention back to Alice. His duty, he explained, was toward the woman, not the fetus.[86]

In the end, the conflicting expert testimony about the status of the fetus proved less relevant to the jury than images of the fetus. If medical professionals and scientists had earlier looked at the fetus as a specimen that might serve scientific advance and the death of which was inevitable in an abortion, the increasingly public debate surrounding the status of the fetus shaped by the dissemination of fetal images had now transformed the fetus into a baby that needed the protection of physicians. By 1975, these modern views of the fetus clashed with older scientific sensibilities and led to a jury verdict where feelings about an image trumped scientific understanding.

The biological, legal, and ethical differences between an early fetus wholly dependent on the pregnant woman and the more developed fetus that might survive outside the womb became particularly sensitive as physicians and ethicists tried to grapple with the implications of the Edelin verdict. While abortion remained legal, physicians grew more cautious, and some refused to perform certain procedures. Some hospitals began to place seventeen-, sixteen-, and even twelve-week limits on abortions. "It's no longer a critical issue as to whether the fetus that's delivered is capable of surviving, which is what the word viability meant," the ob-gyn chief at Beth Israel in Boston noted, "but whether or not it's actually alive, regardless of whether it's capable of surviving. . . . And if it's alive, we are now bound by the Edelin verdict to make every effort to salvage it, even if its possibility of being salvageable is negligible."[87]

Live Birth as a Complication: The Question of Viability

As jurors were deliberating the status of the fetus that Edelin had removed from Alice Roe, officials at the NIH continued their deliberations about fetal research. To guide their debates, the commission asked a group of bioethicists to discuss the status of the fetus, whether or not it was considered a person, and whether or not it was entitled to rights and protections.[88] The fetus, some argued was not a person but an "object" that had value only insofar as it was wanted by its parents. Only once it became a live-born baby, capable of independent existence, did it acquire personhood.[89] Since a nonviable fetus scheduled for abortion had no potential to develop into a human being, philosopher Richard Wasserstrom argued, research on such a fetus was permissible if it would yield information otherwise unobtainable. Philosopher and ethicist Sissela Bok included in the category of permissible research experiments on viable fetuses if the research sought to benefit the fetuses used as subjects or their families, sought to develop new techniques for helping premature infants survive, or sought to test new diagnostic techniques that could not be tested at an earlier gestational age.[90]

As the group of bioethicists, researchers, and policymakers struggled to propose solutions, they mirrored the original proposals for fetal research policy that had caused so much controversy and had differentiated between fetuses scheduled for abortion and fetuses to be carried to term.

Now the commission defined a dead fetus in the same category as organs or tissue, which meant that it escaped the stringent regulations governing research on the fetus or abortus. But a group of ethicists strongly disagreed with this differentiation. Ethical standards governing fetal research, LeRoy Walters and Paul Ramsey argued, should be the same as those governing research on children or other vulnerable subjects.[91] Because abortion was immoral, Richard A. McCormick concluded, investigators should only conduct research on a fetus for which abortion was not contemplated.[92]

In addition to individual reports by eight ethicists, the commission also organized public hearings to solicit further opinions. A number of speakers, many of them medical researchers, praised the accomplishments of fetal research, pointing to advances in fetal therapeutics that had resulted from research on the fetus. Much more was needed, they argued. A member of the American Society of Experimental Pathology noted that the developing fetus faced special problems. By helping to solve these problems, fetal research provided medical justice to the fetus.[93] But others could find no justice in fetal research. In fact, many denounced research on the fetus as dehumanizing and feared its implications for society. Monsignor James T. McHugh of the U.S. Catholic Conference called pre-abortion research inconsistent with human dignity and therefore unacceptable.[94] A professor of neurology at George Washington University sarcastically demanded that the fetus be protected from experimentation "without its informed consent."[95] And a number of speakers expressed the fear that research on the fetus might persuade women to have an abortion in order to contribute to the cause of science.[96] "If science becomes dependent on abortion for research subjects," the president of Pregnancy Aid Centers cautioned, "scientists and society will be even less inclined to develop viable alternatives to abortion."[97]

In the end, the 1973 guidelines sought to strike a compromise between the pro- and antiresearch factions by introducing different classifications for fetal bodies that would restrict research for some but not for others. The guidelines differentiated between the "abortus"—defined as a nonviable living fetus outside the uterus—and the "fetus"—defined as any product of conception inside the uterus—and placed restrictions and oversight on research with both. But the dead fetus and fetal tissue were excluded from the above definitions, so the guidelines permitted research on the placenta, macerated fetal material, the dead fetus, and isolated fetal tissue or organs excised from a dead fetus. As a result, policymakers at the NIH separated the fetal research debate from the debate surrounding research on fetal tissue. Further revisions over the following years reiterated and completed this separation while easing some of the oversight.

But as the Edelin case indicated, antiabortion activists did not just attack fetal research; they also focused on fetuses still showing signs of life following abortion. They charged abortion providers with neglecting or outright killing fetuses that had survived the abortion procedure. The suspicion that these fetal bodies would then be used for fetal research cast a particularly sinister light on abortion providers. If Kenneth Edelin was the first physician in the United States to face a lawsuit charging manslaughter for a legal abortion, he was not the last. Edelin's case became one in a long row of so-called live birth lawsuits. As states began to enact post-*Roe* abortion statutes, viability determination and the physician's duty to the fetus became key issues. In the early 1970s, viability was usually placed at about seven months or twenty-eight weeks' gestation, although the Supreme Court acknowledged that it might occur earlier, even at twenty-four weeks. Depending on technological progress, however, viability varied with both time and place. Throughout the 1970s, states attempted to pass laws fixing viability at a specific point in the pregnancy and requiring doctors to choose abortion techniques which would best preserve fetal life. State authorities across the country charged doctors under newly enacted statutes prohibiting abortions when the fetus had reached viability and requiring physicians to take all reasonable steps to preserve a fetus with any chance of survival. But while the Edelin case involved a fetus which never showed any signs of life, subsequent cases involved fetuses which briefly survived after the abortion. Only 1 percent of abortions in the 1970s took place after twenty weeks of gestation, and very few of those resulted in live births. Yet these live births produced a disproportionate number of criminal and civil charges. Although most indictments were eventually dismissed, the threat of prosecution contributed to a chilly climate for abortion providers and inhibited the performance of late midtrimester abortions.[98]

With the emergence of live birth lawsuits, physicians began to describe live births as a medical complication of abortion. Live births, a 1976 study found, were indeed a rare event. Documenting the occurrence of live births for 15,671 abortion procedures performed between July 1970 and December 1972, the authors found a total of thirty-eight live births, a rate of 0.25 per 1,000 pregnancy terminations—8.5 for every 1,000 hysterotomies and 1.7 for every 1,000 saline instillations. Moreover, the authors noted that most infants showing signs of life were so immature that they died shortly after. Thirty-seven out of the thirty-eight infants died, most within twenty-four hours.[99] Nevertheless, these findings were disturbing. By the end of the decade, researchers concluded that "the live-born fetus has become one of the most difficult medical, legal, and ethical problems associated with midtrimester abortion."[100]

What to do about the live-born fetus in an abortion was further complicated by issues that also haunted prematurely born infants: questions about viability and an infant's quality of life. If some advocated saving any infant with a heartbeat, others pointed out that signs of life did not guarantee fetal viability. While vital statistics might require a physician to designate a five-ounce fetus as live born for statistical purposes, one physician argued in the mid-1980s, this was not useful for medical purposes because no technology available could sustain life at such an early stage. Others did not believe an infant viable—and thus subject to the most advanced treatment—if it was seriously deformed or had been determined to have less than a 20 percent chance of survival. Commenting on a 1976 California statute that required physicians performing abortions to take "all reasonable steps . . . to preserve the life and health of the live-born person," one physician pointed out that only a tiny percentage of fetuses live born as a result of abortion would survive, most with severe brain damage. "To force such an existence on the nonviable fetus, or to protect its living death, is a matter of very serious ethical dispute," he noted and warned that "the nightmare of hundreds of isolettes filled with incubated twitching, demented fetuses will become an actuality."[101]

While bioethicists did not participate in debates over fetuses that survived an abortion, they did deliberate the use of life support and medical intervention in neonatal care. When to sustain the life of premature or seriously compromised infants became the topic of conversation among bioethicists in the early 1970s. At a symposium on human rights, retardation and research, organizers screened a teaching film, *Choices on Our Conscience*, which told the story of two young parents who refuse to permit a simple lifesaving operation for their newborn baby with Down syndrome. The film, which thrust neonatal care into the ambit of the early bioethics movement, prompted vociferous debate. In 1974, conference participants from medicine, law, theology, philosophy, and the social sciences affirmed that it was morally legitimate for physicians to forgo life support for compromised infants and that parents had the right to make such decisions. Indeed, conference attendants found that in exceptional cases, it was legitimate to hasten an infant's death.[102]

Not surprisingly, however, such conclusions were controversial. In a 1976 forum in the *Hastings Center Report* entitled "The Unwanted Child," several bioethicists called for the introduction of gestational limits after which abortions would no longer be permissible. In cases where pregnancy termination resulted in live birth, physicians should treat the fetuses like all prematurely born infants, employing all possible lifesaving measures. Indeed, some of the authors suggested that rather than try to avoid live births, physicians should choose abortion procedures that carried the highest chance of fetal survival, allowing as many fetuses as possible to be saved. "If a legislature can limit the amount of fetal damage caused by abortion without endangering the life or health of the pregnant woman," bioethicist LeRoy Walters concluded, "then in my view it should do so."[103] Others, however, worried about providing care to infants so compromised that such care only meant the prolongation of suffering. Commenting on the passage of the California bill earlier that year, Sissela Bok cautioned that physicians must be allowed to exercise their own judgment. "They must be allowed to make a realistic appraisal of the chances of survival and of quality of life after the abortive procedures, and not be forced by legislation and fear of repercussions into providing care they would never give to a similarly burdened premature."[104]

While this bioethics discourse addressed significant moral dilemmas, it failed to resolve many of the issues. Although bioethicists frequently emerged with lists of guidelines and recommendations that might offer physicians a blueprint on how to act, these resolutions did not constitute a consensus. In addition, despite the public hearings, these debates took place among a small group of academics who often did not represent popular opinion. Participating ethicists, to be sure, found their own involvement in these debates valuable. Arthur Jonsen, who had been a member of the National Commission for the Protection of Human Subjects of Biomedical and Behavioral Research and who participated in the debates on the care of "seriously compromised infants," commented that these discussions transformed a private argument within the world of medicine into a broad scholarly discourse.[105] But if Jonsen took the inclusion of philosophers and religion scholars to indicate a broadening of the discussion, many did not share his optimistic view of the process. Indeed, abortion opponents complained that the medical community simply ignored the concerns of the public. Even with public participation, journalist Suzanne Rini commented on the fetal research debate, the medical research community "showed itself to be obsessed with its own logic, unable, despite its scientific accomplishments, to doubt the wisdom of its moral aims. It ignored the public's concern for the weakest members of society and exposed itself as a community to be feared."[106] Researchers' ability to forge ahead, she concluded, indicated that we were now living in a "biocracy," where science was more valued than the democratic process.

OVER THE COMING YEARS, antiabortion activists created their own counterdiscourse to abortion and fetal experimentation that elaborated on the Wilkes' *Handbook on Abortion*. The medical ethics journal *Linacre Quarterly*, published by the National Federation of Catholic Physicians' Guilds, regularly printed essays by physicians and clergy with titles such as "Proposed Abortion Laws: 'Slaughter of the Innocents,'" "Who Speaks for the Fetus?," "The Physician and the Rights of the Unborn," and "Man Plays God."[107] Ultimately, however, the inclusion of images spoke louder than just the written word. Antiabortion activists flocked to the writings of Francis A. Schaeffer, an American theologian who gained prominence in the 1950s for establishing the L'Abri community in Switzerland.[108] In his 1979 book *Whatever Happened to the Human Race?* Schaeffer created the intellectual foundation for abortion opponents' arguments against abortion and fetal research. Coauthored with his friend C. Everett Koop, a born-again Christian pediatric surgeon who served as surgeon general under President Ronald Reagan, the book was accompanied by a five-episode film documentary produced by Schaeffer's son Frank. Images in the book showed physicians bending over tiny infants who were hooked up to an array of machines or surgeons performing surgery on infants. It was unclear from the images if these physicians were saving lives or conducting research. Photos of discarded dolls thrown across a desolate landscape and images of a car graveyard lend the narrative a doomed quality and suggested the disregard society held for the lives of people and things. In the accompanying film, the camera slowly panned a row of cages with rabbits, followed by a row of cages with rats, to finally rest on a cage that held a crying toddler. Set in this context, images of physicians and infants conveyed the enormous power these professionals held over human life: a power that might be used for good but was increasingly used for bad. Both book and film offered a detailed indictment of American society for its decision to accept abortion.

Abortion, Schaeffer and Koop argued, eroded the sanctity of human life and would inevitably lead to infanticide and euthanasia. Society's tolerance of legal abortion indicated a loss of humanness and a devaluation of human life comparable to that of the Nazis. "Once the doors are open, there is no reason why the aged, weak, and infirm will not find that as they become economic burdens, they will be eliminated under one pretext or another," they warned.[109] Indeed, American society already allowed for infanticide when physicians and parents chose to let "malformed babies" die. "The next step is to destroy human individuals or groups of individuals because they are unwanted, imperfect, or socially embarrassing. Senility, infirmity, retardation, insanity, and incontinence are conditions that come to mind."[110] Genocide and selecting who should die, they concluded, marked the logical end.

Accompanied as the book was by a careful selection of photographs and film scenes illustrating the power of physicians and scientific researchers over human beings, especially infants and children, it powerfully illustrated the dangers that American society was facing. For an audience steeped in narratives of fetal research, the message here was unmistakable. Over the coming decades, *Whatever Happened to the Human Race?* offered antiabortion activists a conceptual framework that was accessible and simplistic. In 1979, Schaeffer and Koop took book and film on a four-month tour of the United States, holding three-day seminars in over twenty cities. Each five-film sequence aired over two or three days in an auditorium, followed by a panel discussion. "The films were essentially on-screen lectures, full of somber narrative and imagery," journalist Cynthia Gorney describes the events. "Here was Koop bent over an ailing newborn on a surgical table; Schaeffer in a junk yard besides a broken baby carriage; Koop on the shores of the Dead Sea, surrounded by the scattered forms of prostrate baby dolls. The text of both films and book ranged through logic, medicine, history, and philosophy; and when it explored theology, it used the language of evangelical Protestant preaching."[111] Schaeffer and Koop's message struck a chord among evangelicals, who mobbed the events like rock concerts. In the early 1980s, when many young, born-again Christians joined the antiabortion movement, the works of Schaeffer and Koop provided them with an entry into antiabortion politics. In the months leading into the 1980 political season, Gorney notes, Schaeffer and Koop's message spread far more widely than the films themselves. It drew evangelicals into the right-to-life cause, which up to then had been the purview of Catholics.[112]

The emerging discourse over the fetus was to hold long-ranging implications for the abortion provider community. Following the Edelin verdict, abortion providers began to feel under attack. Over the second half of the 1970s, they looked to science to establish abortion services as legitimate and safe and to integrate abortion into the larger mainstream medical community. They also came together at conferences and meetings to share their experiences and research findings. At these meetings, they began to discuss the formulation of basic standards that should undergird abortion services across the country. While the standardization of abortion care was part of a crucial process of professionalization to strengthen the image of abortion as a legitimate medical procedure, the debates surrounding the formulation of standards and the meaning of professionalism were highly contested, pitting not only antiabortion activists against the abortion provider community but also abortion providers against one another.

3

The Formation of the
National Abortion Federation
and the Standards Debate

In 1973, Warren Hern, a physician and epidemiologist, was approached by a psychotherapy group seeking to open an abortion clinic in Boulder, Colorado. Hern had become interested in abortion in the 1960s, after practicing for several years in Peru, Panama, and Brazil. In the late 1960s, he returned to the United States to earn a master's degree in public health and then worked for two years at the family planning program in the Office of Economic Opportunity in Washington, D.C., before returning to his hometown of Boulder. While in Washington, Hern also visited Preterm and learned how to perform abortions. Spurred by the recent *Roe v. Wade* decision, Hern decided to accept the psychotherapy group's offer to join them in establishing an abortion clinic. The group leased and remodeled a house, and Hern ordered the equipment and developed a program plan and charts. In November of 1973, the Boulder Valley Clinic opened with Hern as the medical director and sole abortion provider. The clinic offered abortions Tuesdays through Saturdays, and the number of patients rose quickly, from 20 patients during the first week to thirty to forty patients per week thereafter.[1]

But Hern soon grew frustrated with the casual atmosphere at the clinic, and his experience there embodied what he would come to define as unprofessional. Most Boulder Valley Clinic employees and volunteers wanted a clinic without the hierarchies that characterized traditional medical offices. Many of the nurses and counselors were volunteers. As a result, staffing was irregular. Volunteers canceled their shifts at the last minute and squabbled with paid staff about cleaning responsibilities. The few paid employees were overworked, and Hern grew increasingly frustrated at the shortage of reliable personnel. What Boulder Valley Clinic saw as a casual form of operating, Hern found counter to basic professional standards: the storage of medical records in an open box in immediate proximity to those sitting in the waiting area, a dirty floor in the procedure room, and the fact that the clinic director had disclosed confidential medical information to a patient's boyfriend without first seeking the patient's permission.[2]

Hern's concern with professionalism was based on his desire to move abortion from the margins to the center of respectable medical care, increasing both the safety of abortion and the respectability of abortion providers. Hern came to the Boulder clinic having performed only half a dozen abortions at Preterm. Concerned about medical safety, he consulted his medical books where he read about laminaria—seaweed sticks that, if inserted into the cervix, will absorb moisture and dilate the cervix. In the early 1970s, most physicians used manual dilation to dilate the cervix, inserting progressively larger metal rods (dilators) that widened the cervical opening until the physician was able to insert the suction cannula or curette to perform the abortion. Dilation by laminaria required that patients come to the clinic twice—once for the insertion of the laminaria and then again the next day for the abortion procedure. But Hern felt that dilation by laminaria was less traumatic and led to fewer complications, outweighing the disadvantage of two required clinic visits. He decided to incorporate it into his practice. "I started developing techniques for doing this, writing things down," Hern remembered.[3] He meticulously recorded data on every abortion he performed, and at night he spent hours poring over data and research studies on the medical safety of abortion procedures. In the fall of 1974, he wrote a paper chronicling his experience of performing first trimester abortions with laminaria on 1,368 patients and presented the paper at the annual American Public Health Association meeting in New Orleans.[4] His insistence on developing procedures, collecting data, and publishing the results applied a traditional scientific procedure to abortion services, ensured valuable feedback from practitioners and researchers, and created a body of knowledge for others to draw on.

But while data collection, interpretation, and the presentation of research results were central to Hern's understanding of his position as an abortion provider and medical director, other clinic members lacked interest in these aspects of medical practice. Indeed, they criticized his approach as hierarchical. When the board of directors decided to abolish the position of medical director to reduce clinic hierarchy—while expecting

Hern to continue his work as the clinic's abortion provider—Hern quit. Furious that he was expected to carry the medical responsibility for abortion procedures without having the authority to enforce standards he felt were essential, he resigned. In January 1975, he opened his own clinic— the Boulder Abortion Clinic.[5]

Abortion providers across the country shared Hern's desire to mainstream abortion as a medical procedure while anchoring it firmly in science and medicine. In March 1975, abortion providers and their supporters met for the first national symposium on abortion since the *Roe v. Wade* decision. The event at the University of Tennessee in Knoxville was organized by Charles Reynolds, an associate professor in the Department of Religion who had been involved with the Clergy Consultation Service, and Candice Adam, a minister who owned an abortion clinic in Knoxville. It brought together about 120 physicians, counselors, clinic owners and personnel, and others working in abortion services. Over three days, attendees visited workshops on clinic administration and funding, legal responsibilities, pregnancy termination techniques, abortion counseling, and birth control. Following the meeting, a group of twenty-five participants from clinics across the country discussed the establishment of a national organization of abortion providers. They formed a committee to plan the creation of the National Association of Abortion Facilities (NAAF), which, committee members hoped, would function as a forum to exchange information, support research, establish standards for abortion clinics, and lobby on behalf of abortion providers.[6]

Buoyed by a sense of enthusiasm over the emerging network of abortion clinics, abortion providers were nevertheless aware that legal abortion services were under attack. Following the Edelin conviction in Massachusetts, juries in a number of other states brought criminal charges against abortion providers, and state legislators around the country sought to undo the gains of *Roe v. Wade*. In Missouri and Ohio, legislators tried to impose a range of restrictions on abortion, including parental consent requirements for minors, a husband's consent to his wife's abortion, a ban on second trimester saline abortions, a twenty-four-hour waiting period, and hospitalization requirements for second trimester abortions. In 1977, antiabortion legislators in the U.S. House and Senate passed the Hyde Amendment, which restricted federal funding for abortion. And when, in October 1977, two months after the ban went into effect, a twenty-seven-year-old single mother, Rosaura Jimenez, died of blood poisoning following an illegal abortion in a Mexican border town, issues of access and abortion safety took on a new level of urgency.[7] Abortion rights advocates considered Jimenez, who had sought the illegal abortion after Medicaid would not pay for a legal one, the first casualty of the Hyde Amendment.

A scientific approach to abortion and the formulation of standards for abortion clinics seemed even more urgent to abortion providers after a 1978 *Chicago Sun-Times* exposé resurrected the image of the greedy and indifferent abortion provider. The tone of the exposé about four Chicago abortion clinics notorious for providing shoddy and unscrupulous services harkened back to reporting from the pre-*Roe* era that described abortion services as dirty and dangerous. "12 Dead after Abortions in State's Walk-In Clinics," the first headline announced, and over the following days, the paper was filled with descriptions of "men who profit from women's pain."[8] Antiabortion activists gloated while abortion providers feared a backlash in their efforts to establish public confidence in the safety of abortion services and the respectability of abortion providers. Abortion providers were advocating for safe services rooted in scientific management and supported nationwide standards for abortion clinics. But they were confronted by local authorities disinterested in enforcing the rules and regulations governing abortion clinics. Although existing regulations could have prevented the existence of shoddy services, Chicago's health authorities had failed to force clinics to comply with inspections and to enforce the closing of clinics that had lost their licenses. And if Chicago authorities jeopardized women's health through regulatory neglect, other towns drafted onerous clinic regulations to keep abortion clinics out altogether.[9] Caught between the twin evils of overregulation, on the one hand, and regulatory neglect, on the other, abortion providers hoped that standards would serve not only as guidelines to abortion clinics around the country but also as a model for politicians and public officials.

As abortion providers set out to challenge the image of the unscrupulous abortionist who performs dangerous procedures in dirty clinics, they worked within their professional organizations to support medical research and formulate standards based on the latest research findings. How to do this, however, was a contested issue among abortion providers. Did professionalism and adherence to medical standards necessarily imply hierarchy and the delivery of abortion care through a traditional model? Or could alternative clinics deliver care that was considered professional? Did the development of new abortion procedures such as the use of laminaria constitute an exploitation of women's bodies for research purposes? And did the collection of data and presentation of medical research surrounding abortion care reinforce medical hierarchies in which physician researchers created information for other physician researchers? Or might such information be accessible and useful to all? Debates that had so far taken place inside abortion clinics now moved into the national forum as members of the new professional organizations carried their positions into meeting rooms at conference hotels.

It Was Like Forming the United States: The Establishment of the National Abortion Federation

In May 1975, two months after the conference in Knoxville, NAAF founding members met in Cleveland to hash out the creation of a national professional organization. Differences over organizational goals surfaced as soon as members sat down together. While independent for-profit providers sought to create a provider service organization, many of the nonprofit clinics and policy organizations, such as Planned Parenthood and NARAL, were primarily concerned with standards of care and abortion access. Independent, for-profit abortion providers felt poorly treated by members associated with the nonprofit and political movement. By the end of the meeting, NAAF had split in two. Frances Kissling of the Pelham Medical Group in New York City corralled a small group of like-minded providers and supporters around her, including, among others, Judith (Judy) Widdicombe of St. Louis Women's Health Services, Jeannie Rosoff of the Alan Guttmacher Institute, Francine Stein of the PPFA, Terry Beresford of Planned Parenthood of Maryland, Karen Mulhauser of NARAL, and Frank Susman, an abortion rights lawyer from St. Louis. Kissling and her followers decided to establish their own organization, the National Abortion Council (NAC), which rapidly expanded to include a variety of providers, researchers, and academics.[10] From her home in Huguenot, New York, Kissling planned a first annual meeting in Atlanta in September 1976. At that meeting, members attended sessions on medical, legal, and social issues and elected a board of directors.[11]

Tensions between the NAAF and the NAC continued to delay the formation of a unified national organization. When the NAAF held its first annual meeting in November 1976, a small group, including staff from the CDC Abortion Surveillance Unit, who had just returned from the NAC meeting, tried to broker an agreement between the two organizations.[12] How clinics would be represented in a national organization stood at the center of concerns. In January 1977, after months of negotiations, the two organizations reached a compromise. They adopted the NAC model of equal representation by clinic categories—Planned Parenthood providers, feminist health centers, doctors' offices, freestanding clinics—and called the new organization the National Abortion Federation (NAF), thus almost pre-serving the NAAF initials.[13] "It was like forming the United States—there are the colonies fighting over representation and bicameral legislators," Frances Kissling, who became the first executive director of NAF, com-mented on the effort.[14] NAF offices moved to East 58th Street in New York, and Kissling began to recruit members.[15] When, in 1977, NAF held its first meeting in Denver, members of seventy-five different clinics and organiza-tions participated. The program featured NAF's first postgraduate courses on counseling and medical aspects of abortion and a keynote speech by Republican senator Robert Packwood from Oregon, who, two years before the *Roe v. Wade* decision, had introduced the Senate's first bill to legalize abortion.[16] In addition, NAF published "A Guide to Abortion Facilities."[17]

NAF brought together a wide assortment of individuals. Members of feminist collectives, owners of for-profit clinics, and abortion providers from diverse backgrounds were joined by researchers, academics, lawyers, and policymakers. All gathered to negotiate the goals and direction of the new organization. "You'd come to board meetings," Frances Kissling re-membered,

> and there would be guys in sharkskin suits, you know, with watch fobs, and black Cadillac limousines, ready to take people out to dinner and spend like crazy. And you'd have radical feminists who were there basi-cally arguing for women's rights, just sort of sixties counterculture, the *least* concern for how they looked. And you'd have button-down Planned Parenthood types, very nice ladies in plaid skirts and white blouses, and you'd have people like Judy [Widdicombe], professional dress and gold jewelry. Sometimes I felt like what's-his-name the lion tamer, Gunther, with the whips, trying to keep the peace.[18]

Indeed, for many attendees these first meetings were eye opening and invigorating. They also contributed greatly to the education of members as they found their individual identities in this diverse group of people. Particularly for the young women who joined NAF as clinic directors, ex-posure to the group of medical, academic, and business men introduced them to a broad range of positions and helped them to clarify their own positions as feminists in the emerging field of women's health care. Renee Chelian remembered her first meeting:

> I was on the cusp of something new. I just didn't know how to be part of something bigger. . . . When I got to the first meeting . . . there was a room filled with people from all over the country, yelling and scream-

ing and arguing and debating. It was the first chance I had to see doctors and feminists, and people arguing about: "well, I am for profit" and "I am a not-for-profit" so "not-for-profits are better than for-profits." . . . And then there were the medical doctors who were concerned that people who were non-physicians were getting into something they shouldn't. They were starting to take over medicine and they had no right to do that. And so there was all of this debating going on. There was also a lot of information. But the one thing that came out of it was that this group of people were going to meet, and they were going to have an annual meeting where everybody who did abortions could get together . . . to talk about counseling and to talk about medical problems and to share ideas and mistakes.[19]

Consolidation did not come easily. From the very start, NAF was plagued by profound disagreements about the best ways to deliver abortion care. Although I could not locate any documentation of the early discussions surrounding standards nor of the first set of standards adopted by NAF, participants vividly remembered the debates, and some of the discussions at later NAF meetings are documented. At a February 1976 meeting of abortion providers and supporters in Denver, panelists had spent considerable time discussing the need for guidelines.[20] Drawing on her experiences with for-profit clinics and for-profit referral services, Jean Pakter, director of the Bureau of Maternity Services and Family Planning in New York, reminded the audience how, when abortion was first legalized in New York, a desire for quick profits often trumped referrals to quality abortion services. "In the beginning, we had a potentially very serious situation because of a proliferation of commercial referral agencies," Pakter noted.

Unfortunately, many of the services that were springing up were concerned about their own interests and the welfare of their own financial status. In a short period of time after July 1970, 29 referral agencies were in existence and they were all commercial and profit-making. We finally had to turn to the Attorney General of the State for help in trying to eliminate these agencies. People were often being referred to inferior services rather than the good ones. We still have referral agencies in existence, presumably non-profit in nature. Some are good, some are not good. It's very difficult to eliminate this practice altogether.[21]

Denver panelists discussed a range of criteria to evaluate abortion clinics. Abortion services, noted Irvin Cushner, associate professor of public health and ob-gyn at the University of California School of Medicine, should be safe, readily available, and humanely delivered. Clinical skills, the ability of a facility to respond to trouble, clinic policy concerning costs and availability, and the internal attitudes, values, and beliefs of those delivering services were all crucial to quality services. Clinics should be required to provide follow-up data indicating acceptable complication rates, to document evidence of patients' medical history, including appropriate laboratory tests, and to offer adequate information and disclosure, including counseling.[22] Some panelists also expressed concern about the way physicians were reimbursed. "I would like to know whether it is piecework or whether they are paid by the session," Judy Widdicombe noted.[23] All panelists urged the implementation of regular site visits. "Before you refer any women to a facility," Widdicombe argued, "it is imperative that you have seen it."[24] Some wished that abortion clinics had an academic affiliation to help establish good standards and teach students and residents abortion procedures. While one physician worried that panelists were trying to "shoot a mosquito with a shotgun," most concurred that with the rapid rise of freestanding abortion clinics, some form of evaluation was urgent.[25] Alluding to the fact that, already in 1973, more than half of all abortions were performed in freestanding clinics rather than in hospitals, Cushner noted: "My hope for free-standing clinics is that they survive stringent program evaluations."[26]

But if panelists at the 1976 Denver meeting largely agreed on the desirability of standards and the shape that such standards might take, debates about clinic standards at later NAF meetings were considerably more contentious. Here, old divisions prevailed as feminists continued to mistrust male doctors, many male doctors were offended by feminists, and many in the movement distrusted abortion entrepreneurs. When a newly established standards committee brought the question of clinic standards up for discussion, delegates from the most radical feminist clinics, the FWHC, objected. Implementing standards, FWHC representatives argued, would be too expensive for feminist clinics. They would drive up the price of abortions and limit women's access to abortion care.[27] Recent restrictions of federal funding for abortion as a result of the Hyde Amendment made issues concerning access to abortion particularly poignant. With the passage of the Hyde Amendment, the number of Medicaid abortions fell from 295,000 for fiscal year 1977 to 194,000 in fiscal year 1978. As a result of the cutbacks, many poor women found access to abortion services difficult, if not impossible. Between 18 percent and 23 percent of Medicaid-eligible women, one study found, would have obtained abortions had funding been available but carried their pregnancies to term when funding was cut off.[28] The restrictions of Medicaid-funded abortions disproportionately affected nonwhite women, 20 percent of whom carried their unintended pregnancies to term in 1978 rather than pay for abortions with their own funds. Those who were able to come up with money for their abortions frequently found that it took them longer to collect the necessary funds, leading to a delay of their abortion procedures and the risk that the cost of abortion procedures increased even further.[29]

Feminist clinics were particularly concerned about these developments and approached the standards discussion with the question of accessibility of foremost importance. The concern with poor clinic services, they further noted, was a problem of capitalism and patriarchy. "The most radical feminists," Merle Hoffman said, remembering the FWHC representatives at NAF, "believed that abortion and all medical procedures should be free of government involvement and free of cost. . . . The idea of making money through providing abortions was deeply antithetical to these feminists."[30] FWHC representatives were pitched against conservative physicians. "You had Carol Downer and the other feminists at one end of the table," Warren Hern recalls one meeting, "and at the other end you would have Burt Colonel, arch male chauvinist, Bill Peterson at the Washington Hospital Center. . . . These people were screaming at each other. And Chris[topher] Tietze [senior fellow with the Population Council] was sitting there saying, 'Now, let's be calm.'"[31] Debates got so heated that a small group of physicians on the standards committee met secretly behind locked doors in a hotel room to prevent a group of feminists from interrupting their deliberations. Feminist representatives, in turn, appear to have felt powerless enough to adopt an obstructionist strategy. While it is difficult to reconstruct the details of the disagreements, profound differences in outlook and experience surely contributed to the heated nature of this fight. At its heart lay competing visions of the nature of women's health care.

I Put My Heart and Soul into the Clinic: Professionalism, Patriarchy, and Capitalism

One of the most immediate concerns of feminist clinics was the lack of women physicians to provide abortions. Fearing that male abortion providers might be insensitive or act inappropriately toward women patients, feminists at the EGC and elsewhere hoped to hire feminist women as their abortion providers. For years, EGC women wrote to any woman physician they knew who had expressed an interest in women's health, and they advertised in local papers and medical journals. But until 1980, their efforts were to no avail. Indeed, the search for a woman physician proved so frustrating that in August 1975 the committee charged with the task disbanded because nobody wanted to be on it.[32] The very first physician hired at the EGC was Dick Winter, a dermatologist whom EGC women had met at Iowa City's Free Clinic. The collective sent Winter to the FWHC in Los Angeles, where he learned how to perform vacuum aspirations.[33] But collective members quickly realized that Winter exhibited negative stereotypes of male physicians. They felt that he lacked in sensitivity and courtesy and conducted himself in an inappropriate manner. He pulled on his surgical gloves in patients' faces, raised patients' anxiety by failing to keep the syringe used for the local anesthesia out of sight, ate during the abortion procedure, and engaged in loud conversations with EGC women about details of the abortion procedure that the women deemed inappropriate for patients' ears. Worse, Winter grew increasingly impatient with patients. As one collective member reported,

My friend Judy was made very upset (brought to tears) by Dick's *attitude* toward her. He maintains she was uptight before he saw her and her muscles were so tight he couldn't do a pelvic. I would like to make it clear that his pelvic is not the issue. The issue is his *attitude*. He raised his voice (seemed angry) and repeatedly told her to relax. His <u>tone</u> and his own tenseness and dissatisfaction with her caused her to become very upset until she nearly cried from frustration. She said all the women were so supportive and relaxed up to the procedure room and she was not uptite [*sic*] until he got so angry at her.[34]

Feminist clinics adopted a variety of strategies to shield women patients from sexist attitudes and behaviors of male physicians. Women at the EGC regularly observed their physicians and critiqued their behavior when they found it offensive. But collective members quickly discovered that their ability to control how their physicians delivered abortion services was limited. EGC women tried to diffuse the situation by suggesting to Winter that he help women relax through breathing exercises and by using a gentle voice. But Winter grew increasingly defensive and unable to deal with his frustration.[35] Because he refused to participate in the process of criticism/self-criticism that provided EGC staff with a structured way to offer and respond to suggestions, some collective members pleaded with him individually. "Dick," one wrote in a long note to him, please eat breakfast in preparation for a long day and please pack a sandwich. We've asked before that you not eat of food trays in the recovery rooms and I really don't feel like being a "mother" and making up food trays for you in the kitchen. I think you're grown up enuff [*sic*] to understand that not eating makes you or anyone feel grouchy, fatigued, energyless, and causes nagging and aches and pains. Please remember your responsibility to the staff to be in good shape for what we do.[36]

Others were less understanding, calling Winter "a classic male pig doctor" who made his patients feel like "unmodified shit."[37]

Winter's behavior was not unusual of male medical professionals at the time. Merle Hoffman, who ran a freestanding clinic, Choices, on Long Island, New York, recalls in her memoir being infuriated by some of the doctors' remarks. "Thinking that casual humor helped relax patients, some doctors would make blatantly sexist remarks. 'Come on, you knew how to spread your legs before you got here, you can spread them for the exam,' a doctor once chided. Another commanded a patient to keep still, saying, 'Keep your backside on the table—you should know pretty well how to do that by now.'"[38] Scholars of the history of medicine have noted that particularly male physicians treating women for conditions related to reproduction and sexuality were frequently sexist and engaged in sexual harassment of their patients.[39]

While EGC women sought to educate their physicians about how to interact with women patients, other clinics decided to reduce the interaction between physician and patient to a minimum. Doctors working at FWHC clinics were asked not to talk to patients at all. At Choices, Hoffman put counselors in charge of educating and psychologically supporting the patients. Physicians had only to perform the abortion procedure. In addition, she drew up a bill of patients' rights that challenged the power of the male medical establishment and posted it in her clinic. "Acknowledging patients as a class with rights and responsibilities seemed to me an appropriate analytical and political vehicle for combating the victimization of female patients by a generally male medical establishment," she explained.[40] The poster reminded all that patients had the right to question their doctor and not to be intimidated by the props of medical power. Rather than passive recipients of treatment, patients should be consumers of medical care. "I called it Patient Power," Hoffman noted.[41]

While some physicians adjusted themselves to the new rules, others refused to comply with the requests of their feminist employers. Hoffman recalls that several physicians became angry when they saw the bill of patients' rights. Others, however, supported her approach. Still, feminists had the doctors talking. Rumors spread that feminists hated men.[42]

Distrust toward male medical professionals was further complicated by suspicions that male physician researchers took advantage of and experimented on women patients. In the early 1970s, health scandals surrounding the first birth control pill and the Dalkon Shield IUD had taught feminists to mistrust physicians and the pharmaceutical industry. The controversy around Harvey Karman—accused of experimenting on women's bodies as he was developing new abortion techniques—reinforced the impression that the use of women's bodies as testing grounds extended to the development of abortion techniques. Women's health activists vehemently debated whether or not feminist clinics ought to embrace the development of new contraceptive drugs and reproductive technologies as liberating to women or condemn them for their exploitative potential. Referring to Harvey Karman, one *Ms. Magazine* journalist pondered where the fault lines of feminist support lay:

> Is the enemy [Karman] of our enemy [the medical and pharmaceutical industry] automatically our friend? Do we endanger abortion rights by exposing potentials for malpractice and physical danger to women? If an apparently feminist health group endorses a method, person, or device, can other women trust this appraisal? And what is an appropriate feminist response when an apparently feminist endorsement is in error? While antiabortion forces work incessantly to limit access to abortion by setting up unnecessary medical guidelines, is there a way to establish necessary standards for high quality care?[43]

By placing the decision making around women's health into women's hands and by questioning the cultural assumption that "professionals" (male) are the only ones capable of delivering routine quality health care, feminist clinics sought to challenge men's control over women's bodies. Feminists saw women-controlled clinics as a direct response to the patriarchal nature of the medical establishment and intimately linked to women's struggle for reproductive freedom. Lay health care workers, an EGC collective member noted, broke down the professional barriers that separated an elite of male doctors from their patients. They were "people's doctors, and their medicine was part of a peoples' subculture."[44]

An examination of the EGC further illustrates the tensions between professionalism and lay health care. For members of the EGC, the details of creating a collective and working within collective structures were of equal importance to providing abortion services. The very creation of a feminist collective and the opening and expansion of women's health clinic collectives across the country were highly political acts that EGC women saw as crucial for the transformation of health care.[45] If the EGC was started because Iowa City's male gynecologists had seemed unwilling to establish abortion services following the *Roe v. Wade* decision, EGC women feared by the mid-1970s that men who were establishing women's health clinics were exploiting rather than helping women. Clinics owned by men, EGC women charged, took advantage of women. They paid them low salaries, offered them only token decision-making powers, charged high fees for services, and absorbed the profits back into their own pockets or into the establishment of more clinics. "Male capitalists," they concluded, are "thriving on the troubles, sweat, and concern of our sisters."[46] As a "feminist socialist collective," by contrast, the EGC paid all women equally, regardless of previous professional training.[47] While these salaries were also low, they indicated that the services of all members were valued equally.

Tensions over professionalism arose early on at the clinic and illustrate that professionalism was not only a problem of gender but also one of education. In the early years of the collective, members taught one another the skills necessary for running a feminist health clinic. One member, for instance, had trained as a medical technician and taught others how to sterilize medical instruments. Another was enrolled in an accounting program and taught fellow collective members the basics in bookkeeping. A third was a registered nurse who taught collective members how to perform pelvic exams and provide basic gynecological care. Each collective member learned to do every job—with the exception of the actual abortion procedure—and a system of job rotation meant that all collective members performed every job at the clinic. "Collective members share equal power and responsibility in every aspect of policy and decision-making. All knowledge brought to the collective is actively shared among us," they explained in a form letter sent to women's groups around the country seeking advice on the establishment of feminist clinics.[48] While all the skills were crucial to the functioning of the clinic, some collective members saw the specialized knowledge of other collective members not as a potential asset but as a threat to lay health care. Indeed, a number of collective members were outright hostile to the medical professionals who worked at the clinic. Teresa McDonald, a registered nurse, who trained collective members in the 1970s, was "phenomenal in what she did," Gina Keating remembers. "She trained so many of us and she was so patient and so persevering and she received a lot of criticism for being professional and it really hurt her."[49] When, in 1980, EGC was finally able to hire Adele

Franks, the clinic's first woman doctor, she, too, became the focus of criticism for her professionalism. Franks had been a member of the EGC collective in the early years before leaving to attend medical school. By the time she returned, however, the women who had known her as a collective member had been replaced by a younger group of women unfamiliar with Franks. Some members soon objected that Franks's status as a physician created problems for them. Several women noted that it took them longer to trust Franks because she was a professional.[50]

With Franks's hiring, the underlying tension between the delivery of lay health care and medical professionals came into sharp focus. Collective members argued over the birth control pill, IUDs, and other services that required a physician's authority—and specialized knowledge—and that could thus not be disseminated within the framework of lay health care. Given the collective's philosophy of alternative health care, many collective members opposed the birth control pill and IUD. Besides concerns over health risks, they argued that distributing the pill meant giving in to "the power." "If we give the pill, the establishment wins, we're playing their game and by their rules," the minutes of one meeting noted.[51] Collective members were additionally frustrated by the fact that clients frequently resisted the pitch for alternative barrier methods and wanted the pill instead. "Women coming here for pills don't always want to hear about the side effects, etc.," Joan noted. "They just want to be handed the pills."[52] Exasperated, the collective voted at one meeting to no longer dispense the pill and the IUD. But Franks disagreed. "True, the birth control pill and IUD have known hazards," she conceded. "But so does smoking, riding a motorcycle, hitchhiking, and sleeping with strange men. Yet we don't disallow any of those."[53] Unless the pill was clearly contraindicated, she argued, patients should be able to choose whichever contraceptive they favored.[54] After the collective voted to continue offering the birth control pill and IUD, several collective members complained that Franks always got everything she wanted. Having a physician on staff, they charged, meant that some women, particularly those on the Gyn Committee, which was responsible for oversight of and recommendations for the gynecological care provided at the clinic, relied too heavily on Franks's opinion. Women also found that Franks was more traditional in her approach to medicine than they had expected and concluded that her presence diminished the importance of lay health care advocacy.[55]

To be sure, EGC's medical professionals and collective members often worked as a constructive team. When EGC's medical professionals were in a position to share their knowledge and physicians and collective members engaged in discussion of medical issues and complications as they related to abortion services, the collective functioned smoothly. The Abortion Committee regularly reviewed cases with clinic physicians, for instance, and collective members posed questions and discussed abortion procedures in detail. Staff members' close observation of physicians led to modifications and improvements of abortion procedures. If women liked a physician's technique, they suggested that other physicians adopt the same technique. As new physicians joined the clinic, they introduced EGC women to newer developments in abortion care. When Franks joined the collective, she suggested that the clinic start using laminaria. EGC women agreed, and within weeks, one staff member had had long conversations with Minnesota abortion provider Millie Hanson about the use of laminaria in abortion care.[56] If such discussions involved a larger group of EGC physicians and the clinic's small abortion committee, they could prove very satisfying and constructive.[57]

At other times, however, the tensions over issues of professionalism became insurmountable. In February 1981, when one abortion patient developed a complication, tensions between Franks and the collective members came to a head. When Franks, who was treating the patient, requested a sharp curette, none could be found. Most of the women working that day had only recently been hired. Because they lacked experience, they failed to understand how seriously Franks felt about the event. Some staff members talked about the emergency in front of patients in the recovery room. When Franks asked for the car to transport the patient to the hospital, women did not respond in an emergency fashion. They failed to take the patient's blood pressure or pulse and failed to get her dressed quickly for the trip to the hospital. Indeed, the clinic lacked a protocol for medical emergencies. The minutes recording the event noted that "everyone was just waiting for her to feel better." Franks argued that she "no longer [trusted] that staff will act [appropriately] in an emergency" and added that the clinic was "just lucky it wasn't more serious."[58] Over the following months, relations between EGC women and Franks soured. Although the collective drew up a protocol for medical emergencies in the aftermath of the crisis and resolved that during abortions at least one experienced person should be in the procedure room, Franks felt increasingly stressed having to bear the medical responsibility for the clinic.[59] Like Hern, Franks thought that her ability to influence clinic details was out of sync with the amount of medical responsibility she was carrying.

While a number of EGC women were sympathetic to her fears, the collective was more likely to train its own members in improved emergency response than to follow Franks's request to hire another expensive medical professional from the outside. It is unclear from the minutes whether any of the EGC women understood that their lack of response during the emergency posed a serious problem. Two women, Deb Nye and Flora Cassilianos, voiced understanding for Franks's frustration and confirmed that constant job rotation meant workers were often inexperienced. At the end of 1981, Franks abruptly left the collective. While she had wanted more professionalism, the clinic had remained in flux and job rotation remained high. Frustrated that EGC women frequently left jobs that they did well to train for new positions in the clinic, Franks felt that she could no longer trust decisions made at the clinic and quit.[60]

The desire to avoid having collective members acquire specialized knowledge and to rely on job rotation instead gave collective members the false impression that all responsibilities in an abortion clinic were equal and carried interchangeable skills and comparable responsibilities. The fact that collective members physically moved through all the spaces in the clinic—from the reception desk, where they might greet patients and answer the phones, to the counseling rooms, where they advised women on the abortion procedure and birth control options, to the procedure room, where they assisted in the abortion and served as patient advocates—was likely to further blur the boundaries between skills that could be performed by lay health activists and those that required specialized professional knowledge. In addition, the overall safety of abortion procedures, the knowledge that women in the underground abortion group Jane had learned how to perform such procedures, and the fact that EGC physicians taught several collective members how to perform abortions in case the procedure should ever become illegal again surely contributed to a lack of acknowledgment that abortion was a medical procedure that could have serious complications, even if those occurred rarely.[61]

To Franks, the level of mistrust must have seemed like an insult. "I put my heart and soul into the clinic," she explained after her departure.

> What other physician consistently went to meetings, did workshops, helped write handouts, provided other services, was constantly available for consultations and then went home to read about clinic related medicine and stay awake half the night thinking about clinic problems? The fact that this ultimately did not work out well is sad for us all. The fact that some collective members did not like my input, my proposals, my personality, and my medical orientation is unfortunate but it does not negate the fact that my intentions were good. I always did what

I thought best for the clinic and I invested a lot of my best energy in clinic affairs.[62]

The collective structure of early 1970s women's health clinics drew the attention of collective members to the political structures of the collective and led particularly young and passionate feminists to downplay the delivery of abortion services. The clinic, it seemed at times, existed primarily to allow young feminists to experience a collective work space—with abortion care being a means to that end. Feminist collectives, anthropologist Sandra Morgen notes, encouraged the integration of personal concerns into the workplace, placing the emphasis on "challenging the boundaries (personal and political, private and public) [that] feminists defined as part of the structure of gender oppression."[63] As a result, the collective clinic, staffed by young, passionate activists, might display a high level of emotional and passionate engagement. This was certainly true for the EGC feminists who were passionate about the political implications of hiring another specialized professional as a backup for Franks. But they failed to address Franks's concerns about responding to medical complications.[64]

While the challenge to male medical authority resonated powerfully among feminists at many clinics, many feminist NAF members felt that challenging male medical authority did not necessitate a separation from them. And many feminists found radical feminists naive in their rejection of "professionalism" or the marketplace. Women such as Merle Hoffman, Susan Hill, or Renee Chelian came to NAF as directors of clinics committed to a medical model. "Why was it necessary for women to forgo all the clinical and technological advances that were part of the medical research and clinical establishment for protective or political purposes?" Hoffman wondered. "Why should we adopt minimalist standards as a defense against the medical industrial complex when we could find a way to incorporate it into our paradigms and use it to our benefit?"[65] Many women clinic directors sought to create a supportive clinic environment by employing physicians who behaved respectfully to patients. While they might have to tolerate sexist behavior at professional meetings, they would try to minimize the damage by refusing cooperation.[66]

Even feminists with the FWHC realized that medical professionals had knowledge to offer that could be of benefit to FWHC. In a 1983 letter to Takey Crist welcoming him as a new member on the NAF board, Carol Downer sought to assure Crist of the constructive relationship between FWHC and male medical professionals. "Although there is a general criticism that feminists have of the medical profession," she wrote, "there is no enmity. . . . I have seen a very beneficial dialogue between owners, doctors, nurses, counselors, administrators, and feminist clinics. . . . I think the feminist clinics have especially benefitted from this dialogue as we are often isolated from the medical institutions."[67] FWHC, she pointed out to Crist, actively participated in professional medical events and drew on the expertise of NAF colleagues. In 1979, FWHC had sponsored a symposium on D&E in Los Angeles, and FWHC had conferred with NAF doctors about complications. Indeed, Dr. Warren Hern, once an opponent in the fight over standards, had recently served as a witness for the Chico FWHC.[68] "Feminists, whether from the Feminist Health Center category or from any other, regard our physician members with great esteem as an essential and, at times, a leading element of NAF."[69]

In 1978, NAF published its *Standards for Quality Abortion Care*, which articulated expectations of professionalism and safety for all NAF members to meet.[70] That year, Uta Landy took over from Frances Kissling as NAF's executive director. Following the death of Rosaura Jimenez, Kissling had decided to join Ellen Frankfort and write about the consequences the Hyde Amendment would have on poor women's access to abortion.[71] Landy sought to "develop the relationship with academics and science behind abortion and research. And sort of mainstreaming in that sense who we were and what we were trying to accomplish. How to act on the one hand . . . on the other hand also expose our membership to that larger view and perspective."[72] At the 1978 annual meeting in San Francisco, which featured a keynote speech by Bella Abzug and set the pattern for future annual meetings, NAF members attended sessions on medical research and practice, on legal issues, contraception, the media, clinic policies, and specialized workshops for nurses. In the following years, NAF received accreditation from the American Medical Association and the American College of Obstetricians and Gynecologists for continuing medical education. NAF also began offering risk management workshops every fall.[73]

This Issue Is Inextricably Linked to the Political Aspect
of Abortion: Implementing Clinic Standards

In November 1978, the *Chicago Sun-Times* ran a two-week-long exposé about four Chicago abortion clinics notorious for providing shoddy and unscrupulous services.[74] Over the course of several months, a group of investigative journalists and local civic investigators had infiltrated the clinics posing as patients or new employees. Reminiscent of journalistic coverage prior to *Roe*—and raising the impression that little had changed with legalization—the articles described abortions that six years after *Roe* were perfectly legal but not safe. Prioritizing profits over women's health and lives, medical staff cut corners, rushing women in and out of unsanitary procedure rooms. Physicians performed abortions in such haste that complications were common, and some women were still pregnant after the abortion procedures.

To be sure, many of the thirteen abortion clinics in Chicago in the late 1970s provided abortion services of high quality—and the *Chicago Sun-Times* noted that the four clinics featured were by no means representative of Chicago's abortion clinics as a whole. But the problems with unscrupulous referral services, which Jean Pakter described at the 1976 Denver meeting, persisted. If women seeking abortions looked in the ad section of the city's local newspapers, they could find ads for many different clinics. But the ads provided only an illusion of choice. The Water Tower Clinic, for instance, identified in the *Chicago Sun-Times* investigation as one of the notorious abortion clinics, ran nine different ads a day, listing the clinic under nine different names with nine different phone numbers. If women called any of the numbers, they reached a telephone operator who—posing as a counselor—was paid by the number of abortions she sold. Rather than asking women whether they wanted to terminate a pregnancy, operators were instructed to ask, "When do you want a termination?"[75] They were further instructed to withhold relevant details and to provide deceptive information. "Don't answer too many questions because the patient gets too nervous and the next thing you know they'll be out the door," a supervisor told the operators.[76]

Staff in all four of the clinics investigated by the newspaper engaged in a range of fraudulent and dangerous practices, jeopardizing women's health and making the abortion experience painful and unpleasant. They misinformed patients about the results of their pregnancy tests, sold abortions to women who were not pregnant, made up entries in patient charts, and failed to inspect the products of conception after an abortion to ensure that the abortion procedure had been complete.[77] Even when clinics sent specimens to a pathology lab, they frequently used laboratories that sent unreliable reports—and clinic staff regularly failed to share the results with patients.[78]

Details of the investigation revealed that many of the concerns articulated in the NAF standards debate were of real significance to patient care. As Widdicombe had warned, paying abortion providers by the procedure led easily to the poor treatment of patients. Women, rushed in and out of procedure and recovery rooms, complained about the assembly-line fashion of their abortion procedure. "I could swear that there was only one doctor and he just went down the line giving abortions," one patient recalled her experience lying on the operating table waiting for her doctor. "I started crying because I could hear that little [suction] machine going on and going off. He just kept getting closer and closer. I heard his gloves pop off in the next room and then he came to me. . . . He didn't say a word. He came in and did it and walked out in three minutes. Then he started down the hall again."[79] Some physicians performed abortions so quickly that the anesthesia did not have time to work. Others gave no anesthesia at all. "The pain was unbearable," one patient noted.[80] "Women who scream are told to shut up," the investigative journalists reported. "Others thrash around and are held down by aides. Even when they ask for additional pain relievers, some doctors don't wait."[81] Rushed through the abortion procedure, women were also rushed through recovery. Rather than take the estimated thirty to sixty minutes of recovery time, patients were hurried out of recovery after ten to fifteen minutes. "I was very weak and woozy in the recovery room," one patient recalled. "I was lying there about 15 minutes when the lady said, 'You aren't going to get any better sitting there sulking. Get up and get dressed.'. . . I couldn't stand. I had to lie down on the dressing room floor for another half-hour."[82]

The enormous profit margins of abortion clinics had the potential to attract entrepreneurs and physicians willing to jeopardize the quality of abortion services in order to maximize income. While the price for abortion services varied by geographic location, most clinics charged between $150 and $200 for abortions performed in the first trimester of pregnancy. Abortions in the second trimester were considerably more expensive, ranging from $250 at the lower end to more than $400 for an induction procedure.[83] Given that vacuum aspirations took only a couple minutes to perform, clinics could schedule many vacuum aspirations per hour for their abortion provider, and some did so. Owners of the clinics described in the Chicago exposé lacked interest in their staff's competency and professional demeanor. Some doctors were drunk while performing abortions; others had come to work at the clinics after losing their medical licenses elsewhere.[84] The owners also employed residents who were not trained to provide abortions. State officials, in turn, did not enforce existing regulations governing the state's abortion clinics. Chicago health authorities failed to seek information that might alert them to poor abortion services, to force clinic compliance with inspections, and to enforce the closing of clinics that had lost their licenses. After Chicago public health officials revoked a clinic license, they neglected to inform the public about the revocation and failed to check whether the clinic had indeed closed down. As a result, at least two clinics continued to operate without valid licenses.[85] When a patient died at Water Tower Reproductive, the state attorney general failed to respond to repeated requests by a coroner to investigate the circumstances of the death.[86] But the investigative reporters also blamed physicians who, unwilling to perform abortions themselves, frequently referred patients to clinics they knew little or nothing about.[87]

The *Sun-Times* exposé elicited a range of responses. Within forty-eight hours of the initial story, Illinois governor James R. Thompson ordered state officials to step up their inspections of abortion clinics and asked State Attorney General William J. Scott for his cooperation on pending lawsuits against two physicians mentioned in the series. Although Senator Don Wooten, who had authored the state's existing abortion regulations, noted that better enforcement of existing regulations would have prevented the kinds of abuses uncovered by the *Sun-Times*, a number of state legislators—eager to crack down on legal abortion—called for tougher regulatory measures.[88] Feminists and members of the abortion provider community worried that the reports of medical abuses in abortion clinics would add fuel to antiabortion sentiments. Indeed, commenting on the immediate closing of Water Tower Reproductive, antiabortion activists used the exposé as an occasion to call for the closing of all abortion clinics. "The only good abortion clinic," Joseph Scheidler, executive director of Friends for Life and later the founder of the Pro-Life Action League, a national antiabortion group based in Chicago, explained to the press, "is a closed abortion clinic."[89] Over the following decade, antiabortion activists incorporated the details about patients' experiences in the four discredited Chicago clinics, weaving these stories into often-repeated, if completely erroneous, warnings in which a handful of unscrupulous providers stood for the norm.

NAF members were alarmed by the *Sun-Times* exposé. They felt it tarnished the reputation of all abortion clinics. "We were all talking to each other on the telephone, and the phone at NAF was ringing off the hook," recalled NAF executive director Uta Landy. "I think that in general everybody felt it was an attack on them, on everybody, that the media was using this opportunity to discredit abortion clinics, period. Everybody was really aware that there were some clinics that were lacking in certain standards, and we were relieved that none of these clinics from the articles were members of NAF. But we also realized that they could have been, as well, because we didn't have a very stringent screening process."[90]

It is likely that both NAF physicians and feminists felt the bad news about Chicago clinics confirmed their concerns and experiences. Physicians who had lobbied for the implementation of clinic standards were affirmed in their conviction that merely formulating standards was not sufficient to separate the wheat from the chaff; NAF needed to find a way to enforce clinic standards among its members. For feminists, on the other hand, the Chicago story seemed to confirm their analysis that patriarchy and capitalism were the problem. The Abortion Profiteers, as the journalists called the Chicago clinic owners and doctors, were ruthless businessmen who sought to profit from women's unwanted pregnancies and who employed other men to perform abortions with little care for women's emotional and physical well-being.

In the immediate aftermath of the exposé, NAF turned to patient education and the dissemination of information about reputable abortion clinics to aid women's search for abortion services. The organization established a toll-free telephone hotline that women could call for referrals to respectable abortion providers. By 1981, the hotline was receiving 3,000 calls annually and offering a vital resource, particularly to poor women, by providing information about organizations and clinics that could help with the cost of an abortion.[91] In addition, NAF issued a brochure, *How to Choose an Abortion Facility*, to help women evaluate different abortion clinics.

The *Sun-Times* exposé lent urgency to the debate over the implementation of clinic standards that NAF had published in 1978. Physicians and members with academic backgrounds pushed for some way to enforce medical standards for NAF clinics, suggesting, for instance, that NAF conduct regular inspections of member clinics and that applicants for NAF membership be required to pass an inspection before they could become NAF members. But such proposals carried a significant price tag, as NAF—or the member clinics—would have to find a way to pay for the inspections. Feminist and freestanding clinics balked at the increase in membership dues that standards implementation implied. Indeed, membership fees were high enough to discourage the EGC from joining. EGC members felt the collective could not afford clinic membership, and even participation at regular NAF meetings was so expensive that collective members had long discussions about whether they could send representatives.[92] This reflected both the financial situation of the clinic and questions of priority. EGC members were more likely to visit a workshop on feminist politics than a meeting by NAF.[93] Indeed, implementing clinic inspections must have seemed daunting, if not impossible. In 1978, NAF listed 120 different abortion clinics on its first membership list. Numbers rose quickly to 144 clinics in 1979 and 176 clinics in 1980–81. The number exploded in the early 1980s, when the election of Ronald Reagan, the political turn against legal abortion, and escalating attacks against abortion clinics put abortion providers on the defensive. By 1984–85, NAF had 269 member clinics in the United States and several abroad. Such growth within six years magnified the difficulty of implementing clinic inspections for the new organization. Still, the Alan Guttmacher Institute counted 2,701 abortion providers in 1984, which meant that only 10 percent of abortion providers joined NAF. Bowing to financial constraints, NAF members had already voted in 1979 not to make on-site evaluation a requirement for membership.[94] And while members remained divided about the issue, some physicians conceded that policing NAF clinics was a logistic and financial impossibility. Instead, in 1980, NAF began to offer regular risk management seminars in the hope that access to continuing education combined with peer pressure would lead member clinics to follow NAF standards.[95]

It fell to the NAF Medical Advisory and Educational Committee to urge member clinics to adhere to NAF standards. These standards required that each member clinic designate a particular physician as medical director. But when the committee reviewed information about member clinics' medical directors, they found that several women's health clinics had failed to designate one. Designating a physician as medical director, they objected, elevated the physician over the rest of the clinic. Committee members suggested possible solutions but were unwilling to compromise. The medical director had a number of crucial responsibilities: the review of medical practice in a clinic, the approval of medical protocols, the approval of standing orders, the review of performance of medical practitioners, and the review of complications.[96]

The Medical Advisory and Educational Committee regularly discussed developments and problems of individual clinics. It sought to exert some control by asking for regular complication reports, ranking individual clinics on the number of complications they had, and issuing notifications if committee members found fault with particular clinic policies.[97] As NAF membership increased over the 1980s, concerns about whether new member clinics met the standards continued to grow. With membership more than doubling in the course of five years, NAF struggled with the issue of how to assure that it not admit members who fell short on clinic standards. When the owner of a New Orleans clinic with several pending malpractice lawsuits against him joined NAF, the Medical Committee complained about the careless admissions process. Members Phillip Darney and Michael Burnhill, who had been asked to testify against the clinic owner, noted that the nature of the complications in question should raise concerns about the clinic's membership in NAF and that the clinic file lacked any information that might support membership. Another clinic, which had recently had two serious complications, applied for inclusion in NAF's malpractice insurance coverage that the federation had begun to offer in the early 1980s. Committee members felt that the clinic could not be approved for malpractice insurance coverage until the details of the complication cases were revealed. NAF, the Medical Committee cautioned, should be careful not to accept unsatisfactory members and should make sure that applicants could offer good references.[98]

As attacks against abortion providers escalated in the 1980s, the political importance of maintaining clinic standards increased. By the mid-1980s, the harassment of abortion providers had significantly intensified. Almost half (47 percent) reported that they had experienced antiabortion harassment in 1985. Freestanding clinics and offices performing more than 400 abortions per year were the most likely target for harassment, and clinics in the Midwest and South fared worse than those in the East or West. Eighty percent of abortion providers reported picketing at their facilities. This was usually accompanied by other forms of harassment: the distribution of antiabortion literature inside the facility, bomb threats, physical contact with or the blocking of patients by picketers, numerous no-show appointments scheduled to disrupt the scheduling of legitimate patients, and demonstrations loud enough to be heard by patients inside the facility. In 1985, demonstrators invaded close to a third of abortion facilities and vandalized almost as many.[99] The pressure from demonstrators was accompanied by state and federal legislative efforts to regulate abortion facilities and, starting with the 1976 Helms Amendment, establish that life begins at conception. In 1981 and 1983, legislators introduced a Human Life Bill and a Human Life Amendment that would overturn the *Roe v. Wade* decision by defining life to begin at the moment of conception, efforts that, by 1985, had won the endorsement of President Ronald Reagan.[100]

With these attacks, maintaining clinical standards suddenly became political as it had not been before. When Charlotte Taft, who ran an abortion clinic in Dallas, Texas, was asked in 1985 to testify against a Texas antiabortion bill, she found to her surprise that one of the star witnesses for the other side was a former Dallas clinic director, Carol Everett. After getting fired from her job, Everett had joined the antiabortion movement and now regularly testified to the poor clinic practices in the clinics she had directed. Indeed, in her attempt to discredit the work of abortion providers, Everett seemed to boast about the illegal and unethical practices that had taken place under her supervision. Abortionists, she noted, had taken advantage of the lack of regulations in Texas. In her own clinics, she had hired physicians without checking their medical licenses, and many of her patients had experienced major complications and had needed hospitalization. And rather than send the fetal remains to a pathology lab as they told patients they would, she and her staff had put the remains down the disposal.[101] Taft worried: "I did not feel as confident as I wanted to feel that none of the accusations was true and could not occur now in clinics in our state and nation, and *within* our organization."[102]

Others agreed. In a 1985 memo, Lewis Koplik, chair of the NAF standards committee, reminded NAF members of the importance of the proper disposal of fetal remains as medical waste. "If an average non-'right to lifer' were aware of how you dispose of abortion tissue, would you feel completely comfortable?" he asked. "Would you feel comfortable discussing tissue disposal before a television reporter's camera or a legislative committee? If the answer to either of these questions is 'no,' then you must reevaluate how you or your institution processes and disposes of your specimens."[103] Koplik reminded members of the damage antiabortion propaganda could do when it focused on inappropriately stored or discarded fetal tissue. Indeed, reports of such finds were increasingly common. In 1982, for instance, authorities had discovered more than 500 fetuses in a storage container repossessed from a California pathologist. Antiabortion activists used the find for its lurid graphic effects in propaganda material that presented the pathologist as part of an American Holocaust. And when the California Pro-Life Medical Association proposed a memorial service for the fetuses, it gained the endorsement of President Ronald Reagan. "Your decision to hold a memorial service for these children is most fitting and proper," Reagan wrote to the organization and suggested that activists take the incident as an occasion to strengthen the resolve to end the "national tragedy" of legal abortion.[104] Abortion providers, Koplik's memo suggested, needed to make sure that none of their actions and practices could cause negative publicity. Koplik called on NAF members to realize that they held the ultimate responsibility for the disposal of specimen. Even if they worked in a large hospital setting, merely trusting that janitors transported the specimen appropriately and that pathology labs promptly disposed of tissues they received was not sufficient. "You cannot assume that all physicians or janitors who may come in contact with the specimen will be supportive of what we do," he cautioned and urged providers to individually investigate tissue disposal and assure themselves that their requirements were satisfied.[105]

Taft, too, implored NAF members to recognize the political danger in the lack of clinic supervision. "No matter what the truth or falsehood of these allegations," she noted about Everett's testimony, "it became clear to me that the hearing was not about the bill—it was a trial of all our clinics. . . . Neither my clinic nor other clinics in Dallas have been evaluated in a very long time. I find this a very worrisome situation and one which directly affects NAF's stated purposes." Taft urged NAF board members to institute on-site visits for any NAF applicant of whom any current member had a negative impression. In addition, she suggested the organization develop a standardized test that would allow clinics to measure their own performance. Finally, NAF should promote consumer awareness by reprinting and redistributing its guide to choosing an abortion facility. Everett's testimony had been followed by a number of patients who had testified about the poor care they had received at Texas abortion clinics. "Hearing woman after woman testify to inadequate services that she received when they [sic] had abortions was a sad experience for me," Taft commented. "The hard work we all do to keep abortion legal is a travesty if women are routinely damaged emotionally or physically in the process."[106]

Within the course of a decade, medical practice had become political in ways never before experienced. Towns used zoning and building regulations to prevent abortion clinics from opening, and a number of localities drafted onerous clinic regulations to keep abortion clinics out. But if some localities overregulated clinics, others—as the *Chicago Sun Times* exposé revealed—neglected to enforce existing regulations or left abortion clinics entirely unregulated. Concerns surrounding safety standards were no longer merely about the provision of quality health care. They carried a significance that reached into the state legislative offices. "This issue," Taft concluded, "is inextricably linked to the political aspect of abortion."[107] As the 1970s gave way to the 1980s and antiabortion activists sharpened their depiction of abortion as murder, abortion providers found that science and professionalism, while crucial to the establishment of safe abortion services, were insufficient as a response to antiabortion propaganda and activism.

4

The Development of Dilation and Evacuation and the Debate over Fetal Bodies

At the 1978 NAF meeting in San Francisco, Minnesota ob-gyn and abortion provider Dr. Millie Hanson, a tiny woman with the energy of a hurricane, got up and gave a presentation on laminaria. Physicians in Japan and England used laminaria to perform a second trimester abortion procedure called D&E, in which the fetus is removed, generally in parts, through the cervix and vagina. In the United States, however, D&E was not an accepted medical procedure. Instead, physicians used manual dilation for first trimester abortions and relied on saline and prostaglandin instillation procedures to perform midtrimester abortions. Hanson had read about laminaria in a medical journal. Frustrated with the four-week period between the twelfth and sixteenth week when women were unable to obtain an abortion in the United States, she took note. "It just seemed like such a great idea," she recalled.[1] She booked a flight to Nagoya, Japan, where she visited a laminaria factory, observed the use of laminaria in a local clinic, and returned with a suitcase full of supplies.[2] Back at her clinic, she began to use the laminaria to perform second trimester abortions, carefully recording her experience. And in 1978, she presented a paper on her experience performing D&Es on over 2,000 patients whose gestational age went up to 20 weeks since their last monthly period. Renee Chelian, who was in the audience, recalls: "I remember doctors yelling that it wasn't a scientific study because it wasn't done in a hospital setting. They were angry that this, I suspect, that this woman took it upon herself to do this without any of their help, certainly not their permission and not their input and guidance. It wasn't a collaborative effort."[3]

Hanson was not the only one intrigued by the laminaria

procedure. Warren Hern, who had read about the technique in the text-book *Techniques of Abortion*, chose laminaria in his Boulder, Colorado, clinic.[4] Hern bought the laminaria from the Milex Company, where he also purchased some of his instruments.[5] He, too, began to collect data on the laminaria procedures—initially to perform first trimester abortions only. At night, he spent hours poring over data and research studies on the medical safety of abortion procedures. In October 1974, he presented a paper at the annual American Public Health Association meeting in New Orleans chronicling his experience of performing first trimester abortions with laminaria on 1,368 patients.[6] And in November 1976, he presented another paper—this one at the Annual Meeting of the Association of Planned Parenthood Physicians on 150 abortion patients whose pregnancies were in the second trimester, ranging from thirteen to nineteen weeks. Midtrimester abortions, he explained to his colleagues, may be more safely performed by D&E than by amnioinfusion techniques.[7]

Among their colleagues, American pioneers of D&E were more likely to find themselves the target of hostility rather than the center of appreciation. Many in the field feared that laminaria might cause infection or even worried that a physician lacking experience and caution might kill a patient performing a D&E. One prominent abortion provider accused Hanson, who displayed laminaria at NAF meetings in a glass of water to illustrate how they expanded, of lying about the gestational age of the abortions she was performing with the help of laminaria. Her Minneapolis colleagues filed a complaint with the hospital, alleging that she was performing "dangerous and hazardous" procedures.[8] Hern, too, faced hostility and opposition. "There were all kinds of people waiting for me to screw up," he recalled.[9] Physicians also objected to the unpleasant nature of the procedure. Renee Chelian recalls first learning about laminaria and D&E through Hanson's presentation at the NAF meeting that she attended with her medical director. "I and the doctor that went to the meeting with me thought it sounded barbaric."[10]

The meticulous recordkeeping of providers such as Hanson and Hern helped to establish a safety record for D&E procedures that belied the procedure's reputation. Hanson not only personally challenged colleagues who claimed D&Es were dangerous and hazardous. When ob-gyn David Grimes with the CDC Joint Program for the Study of Abortion failed to include the use of laminaria in an article that evaluated safety and adverse events of different abortion techniques, she invited him to her clinic to watch her demonstrate her method. Indeed, many people came to watch Hanson perform D&Es, and Hanson taught the method to some of the most prominent abortion providers in the country.[11] In 1977, David Grimes and his coauthors compared complications in 6,213 midtrimester curettage procedures to 8,662 saline abortions and concluded that D&E was not only "considerably safer" than saline abortion but also "direct, rapid and convenient for the patient."[12]

Following the 1977 establishment of NAF, which provided a forum for support and information exchange, abortion providers turned their attention to the development and refinement of abortion procedures. Over the next decade, they created a scientific discourse surrounding pregnancy termination procedures that included the comparison of different procedures and the development of support systems and counseling techniques for patients and clinic staff. Steeped in traditions of scientific data collection, interpretation, and dissemination, this discourse established an ordered way to rank abortion procedures and mainstream the development of new abortion methods. Providers not only discussed medical safety but also voiced their feelings about the performance of particular abortion procedures. As antiabortion propaganda increased and the nature of fetal bodies became more and more politicized, abortion providers lost their ability to openly discuss their work experiences and their concerns. Any unease an abortion provider expressed provided antiabortion activists with material to use in the fight against abortion, effectively silencing important discussions in the abortion provider community.

A Complex Medical Problem: From Saline Procedures to D&E

In the 1970s, Judy Widdicombe, who had started Reproductive Health Services in St. Louis in May 1973, traveled to New York and Kansas to observe several saline units in local hospitals. Such programs offered the most widely used method of second trimester abortions at that time. Physicians induced patients with saline or prostaglandin, leading the pregnant woman to miscarry. Observing the programs, Widdicombe found it hard to contain her own revulsion. "This was an *advance*?" journalist Cynthia Gorney described her response. "Ashen women in hospital gowns pushing IV poles down the hall and stopping long enough to grab their bellies and double over in pain—it was as though someone had hospital-gowned the women she and Art [Widdicombe's husband] used to pick up on street corners during the illegal days."[13]

Widdicombe was not alone in her lack of enthusiasm for saline programs. Instillation procedures came with a host of problems. First, there was the four-week period in which women were too far along for a first trimester vacuum aspiration but not far enough along for the instillation procedure. Then there were the risks and unpleasant side effects for the pregnant woman. Finally, the procedures could lead to the delivery of a fetus still showing signs of life. Such outcomes were rare—only 1 percent of abortions in the 1970s took place after twenty weeks of gestation, and only one in 4,000 of those resulted in a live birth. When live births did occur, most of the fetuses were so immature that they died within twenty-four hours.[14] Nevertheless, such events were disturbing.

Live births as a result of abortion led to a disproportionate number of criminal and civil charges against abortion providers. While most of these legal indictments were eventually dismissed, the threat of prosecution contributed to a chilly climate and further inhibited the performance of abortions in the late second trimester. Since physicians frequently left after performing the amniocentesis (the withdrawal of amniotic fluid) and inserting the medication to begin labor, nurses were usually the ones having to deal with the fetus. As the authors of a study on the emotional demands of midtrimester abortion procedures commented: "Amnio abortions [saline instillations] are viewed by the nurses as the most upsetting experience which occur [sic] and a symbol of abandonment by the medical staff. The ward nurses' comments speak clearly to the point of being left to cope with an upset patient who delivers late at night. The nurses found the physical contact with the fetus particularly difficult."[15] By the end of the decade, researchers concluded that "the live-born fetus has become one of the most difficult medical, legal, and ethical problems associated with midtrimester abortion."[16]

Physicians and nurses were frustrated with saline procedures, but in the United States, D&E was considered an unsafe procedure. The technical challenges of "removing something larger (the fetus) through something smaller (the cervix) with minimal risk to the patient" seemed insurmountable.[17] In addition to technical problems, midtrimester abortions were beset with medical, aesthetic, and social problems not present in first trimester abortions. As Colorado abortion provider Warren Hern, author of *Abortion Practice*, then the nation's most widely used textbook on abortion, explained: "The signs of fetal life on expulsion and the repugnance of dismemberment plague the alternatives in midtrimester abortion. It is certainly one of the more complex medical problems of the 20th century, and its complexity is intensified by the milieu of social controversy."[18]

Nevertheless, by the mid-1970s, some abortion providers began to look for alternatives—in particular, the use of laminaria. While dilation by laminaria required patients to come to the clinic at least twice—first for the insertion of the laminaria and then again for the abortion procedure—the procedure was less traumatic and promised to lead to fewer complications and to open the door to abortion procedures between the twelfth and sixteenth weeks. In addition, instillation procedures required a hospital stay of forty-eight to seventy-two hours. D&E procedures could be performed on an outpatient basis, moving second trimester abortions from hospitals to freestanding clinics. Intrigued, several physicians decided to incorporate the use of laminaria into their practice.

The use of laminaria allowed abortion providers to slowly extend the gestational age past the traditional twelve-week cutoff. Prior to the introduction of ultrasound in abortion clinics, abortion providers had to estimate fetal age. Sometimes the fetal age was a week or two further along than their estimate had indicated. Providers' ability to meet these unexpected challenges contributed to their confidence and skills and increased the willingness of some physicians to perform abortions at more advanced gestational ages. "The way I got gutsy or adventurous about the whole thing," Hanson remembered, "[was] when I knew I was doing a 14-weeker and when I had the fetal remains I had a 16-weeker and I thought: 'well, that went pretty well.' And then I would do a 16 weeker that would turn out to be a 17-weeker and finally I was doing 20-weekers. And sometimes a 21-weeker."[19]

A 1979 study at the University of California at San Francisco on the impact of abortion techniques on physicians, nurses, and patients further hastened reform. The study found that physicians preferred amnioinfusion abortion, whereas nurses and patients preferred D&Es. D&E shifted the emotional burden away from nurses and patients to the physician performing the procedure.[20] In the end, the refusal of an increasing number of nurses to assist in instillation abortions and the continued threat of live birth lawsuits forced hospitals to either limit second trimester abortions or adopt D&E. And the development of larger cannulas through which material of a more developed fetus could pass more easily improved physicians' experience when performing D&Es.

The shift from instillation procedures to D&E meant that doctors prioritized a female patient's safety and the emotional well-being of patients and staff over their own experience performing abortion procedures. Since D&E involved the extraction of recognizable fetal parts, the procedures took an emotional toll on the doctors. "A physician performing a D&E," a study on the emotional impact of D&Es pointed out, "must deal with the second trimester fetus in an intimate, physical way, using methods of evacuation that often take longer than amniocentesis and that may be distasteful to the medical staff. Ossified parts, such as the skull, must often be crushed. The bone fragments must be extracted carefully to avoid tearing the cervix. Reconstruction of the fetal sections after removal from the uterus is necessary to ensure completeness of the abortion procedure."[21] NAF began to sponsor continuing education seminars to encourage abortion providers to switch from instillation procedures to D&E and to develop supportive services to abortion providers and staff involved in D&E procedures. In cooperation with the Department of Obstetrics and Gynecology at UNC, NAF held a meeting on second trimester abortions in September 1979. For two days, attendees listened to presentations on second trimester pregnancies and the medical, ethical, psychological, and legal issues surrounding them. On the third day, a small group of abortion providers from across the country offered a workshop on the technical aspects of D&E and amnioinfusion techniques.[22] Organizers addressed the challenges of D&E and the emotional and counseling issues providers would have to face. Staff who did not understand and support a patient's decision to have an abortion, panelist Judith B. Rooks cautioned, were more likely to suffer emotional stress as a result of the procedure.[23] Conceding that it was impossible to control physician and staff feelings regarding D&E, Rooks urged that staff be well trained, participate in abortion voluntarily, and work in a cohesive group with open communication so that all staff members could verbalize negative feelings and still feel respected. By 1980, D&E had emerged as the most frequently used method of second trimester abortion. "Second trimester abortion techniques," David Grimes noted hopefully, "have shifted from those in which a live birth may be possible, such as hysterotomy or instillation, to D&E, in which it is not."[24]

Over the following years, the use of D&E procedures continued to expand. To be sure, 90 percent of abortions took place in the first trimester. In 1981, when 9.7 percent of all abortions were performed after the first trimester, 36 percent of these were induction procedures; by 1988, when 10.5 percent of all abortions were performed after the first trimester, induction procedures had fallen to 13 percent.[25] The procedures had also become safer. The wider use of ultrasound meant that providers could more accurately date gestational age. The invention and trial of synthetic dilators, which worked more quickly than laminaria, and the development of new antibiotic agents which were more effective against organisms common in gynecologic infection further improved the safety record. An amicus brief in the 1983 U.S. Supreme Court case *Planned Parenthood v. Ashcroft*, which challenged Missouri statutes regulating second trimester abortions, addressed the safety of abortion practices and highlighted the role that

NAF members had played in the advancement of pregnancy termination procedures: "Technological advances in the provision of second trimester abortions, pioneered by NAF members, have resulted in the availability of D&E abortions, which were virtually unknown in 1973."[26]

While the shift from instillation procedures to D&E made pregnancy terminations after the first trimester significantly safer and easier to perform, it did not solve the ethical and aesthetic issues surrounding the procedure. Indeed, not all abortion providers felt comfortable performing D&Es. In the late 1970s, Judy Widdicombe decided to offer D&E abortions in her St. Louis clinic. Widdicombe had read medical articles and listened closely at NAF seminars. In 1979, she took Michael Freiman, who performed first trimester abortions at her clinic, and another clinic doctor to Washington, D.C. At the Washington Hospital Center, they discussed the expansion of her services with physician William Peterson, one of the few doctors Widdicombe knew who was skilled at performing D&Es. Like Hern and Hanson, Peterson used laminaria and offered D&Es to his patients, most of whom were fourteen to fifteen weeks pregnant. The three visitors accompanied Peterson into the surgery room for a demonstration of his technique. Freiman struggled as he watched Peterson perform the procedure. Cynthia Gorney recounts his response after he watched a small arm with a hand drop into the surgical pan:

> When the abortion was finished and they walked away from the procedure table, he found that all he could remember was that first single hand. He felt sick around his midsection still, although he was sure now that he was not going to throw up or otherwise embarrass them all, and he listened in wonder as Judy and Bill Peterson reviewed in their intelligent medical way some of the fine points of D and E. What was wrong with him? Why was he suddenly thinking about Nazi Germany? Freiman had been the chief abortion doctor at RHS [Reproductive Health Services] for six years and he knew he had observed his share of bloodied parts. . . . But never before had his work at the clinic required him to consider so plainly the mechanics of dismemberment.[27]

Freiman told Widdicombe that he was happy to defend her plans to expand to second trimester procedures, to sign the documents, to testify in court, if needed. But emotionally, he would not be able to perform D&E procedures.[28] Others, however, did not share Freiman's response. Robert Crist from the University of Kansas Medical Center, whom Widdicombe hired in Freiman's place to provide D&Es at her clinic, had spent a decade developing a reputation as one of the nation's accomplished D&E

doctors. Crist performed abortions as a routine part of his gynecological work. In contrast to Freiman, Crist did not find D&Es hard to perform. He found cancer surgeries much harder. "When he did his oncology procedures," Gorney writes, "Crist had to take out vaginas, bladders, small intestine sections, whole swaths across the pelvic area; he had to leave women maimed and still terrified of cancer. When he did his abortions, the women were relieved, they were whole, they went back to their families or their military careers or their high school cheerleading squads, they sent him Christmas cards at the end of the year and told him in their own handwriting how grateful they were."[29]

In January 1980, Widdicombe began to offer second trimester D&E abortions at Reproductive Health Services. Crist brought his own nurse and counselors and several nurses at RHS volunteered to help. Widdicombe took NAF's advice on staff training to heart and gave her staff members the opportunity to talk about their feelings and ambivalence.[30] Renee Chelian, too, was deliberate and cautious about the involvement of staff when she decided to expand her services from first to second trimester abortions by integrating D&E services into her clinic. Chelian made the decision to provide D&E as an outpatient procedure in her abortion clinics after two patients of Detroit colleagues experienced severe complications when the saline entered their bloodstream during instillation procedures. One woman died; the other suffered permanent brain damage. Suddenly, the need for a safer method outweighed any other concerns. Worried that some staff members might quit if they were asked to participate in D&E abortions, Chelian organized a voluntary D&E team that performed D&Es early in the morning before other staff arrived. Once the service was established and running smoothly, however, Chelian integrated D&E services into the regular clinic. While staff who had worked at the clinic prior to the introduction of D&E were not required to help with second trimester abortions, staff members hired after the introduction of D&E were expected to participate in all aspects of the clinic. Chelian explained to her staff why second trimester abortions were necessary. "I decided that I needed to make sure that—because this was so fresh in our mind about why we did D&Es—that we needed to explain to all of our staff and anybody new who was hired why we did second trimesters. Because all I could hear in my own head was 'why be involved with that.' And it was important to be involved because it was safer for the patient."[31]

NAF addressed the issue of the emotional burdens of D&E head on. It offered seminars on abortion complications, including a workshop on complications that could lead to lawsuits and a workshop on preexisting conditions that might raise complications rates. Its seminars on D&E services included workshops on ethical considerations, operative technique, the use of laminaria, the development of standards for D&E services, and counseling and staff training. A 1984 risk seminar on D&E, for example, not only addressed technical and administrative considerations surrounding the integration of D&E into clinic services but also devoted extensive attention to staff support. Faculty gave advice on how to prepare staff for the performance of D&Es, how to facilitate staff acceptance of second trimester abortions, how to present second trimester abortions to patients, and how to help staff voice their feelings, identify emotional barriers, and select coping techniques to handle the stress of providing D&E services. Such a broad approach meant that physicians and clinic staff not only gained valuable skills but also received important emotional support

Developed against the backdrop of attempts to introduce a Human Life Amendment to the U.S. Constitution that would define life to begin at the moment of conception, D&E procedures brought questions about fetal development into sharper focus. Even if abortion providers had no question about the ethical implications of their work, the public discussion surrounding the human life amendments meant that abortion patients, clinic staff, and the abortion providers themselves needed a moral framework to guide them through this work. At the 1983 annual NAF meeting, the issue of moral and ethical dilemmas of abortion stood front and center. "We believe it serves us well to ponder complex moral issues, to sharpen our sense of moral rightness and to become aware of how our personal moral limits affect our interactions with patients," Uta Landy noted as she introduced the first panel.[32] In the following hours, NAF members listened as panelist Ruth van Hosen, a nurse from Midtown Hospital in Atlanta, which specialized on abortions after the first trimester, explained how her hospital dealt with the ethical dilemmas raised by midtrimester abortions. Van Hoesen urged NAF doctors to provide a role model to their staff by dealing in a professional manner with the fetal tissue. Moreover, she emphasized that all involved with D&E abortions should complete a value assessment in which staff members reflected on their personal moral values, because none of these skills were taught as part of the professional training in medical or nursing school.[33]

Panelists Marjorie Reilly Maquire, a Ph.D. and fellow in ethics and theology at Catholics for a Free Choice, and developmental biologist Clifford Grobstein suggested ways to think about the concept of personhood. Maquire proposed that personhood be thought of in relational terms, suggesting that a fetus became a person "at the moment when the mother gives consent to the pregnancy. Before this point, what you have is a purely biological development going on within her body." Grobstein noted that the concept of person was only partly biological, and even those of its components that are biological, he observed, came gradually into existence. "Forceful and integrated behavior," he assured the audience, "such as we associate with persons in the usual context, seems first to appear midway in the third trimester—along with maturational changes in the upper brain. Professional behavioral observers have described this behavior as though it indicated a rudimentary and fluctuating subjective awareness, possibly the first appearance of a consciousness of self." But, he concluded, "science cannot now, and perhaps never will[,] answer all questions about human life, whether they relate to origins, characteristics or terminations."[34]

NAF events in the 1980s addressed not only the ethical issues surrounding D&E abortions. In a range of risk management and quality assurance seminars, NAF also drafted standards for D&E in the later second trimester and made sure that its members were able to acquire the skills and resources to meet those standards. These seminars functioned both as continuing education events—starting in 1981 attendees could receive postgraduate accreditation from the Accreditation Council for Continuing Medical Education—and as a reminder of proper abortion care.[35] Seminar topics ranged from abortion complications to workshops on ultrasonography and D&E services. A 1983 seminar taught abortion providers the latest skills in ultrasonography for abortion care, complete with demonstrations of the most recent ultrasound machines on which seminar members practiced.[36] The following year, NAF members drew up standards for second trimester abortions which specified that physicians who performed later midtrimester abortions "must be experienced in the use of ultrasonography and specialized instruments."[37]

The educational mission that NAF carried out through these seminars was essential to building and maintaining abortion services that would meet the highest standards. Abortion providers, nurses, counselors, and other clinic staff were unlikely to pick up the necessary technical and counseling skills in their regular training. And workshop participants made it clear how helpful NAF seminars were for their work. The workshop discussion, one participant noted, "started some thought probing and soul searching on my own part. It also helped me to realize where some of my co-workers are coming from. I feel we will be more supportive of each other."[38] Staff particularly appreciated those aspects of the workshops that helped them cope with burnout and the stress of an emotionally demanding workplace that was becoming increasingly politicized. They asked for help on handling issues such as abortion at more advanced gestational ages and complimented workshop information that helped them gain emotional distance from the problems of their patients. "It helped to see how I was interjecting my own feelings into a situation, rather than just seeing it as it is," another attendee praised the experience.[39] The workshops did not merely teach skills; they also provided attendees with emotional support. Many commented that they appreciated the opportunity to meet and interact with people from other clinics.[40]

But attempts to articulate the persistent problems with D&E abortions and discuss ways to help staff cope with the aesthetic problems of abortions in the late second trimester were exploited by antiabortion activists. During the early years of NAF, annual meetings were advertised and open to anyone. By the early 1980s, antiabortion activists had begun to attend. "During that time," Uta Landy recalled,

> [Joe Scheidler] started to come to our meetings and he was very infamous. Some people on the board thought that he shouldn't be allowed in. I remember that very first time when we were just at the very beginning of our annual meeting, the plenary session, and we were just getting organized, starting to sit down, and somebody from the staff came and asked about this and was very excited. And I just said, "No, I don't want to keep him out. Let him in. We have nothing to hide." And he came with another younger man who had a big bullhorn that he put in front of him. And they always sat in the front row, maybe trying to intimidate us. But I thought, "You are not going to intimidate us." Nobody had any fear at that time. . . . It was a little bit uncomfortable. On the other hand, I thought I'd rather tolerate the discomfort.[41]

Scheidler attended a number of annual meetings and listened to the presentations and discussions. Staff workshops, too, were occasionally attended by antiabortion activists. One staff member complained about the presence of antiabortion activist Olga Fairfax, who attended a NAF-sponsored media workshop: "I didn't feel comfortable sharing too much as a clinic that is picketed by Fairfax's forces every Saturday."[42] Antiabortion activists freely followed the discussions about ethical and aesthetic issues surrounding abortion procedures and misappropriated the words of abortion providers for their own purposes. In 1980, Warren Hern published an article in *Advances in Planned Parenthood* analyzing staff reactions to D&E procedures. "We have reached a point in this particular technology," Hern commented about D&E, "where there is no possibility of denying an act of destruction. It is before one's eyes. The sensations of dismemberment flow through the forceps like an electric current."[43] These procedures, he found, took their toll on staff. Some tried to avoid viewing the fetal parts. Others responded with shock, dismay, disgust, fear, amazement, and sadness. Many reported disturbing dreams.[44] In 1986, Hern's words offered fodder for Joseph Scheidler, who, in a speech in Atlanta, Georgia, quoted them as proof that abortion providers knew that abortion was murder.

> When they say, "Well, abortion isn't really murder, it isn't really killing," I say, wait a minute, don't take my word for it. Let's take the biggest abortionist, the one who writes all the books, Warren Hern, and let's see what he says: "We have reached a point in this particular technology where there is no possibility of denial of the act of destruction on the part of the operator, even before his eyes the sensation of dismemberment flow of the forceps like an electric [current]." . . . Abortionists know that it is killing, they know it is murder. They are willing to live with it.[45]

Antiabortion activists stripped the words of abortion providers of their larger context and wielded them against the physicians who performed the procedures. Providers, struggling with the implications of the procedures they performed but committed to a pro-choice position, had no space to voice their thoughts without the risk that such discussion would be exploited by the antiabortion movement.

The stifling of discussions surrounding D&E was the more devastating as concerns about the procedure continued to plague the field. Despite the procedure's excellent safety record, researchers cautioned throughout the 1980s that second trimester procedures raised complex medical, legal, and ethical problems. While it was now possible to safely terminate pregnancies at later and later gestational ages, a 1984 article in the *New York Times* noted, medical technology was pushing fetal viability earlier and earlier. If in the early 1970s the point of fetal viability was generally twenty-eight weeks after conception; a decade later it was possible to sustain the lives of infants as early as twenty-three weeks.[46] The emotional burden of abortion increased with more advanced pregnancies and was particularly high for staff who had close contact with the fetus—the physician performing the procedure and the lab assistant reconstructing the fetal sections. "Any procedure at this stage is pretty gruesome," one specialist of high-risk pregnancies commented. "When I did second-trimester abortions, I did them late in the day, and when I'd get home, my wife would say, 'You did one today, didn't you?' It would be all over my face."[47]

The situation was further complicated by the development of procedures that could detect fetal defects before birth. Since many of these diagnostic procedures could not be performed until relatively late in pregnancy, decisions about abortions due to fetal abnormality were often made just at the edge of fetal viability.[48] Alerting abortion providers to the moral complexity of pregnancy terminations in the late second and third trimester, David Grimes noted: "Technological advances in pediatrics continue to lower the threshold of viability for newborns, so that the distinction between a late-second trimester abortion and the premature birth of a potentially viable fetus may soon be blurred. The conflict between the interests of the pregnant woman and those of the fetus escalates as the pregnancy progresses and as the fetus develops a capacity for independent life."[49] "It makes us all schizophrenic," one professor of ob-gyn commented. "Nowadays we are asked to terminate a pregnancy that in two weeks doctors on the same floor are fighting to save."[50] Physicians concluded that abortions at or after the late second trimester were among the most difficult. Given medical technology, they were also surrounded by questions lacking an easy answer.[51] Physicians disagreed on the implications of this development. Some chose not to offer abortions beyond twenty weeks' gestation—a point when it was impossible to sustain fetal life. Others stuck to the viability threshold of twenty-five weeks noted in *Roe v. Wade*.

I Am Entitled to My Feelings: Abortion Providers and Their Doubts

The political appropriation of any discussion of the complications of abortion work further narrowed abortion providers' ability to discuss a topic that was difficult to talk about in its own right. Ultimately, the politicization of this debate drove the conversation about doubts and feelings of clinic workers underground. Antiabortion activists not only misappropriated the statements of abortion providers but they also invited those who decided to leave abortion clinics to join the antiabortion movement. As a result, the only visible discussion of abortion provider ambivalence took place within the antiabortion movement.

The first abortion provider who publicly articulated his reservations about the work he was doing was Bernard Nathanson. Nathanson had been an early and prominent member in the abortion reform movement.

In the 1960s, he participated in the establishment of NARAL and actively lobbied for the legalization of abortion. After New York legalized abortion, he established the Center for Reproductive and Sexual Health, the largest freestanding abortion clinic in New York City. In late 1972, he resigned as director from the center and began to reflect on his work of the past three years. Then, in 1974, Nathanson distanced himself from the pro-choice community in a very public manner. In an editorial in the *New England Journal of Medicine*, he explained that after his resignation from the center, he had supervised the establishment of a perinatology unit at St. Luke's Hospital Center. In the process, he had learned details about fetal development that led him to conclude that abortion really constituted murder. During his tenure as director of CRSH, he stated, "the Center had performed 60,000 abortions with no maternal deaths—an outstanding record of which we are proud. However," he now concluded, "I am deeply troubled by my own increasing certainty that I had in fact presided over 60,000 deaths."[52] The editorial ignited a firestorm, drawing media attention from across the country. It became a starting point for abortion providers who decided to rethink their position. And it laid the intellectual framework for those responding to such retractions.

Nathanson framed his "coming out" as resulting from a rational rather than an emotional process: he had begun to reconsider the morality of abortion after learning about the most recent findings in perinatology. In his editorial, he pointed to the existence of heart function in embryos as early as six weeks and brain activity at eight weeks. "Our capacity to measure signs of life is daily becoming more sophisticated," he marveled. "And as time goes by, we will doubtless be able to isolate life signs at earlier and earlier stages in fetal development."[53] While he did not yet question the legality of abortion in his 1974 reflections, Nathanson urged his readers to acknowledge the "infinitely agonizing truth" that abortion was the taking of life and hence an "irrepressibly serious matter."[54]

Who, then, has the moral agency to decide about abortion? Nathanson made it clear that women, themselves, were not suited to this task. If his editorial showed any emotion, it was a bristling contempt for women who advocated for a woman's right to abortion. The issue of abortion, he lamented, was distorted by "fierce militants of the Women's Liberation [Movement]" on the one side and "ferocious Right-to-Life legions" on the other. Neither, he claimed, had the capacity for reasoned thought. The medical profession itself could not shoulder the burden either, as doctors were "only the instrument in her [the woman's] decision."[55] Instead, Nathanson suggested the establishment of a body of specialists—such as a psychohistorian, a human ecologist, a medical philosopher, and an urbanologist-clergyman—to advise women on their abortion decisions. His suggestion harkened back to therapeutic abortion committees that, prior to legalization, had placed the decision over therapeutic abortion into the hands of a group of "experts" who served as gatekeepers to abortions performed in hospitals.[56] Such a committee structure had institutionalized conservative medical views about abortion and reasserted the (male) doctor's authority over the woman patient. Nathanson's discomfort with women's rights and the implicit loss of male authority probably contributed to his turn against abortion.[57]

In 1979, Nathanson wrote *Aborting America*. In this book, he laid out the basic argument for physicians seeking to create a narrative for themselves as they justified previous activity in abortion from which they were now distancing themselves. Noting his exhaustion by years of frenetic activism around abortion, Nathanson expressed a sense of being overrun by something larger than himself that had pulled him into abortion work. He complained about the "dogma" of NARAL and militant feminists. "Until 1973," he noted, "I was sold a bill of goods. No—let me be honest—I was selling a bill of goods."[58] His revelations were met with attention from across the country. Members of NARAL demanded his immediate expulsion from the organization, while writers for the antiabortion movement began to quote him and antiabortion activists courted him with speaking invitations. But in his 1974 editorial, Nathanson had still distanced himself from the antiabortion movement. "Their organs somehow neglected to report that I had endorsed 'abortion on demand' in the article," he reflected in *Aborting America*. "I turned down their innumerable speaking invitations. I did not want them to use me; I didn't even like them quoting me. I was left in a lonely no-man's land between the two factions."[59] It is difficult to feel sorry for Nathanson, who, in subsequent years, produced some of the most damaging and manipulative antiabortion materials. While he eloquently agonized over the moral dilemmas surrounding the fetus, he seemed impervious to the agony of women with unwanted pregnancies. Indeed, his bristling contempt for feminists not only indicates a generational gap but also harkens back to the male chauvinism of some medical professionals that surely contributed to his experience of a "lonely no-man's land."

In the mid-1970s, a new body of literature based on interviews and first-person accounts offered growing material about the disturbing nature of abortion. Written by authors who professed to favor abortion—frequently women who had had abortions themselves and interviewed other patients and health professionals afterward—the works were at best ambivalent about abortion, at worst hostile and distorting. An abortion clinic, suggested Magda Denes in her 1976 book *In Necessity and Sorrow: Life and Death in an Abortion Hospital*, was reminiscent of Dante's Inferno. Denes, a clinical psychologist, who described herself as a "pro-abortionist with a bad secular conscience," painted a picture of a clinic in which all occupants were deeply tormented by abortion and clinic space itself elicited physical revulsion from those who occupied it.[60] "From time to time, gripped by unmanageable and otherwise inexpressible revolt," she notes in the book, "someone vomits in the corridor on one of the yellow plastic chairs or in the middle of the vinyl covered floor."[61] The most positive abortion provider quoted by Denes revealed deep ambivalence toward abortions, while the vast majority of her subjects expressed sheer horror. Over the following decades—and in keeping with pre-*Roe* beliefs about abortionists and women seeking abortions—the first-person testimonials provided in this literature offered antiabortion activists with the "proof" that abortion providers and their patients were truly mentally disturbed.[62]

Nathanson's editorial also ignited a public discussion about the ways abortion providers felt about their work—and the exploitation of the words of providers who expressed ambivalence toward pregnancy termination procedures. Authors began to write about a new "abortion trauma" that could be found, as Norma Rosen noted in a 1977 *New York Times* article, "not where one expects it, in the psyche of the pregnant woman, but in the psyche of the doctor who performs this legal and much-desired operation."[63] Inspired by Nathanson's 1974 editorial, Rosen and others like her interviewed abortion providers about their feelings. What they found, they concluded, spelled trouble. Some abortion providers, Rosen noted, derived great gratification from their work. Others, however, expressed

> guilt and despair; the doctors admitted to heavy drinking and complained of nightmares which they ascribed to the nature of the work, the sheer monotony of it and the pressure of performing great numbers of abortions. One doctor had a fantasy in the midst of every abortion: He imagined that the fetus was resisting its own aborting, hanging onto the walls of the uterus with its tiny fingernails, fighting to stay inside. The doctor said he suffered the fantasy in silence, worked steadily from procedure to procedure, completed the operation and then went on to the next patient and the same fantasy.[64]

The fact that such a fantasy was clearly that—a fantasy (or nightmare) that was in fact impossible, because a fetus lacks consciousness of the abortion procedure and fingernails with which to hang from a uterine wall—did not diminish the image's emotional power. Indeed, it was so visual and gruesome in nature that it became a mainstay of the antiabortion literature.

Rosen, and those who followed in her footsteps, described abortion providers who were tortured by their work. At length, Rosen reported on the feelings of William Rashbaum, chief of family planning services at Beth Israel Medical Center and a faculty member of the Albert Einstein College of Medicine, who had shared his uncomfortable feelings about the clinging fetus with her. Rashbaum eloquently defended his continued work as an abortion provider by noting that he had seen too many troubled unwanted children and had spent years delivering not only wanted but also unwanted babies. Indeed, Rashbaum explained to Rosen that he felt his contribution to society was greater through abortion than when he was doing obstetrics. But his interview with Rosen became fodder for antiabortionists who painted him as a callous individual driven by greed. Over and over again, they quoted Rashbaum's comments on the troubling aspects of his work, but robbed his reasoning of its complexity by omitting crucial parts of his explanation. As a 1987 book on women who regretted their abortions quoted the story: How, Rosen had asked Rashbaum, had he managed while enduring this fantasy?

> [Rashbaum replied,] "Learned to live with it. Like people in concentration camps." [Rosen asked,] "Did he really mean that analogy?" [Rashbaum replied,] "I think its apt—destruction of life. Look! I'm a person. I'm entitled to my feelings. And my feelings are: Who gives me or anybody the right to terminate a pregnancy? I'm entitled to that feeling but I also have no right to communicate it to the patient who desperately wants that abortion. I don't get paid for my feelings. I get paid for my skills. . . . I'll be frank. I began to do abortions in large numbers at the time of my divorce when I needed money. But I also believe in the woman's right to control her biological destiny. I spent a lot of years learning to deliver babies. Sure, it sometimes hurts to end life instead of bringing it into the world."[65]

In this passage, Rashbaum had become greedy and callous, aware that abortion took life, yet willing to perform the procedure for the money. The humanitarian concerns that made him a committed abortion provider were absent from this narrative. In fact, this and subsequent authors used such passages to argue that abortion providers were deeply disturbed individuals. How else, these works noted, could physicians continue providing abortions while also understanding that they were taking life. Anti-abortion authors' contention that abortion providers were really monsters seemed further supported by the fact that, as Rosen reported, some abortion providers "[derived] great gratification from their work."

By the 1980s, Joseph Scheidler of the Pro-Life Action League began to collect narratives of abortion providers, abortion assistants, and clinic owners who had once worked in abortion clinics but had since concluded they could no longer do this work and were willing to speak publicly about their experiences. Antiabortion activists had always relied on the voices of physicians and nurses who could talk about abortion with professional authority. Under the auspices of the Pro-Life Action League, Scheidler invited former abortion providers, clinic owners, and clinic employees to several roundtables to discuss their experiences. "I got [an invitation] from Joe Scheidler of the Pro-Life Action League to come to Chicago and tell people why I didn't do abortions any more," Paul Levatino recalled. "I had no involvement with any kind of pro-life activity prior to that. I decided to take up the invitation more out of curiosity than anything else. . . . I had no idea that Mr. Scheidler was planning to market this, but anyway he put out a video tape that included myself and other physicians talking about their experiences."[66]

Unlike Nathanson, these physicians and former clinic employees described their conversion not as rational but as emotional and spiritual decisions. The testimonies of Scheidler's panelists shed some light on the emotional struggles that accompanied abortion providers' decisions about when to perform abortions—and when to stop. Providers described how they had learned to provide abortions, how they had ignored feelings of discomfort and integrated abortion procedures into their practices, and how they had finally come to the point where they were unable to continue their work. "I learned to do D&Es in Chicago, and boy did that make me feel uncomfortable," one presumably former abortion provider confessed in an interview in the late 1980s.[67] Most of the abortion providers on Scheidler's panels noted that they did not set out to learn how to provide abortions but did so as a result of their medical training in the early 1970s. David Brewter recalled the time during his medical training when he watched his first vacuum aspiration and was then asked to identify the contents of the suction container. "It was kind of neat, learning about a new experience," he remembered. His excitement abated as he recognized a number of fetal parts, a moment he recalled as physically painful: "It was like somebody put a hot poker into me," he explained. "I had a conscience and that hurt." Unsure how to respond,

I did what a lot of us do in our life. We don't do anything. I didn't talk with anybody about it. I didn't talk with my folks about it. I didn't think about it. I didn't look in the bible because I wasn't a Christian and so I did nothing. And you know what happened? I got to see another abortion. And you know what? That one hurt too. But I didn't do anything again and so I kept seeing abortions. And you know what? It hurt a little bit less every time I saw one. And you know what happened next? I got to sit down and do one. Because you see one, you do one, and you teach one. . . . Well, the first one I did was kind of hard. It was like hurting again like a hot poker. But after a while it got to where it didn't hurt. My heart got calloused.[68]

After their training, these physicians continued to provide abortions because they were employed in clinics or hospitals that routinely provided the service.

Some of the physicians and a number of the other health professionals described coming to their work as feminists, convinced that women should have the right to choose an abortion. "If you are pro-choice and you happen to be a gynecologist," Anthony Levatino explained to the anti-abortion audience, "then it's up to you to take the instruments in hand and actively perform an abortion. It's the most natural association in the world."[69] Several nurses and clinic administrators mentioned that they had joined abortion clinics while being active members of the National Organization for Women (NOW). "I thought that I had a wonderful opportunity as a nurse and as a firm believer in choice to be able to actually practice my political beliefs," former nurse Joan Appleton explained.[70] But most health professionals noted that they performed abortions without conviction. Brewter explained that he was "caught in the middle" when he became involved in abortion as a young resident, and McArthur Hill, who provided abortions as a young Air Force surgeon, offered the following disclaimer to his story: "As I make my presentation to you today it should be obvious to you that my participation in abortion was not as an avid abortion proponent, but as a reluctant puppet in a world gone berserk."[71]

Many of the panelists vaguely pointed to recurring nightmares and religious conversions to explain their decision to leave the field of abortion care. Some suffered from depression, which they attributed to their work. Others seemed simply burned out. Eventually, their feelings bothered them so much that they felt the need to stop providing abortions. At least one, Anthony Levatino, pointed to a traumatic personal experience—the death of his daughter—to explain his withdrawal from abortion provision.

Levatino had learned how to perform abortions while in medical school, had subsequently joined the practice of another ob-gyn who offered abortions in upstate New York, and had then begun to perform abortions himself. While he describes how he struggled with his work as he and his wife were trying to have children, his testimony also makes clear that he was committed to providing abortion services and understood the two issues to be separate from each other. Eventually, the couple adopted a daughter, ending Levatino's frustration. Things changed, however, when his daughter was hit by a car and died. "When you lose a child, your child, life is very different. Everything changes," Levatino explained. "My own self-esteem went down the tubes."[72] After several months he realized that he was no longer emotionally able to perform abortions and decided to quit. "I began to feel like a paid assassin. That's exactly what I was. It got to the point where it just wasn't worth it to me anymore. It was costing me too much personally. All the money in the world wouldn't have made a difference."[73]

While it is relatively easy to identify why physicians might decide to stop performing abortions, it is harder to understand why some felt the need to join the antiabortion movement. Clearly, the choice to move from abortion clinic to antiabortion movement was not the only option available. As in any other employer-employee relationship, workplace tensions and personal resentments played a role. Employees of abortion clinics complained about pay and dissatisfaction with their former work environment. Several former clinic workers had been fired and might have sought revenge. Some clinics had to rely on temp agencies to fill certain positions and were forced to hire staff who were emotionally unprepared for the work. Clinics that offered pregnancy terminations after twenty weeks' gestation, especially, needed fully trained staff. The two former temp workers on Scheidler's panels worked at such clinics. Others were drawn to work at abortion clinics because they sought the drama of an intense and highly emotional workplace. Disappointed by what they found, they looked to the antiabortion movement to fulfill their emotional needs.[74]

While joining the antiabortion movement was clearly not the only choice these former abortion providers and clinic employees had, it was a visible place to turn for those who felt they could no longer do this work. Abortion providers might discuss their doubts among themselves. But to participate in such discussions, those who worked at clinics had to be integrated enough in the abortion provider community to know where to locate others who might understand these doubts. Because only about 10 percent of abortion providers were members of NAF, most lacked a professional circle that might bring them in touch with fellow abortion providers.[75] A number of staff members were clearly burned out but lacked a framework to deal with their doubts and frustrations. And while providers did occasionally discuss the challenges of their work with one another, these discussions took place in a context in which providers sought to continue their work, not leave the field of abortion provision. For those providers and clinic staff whose doubts made them want to stop doing the work, there was no place for discussion. The "lonely no-man's land" that Nathanson had described in 1974 drove some directly into the arms of the antiabortion movement. When Joan Appleton, a NOW member who had identified as a feminist and was a nurse in a Washington, D.C., abortion clinic, experienced increasing doubts about her work, "she felt that she couldn't go to a feminist leader such as [the president of NOW] Molly Yard and say, 'Molly, you got a minute?'"[76] Appleton's work environment was particularly stressful, since she worked at a clinic beset with demonstrators. It is possible that the demonstrators also singled out and followed clinic staff members, including Appleton.[77] Feeling unable to discuss her doubts with friends or colleagues, Appleton befriended an antiabortion demonstrator who regularly stood in front her clinic. The two had many conversations over the course of several years, leading Appleton to eventually leave the clinic and join the antiabortion movement. For those who decided they could no longer work in an abortion clinic, the antiabortion movement offered a framework in which their feelings found validation—indeed, were praised.

Individuals who defected to the antiabortion movement harmed the pro-choice movement significantly. Once on the other side, these former abortion workers did not hesitate to embellish and distort their experiences at the clinics to discredit the work of abortion providers. The narratives of former abortion providers served to reinforce traditional antiabortion claims: that abortion providers were murdering children, that they were motivated solely by financial gain, that they did not care about the well-being of women and, indeed, were willing to jeopardize women's lives and health for the sake of profit, and that abortions were dangerous procedures. In their testimonials, former providers described themselves over and over again as murderers. Brewter, who had testified about his time as a medical resident and his subsequent work providing abortions as a military physician, concluded his testimony with the formulaic statement: "My heart was calloused against the fact that I was a murderer. I was just simply uncommitted."[78] Others also embellished their testimony with dramatic self-confessions. "I am a murderer," former air force physician McArthur Hill testified before the antiabortion audience. "I have taken the lives of innocent babies and I have ripped them from their mothers' wombs with a powerful vacuum instrument."[79]

Abortion, these former providers testified, not only killed babies but also hurt women. In an effort to discredit the abortion provider community, panelists boasted about the number of complications they had caused and bragged about the irregularities at their former places of employment. Carol Everett, who had testified in favor of clinic regulations before the Texas legislature, was among them. Her testimony essentially repeated the same allegations against abortion clinics that she had made at the legislative hearing. Everett and another panelist had worked at clinics that provided disreputable services and had themselves engaged in conduct that was unethical or illegal. Their testimony here was clearly self-serving. Abortion, these panelists concluded, harmed women. As Joan Appleton explained:

> I started out in the pro-choice movement believing that I was helping women, believing that women had a right to choose. They had a right to life. They had a right to go on. I thought when I was counseling women, I was helping them through a difficult situation so they could go on with their lives. . . . But I had to stop and say, "What's going on? Why isn't this happening? Instead, you're going out and getting pregnant again. You're getting diseases. How am I helping you?" Those are the questions that kept gnawing at me. . . . I didn't like what was going on. I didn't like what "Our Bodies, Ourselves" had turned into. I didn't like what we were doing for women. If it was right, why were they suffering? What had we done? We created a monster and didn't know what to do with it.[80]

I Saw Life Avulsed: Narrating Fetal Death

Antiabortion activists spent the late 1970s and 1980s creating increasingly gruesome abortion narratives. The narratives positioned the abortion procedure as a heinous process that caused agony for the woman and an agonizing death for the fetus. The narratives further positioned the fetus as a baby who was being killed and the pregnant woman as a murderer. Based on John Wilke and Mrs. J. C. Wilke's *Handbook on Abortion* and C. Everett Koop and Francis A. Schaeffer's *Whatever Happened to the Human Race?*, antiabortion activists produced a body of propaganda that was disseminated in pro-life newsletters and magazines and in educational materials distributed on picket lines and at pregnancy crisis centers. These materials proved crucial in the recruitment of antiabortion activists, many of whom joined the movement in the 1980s after viewing the images and movies produced in the 1970s. And they served as a rallying cry to a growing number of militant antiabortion protestors who hoped to garner publicity and to provoke public action that might further discredit abortion.[81]

The new generation of narratives described vacuum aspiration machines as monstrous, endangering the life of women and leading to the gruesome death of the fetus, here redefined as a baby. Descriptions frequently compared vacuum aspiration machines to vacuum cleaners—a household machine with which all readers were sure to be familiar. In antiabortion narratives, this machine-turned-monster took on an eerie quality. Twenty-nine times more powerful than a home vacuum cleaner, one 1978 article claimed, the suction machine "first sucks out the fluid in the bag of water surrounding the baby. The patient, enduring severe cramps, perspires heavily as the tube probes and licks her womb, inhaling the tiny boy or girl swimming there, tearing the perfectly formed body limb from limb and sucking the pieces into a jar at the other end of the tube. . . . The nurse covers the torn shreds of what moments earlier had been a living, feeling, eating, drinking baby."[82]

Vacuum aspiration machines in these accounts not only tore babies apart but also seriously hurt and sometimes even killed women. If the patient in the above narrative merely endured cramps, other narratives emphasized that women experienced unimaginable pain. In a 1987 visit to Birthchoice, a pro-life center, counselors seeking to discourage women from having abortions screened a movie about pregnancy termination intended to scare viewers. One visitor explained, "It was stressed that during any of the abortions, anesthesia was not given to either the mother-to-be or fetus, and that the fetus feels great pain, feels itself being ripped apart."[83] If the fetus could feel great pain, the insinuation was, the woman must feel great pain as well, and the movie visuals supported this contention. "The [operating] table [was] shaking visibly with the patient and her legs shaking to a severe extent, greatly exaggerated. It almost looked as though the camera was shaking itself."[84] Ultimately, vacuum aspiration machines might also malfunction and kill the patient. A visitor to another antiabortion counseling center described a slide show presented at the counseling session: "There was a slide of what they said was a dead woman lying under a sheet. All you could see was her hair. The voice said this woman went into the hospital thinking she was getting a safe and legal procedure, a suction abortion, but the suction machine was hooked up wrong; it blew the pressure into her body, causing her uterus to explode and for her to suffer cardiac arrest."[85]

In the imagination of antiabortion activists, the terror of pregnancy termination culminated in narratives that collapsed the different abortion methods into one improbable tale of horror that combined all the different elements of antiabortion stories. At the 1983 state convention of North Carolina Right to Life, for instance, Donna Turner, director of the North Carolina chapter of Women Exploited by Abortion (WEBA), an organization of women who regretted their abortions, told about her own abortion.[86] Turner wove a medically impossible tale that collapsed vacuum aspiration and saline instillation into one procedure and conjured up all of the worst elements of antiabortion narratives:

> The [vacuum aspiration] machine starts sucking, takes out some umbilical fluid, and then they turned the same machine, did something down there and started pushing some salt solution some Drano, like putting Drano on your children, into my uterus. . . . The baby kicked and thrashed inside of me quite a while. . . . I gave birth to him in the back seat of a car. . . . I got to hold him, he had chemical burns all over his body, his eyes were burned out of their sockets. By the expression on his face, he died a horrible, horrible death, and I did it.[87]

The machine gone mad, the equation of saline with Drano, the description of chemical burns over an infant's body, and the allegation that, ultimately, women were left unattended and uncared-for at the moment of delivery combined all the prominent narrative elements in antiabortion rhetoric.

To further highlight the gruesome nature of abortion and the humanity of the fetus, antiabortion activists created a line of fetal narratives that recounted the abortion experience from the perspective of the fetus. Even before the spread of ultrasound technology led to the proliferation of fetal imagery, narrators had breached the uterine wall to describe the abortion experience from the fetal perspective. This proved an effective technique for making visual the horrors of abortion techniques such as prostaglandin, which did not offer any gory images of severed limbs or blotchy skin. In a 1976 description of a prostaglandin abortion, for instance, the narrating physician took on the perspective of the fetus to describe its struggle against the needle injecting the prostaglandin into the uterus. Starting out from his perspective as a physician, he explained,

> I see something other than what I expected here. I see a movement — a small one. . . . And now I see that it is the hub of the needle in the woman's belly that has jerked. First to one side. Then to the other side. Once more it wobbles, is tugged, like a fishing line nibbled by a sun-

fish. Again! And I know! It is the fetus that worries thus. It is the fetus struggling against the needle. Struggling? How can that be? I think: that cannot be. I think: the fetus feels no pain, cannot feel fear, has no motivation. It is merely reflex. I point to the needle. . . . A reflex, the doctor says. I hear him. But I saw something . . . in that mass of cells understand that it must bob and butt. And I see it again! . . . I close my eyes. I see the inside of the uterus. It is bathed in ruby gloom. I see the creature curled upon itself. Its knees are flexed. Its head is bent upon its chest. It is in fluid and gently rocks to the rhythm of the distant heart-beat. It resembles—a sleeping infant. . . . It is sudden. A point coming. A needle! A spike of daylight pierces the chamber. Now the light is extinguished. The needle comes closer in the pool. The point grazes the thigh, *and I stir. Perhaps I wake from dozing. The light is there again. I twist and straighten. My arms and legs push. My hand finds the shaft— grabs! I grab. I bend the needle this way and that. The point probes, touches my belly. My mouth opens. Could I cry out? All is a commotion and a churning. There is a presence in the pool. An activity! The pool colors, reddens, darkens.* I open my eyes to see the doctor feeding a small plastic tube through the barrel of the needle into the uterus. . . . A nurse hands the physician a syringe loaded with a colorless liquid. He attaches it to the end of the tubing and injects it. Prostaglandin, he says. Ah, well, prostaglandin—a substance found normally in the body. When given in concentrated dosage, it throws the uterus into vigorous contraction. In eight to twelve hours, the woman will expel the fetus. . . . There is the flick of that needle. I saw it. I saw . . . I felt—in that room, a pace away, life prodded, life fending off. I saw life avulsed—swept by flood, blackening—then out.[88]

In this account, the physician's critical medical commentary alternated with an account of fetal experience that bestowed consciousness of the event on the fetus's mind. The fetus, the account insinuated, understood the full danger of the needle appearing in the uterus and fought against it with all its might—including trying to grab the shaft of the needle and bend it away.

In the following years, fetal narratives proliferated in antiabortion literature. Most commonly, these stories were told by the women who had had the abortion and could presumably speak with authority to the fetal experience. Nancyjo Mann, for instance, the founder of WEBA, told of her fetus's response to a saline procedure. Drawing from descriptions in antiabortion materials which provided gruesome portrayals of saline abortions, Mann projected these depictions onto her fetus.[89] After the abortion provider had injected the saline solution, "my baby began thrashing about—it was like a regular boxing match in there. She was in pain. The saline was burning her skin, her eyes, her throat. It was choking her, making her sick. She was in agony, trying to escape. She was scared and confused at how her wonderful little home had suddenly been turned into a death trap."[90] Narratives such as these offered the opportunity to combine a story of trust with one of betrayal, disbelief, and destruction.

Antiabortion activists in the mid-1970s were unable to provide a visual view of abortion from the fetal perspective; they had to rely on fictionalized accounts. This situation changed drastically in the 1980s with the rise of sonography. The use of ultrasound in medicine traces back to the 1930s, when clinical researchers in several countries began to experiment with it. The Austrian Friedrich Dussik began using ultrasound to diagnose neurological conditions, and a Scot, Ian Donald, mobilized it as an obstetrical tool, thus expanding the diagnostic scope of the technology. By 1970, despite ongoing disagreements about the meaning and interpretation of ultrasound images, sonography had become integrated into reproductive medicine. Physicians used ultrasound images to detect anomalies in fetal growth, expose birth defects, establish how many fetuses there were, determine gender, and otherwise ascertain "normality" in pregnancy. In addition, medical professionals assumed that ultrasound increased bonding between patient and fetus and provided reassurance to the patient that her pregnancy was normal. The cost of ultrasound machines and staff able to properly read the images, however, delayed the use of ultrasound in abortion clinics until the 1980s, when the percentage of pregnancies scanned by ultrasound more than doubled, from 35.5 percent in 1980 to 78.8 percent in 1987.[91]

While sonography was developed as a medical diagnostic technology, ultrasound images of the fetus also acquired broader cultural meaning. The very sight of the ultrasound image was expected to work an emotional transformation upon the viewer. Indeed, the idea that knowledge of fetal life and the confrontation with the visual image would convert a woman to a pro-life position has been a central theme in right-to-life activism from the very beginning.[92] Fetal images had already surfaced in the early 1970s Wilkes brochure, "Life or Death," which featured a greatly enlarged photograph of a fourteen-week-old fetus.[93] In the 1980s, antiabortion activists turned to the increasingly sophisticated ultrasound imaging and familiar pictures to provide the public with a view of abortion from the perspective of the fetus. By the late 1980s, the diffusion of these images to the larger

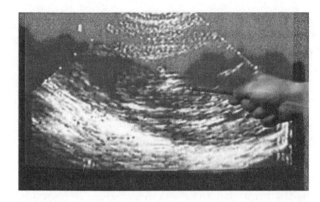

Ill. 4.1. This image illustrates Bernard Nathanson's description of the silent scream. From *The Silent Scream* (1984).

public contributed to the increasing violence of the antiabortion movement. Indeed, many activists reported that the pictures further radicalized them.[94]

The 1984 movie *The Silent Scream* offered viewers a supposedly real-time ultrasound image of a first trimester abortion. Former abortion provider, now antiabortion narrator Bernard Nathanson explained to viewers watching the ultrasound of the vacuum aspiration procedure that the suction tip "has now been firmly clamped to the child's body . . . and the body is now being torn systematically from the head."[95] The ultrasound images culminated in a freeze-frame of the fetus with its mouth wide open (see ill. 4.1). This, Nathanson commented, "is the silent scream of a child threatened imminently with extinction."[96] While the images were so grainy as to make them impossible to identify by the untrained eye, Nathanson's authoritative narrative seemed to leave no doubt about their meaning. Ironically, the power of the images lay less in what viewers actually saw and more in what Nathanson told them they saw—and what they had heard and read since the early 1970s. Distributed to all members of Congress in early 1985 and screened by President Ronald Reagan to a select audience in the White House, *The Silent Scream* raised a storm of controversy. Pro-choice advocates criticized the movie as medically inaccurate, exaggerated, and misleading.[97] However, during the mid-1980s, *The Silent Scream* became the antiabortion movement's most successful piece of propaganda.[98] Its use as a recruiting tool and its ability to incite increasingly violent protests is well summed up in Paul Hill's statement at his sentencing for the 1994 murder of Dr. John Britton and Britton's bodyguard, John Barrett, outside a Florida abortion clinic that in order to understand his motivations, the judge need only watch an ultrasound of an abortion being performed.[99]

Aborted Women of an Unwanted Society: Patient Narratives

Completing the arc of antiabortion narratives were the stories of women who had had abortions and told about their experiences. Already in the late 1970s, journalists probed into the psyche of women who had had abortions. Linda Bird Francke's 1978 book, *The Ambivalence of Abortion*, based on interviews with abortion patients, their partners, and family members, did for this cohort what Magda Denes had done for abortion providers.[100] While Francke's subjects did not express the same sense of revulsion and horror as Denes's interview partners, the vast majority seemed to be poorly functioning adults, giving the impression that women who chose abortion were irresponsible and self-destructive.

The discussion of women's experience took on a more systematic approach in the early 1980s, when Nancyjo Mann, a singer in the Christian hard rock band Barnabas, founded the organization WEBA to give voice to women who regretted their abortions. Mann had had an abortion in 1974, at the age of 21, when she was pregnant with her third child and her second husband had just walked out on her. While she had wanted to keep the pregnancy, Mann had followed the advice of her mother, who, worried about her daughter's ability to support herself and her two children with no more than a high school degree, urged her to end her third pregnancy. Mann, at that point 5½ months pregnant, describes herself as traumatized by her abortion. Concluding that she had murdered her child, her life spiraled downward. She began to deal drugs and burglarize houses and turned to prostitution. Only after finding God, Mann maintained, was she able to regain control of her life. "We are the victims, the aborted women of an unwanted [*sic*] society," she concluded.[101] WEBA was made up solely of women who, like Mann, had had abortions and regretted them. The organization provided its members with a group of like-minded women to whom they could express their regret. Members were encouraged to speak publicly about their experiences and find reconciliation and healing through their engagement in the antiabortion movement.

In the mid-1980s, psychologist David C. Reardon conducted a survey of 252 WEBA members and published his research results. In his 1987 book *Aborted Women: Silent No More*, Reardon constructed a story of women's abortion experiences that simultaneously presented the women as passive victims of abortion—and hence not responsible for their own actions—while also asserting that abortion was the killing of children and that these women were murderers. Because they were victims of abortion, WEBA members were not responsible for their abortions, nor for any criminal activity or child neglect they committed as a result of their postabortion trauma. Being a passive victim represented the one acceptable role they could play in relation to abortion and its aftermath. Indeed, to emphasize their passivity, Reardon referred to WEBA members as "the aborted." This stood in sharp contrast to his characterization of women who did not regret their abortions as "aborters," emphasizing their active participation in the process.[102]

WEBA members, in cooperation with Reardon, constructed a story line for women who had had abortions that defined how women were to think about and experience the event if they were seeking acceptance from the antiabortion movement. Passive participants in their own abortions, WEBA members described themselves as devastated by the event. Reardon offered extensive quotes from WEBA members, and the stylistic similarities between the narratives are striking. It is difficult to ascertain how Reardon's questions influenced the stories WEBA members told him. While Reardon might have elicited certain story lines by the questions he asked, WEBA members also learned how to tell their abortion stories by listening to others around them. In this conversation, the acceptable story line for women who discussed their abortion experiences for an antiabortion audience was narrow — and the abortion experience was always negative.

Most WEBA members alleged that they had been pressured to have an abortion. Many were already opposed to abortion prior to their experience. Sixty-four percent of WEBA members, Reardon noted, described themselves as "forced" into abortion because of their particular circumstances at the time. While 51 percent pointed to pressure from boyfriends or husbands, 35 percent blamed the abortion counselor. Others described themselves as lacking any clear conviction or knowledge about abortion. Seventy-three percent did not feel in control of their own lives when making their abortion decisions. Instead, they felt rushed into their decisions — most had had the abortion within four days of discovering that they were pregnant.[103]

Once at the abortion clinic, women contended that they had naively trusted the assurances of abortion counselors and doctors — that abortion was safe, quick, and simple — only to find, as the antiabortion literature suggested, that they endured excruciating pain. Typical was the narrative of one woman who noted that her physician told her she would only feel a "little pinch." "But it hurt an awful lot!" she noted. "It felt like they were pulling my insides out. I don't think I've ever felt that much pain."[104] Women described the actual abortion procedure as horrendous and noted in particular their confrontation with the fetus. This confrontation—a crucial moment in the narratives—represented the moment WEBA members suddenly concluded that the procedure was killing their child. "I saw the bits and pieces of my little child floating in a pool of blood," one WEBA member recounted her abortion of a twelve-week fetus. "I screamed and jumped up off the table. They took me into another room and I started vomiting."[105] In overwrought language, Nancyjo Mann described the process following her saline injection:

> When that needle entered my womb, when it pulled out the nurturing fluid of motherhood and replaced it with that venom of death, when the child I had abandoned suddenly began its struggle within me, I hated myself. It was that fast. Every bit of self-esteem, every value I held dear, every hope of which I had ever dreamed—all were stripped away by the poison of that one vain act. Every memory of joy was now tainted by the stench of death. That moment of desperation which had led me to this "healer's table" had now positioned itself as ruler of my life. I had abandoned myself to despair and despair was my future. There was no way to stop it. There was no way to put everything back the way it had been. I no longer had any control, any choice. I was powerless. I was weak. I was a murderer.[106]

Abortion providers, the women agreed, had failed to offer them enough information to make an informed choice. Indeed, women's striking naïveté about pregnancy and abortion was central to their ability to claim the status of victim. Although Mann had already had two children and was thus familiar with pregnancy, she noted that only after the saline injection to end her 5½-month pregnancy did she "learn that what he [the abortion provider] described as 'cramps' was actually the labor process. These 'severe cramps' were not just going to make my pregnancy magically disappear. Instead, I was going to go through all the motions of normal childbirth—water breaking, labor pains, etc. The only difference was that the baby I would deliver would be dead."[107] Another complained after her first trimester suction abortion:

> I feel that women are being deceived when they go in to have an abortion because they aren't being shown pictures of what their child looks like. Women are being deceived before they get to that place in that they're being sheltered from this truth. Women are being deceived about the procedure they will undergo. I wasn't told that it would be a blind procedure, that the physician cannot see inside my uterus. . . .

Women aren't being allowed to make a truly informed decision about their abortion.[108]

Had they known, these stories implied, these women would not have had abortions.

WEBA members emerged from the experience feeling deceived, filled with guilt, and suffering physically and psychologically for years to come. Many described physical complications, ranging from postoperative hemorrhage to infection. Following the abortion, they had experienced hysterectomy, sterility, cervical cancer, miscarriages, and cervical incompetence. Half of them also suffered from psychological complications that they attributed to their abortions. Unable to deal with their guilt feelings, their lives spiraled down into bouts of drinking, drug abuse, sexual promiscuity, sexual coldness, and child abuse and neglect, until they had finally been able to find forgiveness and redemption through religion and their activism in organizations such as WEBA.[109] Lest the reader think that WEBA members' reactions were unusually negative, Reardon assured his audience that "WEBA members represent a matured, reflective point of view of their abortion experiences."[110] By his very definition, women who had no negative feelings about their abortions had not yet finished the process of postabortion response and reached the natural state of regret. "Abortion," Reardon claimed, "is *typically* followed by a long period of denial and unrecognized reactions."[111] Eventually, he assured his readers, a negative response was virtually unavoidable.

In creating women's narratives of their abortion experience, antiabortion activists skillfully co-opted strategies of second-wave feminists. Harkening back to the feminist tradition of women speaking out about their abortion experiences before legalization, antiabortion activists again encouraged women to speak out—this time about their experiences with legal abortion. And like women's health activists who had demanded that physicians provide them with all information about their medical care, antiabortion activists suggested that a lack of information was at the root of women's abortion experiences. If they only had had sufficient information, they would have understood the dangers of abortion and chosen differently. This time, however, the strategies were not deployed in the name of increasing women's choices but in an attempt to discourage women from choosing abortion. Over the coming decades, antiabortion organizations systematically solicited testimony about women's negative abortion experiences, including testimony from the two plaintiffs in *Roe v. Wade* and *Doe v. Bolton* who now claimed to regret their abortions. By the 1990s, conservative lawyers began to harness these testimonies, hoping to reopen and overturn *Roe v. Wade* and *Doe v. Bolton* and to pass legislation that would restrict women's access to abortion so as to protect women from making the "wrong" choices.[112]

The women described in Reardon's book are striking in their inability to take responsibility and choose for themselves. Indeed, *Aborted Women* paints portraits of women who are either so needy and dependent as to be paralyzed in their decision making or who, having chosen to have an abortion against the counsel of husbands or parents, were ready to blame others, usually the abortion provider or counselor, for their making the wrong choice. What the portraits have in common is the suggestion that women were, indeed, unable to make the abortion decision. "Most of all the stories of aborting women are stories of isolation and despair," Reardon noted. "What they are saying is that they did not really need a 'solution' to avoid their problems; rather they wanted love and support to face their problems."[113] Indeed, Reardon warned that the expediency of abortion encouraged women to be weak, dependent, and incapable of dealing with unexpected challenges.[114] Mann complained ambiguously that WEBA women were the "aborted women of an unwanted society." Reardon argued that society victimized women by offering abortion, rather than love and support to help them raise their children.

IN JANUARY 1985, the TV news program *20/20* opened with a report on the abortion conflict in Fargo, North Dakota. The small town in the Midwest was quickly becoming a center of the abortion controversy. "You will see how one town is being torn in two," anchor Hugh Downs announced to the camera. Journalist Geraldo Rivera, who narrated the Fargo segment, opened with images from the January 1985 pro-life march and President Ronald Reagan's welcome and endorsement of pro-life protestors in Washington, D.C. Images of the marchers were followed by pictures of bombed abortion clinics and a shot of Bernard Nathanson describing the ultrasound images in *The Silent Scream*. The camera finally settled on a group of antiabortion activists gathered on a wintery day in front of the Fargo abortion clinic. Here, the program suggested, the country was witnessing the convergence of antiabortion activists who, spurred into action by illustrations of abortion as an act of violence, protested in new and disruptive ways.

In the course of the 1980s, antiabortion activists sharpened their depiction of abortion as the murder of a child in both narrative and visual form. They tapped into a store of narratives stretching back to the pre-*Roe* era that depicted abortion providers as greedy and unscrupulous murderers and women choosing abortion as irresponsible and mentally deranged. As former abortion providers and clinic staff members confessed to the brutal dismemberment of fetal bodies and women regretting their abortion recalled their painful confrontation with the dying or dead fetus, fetal images became a mainstay on picket lines and at marches. Protestors regularly brought fetuses to antiabortion protests to confront women with the fetal bodies.

As antiabortion narratives of pregnancy terminations depicted abortion procedures in increasingly violent terms, protestors escalated their aggressive strategies to intimidate patients and clinic staff. While picket lines in front of abortion clinics had been relatively small in the 1970s, during the following decade they gradually grew, reaching into the hundreds after the rise of a new antiabortion group focused on direct action tactics: Operation Rescue (OR), founded by Randall Terry in 1986. Unlike their largely peaceful predecessors, demonstrators of the 1980s, armed with posters, plastic fetuses, and specimens in jars, aggressively approached clinic staff and patients, frequently screaming at patients and family members. They fetishized the fetus and systematically escalated antiabortion tactics.[115]

The opening shots of the Fargo *20/20* segment summarized the state of antiabortion protest in the mid-1980s. Clinics were regularly beset with protestors who engaged in so-called sidewalk counseling, harassed patients, and disrupted clinic operations by blocking clinic entrances or invading clinics. Fetal images featured prominently in this fight. Antiabortion activists hoped that *The Silent Scream* would persuade everyone of the violence of an abortion. Such imagery, President Ronald Reagan noted, should lead the American nation to the realization that *Roe v. Wade* needed to be overturned. "It is said that if every member of the Congress could see this film of an early abortion," Reagan was heard commenting in the *20/20* segment as images of protestors at the 1985 pro-life march carrying a makeshift casket rolled across the nation's TV screens, "that Congress would move quickly to end the tragedy of abortion. And I pray that they will."[116] Even if most congressional members and the American public disagreed with President Reagan's assessment, for some antiabortion activists these images and fetal bodies that appeared on picket lines provided incontrovertible evidence of the violence of abortion.

The political implications that the antiabortion narratives of the 1980s held for pregnancy termination procedures, particularly D&E, were not lost on abortion providers. As protestors stood outside the Crist Clinic for

Women in Jacksonville, North Carolina, charging that abortion providers dropped live babies into meat grinders to make them into tissue cultures, Takey Crist worried about the impact that a new variation of D&E might have on abortion providers' ability to do their work. "I think this is the kind of surgery that will bring more and more attention to us and create greater problems in setting the movement backwards," he wrote to Philip Stubblefield. "I am scared that physicians attempting this with no experience would create a lot of problems for all of us. It needs to be put on the back burner for when the fundamentalistic Ronald [Reagan], [Jessie] Helms, and [Jerry] Falwell endeavors are over."[117]

In the face of the politicization of medical procedures, abortion providers looked for help to alliances that emphasized the professional nature of abortion care. The adoption of laminaria, the development of D&E, and the eventual switch from saline to D&E as the preferred second trimester abortion procedure took place within a scientific process that followed the best process for the development and evaluation of medical techniques and treatment methods. Hern's and Hanson's collection of data, their presentation of their research findings at professional meetings, their publication of articles evaluating the use of laminaria in medical journals, and their training of colleagues in the use of laminaria and D&E procedure was part of a larger scientific process that spoke to the professional nature of abortion care.

In the end, decisions whether or not to perform D&Es remained an individual doctor's choice. Physicians' level of discomfort with the procedure and their own sense of ethics determined whether they were willing to perform D&Es, how late they were willing to perform the procedure, and which indications they felt justified an abortion at an advanced gestational age. Some chose not to offer abortions beyond twenty weeks' gestation—a point at which it was impossible to sustain fetal life. Others performed abortions after twenty weeks' gestation when the fetus had serious defects, such as Down syndrome and spina bifida, but would not perform terminations for "frivolous reasons."[118]

Those willing to perform D&Es emphasized the interests of their women patients. "I do D and Es because I think it is safer," one gynecologist explained. "It is a horrible procedure. Staff burnout is a major problem. But are you functioning in the interests of taking care of your staff or taking care of your patients?"[119] Another stressed that parents should be able to decide the conditions of parenthood. "The idea that we have to salvage every individual no matter how impaired is really crazy," he argued. "Some people feel that taking care of an impaired child is ennobling and that's fine for them. But it's not for everybody. It's oppressive to say that everyone has to do this."[120]

While the risk management seminars, organized by NAF, contributed significantly to the acceptance and safe performance of D&E procedures, NAF was unable to influence the political impact of the redefinition of "fetus" into "baby." Indeed, as we will see in Chapter 6, Crist's worry proved prophetic. When Cincinnati abortion provider Martin Haskell presented a new variation on D&E, the intact D&E, at a 1992 NAF risk seminar, anti-abortion activists were prepared. They redefined the procedure as a partial birth abortion and began a concerted campaign to have it outlawed. Politics, again, would define what happened in the surgery room.

To Protect the Lives of American Babies

The Escalation of Antiabortion Activism

In February 1988, four antiabortion activists stole onto the premises of Vital Med, a Chicago pathology lab. It was after business hours, and the place was dark and deserted. The four snuck through the garage door and approached a loading dock in the back. On the dock, stacked in boxes, on shelves, and in trash barrels, were hundreds of sealed plastic bags and specimen jars with fetal remains waiting to be picked up for incineration. Some had stickers bearing the name of the abortion clinic, the abortion provider who had performed the pregnancy termination, the name of the woman who had undergone the abortion, and the gestational age of the fetus. Fort Wayne Women's Health Organization, one of them read (see ill. 5.1). The activists grabbed several of the boxes, loaded them into their car, and within five minutes they were gone. Over the next nine months, they returned every two to three weeks to take more fetuses, and by November of that year they had stolen between 4,500 and 5,000 fetal remains.[1]

Back at her apartment, Monica Migliorino, one of the activists, carried a box of remains into a small side room, opened it and slowly took out one plastic bag after another. Inside each bag was a fetal body submerged in formalin solution to prevent disintegration (see ill. 5.2). Over the following weeks and months, the group of activists selected specimens that were most recognizable as fetuses, removed them from their containers, and laid them out. They reassembled the fetal parts and photographed the specimen with close-up lenses. Sometimes the images included tags with the place of origin, fetal sex, and gestational age. At other times, activists named the fetuses and included little nametags (see ill. 5.3).[2] At the same time,

Ill. 5.1. Fort Wayne Women's Health Organization mailing label. Courtesy of Citizens for a Pro-Life Society, www.prolifesociety.com.

they continued their regular trips to Vital Med's loading dock, bringing home more and more boxes of fetal remains. By the summer, around 500 fetuses were cluttered on the shelves and floor of Migliorino's spare bedroom. When she ran out of space in her apartment, she began to take the fetal remains to the house of a friend in Milwaukee.

Intent on returning the fetuses to their place of origin, the activists began to send the bodies to other antiabortion activists across the country. Migliorino and her future husband, Edmund Miller, drove 729 specimens to Tallahassee, Florida. Twelve hundred bodies went to Milwaukee; 150 bodies were flown to Fargo, North Dakota; 200 went to Indiana; and 157 went to Chapel Hill, North Carolina. Antiabortion activists in Philadelphia requested some bodies and received 200; another 100 went to New Jersey. The remaining bodies, about 2,000, stayed in Chicago.[3] Like Migliorino, other activists were scrambling for storage space as well. Joseph Scheidler kept his fetuses in his doghouse. Lucy O'Keefe, an antiabortion activist in Chapel Hill, North Carolina, stored her fetuses in her kitchen cabinets.[4]

By March, when some of the fetuses started to rot, Migliorino and the group of antiabortion activists began to organize burials for the bodies. On March 25, 1988, activists held the first of about twelve funerals—this one in Milwaukee. They took the plastic bags to a funeral home, where Migliorino, with the help of several others, packed them into children's coffins donated by the Milwaukee Casket Company. Packed tightly, the coffins could hold several hundred specimens (see ill. 5.4). Migliorino carefully

Ill. 5.2. Whirl paks with fetal remains. Courtesy of Citizens for a
Pro-Life Society, www.prolifesociety.com.

chose four fetuses to place in an open casket for the wake service. One
of the fetuses was of about six months' gestational age; the other three
were first trimester bodies in relatively good condition. The funeral director placed all the coffins into three hearses, and following the service, the
bodies were buried at Holy Cross Catholic Cemetery.[5]

Activists conducted these rituals to construct a story about abortion
that depicted the procedure in stark contrast to medical understanding:
abortion, they argued, was not a medical procedure but an atrocity comparable to the Holocaust, and the fetal remains were not medical waste but
the victims of this atrocity. The rituals with which antiabortion activists
surrounded the remains were intended to create an origin story that confirmed that the fetal remains were indeed babies. Activists claimed that
the arrangement of the fetal remains on the loading dock indicated that it
was their responsibility to retrieve the bodies. In the beginning, according
to Migliorino, "dozens and dozens of boxes of fetal children were strewn
haphazardly about."[6] As the weeks went by, however, the placement of
the boxes became systematic, neat even, giving the bodies, she believed,
a purpose. "There was more of a deliberate intelligence . . . of how the fetal bodies were being placed on the loading dock," Migliorino explained.
"Somebody wanted us to retrieve them. Somebody wanted us to give dignity to the babies."[7]

Ill. 5.3. Reassembled fetal parts. Courtesy of Citizens for a Pro-Life Society, www.prolifesociety.com.

The rituals that the activists performed with the fetal remains identified them as bodies of babies who were victims of an atrocity. By removing the fetal parts from the plastic bags, putting them back together, naming them, and then taking photographs, activists both conveyed individual identity on the bodies and linked them to Holocaust victims. As the images of Holocaust victims are intended to show the atrocity of the Nazi regime, photographs of fetal bodies were intended to "show society the atrocity of abortion."[8] Returning the fetal remains to the cities from which they had come was intended to erase the abstraction of abortion and prepared the bodies for the last ritual: the public burial.

It was the public burial that lent fetal bodies their ultimate meaning, not only confirming their identity as babies but also establishing the originally private bodies as public entities. Activists simultaneously claimed their right to bury the bodies and to do so publicly by arguing that the fetal remains were babies "killed under the law."[9] "These are the actual victims killed under *Roe v. Wade*," Migliorino argued. "To treat them as if

Ill. 5.4. Coffin with whirl paks. Courtesy of Citizens for a
Pro-Life Society, www.prolifesociety.com.

they had no public significance . . . I felt was deeply contrary to the dignity and meaning of those babies' deaths."[10] And since they were "babies,"
she continued, they had "a right to be buried as human beings."[11] Over the
summer and fall, activists staged the burials as large public events. They
announced the events by sending out press releases and spoke to reporters who covered the services. At several services, they displayed carefully
selected bodies for public view. Commenting on the selection of fetuses
for the open casket in Milwaukee, Migliorino explained: "We laid out—
like lying in state—the six month old aborted baby and the three first trimesters to show that there was essentially no difference in humanity between the early fetal children and the six months aborted baby."[12]

The public might have reacted to the theft of fetal remains, their storage in bedrooms and doghouses, their photography and transportation
around the country with distaste and revulsion, but such rituals so con-
vincingly transformed remains into dead babies that those who questioned
the public memorial services could now be depicted as amoral. Joseph
Scheidler responded to critical questions about the origin of the bodies:
"If our society has reached the point that it's more interested in how we
got the bodies than how the babies got there, then we are sick, real sick."[13]

His response indicated the transformative power of the ritual: they had retrieved bodies but were burying babies. Local newspapers were eager to cover the events. "Mass for 157 Fetuses Draws 350 Mourners," announced the *Raleigh News and Observer* on August 24, and the *Milwaukee Journal* followed less than three weeks later with "500 Give Fetuses an Emotional Burial."[14] Reporters described the ceremonies in detail and gave voice to activists' justifications of their actions. "These are human beings," Migliorino was quoted as saying. "They never should have been killed in the first place; they never should have been thrown in the trash in the second place; and now that they're dead, they deserve to be buried."[15]

The redefinition of fetal remains as dead babies was the result of a process that spanned a period from the late 1970s into the 1980s. The politicized nature of fetal bodies and the manipulation of narratives of the abortion experience that turned medical procedures into murder contributed significantly to the stigmatization of abortion. The escalation of antiabortion protests in the 1980s had a devastating impact on abortion providers and patients and influenced the experience of providing and receiving abortion care for decades to come. The number of physicians willing to provide abortion declined significantly through the 1980s. From a high in 1982, when the country counted 2,908 abortion providers, the number fell to 2,582 in 1988 and to 2,434 by 1991—a 16 percent decline in less than a decade.[16]

In the face of growing antiabortion violence, abortion providers educated one another about ways to respond. Equally important, they educated local law enforcement and complained to their legislative representatives if local law enforcement was unresponsive or the response was insufficient. As abortion providers appealed to sympathetic lawmakers, legislators opened hearings on the nature and extend of antiabortion violence, creating a public forum to educate legislators and the general public. At these hearings, abortion providers, clinic staff, and occasionally patients voiced their concerns about the real life implications of the escalating antiabortion protests and lobbied for new police and legal protections. Whether or not abortion clinics were able to successfully defend themselves against antiabortion protests and attacks depended largely on the willingness of local law enforcement and prosecutors to come to their aid. But even in locations where the community proved supportive and defended accessible abortion care, the costs to clinics and patients were tremendous.

Fort Wayne, Indiana, and the Anatomy
of Antiabortion Demonstrations

Protests against abortion clinics date back to the early years of legal abortion and accompanied the opening of the first abortion clinics. Indeed, in some locations, antiabortion activists fought abortion clinics from the moment a clinic owner sought the initial permits to open a clinic. Once clinics opened, protestors took advantage of the growing body of visual and narrative materials depicting abortion in increasingly gruesome ways and used the materials to "educate" abortion patients about what they saw as the realities of abortion. The power of the grisly descriptions relied on viewers identifying the fetus as a baby. Antiabortion activists distorted the developmental level of the fetus by referring to it as a "baby" or "unborn child." Nathanson, for instance, described the procedure depicted in *The Silent Scream* as "the abortion of a 12-week-old unborn child," erasing the nine months of development between a twelve-week fetus and a twelve-week-old baby to suggest that vacuum aspiration was killing a three-month-old infant. Over the course of the 1980s, the belief that abortion was really the killing of a child motivated protestors to adopt increasingly aggressive tactics.

While in the 1970s most clinics experienced only the occasional group of picketers, some like the NJWHO and the Delaware Women's Health Organization were inundated with protestors before they even opened. And when Susan Hill received the first requests from local feminists to open a clinic in Fort Wayne, Indiana, in 1977, massive opposition emerged almost immediately, delaying the opening of the Fort Wayne Clinic by more than six months. Hill had purchased an old house on 827 Webster Street, a downtown building one block north of the public library, across the street from a church and right next to a little park. In order to start renovations, Hill needed a zoning variance. But city officials quickly indicated that they would not cooperate. As news of the planned clinic reached city hall, Fort Wayne's mayor announced at a news conference that "women in Fort Wayne do not need abortions. This clinic will never open."[17] Over the following months, Hill and Barbara Fishel, Hill's regional director at the NWHO, immersed themselves in the jungle of regulations and permits required to renovate and open the clinic. Antiabortion forces summoned local Catholic congregations, nuns, and priests. At a hearing of the zoning board in Fort Wayne, usually a sparsely attended event, hundreds gathered to protest the zoning request for the abortion clinic. Hill had brought her New York attorney, Roy Lucas, to the hearing. They were met by an audience of 500, packed into rows of folding chairs, all watched over by guards who were as surprised as they were intimidated by the crowds. When the board got to the FWWHO application, the audience began to protest. The clinic was going to kill babies, people screamed. Once the zoning permit was in place, city officials dragged their feet about issuing a building permit. When construction finally began, protestors tried to stop the renovations by harassing the construction workers. When the building was finally ready for inspection, the city sent unsympathetic building inspectors who refused to give a green light for the clinic to open. The Fort Wayne clinic finally opened its doors in June 1978.[18]

From the very beginning, the sidewalk in front of the Webster Street clinic was beset with demonstrators. Patients were met by protestors who pointed to gory photographs of aborted fetuses reprinted in the classic antiabortion *Handbook on Abortion*. "Do you know that they are killing babies in there?" protestors asked patients. "Are you going to kill your baby?" Picketers handed patients antiabortion literature and, if patients did not stop, grabbed their arm or elbow to get their attention. "Do you know that Hitler started out this way?" they challenged. The harassment continued when patients left the clinic. "No wonder you are shaky," one protestor told a patient who, after her visit to the clinic, was standing on somewhat unsteady legs at the curb waiting for a cab. "You just killed a baby."[19] Although the clinic quickly accepted the offer of a local feminist group to escort patients into the facility, the harassment continued. With escorts now posted in front of the clinic, protestors approached patients a block away. This gave protestors an entire block to walk alongside patients, urging them to take antiabortion literature and talking to them about killing their babies.

Within months, protestors lured patients away from the clinic and visited abortion patients at home, feigning concern about the patient's mental health following the abortion. In September 1978, protestors Phyllis Avila and Phyllis Morken intercepted two teenage sisters on their way to FWWHO. Suspecting that her younger sister was pregnant, the older one was accompanying her to the clinic for a pregnancy test and information about abortion. Avila and Morken convinced the girls to accompany them to a nearby McDonald's. There, they led the sisters into the bathroom, took a urine sample from the younger one, and falsely told her that she was not pregnant. All the while, they talked to the girls about abortion being murder.[20] When the sisters finally made it to the clinic and reported the incident, clinic staff were furious. "That was it," Susan

Hill recalled. "We said, we're not letting this happen. We were going after them. Because we knew they were taking other people."[21] On January 15, 1979, FWWHO filed suit in U.S. District Court against Nurses Concerned for Life and several of its members, including Phyllis Avila and Phyllis Morken. The suit was one of the first lawsuits in the country against anti-abortion protestors.

Patients were devastated by the violation of their privacy. Some were so frightened by the aggressive behavior of protestors at the clinic that they ran away. One patient wrote the clinic that she was devastated and broke into tears when two protestors, claiming to be worried about her mental health, visited her home. The patient's parents, with whom she was still living, knew nothing about the abortion. "For them to find out in that manner would have been disastrous," she noted in a letter to the clinic. "Emotionally, and physically, I just would have been unable to handle an angry confrontation with them."[22]

Demonstrators also harassed FWWHO physicians and clinic staff. Within the first nine months, antiabortion activists prompted the departure of three medical directors from FWWHO. After Hill hired Dr. Eliot Breslar as the clinic's medical director in June 1978, antiabortion activists called Chicago's Holy Cross Hospital, where Breslar had admitting privileges, to inform administrators that Breslar performed abortions. Breslar was forced to resign after the hospital presented him with a choice to stop providing abortions or lose hospital privileges. In October 1978, Hill hired Dr. Rhamesh Bhat, who had a private medical office in Fort Wayne. Protestors contacted St. Joseph's Hospital and Lutheran Hospital where Bhat had privileges and showed up in front of his private office. Both hospitals threatened to deny care to Bhat's patients and to suspend his privileges unless he stopped providing abortions. Bhat, too, was forced to resign from the clinic, leaving FWWHO without a physician by the end of the year. In early 1979, Hill hired Dr. Frederick Cravens from Indianapolis as the new medical director. He only stayed for a couple of months.[23] Finally, Hill decided to fly physicians in from New York City. In addition, the clinic reached some stability when Hill found an African American physician who had a big practice in Fort Wayne and lived in one of the black neighborhoods. Scared to go into the black neighborhood, the white protestors left him alone.[24] Picketers also harassed clinic staff. They screamed "murderers," "killers for hire," and "owners of a baby death chamber" whenever staff entered the clinic and made anonymous phone calls to the private homes of staff. "You will be taken care of," one caller threatened Susan Hill. "We will run your doctors and business out of town."[25]

When, in July 1979, a twenty-year-old clinic patient died as a result of a local hospital's refusal to provide proper backup emergency care, the situation deteriorated even further. Internal hospital policies restricting physicians' ability to provide whatever care they judge most appropriate for a clinical situation are commonly associated with but not limited to Catholic hospitals. Such restrictions frequently apply to the management of pregnancy-related complications and regularly violate best medical practice as spelled out by professional medical associations such as the American College of Obstetricians and Gynecologists.[26] The physician on staff at the FWWHO that Saturday had performed a vacuum aspiration, and dissatisfied with the amount of tissue he had retrieved, he had resuctioned the patient. But he continued to have doubts that he had gotten all of the fetal tissue and admitted the patient to Lutheran Hospital for observation and further tests. There, Dr. Ramesh Bhat, who had worked for FWWHO earlier in the year, took care of her. Normally, the attending physician would perform a D&C to clean out any remaining tissue. But hospital policy dictated that physicians could perform a D&C only if the patient had an apparent infection. On Saturday, however, the patient was doing well. Bhat performed a sonogram, but the sonogram results did not become available until Monday, when the images revealed that the patient was still pregnant. Due to the delay in medical care resulting from the hospital policy, by Monday the patient had developed an infection and low-grade fever. Bhat was finally able to perform a D&C to clean out the remaining fetal tissue. Yet, by that time it was too late. Despite antibiotics and the combined efforts of medical specialists, the patient died of an overwhelming infection on Wednesday morning.[27]

Shortly after the death, the clinic began to receive bomb threats. The first one came on the morning of August 11, 1979, as staff were in the middle of a busy day. The counseling, recovery, and waiting rooms were filled with patients and family members. Outside, protestors were in full swing. On that day, Joseph Scheidler had joined more than thirty picketers in front of the clinic. Indeed, the first picketers had shown up at midnight the previous day to conduct a prayer meeting outside the clinic. By mid-morning, demonstrators blocked both the entrance and exit of the clinic. Scheidler yelled into a megaphone: "Women are killing their babies." "Your cervix will be cracked," he shouted at one patient trying to enter the clinic. "What kind of mother will your children think you are when they learn you killed their brother and sister?" he hollered at another. Then he tried to rile up the protestors. "If we are going to be sued for walking in front," he shouted, "we may as well go in and chain ourselves to the tables."[28] When security guards approached the escorts in front of the building to inform them of the bomb threat and to ask for their help with the evacuation, all hell broke loose. "Oh my god, there has been another death," Phyllis Avila yelled to other protestors. Several protestors shouted "Butcher! Butcher! Get the butcher! Kill the butcher."[29] Scheidler roared into the megaphone, "Remember August 11, the day you killed your baby."[30]

As patients, relatives, and staff emerged from the front and back doors, picketers blocked the way. With nowhere else to go, staff led patients into the park across the street, and escorts formed a circle around patients and their relatives to protect them from the onslaught of protestors. "You are having this abortion for your own convenience," Scheidler bellowed through his megaphone as he approached the circle. "Abortion is murder. There is no way you can escape from that."[31] Picketers tried to break through the circle of escorts surrounding the patients. One offered a patient $100 in cash, telling her that this would help her raise her child.[32] Another tried to take pictures of the patients. "You have no respect for the father of your child," Scheidler yelled. "You are being selfish."[33] Patients began to cry.[34] Protestors also blocked the back door of the clinic through which staff and escorts evacuated medicated patients and the physician. It took ten people to evacuate the physician to a house two doors down. "Bring out the butcher, bring out the butcher," picketers yelled, and "Here comes the butcher, here comes the butcher," when he emerged.[35] "Fifty bucks and I'll slit your throat," one male picketer volunteered, while another yelled, "God knows the people who kill."[36]

The city of Fort Wayne refused to dispatch police and fire officials in response to the emergency. The only person to respond to the clinic's 911 call was a technician from the bomb and arson squad, who refused to search the facility for any explosive device because he was "unfamiliar with the contents" of the clinic. Instead, the clinic administrator and a staff member searched the clinic, while the technician waited in his car. Thirty minutes after the initial alarm, staff and the security guards were able to move patients and relatives back into the building.[37]

The lack of police response indicated how vulnerable staff and patients could be in locations where local officials opposed abortion facilities. When, two days later, a FWWHO staff member with a lawyer and city councilwoman in tow visited the offices of the Fort Wayne chief of police to express concern for the safety of patients and staff, Chief of Police Kenneth Buckmaster conceded that the police department had not followed standard operating procedure. But although he promised more help should there be future bomb threats, only one police officer appeared when the clinic received a second bomb threat the following week. It was again left to the clinic security guards and escorts to evacuate the building and guide patients to safety.[38]

Fortunately, this time the scene in front of the clinic was quieter. Frank Avila was walking up and down the sidewalk. Referring to the death the previous month, he yelled at every patient: "You have to know your rights, so that you won't die of gas gangrene like the woman who died here." But there was no Scheidler present to rile up the crowds.[39] This time, staff avoided the park next door and took patients directly across the street to the First Presbyterian Church. Medicated patients and medical staff were guided to the house two doors down. Officer Davis, the one policeman who had responded to the bomb threat, helped staff members and the private security guards conduct a search of the building. He also assisted with the evacuation of patients. Just before noon, Davis cleared the building, and the clinic day resumed.

Susan Hill was incensed at the feeble police response. Although Officer Davis performed his required duties, she wrote to Buckmaster the following week, the Fort Wayne Police Department had again failed to dispatch the personnel required by their own guidelines. Violence against clinics, she reminded Buckmaster, was a real threat. Only ten days earlier, a facility in St. Paul, Minnesota, had been firebombed. FWWHO patients and staff, she insisted, needed the help and prompt cooperation of the police.[40]

In the late 1970s, clinic protests like the one in Fort Wayne were only one tactic in a range of antiabortion strategies to end legal abortion. In local and national elections, antiabortion activists promoted candidates who would support the elimination of public funding for abortion and restrict access to abortion services. After passage of the Hyde Amendment in 1976, antiabortion activists renewed their lobbying efforts for a Human Life Amendment that would undo *Roe* altogether. By the end of the decade, however, it became increasingly clear that while Congress was willing to ban public funding for abortion services, it was unwilling to pass a constitutional amendment prohibiting abortion.

An influx of fundamentalist Protestants into the antiabortion movement quickly radicalized it. With the 1980 election of President Ronald Reagan to the White House, antiabortion activists emerged onto the national stage as a serious force.[41] Reagan appointed a number of antiabortion leaders to positions in his administration. C. Everett Koop, known in antiabortion circles for coauthoring the 1979 book and film series *Whatever Happened to the Human Race?*, which served as the intellectual foundation for many evangelicals in the antiabortion movement, became Reagan's surgeon general. Reagan appointed Robert Billings, a former executive director of the Christian Right organization Moral Majority, to the Department of Education. Marjorie Mecklenburg, founder of Minnesota Citizens Concerned for Life and, with her husband Fred Mecklenburg, an early prominent leader in the antiabortion movement, was appointed to the Office of Adolescent Pregnancy Programs.[42] For the first time, antiabortion activists felt that they had an ally in the White House. Newly invigorated by these developments, they approached the fight against legal abortion with a new sense of optimism and boldness. The example of Fargo, North Dakota, depicted in the January 1985 TV news program *20/20* as the town "being torn into two," illustrates how, within a couple of years, antiabortion activism became significantly more aggressive and intrusive.[43]

A Year of Pain and Fear: From Prayer Vigils to Sidewalk Counseling

When Susan Hill opened the clinic in Fargo, North Dakota, in 1981, she did so with some hesitation. Her experience during the previous three years opening abortion clinics in Wayne, New Jersey; Wilmington, Delaware; White Plains, New York; Fort Wayne, Indiana; and Raleigh, North Carolina, had taken their toll. Indeed, by the end of that decade, more and more clinics had become the site of attacks. Between 1977 and 1979, seven abortion clinics in the Midwest alone experienced arson attacks, and by 1980, the climate for abortion clinics had become much more hostile. Merely finding a suitable building had become difficult. But in the late 1970s, Hill met Fargo feminist Jane Bovard at a NARAL board meeting. Bovard, who had been actively involved with La Leche League, a national organization promoting natural childbirth and breastfeeding, had developed an interest in feminism and abortion rights. She participated in the establishment of a NOW chapter in North Dakota and founded a local chapter of NARAL. Bovard repeatedly urged Hill to come to Fargo, and in 1979 Hill finally agreed. It took Bovard and Hill two years to find a location for a clinic in Fargo. They finally rented an old house on the corner of 14th Street and Main Street.[44] To protect the landlord's identity and minimize the potential for harassment, they established a blind trust from which the clinic rented the building. Seeking to avoid a repeat experience of demonstrators such as those in Fort Wayne, who had harassed contractors before the clinic even opened, Hill kept the intended use of the building vague—neither in the documents filed with the city nor in conversations with contractors did she specify that the clinic would offer abortions. But once Hill and Bovard began to interview physicians and nurses to staff the clinic, word of the impending opening of an abortion clinic spread quickly. Tipped off by a nurse who had responded to an ad for a gynecological nursing position, antiabortion activists called a press conference to alert Fargo residents.[45] On August 25, an overflowing crowd attended a city commission meeting to challenge the clinic's building permit. City commissioners temporarily suspended the permit, but warnings from one city commissioner that Fargo made itself liable to a lawsuit for the suspension and the support of the clinic by Fargo mayor John Lindgren meant the permit was reissued within twenty-four hours.[46]

Over the following month, as Hill and Bovard prepared for the opening of the Fargo Women's Health Organization (FWHO), two antiabortion groups emerged in Fargo: Life Is For Everyone Coalition (LIFE) and Partners in Vision. LIFE was led by Susan Richards, a twenty-seven-year-old mother of two who, after the birth of her children, had left her work as a convention director and devoted her energies to antiabortion activities. Partners in Vision was established by evangelist Lyn Sahr, a newcomer to Fargo, and Darold Larson, a special assistant to televangelist Jerry Falwell. Sahr opened a Christian coffee shop, the Holy Smoke shop, from which the two initially conducted their antiabortion activities. Activists began to mail out antiabortion materials and called for a rally in the Civic Center Mall. Accompanied by music from a six-piece polka band, around 500 protestors gathered on September 27 for a march and prayer vigil.

With the opening of the Fargo clinic on October 1, 1981, women's access to legal abortion increased significantly. Until then, area hospitals had performed only "therapeutic" abortions in cases of rape or incest or if the woman's life or health was in danger.[47] In the eight years between the legalization of abortion and the opening of FWHO, Fargo women who had sought to end a pregnancy had had to travel at least two hours to Grand Forks or Jamestown, North Dakota, where two physicians in private practice were willing to perform abortions. Women could also drive to Minneapolis, but that trip of several hundred miles took at least four hours. Once open, FWHO staff performed about twenty abortions per week. In addition, the clinic offered counseling, birth control, gynecological examinations, information, Pap smears, and pregnancy tests.[48]

Over the following year, LIFE and Partners in Vision organized regular protest activities at the new clinic. Starting on the day of opening, two LIFE members conducted a silent prayer vigil outside the clinic.[49] To foster an image of moderation, LIFE permitted only two volunteers at a time to participate in silent prayers lasting two hours. "DO NOT: argue, explain, discuss, answer questions with anyone including the press," instructions to LIFE volunteers read.[50] Such public display quickly attracted a thousand members to LIFE.

Partners in Vision chose a more public and confrontational approach. Within a week of the clinic's opening, the group presented a petition rife with allegations about the clinic's disposal of fetal remains to the Fargo City Commission, asking for an injunction to close FWHO until the city could pass laws regulating abortion clinics. "The bodies of the aborted babies," the plaintiffs alleged, "are to be ground up and flushed into the Fargo sewer system without proper burials, and would be eventually dispersed into the Red River which could subject this City to lawsuits for contamination and pollution of the River by adjoining cities upstream [sic]."[51] Insinuating that employees of abortion clinics, like guards in Nazi concentration camps, treated bodies with a lack of respect and sought to commercialize as much of the business as possible, the petition further asked "if the human placenta will be sold commercially from the clients they operate on in performing abortions."[52] As a dramatic addition, petitioners attached a bottle of hair conditioner "purchased in a local drug store in which the hair conditioner is made in part from human placenta."[53] Hill protested allegations that FWHO provided substandard care. All NWHO clinics, she noted, voluntarily complied with standards set by the PPFA and NAF.[54] City commissioners declined the request for a public hearing on the issue and refused to issue an injunction against the clinic. While antiabortion activists in Fargo were unable to close FWHO, the publicity garnered by their appeal and prayer vigils educated Fargo residents to the tactics and arguments of antiabortion activists and attracted members to build an organizational framework.

By 1983, the national "right to life" movement experienced a series of setbacks that contributed to a significant radicalization of movement activists. To be sure, passage of the Hyde Amendment had made poor women's access to abortion more difficult, and nonwhite women were particularly affected by the new restrictions. Most states eliminated Medicaid funding for abortions in late 1977, and when in October of that year a twenty-seven-year-old single mother died in Texas of blood poisoning after seeking an illegal abortion in a Mexican border town, the impact of these funding cuts on poor and nonwhite women raised immediate concern among abortion rights supporters.[55] In 1978, an estimated 20 percent of the women affected by the Medicaid restrictions carried their unintended pregnancies to term, unable to pay for abortions with their own funds. The restriction of Medicaid funding for abortions—a restriction that took effect in most states in late 1977—affected nonwhite women disproportionately. Between 1977 and 1980, the abortion rate among white women increased by 16 percent, while the rate fell by 4 percent among nonwhites. Nevertheless, the abortion rate was nearly three times higher among nonwhite women than among whites—a result of a much higher incidence of unintended pregnancies among nonwhites.[56] Despite a White House supportive to antiabortion causes, legislators had defeated several versions of the Human Life Amendment. Although most antiabortion restrictions in the early 1980s passed on the state level, the movement failed to gain significant support on the national level or elect additional candidates in the 1982 midterm elections. In June 1983, the Supreme Court handed the antiabortion movement a further defeat when it ruled in *City of Akron v. Akron Center for Reproductive Health* that various state and local ordinances designed to restrict abortion practice were unconstitutional.

The antiabortion activists, who had spent years fighting against abortion through political and legal channels in hopes of one day overturning the *Roe v. Wade* decision, grew frustrated and impatient with ineffective electoral and lobbying strategies. They shifted their protest style to methods that were much more confrontational and incorporated direct action. While attendees of the 1978 annual National Right to Life Committee (NRLC) in St. Louis had argued back and forth about sit-ins, for instance, by the early 1980s antiabortion activists had begun to incorporate direct action techniques. Many of their new tactics were developed by Joseph Scheidler, the Chicago activist who had wielded his bullhorn in front of FWWHO and who gained legitimacy as a leader in the antiabortion movement when the NRLC invited him to address its annual convention in 1983.[57] When, in January 1984, President Ronald Reagan welcomed a handful of antiabortion leaders, including Joseph Scheidler, to meet in the White House, antiabortion leaders felt emboldened and legitimized by the political gesture. "[Reagan] gave us a lot of moral support," Scheidler noted about a visit to the White House. After getting arrested at a St. Louis picket, a protestor observed that the demonstrators "got a president and a justice department that supports everything we are doing here."[58] In May 1984, antiabortion activists held their first national convention in Fort Lauderdale, Florida, at which Scheidler presented a workshop on effective confrontation. As part of the training, 200 participants went to Women's Awareness Clinic in Fort Lauderdale and blocked all clinic entrances.[59] A rash of clinic bombings that year further indicated that antiabortion activists were escalating their tactics. The following year, antiabortion activists reconvened for a second conference in Appleton, Wisconsin. Under a motel marquee that encouraged participants to "Have a Blast," activists pledged to create a "year of pain and fear" for abortion providers and women seeking abortions. "The old movement is dead. There is a new movement of action and prayer," Scheidler told participants. "We are going to protect those children. We are going to make this year 12 months of pain and unpleasantness from those who are destroying our posterity."[60] Across the country, protestors began to adopt more aggressive picketing techniques.

Demonstrations became dramatic performances directed at abortion providers and women seeking abortions. Antiabortion rhetoric—such as Scheidler's call to "protect those children"—encouraged the total identification of a fetus with a baby and abortion with killing. Indeed, activists adopted a vocabulary that conveyed the violence of abortion in every term. They referred to "baby" rather than fetus, "deathscorts" rather than clinic escorts, "death culture" or "abortion culture" rather than American culture, "murder" or "child killing" for abortion, "abortuary," "killing center," or "child killing industry" for abortion clinics, and "killer" or "mass murderer" for abortion providers.[61] Protestors accosted women entering abortion clinics, blocked their access, confronted them physically and verbally, followed them, traced license plate numbers, called their homes, entered clinics and disrupted procedures, poured glue into front door locks, picketed the homes of abortion providers and clinic personnel, sent threatening letters, and made threatening phone calls. Violence against abortion clinics also escalated. In 1982, three men, claiming to be part of the Army of God, a loosely affiliated group of antiabortion activists who sanctioned the use of violence against abortion clinics and providers, kidnapped Illinois abortion provider Dr. Hector Cevallos and his wife and held both hostage for eight days.[62] Clinic vandalism increased to such an extent that by the mid-1980s, security guards, bomb checks, and escorts for patients were considered essential at many abortion clinics.[63] NAF, which had in 1977 begun to collect national statistics on the nature and amount of harassment at abortion clinics, noted "a precipitous increase in the antiabortion harassment of providers and patients" in their 1983 annual report. In response, NAF embarked on the establishment of a data bank to track antiabortion harassment and violence, intensified cooperation with law enforcement officials, and developed a handbook to help abortion providers deal with harassment. By 1986, NAF had also established a legal clearinghouse to provide information to members who wanted to pursue legal remedies to antiabortion harassment and violence and had distributed thousands of copies of fact sheets about abortion.[64]

Fargo activists, frustrated at their apparent inability to close FWHO or convince women visiting the clinic not to have an abortion, stepped up their protest activities as well. Under criticism that they were not sufficiently active in fighting the clinic and showed no compassion for women seeking abortions, LIFE members initiated a sidewalk counseling program. Started in the early 1980s in Chicago, sidewalk counseling was intended to present abortion patients with information that would make them change their minds before they entered the abortion clinic. The strategy won prominence with the publication of Joseph Scheidler's 1985 book *Closed: 99 Ways to Stop Abortion*. In his very first chapter, Scheidler described sidewalk counseling as "the single most valuable activity that a pro-life person can engage in. . . . Counseling goes to the very heart of the abortion problem. The problem of abortion is the problem of killing babies. They are killed in abortion clinics or hospitals or doctors' offices, and pro-lifers go there to intercede for the baby's life. The aim of the Pro-Life Action League and other activist groups is to get more people out on the streets to stand between the killers and the victims."[65] Such counseling was urgent—Scheidler compared it to trying to physically stop someone who has rushed into your living room to kidnap your three-year-old child—and, he claimed, it was effective. In one thirty-day period, he insisted in his book, half a dozen sidewalk counselors at a few clinics had been able to stop 90 women from having abortions. "Seventeen were stopped in a single morning at a clinic on Michigan Avenue. While a few of these women may have gone back to have their abortions later, more than ninety percent did not return and they kept in touch with the pro-life counseling center."[66] While Scheidler noted that the sidewalk counselor had to know something about human nature to understand why a woman might decide to have an abortion, he emphasized there was no one right way to engage in sidewalk counseling. In general, sidewalk counselors were to inform patients of the alleged dangers of abortion and the stages of fetal development in hopes that women might, at the last minute, change their mind about abortion. "You might say, 'Are you going into the abortion chamber?' or 'Can I talk to you for a moment?' or 'I would like to offer you our help and this is our literature,'" one educational pamphlet advised would-be sidewalk counselors. "Ask her how far along she is in her pregnancy and show her a baby at that gestation. Talk to her lovingly and gently, but continuously. . . . If you do lose her, if she goes into the abortion chamber, continue to pray for her, as God many times will touch women's hearts even on the operating table and they will change their minds and come out to you to accept your help."[67] With some encouragement and education on the facts of fetal life, the training material implied, women seeking abortions might change their minds.[68]

The line between sidewalk counseling and regular protest activities became impossible to draw. Encouraged to think of the "rescue" of a fetus as equivalent to the rescue of a baby or toddler, some sidewalk counselors did anything they could think of to discourage women from entering the clinic. They blocked clinic entrances, yelled at women seeking to enter clinics, and attempted to show women dead fetuses. "We feel that it's important to visualize and to educate and inform people," Reverend Norman Stone, who regularly traveled with fetal remains to abortion clinics, explained at a 1985 demonstration in St. Louis. "So, sometimes it takes this kind of demonstration to make that point."[69] Antiabortion activists regularly intimidated women, trying to scare them away from the clinic. "They started yelling at people to get their attention. They said hateful, hurtful things to people," a Planned Parenthood staff member recalled.[70] One sidewalk counselor explained to a couple whom he intercepted how God looked at abortion. "Women who reject his gift, his children," he argued, "he makes them barren. Because women have become sterile out of abortion. That's obvious, that happens all the time. I just want to let you know," he added, turning to the woman, "that the consequences of your decision is, before God you have now become a murderer."[71]

Administrators at clinics across the country reported that on some days they counted as many as 100 protestors in front of their clinics. Even when the numbers were much smaller, protestors were aggressive and disruptive. At the Northeast Women's Center in Philadelphia, demonstrators walked up and down the public sidewalk, praying and carrying signs with large photographs of mutilated fetuses and slogans such as "Abortion is Murder" and "Northeast Women's Center does Back Alley Abortions." One or two picketers typically followed anyone entering the building to offer antiabortion literature. Protestors blocked access to the parking lot and refused to move until someone in the car rolled down the windows to accept antiabortion literature. If women refused to acknowledge the demonstrators, protestors grabbed women's arms and yelled at them: "Don't murder your baby. They'll rip your baby's eyes out."[72] Picketers at other clinics were even more aggressive. At the Hillcrest Clinic in Baltimore, antiabortion activists staged almost daily protests in which one demonstrator, dressed as a doctor and carrying a paper hatchet, chased women around the public easement in front of the building. Here, too, protestors followed patients and verbally assaulted them. They snuck into the clinic waiting room, where they harassed patients and family members, stuffed magazines in the waiting room with antiabortion literature, and taped pictures of dead fetuses in the downstairs lobby. And at the FWHC in Yakima, Washington, protestors played a recording of a fetal heartbeat outside the clinic and shouted such threats as, "If you go in there for an abortion, they will rip it up and burn it. They will burn their eyes out."[73] Several times, FWHC picketers formed a twenty-two- to thirty-five-foot gauntlet in front of the clinic by holding hands and forming two lines on both sides of the sidewalk. Anyone approaching the clinic on the front sidewalk would have to pass through this gauntlet to enter the clinic. Patients had to seek the help of escorts to enter the clinic. In one instance, the picketers also interfered with an ambulance transport to a hospital and took pictures of the patient.[74]

Confrontations were not limited to patients—picketers also harassed clinic staff. They blocked entrances in an attempt to dissuade employees from entering work and followed them into the building. They threatened staff, shouting, "I will pull your hair out. Butcher! Slime!" and "Your time is limited. I promise you. Your time is limited."[75] Antiabortion activists also showed up at the homes of clinic administrators, staff, and abortion providers. In Philadelphia, they scared the twelve-year-old son of a clinic administrator when they unfurled banners in front of the family residency that read: "Mary Bannecker Thrives on Innocent Blood" and "Bannecker's Business Brutally Butchers for Big Bucks."[76] In Elizabeth City, North Carolina, they organized demonstrations against an ob-gyn who regularly traveled to Hillcrest Clinics to provide abortions, conducting biweekly pickets at his regular group practice in Elizabeth City until his partners asked him to leave the practice. Antiabortion activists identified one Hillcrest clinic employee in a shopping area and verbally assaulted her.[77] The FWHC in Yakima, Washington, and its employees received hate mail and harassing phone calls at both the clinic and their private residencies—often 300 to 400 calls a day, but on some days more than 700. "Don't make me hurt you," the male caller threatened clinic staff.[78] At least one letter warned the recipient to "never go out alone, by day or night, and to never be alone at the office."[79]

Patients, their family members, and clinic staff were angry and scared. One study reported that more than one-third of patients encountering sidewalk counselors at one clinic were upset by the confrontations. Three-quarters of the patients in another study reported that demonstrators had talked to them, and 42 percent stated that demonstrators had tried to prevent them from entering the clinic. Only 1 percent of patients reported being interested in what the pro-life activists had to say.[80] "The antiabortion activities created a stressful and tense atmosphere in and outside the clinic," explained Beverly Whipple about responses to protestors at the FWHC Yakima clinic: "It caused some clinic employees to quit, cut back hours and change their residences. Patients have entered shaking, trembling, and crying. There have been cancellations, no shows, requests for referrals to other clinics and patients afraid to enter or leave the clinic without an escort."[81] Intimidated, some women decided not to come to clinics with picketers and asked to be referred to other abortion providers. One woman, concerned about her privacy, asked if she could wear a mask to the appointment since picketers might be taking pictures. Another requested a referral to another abortion provider because her mother was a picketer. Some asked about alternative entrances into the clinic or called the clinic for help getting through the picket line.[82] As a representative of Hillcrest Clinics complained: "These professed Christians continually demean and cruelly harass our patients. By the time the patients endure the verbal assault, they are an emotional wreck. When the picketers are present, the patients are more difficult to counsel and have a much longer post-procedure recovery time. Our very basic freedoms are being violated under the guise of 'peaceful protest.'"[83]

Patients complained about the harassment they endured. Occasionally, they were so angry at protestors that they were willing to speak publicly about the experience. One woman who sought an abortion at the FWHC in Portland, Oregon, testified before the Subcommittee on Civil and Constitutional Rights. She explained to the committee members how she had seen about thirteen people picketing on the sidewalk when she approached the clinic. "They started yelling things at me like 'two lives go in and one comes out.' Each sign they were holding had the word 'murder' written on it somewhere. One sign had . . . pictures of the dead babies in the garbage can. . . . I just had to keep saying to myself that 'this is my choice and I don't have to look at or listen to these people.' . . . While we were in the clinic I could still hear one woman outside yelling 'Auschwitz' continuously."[84] Staff members, too, suffered under the strain of constant harassment. At times it was so bad that family members questioned whether their loved ones should work at an abortion clinic. Some staff members withdrew; all were profoundly shaken. The 1985 hearings before the Subcommittee on Civil and Constitutional Rights, chaired by Representative Don Edwards, a Democrat from California, became the first televised forum at which abortion clinic staff and patients could voice their concerns publicly. Frustrated that the federal government and Department of Justice had so far refused involvement in investigating antiabortion violence, abortion providers and their supporters clearly hoped that their testimonials would result in greater law enforcement support.

Abortion providers and their patients also noted the specific use of race-based arguments in antiabortion propaganda. White protestors picked up black nationalist charges that abortion was a form of racial genocide when approaching African American patients and staff. "Don't you know that they are trying to kill the black people? That slavery is over?" protestors in front of the FWWHO asked when encountering a black patient.[85] An African American staff member at the Atlanta FWHC noted that white Operation Rescue demonstrators regularly referred to issues of race genocide, telling her that "'the Reverend Dr. Martin Luther King would be very upset because you're creating genocide on your people.' . . . They try to make me feel responsible for my whole race of people. . . . If I go in there and have an abortion, I'm going to just stop the whole black race."[86] But African American patients and abortion providers were unconvinced by the appropriation of race suicide arguments by white demonstrators. Pittsburgh's African American providers recalled these arguments as incoherent and peripheral—held and vocalized by the editor of the *Pittsburgh Courier*, but a minority opinion in the black community nonetheless. Both Morris Turner and his colleague Robert Thompson described the African American community as pragmatic, realizing that "people need access."[87] "People were having significant medical problems and needs," Thompson noted. "And the difficulties with these unwanted pregnancies throughout the populations in general and the black population specifically were tremendously endangering the capabilities and the progression of some of these young women. It would stifle their life and they were locked in poverty for the rest of their lives. . . . The genocide was on the side of the women that were having these kids and whose life was ruined, [who were] dying earlier, [who] certainly injured their health."[88]

African American patients and staff were not only unconvinced by white demonstrators' attempts to appeal to their racial pride, but they also framed their resistance to white demonstrators explicitly as a civil rights struggle. When, in the 1980s, 250 demonstrators gathered to protest in front of Preterm in Washington, D.C., several patients insisted on proudly walking through the hostile crowd of antiabortion activists that included Joseph Scheidler, who was screaming through his bullhorn. Clinic director Terry Beresford had secured the help of local police to allow patients, whose abortion procedures had been completed, to leave the clinic through the back door where a paddy wagon would drive them away from the clinic site. But one patient, an African American schoolteacher, was unwilling to leave through the back door. Beresford recalled: "And the counselor said to them [the schoolteacher and two younger women patients], 'You can leave now and I'm going to escort you out the back door where the police will provide you protection.' And this teacher stood up and she said, 'I'm not going out the back door, never again.' And these other two women said, 'Well, I guess we have to go with her, don't we?' The three of them hooked arms and walked out the front door."[89] Abortion provider Morris Turner responded similarly when confronted with demonstrators on his walk to the Pittsburgh clinic where he provided abortions. Demonstrators regularly lined up for three blocks to observe and protest his walk from his parking spot to the clinic.

> They'd take pictures of you and they often had your picture on their signs. And they used that as propaganda, all over. "This is the abortion provider." They knew all of us. And they ultimately found out our home addresses and our office addresses. There were occasions when they would demonstrate outside of the office, they'd been on the street here [his home] and certainly in front of the clinic. . . . Initially it's a little unnerving, because they are yelling at you: "Murderer!" "How could you do this? These women are suffering!" . . . Then they would have some of the more radical, usually some men . . . who would actually come face to face with you to impede your way. Again, a little bit unnerving. . . . And then, of course, along the way there were fights, there were physical fights. Some of the men who would accompany women to their procedure—these folks would approach them and sometimes tempers flared and you actually would have physical confrontations.[90]

Walking through the gauntlet, Turner recalls, took some getting used to. "But the more you did it, the more you got used to it and the more you expected it."[91] Like civil rights activists in the South, African American physicians and patients framed abortion as a civil rights issue and chose to defy protestors by holding their heads high and moving on.

The fact that antiabortion protestors were almost always white surely contributed to a situation in which parallels to the civil rights struggles of the 1960s were hard to escape. Turner recalls that in Pittsburgh he could count African American antiabortion protestors "on one hand." He remembers only one African American woman protestor who would join the antiabortion demonstrators to read Bible verses out loud. While he made it a point never to acknowledge or engage the protestors, he did "look at her at one occasion, as if to say 'why are you here? Do you see any other black people out here?'"[92] None of Pittsburgh's black churches preached against abortion. Indeed, the counseling services of a number of churches, including black churches, regularly referred members to Alleghany Reproductive Health Center and offered postabortion counseling to congregation members in need of such services. "They would openly defend what we were doing," Turner recalled.

While abortion providers and some patients and staff tried to cope with antiabortion harassment by ignoring the presence of demonstrators, others found informal ways to relieve the tension and gain some space for themselves. Young female staff often tried to shock or stymie antiabortion activists, frequently resorting to jokes about sex. As one Atlanta FWHC staff member recalls, "One time I was out there and this man and his son—who was probably about fifteen—came up and the man was saying all these mean and nasty things . . . [and I said] to the fifteen-year-old son—I was like, 'Do you know your father masturbates?' And the father just looked at me and looked at his son and they just left."[93] As sociologist Wendy Simonds notes, "trying to rile and annoy the antis made some of the women [staff members] feel a brief flash of satisfying vengeance; at the same time, it provided comic relief and diminished the threat the antis presented for the time being."[94] Because of his regular presence on antiabortion picket lines and his bullying behavior, successfully intimidating Joseph Scheidler gave providers both pride and courage. Susan Hill gained some fame in the abortion provider community for making Scheidler move across the street and away from the clinic entrance by staring provocatively at his crotch.[95] Renee Chelian learned about the importance of fighting back when her brother, a bodybuilder whose hero was Arnold Schwarzenegger, taunted Scheidler until he left a training site for clinic escorts. When Scheidler started to threaten staff who tried to prevent his entering the training site, her brother went up to Scheidler and said: "'You want to mess with anyone motherfucker, you have to mess with me.'"[96] Her brother followed Scheidler as he took off, pacing him outside the door and all the way down the street, taunting him while he followed him. "That's when I learned that you fight back," Chelian concluded.[97]

Clinic owners sought the help of the courts and police in order to curb the harassment they experienced. In some cities, close collaboration with city officials and community support led to a productive relationship between clinic owners and the police. Claire Keyes, who ran the Alleghany Reproductive Health Center in Pittsburgh, was careful to maintain cordial relations with members of the city council and the police chief. In turn, the local police precinct responded quickly when called and regularly assigned an officer to stand guard on procedure days.[98] Terry Beresford, too, had positive experiences with the police in Washington, D.C., where she directed the Preterm Clinic.[99] But police forces were not always responsive to abortion clinics. While some abortion clinics praised their local law enforcement officials, others noted that the amount of protection they received depended on the politics of the officers on duty. Some clinics were unable to get any help from the police. Up to a third of police officers ignored antiabortion activists who violated the law, and some even sided with the protestors. They offered antiabortion protestors coffee and told them to "keep up the good work."[100] One officer rented an airplane and, carrying pro-life messages, flew over a clinic while protestors were picketing below. Another showed Joseph Scheidler where patients were sneaking into a clinic during a sit-in.[101] But police officers were more likely to do nothing than actively aid antiabortion protestors. In the majority of cases where law enforcement officials were uncooperative, officers failed to show up when called, failed to act on or lost complaints that clinics had filed, refused to search for explosive devices when called to a bomb threat, refused to enforce injunctions and merely watched antiabortion activities from the sidelines, even when protestors violated the law. At other times, officers enforced the law so slowly that antiabortion activists still achieved their goals. They arrested protestors who blocked a clinic to prevent its opening, for instance, but acted so haltingly that the clinic was closed for the entire day.[102] Police departments frequently excused their lack of action by claiming that they had to stay neutral. In Fargo, North Dakota, for instance, officers watched protestors pound on patients' cars and stuff papers into their windows as patients drove toward the clinic entrance. "Our job is to maintain the peace in the community," Fargo's police chief argued, "and we are doing it. We're not taking sides at all."[103] City officials and law enforcement in Yakima, Washington, failed to take the threats to the Yakima FWHC seriously until the clinic burned down in its third firebomb attack. Only then did Yakima's mayor finally speak out in support of the clinic, noting that "the severity of the situation requires that police provide the clinic security during non-office hours when it reopens."[104] By that time, clinic director Beverly Whipple dryly noted, there was no clinic to protect. The law, it was clear, was only as good as those who enforced it.

Clinics filed temporary injunctions and sued antiabortion protestors to establish guidelines that would prevent picketers from using insensitive and graphic language and interfering with patients' access to the clinic and would prevent protestors from intercepting patients on the way to the clinic or following them home.[105] The verbal harassment of patients and staff, however, continued. Even when antiabortion activists were arrested, they often escaped punishment. Of 1,000 arrests during an eight-year period spanning the late 1970s to the mid-1980s at clinic sit-ins in St. Louis, only thirty people were convicted. When in court, activists used their cases as a forum for their cause and as another way to distract clinic owners. Countless legal loopholes and court backlogs meant that activists could frequently postpone sentencing indefinitely.[106] "We are in the right legally, but I feel so helpless," noted Judith Widdicombe who headed Reproductive Health Services in St. Louis. "The legal remedies aren't working."[107]

Abortion clinics might win their legal cases against antiabortion activists or against townships that sought to deny clinics the necessary permits. But they did so at tremendous financial and emotional cost to clinic owners and staff. Susan Hill, who regularly went to court on behalf of NWHO's ten clinics, won almost all her cases against townships and antiabortion activists. But NWHO legal expenses for individual clinics could far exceed the clinic's annual profits.[108]

The lack of legal response meant that the protection of abortion clinics and women's access to reproductive health care became privatized, the responsibility of abortion clinics. Clinics were forced to shoulder the costs of clinic protection themselves. Many clinics turned to volunteers who helped to escort patients into the clinic. But at some clinics, antiabortion protestors shoved escorts into bushes, swung protest signs at them, and endangered their physical safety in other ways, forcing clinics to discontinue the use of volunteer escorts due to safety concerns.[109] Many clinics hired security guards to add to or replace clinic escorts. In addition, clinics installed alarm systems. These steps were expensive and turned clinics into fortresses.[110] The escalation of antiabortion violence had another costly effect: almost 80 percent of clinics lost their property and liability insurance, and some clinics lost their leases and were forced to close. New insurance policies were often ten times more expensive. The financial burden forced some clinics to cut employee salaries, eliminate extra programs, and raise the price of abortion.[111]

Crisis Pregnancy Centers and the Education of Pregnant Women

Alongside sidewalk counseling, antiabortion activists also turned to the establishment of crisis pregnancy centers (CPCs) to educate women about the dangers of abortion and discourage them from terminating a pregnancy. CPCs trace their roots back to the early 1970s, when a number of states began to liberalize their abortion laws. Established to provide pregnancy options counseling, the number of centers increased significantly in the early 1980s when antiabortion activists intensified their efforts to reach out to women seeking abortions. One estimate notes that at the end of 1984, there were at least 2,100 CPCs around the country. Many of them were established by conservative Christian foundations. The Christian Action Council, which operated eleven centers in the United States, Canada, and Japan in 1981, had increased the number of its centers to 240 by 1986. And the Pearson Foundation, a Catholic antiabortion organization based in St. Louis, had set up an estimated 200 facilities in the United States by the end of that year. North Carolina, alone, had about twenty "bogus abortion clinics" in 1986.[112] Some of the centers started out with the intention of providing women with broad options counseling and the resources to continue their pregnancy. But as a spokesperson from Planned Parenthood noted, by the mid-1980s "many of these centers over the last five years have decided that it is ok to deceive women."[113] The Pearson Foundation, for instance, distributed a manual, "How to Start and Operate Your Own Pro-Life Outreach Crisis Pregnancy Center," that advised CPCs to find office space near the entrance of an abortion clinic and adopt a name similar to that of the abortion clinic. "If the girl who would be going to the abortion chamber sees your office first, with a similar name, she will probably come into your center," the manual noted.[114] Fargo activists and many others across the country followed suit. To back up its sidewalk counseling program, the LIFE Coalition announced in the spring of 1984 that it planned to open a crisis pregnancy center. By the end of 1984, Fargo boasted three CPCs run by the LIFE Coalition, Birthright, and Partners in Vision, respectively.[115] To confuse women who were looking for the Fargo Women's Health Clinic, Partners in Vision activists Pat and Darold Larson named their center the Women's Help Clinic. In Yellow Pages ads, the Women's Help Clinic promised "free and confidential counseling" and financial help to women seeking abortions.

CPCs attracted potential patients with the promise of free walk-in pregnancy tests. During a thirty-minute wait for the test results, a staff member was to show the woman a film or narrated slide presentation detailing the horrors of legal abortion. The manual from the Pearson Foundation emphasized the importance of the presentations and the use of graphic pictures. "If the killing of whales and seals can be shown very emotionally and graphically on t.v. to stop their deaths, then this is the least that can be done for the preborn baby and for the mother considering abortion," the manual noted and continued: "It's ludicrous to leave the life of a baby as a free and open 'choice' for the mother."[116] So-called bucket shots of fetuses were a staple in presentations at CPCs. "It was on all the evils and horrors of abortion," Susan, a woman who mistakenly visited the Fargo Women's Help Clinic, explained. "It had violent music with fetuses in trash cans and stories about young girls who committed suicide after having abortions because they couldn't live with the decision they made."[117] After the conclusion of the slide presentation, Pat Larson showed Susan a fetus in a jar to illustrate its similarity to a baby. "I was devastated," Susan recalled about the visit.[118]

CPC staff drew on the antiabortion narratives of women who now regretted their abortions and on the stories of fetal death to convey the alleged dangers of abortion and scare clients away from abortion clinics. Narratives of agonizing pain and death—for the fetus and the mother— were a central part of this information. One teenage couple who visited a Birthchoice Center in Jacksonville, North Carolina, reported that the counselor had told them "the Dr. would go in with a knife and making an x would cut the baby in quarters and then the Dr. would go in with his hand and arm and pull the parts of the baby out. She was also told that she would lie for hours in extreme pain while having the procedure done. She was told that she would have a 50-50 chance of dying during the procedure and was told that if she didn't die, that all manner of complications could occur."[119] Another student, who went undercover to the same Birthchoice Center in Jacksonville, reported about the presentation:

> They used a lot of terms like "ripped apart," "torn to shreds." They said that the suction machine used in D&Es was 29 times stronger than a common household vacuum cleaner. They also said that when the fetuses were not ripped apart or torn in the procedures (in other words when the procedures didn't work) the doctors reached in and sliced them apart. With the saline abortions they showed fetuses which had been expelled that were quite red and burned. They then stopped the movie at that point, and talked to me about burning children and any moral associations with that. They also mentioned that with hysterotomies that it was not uncommon that some fetuses were alive after the procedures, in which case the technicians would then coldly take the fetuses and asphyxiate them with the placenta or strangle them. [Note that the procedures were always done "coldly."] It was stressed

that during any of the abortions, anesthesia was not given to either the mother-to-be or fetus, and that the fetus feels great pain, feels itself being ripped apart.[120]

CPC staff and sidewalk counselors drew on a growing body of antiabortion literature to write their own pamphlets, including works such as Ann Saltenberg's 1980 book *Every Woman Has a Right to Know the Dangers of Legal Abortion*. Full of misleading information about abortion, the book claimed that all abortion procedures, even those during the first trimester, posed a serious hazard for the woman—a risk that was even higher for teenagers.[121] The book included detailed sections on fatal complications and a five-page list of physical and psychological complications. Counselors handed pamphlets with this information to women who came to the CPC or distributed them to prospective abortion patients in front of abortion clinics.[122]

CPCs were most likely to attract young women who found themselves pregnant for the first time. Most were determined not to let their parents find out that they were pregnant and many of them sought an abortion alone or with the help of a boyfriend or girlfriend. Scared and intimidated by what lay ahead, they were an easy target for CPCs. They frequently did not realize that they had gone to the wrong place, failed to recognize that the counseling at CPCs was biased, and were too shy to just leave the fake clinic if they recognized their mistake. Many young women looking for Fargo's abortion clinic, for instance, mistook Fargo Women's Help Clinic for the counseling arm of the Fargo Women's Health Clinic. After receiving a positive pregnancy test at FWHO, Lindsey, a teenage girl, thinking that Pat Larson was the counselor at FWHO, met Larson at the Women's Help Clinic to discuss how to get a judicial bypass for parental consent. Larson, however, handed her pamphlets warning about the dangers of abortion, cautioned her that she would feel like a murderer, and predicted that Lindsey would break up with her boyfriend if she had an abortion. Then Larson showed Lindsey and her boyfriend a slide presentation with the gruesome images of fetal remains and discussed the alleged problems of abortion.[123] For the following week, Larson pretended that she was trying to call Lindsey's sister to arrange for the judicial bypass. When Lindsey and her sister finally discovered their mistake, Larson had delayed Lindsey's abortion by a week.[124]

Indeed, delaying the procedure until women could no longer obtain a first trimester abortion at FWHO was another tactic at the Fargo Women's Help Clinic.[125] Ellen, an eighteen-year-old college student, spent a month in various appointments with pro-life counselors and physicians in the mistaken belief that she was in the care of FWHO. At her initial appointment, Pat Larson sent her to Dr. Perry, a member of Fargo's pro-life community, to confirm the positive pregnancy test. While Ellen believed that Dr. Perry would give her information about abortion, he talked about his children instead. Too scared to ask him about the abortion, Ellen requested at her next appointment that Larson refer her to the abortion clinic. Larson, however, sent her to Birthright, where Ellen had an argument with the staff over her right to have an abortion. "I was extremely distraught and confused," Ellen noted. "I began questioning my own sanity and did not know where to turn."[126] She was in her fourteenth week of pregnancy when she finally realized her mistake and, with the help of a friend, found the Fargo Women's Health Clinic. The experience left her upset and feeling deceived at having discussed her intimate problems with a number of pro-life activists who did not intend to help her. "When I got to the Fargo Women's Health Center, I was very scared after all the things the other two places had told me. At the time of my abortion, the physician informed me that I was 14 weeks along and that the abortion had been done on the absolute last day it could possibly be performed at Fargo Women's Health Organization."[127]

Staff at Fargo Women's Help also called clients who had been to their clinic at home and sent clergy to clients' homes in hopes of changing their minds. After finding that she had become pregnant by her twenty-two-year-old boyfriend, thirteen-year-old Bridget visited the Women's Help Clinic. Bridget and her mother had agreed that abortion was the best solution, and Bridget continued to think so even after her visit to Fargo Women's Help. Then the telephone calls began. "They just called me on the phone and they said that the baby will never have a chance to live and that I can just go to a place and give it up for adoption and get my schooling there. And I said I didn't want to. They just got madder and said the baby can feel it and he has nerves and his heart beats," Bridget remembered. "They sent a pastor over to my house and the pastor told me they use a knife to cut up the baby and then they put it together after you are all done with the abortion."[128] Occasionally, clients got up and walked out of counseling sessions they perceived as biased. But at least one client alleged that clinic personnel tried to block the exit when she wanted to leave.[129]

The experiences with CPCs left patients extremely disturbed. "When my daughter returned home after her visit to the center," the mother of a thirteen-year-old who had visited a crisis pregnancy center in Fayetteville, North Carolina, complained to Takey Crist, "she was crying and very upset, almost hysterical. She then told me where she had been and that she was pregnant. She told me that they had made her watch a horrible film about killing babies and had preached to her about her sins and how it was wrong to have an abortion and that the people who performed the abortions were killers and had no feelings for the patient and would hurt her and treat her horrible [*sic*] at the abortion clinics."[130] Patients' emotional condition after visiting a CPC increased their risk of abortion complications. "The women we see who have been to Women's Help Clinic are much more anxious, scared, frightened, and tense which results in the procedure being more difficult and dangerous to the patient," Jane Bovard noted.

> These patients inform us that the people at Women's Help Clinic tell them that they can hemorrhage to death on the table, that they can have their insides sucked out and that if they have any complications, Fargo Women's Health Organization will not help them and that once they leave Fargo Women's Health Organization, Fargo Women's Health Organization will have nothing more to do with them. In reality, none of these complications have arisen although our doctors have performed over 3,000 procedures since opening and in addition we have 24 hour medical backup and we have assisted every patient who has informed us of any complications.[131]

Furious at the number of women deceived by Fargo Women's Help Clinic, FWHO sued the clinic in 1985 hoping to stop their false and deceptive advertising.[132] Indeed, by 1987, abortion providers in Los Angeles, New York, Fort Worth, Texas, and Worcester, Massachusetts, had filed suits against CPCs, charging the clinics with deceptive trade practices. And judges frequently sided with abortion providers. In the Fargo case, for instance, the judge noted that the advertisements of Fargo Women's Help Clinic were "untrue and misleading" and made with the intention of "deceiving pregnant women into believing that the defendants performed abortions. . . . The Defendants calculated that they could convince the woman not to have an abortion."[133] He fined the Fargo Women's Help Clinic and its individual staff members. Other clinics also won cases against CPCs. In Massachusetts, Planned Parenthood won a trademark infringement suit against the Problem Pregnancy Center in Worcester.[134] Despite these court victories, however, CPCs were there to stay.

Ultimately, abortion providers recognized that they could not control the presence of CPCs. In hopes of combating their impact, providers embarked on a public education campaign to inform women about the existence of CPCs. Charlotte Taft, who was confronted with a CPC that had opened next to her Routh Street Clinic in Houston, Texas, recommended that her colleagues contact the Yellow Pages, their state attorney general, the Better Business Bureau, and their Chamber of Commerce to point out the misleading advertisements of CPCs and alert officials to possible consumer fraud and deceptive trade practices. In addition, she advised that clinics embark on a publicity campaign involving the local media to alert the community to the presence and nature of local CPCs.[135] NAF, too, launched a campaign to counter the misinformation that antiabortion activists were disseminating on picket lines and inside fake clinics. In 1985, NAF issued a number of fact sheets with such titles as "Women Who Have Abortion," "Economics of Abortion," "Safety of Abortion," and "What Is Abortion?," which educated readers on the effects of funding cuts, the nature of abortion procedures and their respective complication rates, and the demographic characteristics of abortion patients. "Do women still die from abortions?" one of the fact sheets asked. "Rarely," the authors of the sheet stated. "In 1981, only 1 of 200,000 women who had legal abortions died." The fact sheet discussed the prevalence of complications in first and second trimester abortions, explained how to recognize complications, and advised women to have their abortions as early as possible. "Don't delay," the fact sheet cautioned. "The earlier the abortion, the safer it is." The fact sheet concluded with the warning that antiabortion claims about the dangers of abortion were untrue. "According to the U.S. Centers for Disease Control," the fact sheet stated, "none of these claims is borne out by medical research."[136] In addition, NAF worked with the mainstream media to offer more accurate coverage of nationwide antiabortion activities. The *New York Times* ran a feature story on NAF member Peter Bours's experiences of harassment in a small Oregon community.[137] *TV Guide* blasted the media for its biased coverage of the abortion debate. CBS's news program *West 57th Street* broadcast a documentary exposing the harassment techniques of sidewalk counseling and crisis pregnancy centers. And the crime drama *Cagney and Lacey* featured an episode which sympathetically covered the investigation of a clinic bombing.[138]

Detroit, the Pope, and Operation Rescue

In the mid-1980s, the rise of new leaders invigorated the antiabortion movement. After the 1985 publication of Joseph Scheidler's book *Closed*, activists across the country began to experiment with the direct action strategies he described. One of these activists was Randall Terry, who emerged in the mid-1980s to organize regular pickets of the Southern Tier Women's Center in Binghamton, New York.[139] In April 1986, Terry attended the Pro Life Action Network conference in St. Louis. At that meeting, participants learned about direct action and staged the largest sit-in to date at an abortion clinic in Regency Park, leading to the arrest of 107 protestors. The protest remained largely nonviolent, although "marred, nonetheless, by the raucous efforts of Joan Andrews [a militant antiabortion activist who later served time in prison], Tom Herlihy [who later became engaged to Andrews while she was in prison], and a few other militants [who wrestled] with and [resisted] police who were attempting to place them in paddy wagons."[140] The event inspired many activists, and following the network conference, Terry, with the help of Scheidler, established an organization to stage antiabortion blockades at clinics across the country. He gave the organization the catchy and somewhat militaristic name Operation Rescue. OR's protests transformed the antiabortion movement. Their clinic sit-ins and blockades drew hundreds of protestors from across the country. In 1987, Terry directed one of the first such blockades at a Cherry Hill clinic in New Jersey. Clinic blockades, of course, were not new to the antiabortion movement. Already in the late 1970s, activists had tried to close clinics by blocking the doors. For participants, these were often heady experiences. When St. Louis protestor Samuel Lee, one of the very early protestors who tried to shut down a clinic by blocking access to it, successfully closed a St. Louis abortion clinic on January 22, 1978, he and his fellow protestors marveled at their success. As journalist Cynthia Gorney recounts in her book, *Articles of Faith*: "They had closed an abortion clinic, only a small clinic and only for one afternoon, but they had done it. . . . In exhilaration they began planning right away to do it again."[141] Activists who regularly participated in sit-ins anticipated these events as pleasurable, exciting, very emotional experiences. "A few of the sit-ins slide close to hysteria," Gorney notes, describing the atmosphere, "with some of the women demonstrators weeping uncontrollably or shouting at the police and the approaching patients."[142] For many this included their arrest and the pat on the back that they regularly received at church the next morning with a "You're doing a great job out there."[143]

By the late 1980s, OR's sit-ins had become the most important form of political expression of the antiabortion movement.[144] In 1988, OR kicked off the "Siege of Atlanta" to coincide with the Democratic National Convention. From July to October, the city became site of the largest antiabortion protests ever as OR brought in busloads of antiabortion activists, largely recruited from across the country by the Christian Broadcasting

Network, to block access to the city's clinics. Following the Atlanta protests, OR took its blockades to New York, Philadelphia, Wichita, and Los Angeles, where the rescues attracted hundreds, and at times thousands, of protestors to a single abortion clinic. The number of OR blockades rose from 182 in 1988 to 201 in 1989 and resulted in 11,732 and 12,358 activist arrests, respectively.

By the end of the decade, however, OR activities declined as quickly as the organization had grown. As clinics and local law enforcement agencies developed counterstrategies and began to challenge the legality of its blockades, OR's ability to amass hundreds of protestors faded. By 1990, the organization was down to a core of professional "rescuers" who traveled from city to city living off free food and lodging provided by antiabortion sympathizers.[145] The quick decline of OR speaks to the resilience of the abortion provider community and to its success in raising the awareness of legislators and in reshaping the politics of police and FBI.

In response to the increasingly aggressive behavior of antiabortion protestors, NAF and its members began to coordinate efforts for clinic defenses. Already in 1981, NAF had started the Clinic Defense Project which surveyed members to gather annual statistics on the nature and amount of harassment. Over the following years, NAF members began to share strategies on how to obtain injunctions, file lawsuits to gain relief from protestors, and organize locally to defend their clinics. By the mid-1980s, NAF held regular workshops on clinic defense. In September of 1984, for instance, the organization offered the workshop "In Defense of Freedom," which brought together family planning and abortion providers, attorneys, local and federal law enforcement agents, and representatives from national pro-choice organizations to discuss how to protect patients, staff, and the premises of abortion clinics. NAF urged abortion providers to build coalitions with the Justice Department; the Federal Bureau of Investigation; the Bureau of Alcohol, Tobacco, and Firearms; and pro-choice organizations. Abortion providers and their allies taught Congress and law enforcement that it was indeed their job to arrest aggressive protestors and those who physically attacked abortion clinics. Practitioners and clinics were not just victims. Instead, they educated legislators, police, and FBI on how to respond.

As protests against abortion clinics intensified in the late 1980s, it took careful planning to assure women's continued access to abortion care. Especially in urban areas, clinics began to coordinate their defensive strategies, sometimes to great effect. Local coalition building proved crucial to a clinic's ability to weather the protests. When Pope John Paul II set out on a ten-city American tour in 1987, abortion providers embarked on a model of organizing that frustrated antiabortion activists' efforts to close down all clinics located along the papal route and provided a model for clinic responses during the years of OR. Providers first learned about the visit and the planned antiabortion protests in the fall of 1986 when the Delta Women's Clinic in New Orleans received a letter from antiabortion activist John Cavanaugh-O'Keefe of the Prolife Nonviolent Action Project. Cavanaugh-O'Keefe had cofounded the organization in 1977 as a means to organize acts of civil disobedience at abortion clinics. A twenty-seven-year-old Harvard graduate who had studied feminist theory and had been a conscientious objector during the Vietnam War, he was emerging as one of the philosophical guides of the sit-in movement.[146] Now he wrote to notify the clinic director of the pope's visit: "We would like to make it possible for you to go hear him," he noted and suggested that the clinic close for the day. "But if abortions are scheduled for days when he is speaking," he continued, "we will do all we can to ensure that generous, gentle, loving people interpose themselves between the abortionists and the intended victims."[147] Antiabortion activists organized a nationwide protest under the slogan "We Will Stand Up" during the pope's visit. Over the following months, local antiabortion groups in cities along the papal route joined this movement. In Detroit, activists with the Pro-Life Action League sent a letter to area clinics repeating Cavanaugh-O'Keefe's request. If clinics did not close, activists threatened, they would shut them down.[148] "This is a war on the unborn and we are God's Soldiers!" Detroit activist Lynn Mills noted in a flyer that called on fellow antiabortion activists to keep legitimate abortion patients from obtaining appointments for that day by making phony appointments and tying up the phone lines of area abortion clinics.[149]

As abortion providers began to organize for the fall 1987 protests, they established a broad coalition on the national and local level to coordinate clinic responses. NAF, NARAL, PPFA, and Catholics for a Free Choice, a Catholic organization established in 1973 to serve as a pro-choice voice for Catholics, offered training, helped plan workshops, advised on media and policy strategies, and made recommendations on dealing with the Catholic Church and working with local and national law enforcement. They also offered legal advice and press interviews, sent national leaders to the cities in question, and organized protest letters to the pope and U.S. bishops calling upon the church to denounce the planned antiabortion demonstrations and work for their cancellation.[150] NAF member Judith Widdicombe, founder of Reproductive Health Services in St. Louis, and

Frances Kissling, NAF's first president and now with Catholics for a Free Choice, offered their expertise and public voice to the organizing efforts. They visited cities on the papal route, trained clinic staff and escorts, and lent their presence as pro-choice celebrities to help with fund-raisers and excite enthusiasm for the organizing efforts.

On the local level, Detroit-area activists brought together a coalition of groups critical of the Catholic Church under the umbrella of the Michigan Organization for Human Rights, whose members trained in clinic defense. Women's groups, pro-choice groups, gays and lesbians, and health activists were all encouraged to participate. Indeed, the coalition extended to a group of Trotskyists from Wayne State University in Detroit, who had organized the Coalition to Defend Abortion Rights, a group of self-described militant abortion rights supporters who were mobilizing to confront the "right-wing Operation Rescue" and to defend abortion clinics from attacks.[151] This widespread network deflected narrow attention on abortion and allowed abortion clinics to draw on a range of voices to defend reproductive rights in front of abortion clinics.[152] Despite the threats of antiabortion pickets, Renee Chelian convinced the majority of her colleagues to leave their clinics open. NARAL sent Judith Widdicombe to Detroit to help with the initial organization effort. National pro-choice leaders emphasized the importance of having clinics stay open despite the protestors. "They told us if you close, this will only be the beginning of a campaign to close you down all the time," Chelian recalled.[153] With help from Widdicombe and NARAL, Michigan activists trained clinic escorts drawn from the broad membership of the Michigan Organization for Human Rights and designated a group of supporters to serve as "fake patients" who could sit in clinic waiting rooms and alert staff to any problem.[154]

With a clinic defense network in place, Chelian made an appointment with the local director of public safety, Rollin Tobin, to inform him of the planned events and ask for police protection. To impress Tobin with the urgency of her request, Chelian took along a number of letters from antiabortion activists threatening to close the clinics on the day of the pope's visit. Despite the fact that protecting the clinic was police responsibility, Tobin dismissed her request. The security measures surrounding the pope's visit, he explained, "have taxed our resources to the level that we are not comfortable with the possibility of a major demonstration taking place on your premises. Also, if a major demonstration were to occur, we would not be afforded normal assistance from both Federal and State agencies with regard to their intelligence information. It would be particularly difficult if clergy and other supportive persons become involved in the escorting of clients into the clinic, as it will become impossible to distinguish demonstrators from supporters."[155] The clinic, he suggested, should close. Within hours, the local American Civil Liberties Union chapter filed a lawsuit. Since Chelian's clinic was located in Southfield, a wealthy Detroit suburb home to several major malls, media attention put the city further on the defensive. Business owners began to protest as Detroit papers announced, "Southfield police cannot protect the citizens of Southfield." By the following Monday, the city had reversed course and promised to provide clinics with police protection.[156]

In the end, the careful planning and coordination paid off. On the morning of the pope's visit, twenty-one out of twenty-four Detroit abortion providers opened their clinics. As early as 6:00 A.M., clinics were in touch with one another, volunteer escorts stood by in case protestors showed up, and additional volunteers sat in the clinic waiting rooms to alert staff if antiabortion activists, disguised as patients, should sneak into a clinic. "We had a [police] bus parked outside of our clinic and a lot of Southfield police," Chelian recalls about her clinic. While Chelian's clinic was spared, protestors—many of whom had come from out of town—descended on Summit Medical Center, blocking both clinic entrances in an attempt to shut the center down. Joseph Scheidler from the Pro-Life Action League had organized the sit-in. He was joined by activists who had arrived from as far away as Philadelphia. "The group clashed with 40 escorts who formed human shields and walked women into the clinic, amid jeers and picket signs," the Detroit News reported the next morning.[157] After police arrived and arrested twenty protestors on disorderly conduct charges, the antiabortion demonstrators moved on to a rally at Grand Circus Park, where they confronted about seventy-five demonstrators from women's organizations, civil rights groups, and the gay community who were protesting the pope's visit. Here, Scheidler encountered Eleanor Smeal, past president of NOW, who was addressing the group. "How dare celibate priests tell us what is natural?" Smeal asked while antiabortion protestors dramatically held up two jars containing human fetuses.[158]

Chelian's success in organizing Detroit clinics became a model effort for clinics across the country. At the annual NAF meeting the following year, Chelian, together with the director of media relations at Planned Parenthood New York City, held a workshop on clinic support that taught attendees communication and media skills.[159] The day-long workshop included a number of breakout sessions in which attendees participated in practical exercises that asked them to think through specific scenarios requiring community building and media strategy.[160] One of the biggest challenges,

Chelian cautioned the audience, was to convey to the media and police why clinics could not just close if antiabortion activists called for a day of protest. The media and the police force "were not interested in our rights or a right to choose," she noted. "They all seemed to feel it [the papal visit] was a special occasion and [that it was] no big deal to close for one day! We needed to do a lot of education to the media."[161] Indeed, clinics across the country faced this issue. In order to convince police to take antiabortion activists' threats seriously, a number of clinics screened the 1987 documentary *Holy Terror*, which described the transformation of the antiabortion movement from largely peaceful, focused on prayer and legal change, to the much more aggressive movement of the mid-1980s in which antiabortion protestors firebombed clinics and coordinated techniques to harass clinic staff and patients.[162] Chelian also warned that spearheading an organizing effort like the one in Detroit was likely to be a thankless task. "The unfair part is someone from the provider community has to take the lead to pull it all together and be careful not to take the glory. It was a lot of work, everyone else reaped the benefits, it was a pretty thankless job but it accomplished what was needed. I did constant follow-up phone calls so I had continuing communication with all the providers until the day the Pope came. . . . You have to be willing to spend some money and keep talking when no one else seems interested."[163]

When OR came to Atlanta the following year, Atlanta clinics and law enforcement followed the example of clinics and police in Detroit as they strategized the defense of the city's abortion clinics. Atlanta's abortion providers were not unfamiliar with antiabortion protests. The Atlanta FWHC, for instance, had had protestors on and off since 1984—also the year Joseph Scheidler visited the city for the first time. But the vehemence of OR protests during the summer and fall of 1988 was far worse than any demonstrations staff members had ever experienced. Law enforcement officials, previously quick to suggest that clinics should just close in the event of a protest, were now appalled at protestors' willingness to break the law and determined to stop antiabortion demonstrators in their tracks. In preparation for the demonstrations, Atlanta clinic administrators regularly met with one another, established ties with community groups, and coordinated their strategy with city police officials.[164] Clinics shared escorts and set up a system to share space, allowing staff and patients to move to a different clinic if their own was closed down by a blockade. Atlanta FWHC staff members described the ordeal as nightmarish, hellish, and extremely anxiety producing.[165] Every morning, hundreds of demonstrators tried to make their way to protest in front of the abortion clinics. As protestors descended on downtown Atlanta, police tracked their vehicles and stopped buses carrying antiabortion activists. Eventually, clinics obtained injunctions to keep demonstrators away from their buildings, and police erected metal barricades to prevent protestors from reaching clinic doors. But antiabortion activists were undeterred and began to crawl underneath the metal barriers and between the legs of law enforcement officials to reach clinic doors — a strategy that quickly became known as the "Atlanta crawl." Demonstrations turned into media spectacles broadcast on the nightly news shows, which further fueled the number of antiabortion protests and clinic blockades around the nation.[166] Police arrested over 1,300 OR protestors in the course of that summer. Instructed to refuse cooperation with authorities, OR protestors clogged up Atlanta's court system by claiming to be "Baby Doe" and refusing to give their names. Only after a Georgia state court judge announced that he would bar the arraignment of protestors and keep them in jail indefinitely until they identified themselves did jailed activists give in.[167]

While Atlanta's clinics survived the summer and fall of 1988, the impact of the protests was devastating. Clinics located in downtown Atlanta were hit particularly hard. Atlanta FWHC was a favorite target of protestors because the clinic's name—displayed prominently in front of the building—allowed demonstrators to protest against abortion and feminism simultaneously. "It was two for one," former clinic director Lynn Randall noted. "They could demonstrate against abortion and against feminism at the same time."[168] Business at the clinic declined between 25 and 30 percent, and in August and October 1988—the two months with the heaviest protest activity—the Atlanta FWHC suffered deficits of $23,000 and $61,000, respectively. Clinic administrators were forced to eliminate staff positions and programs. They closed a satellite clinic in Athens, Georgia, where college students from the University of Georgia had been able to receive pregnancy tests and contraceptive advice, and discontinued daycare services for their employees due to protestors' hostile demeanor at the daily arrival of employees with their children.[169]

Clients and staff were overcome by the protests. During the 1988 blockades, some clients entered the clinic crying and shaking, while others—too frightened to confront the crowd of screaming demonstrators—asked to be rescheduled or referred to another clinic.[170] While antiabortion activists claimed they intended to deter patients or convince them that abortion was murder, evidence was lacking that they did anything more than upset patients. "I don't really know that anybody has ever *not* come in and had an abortion because of them," one staff member noted. "[Patients are] clear about their decision, and they know that those people [demonstrators] are telling them lies and that they're wrong and that they're so horrible. . . . It just makes them [patients] feel worse about a situation that may already be painful or difficult."[171]

Despite the fact that OR's Siege on Atlanta officially ended in the fall of 1988, clinic protests continued through the early 1990s. This was true for other cities as well. Detroit, for instance, was overwhelmed with protestors through the late 1980s and early 1990s. Every day during this time period, staff at the cities' abortion clinics had to be prepared for the arrival of hundreds of demonstrators. "It was very stressful for everybody," Lynn Randall of the Atlanta FWHC remembered. As staff members approached the clinic during the morning, "everybody had this pit in [their] stomach coming closer and closer," not knowing whether to expect protestors or a peaceful workday.[172] Clinic workers felt enraged, anxious, and emotionally overwhelmed. Many quit.[173] In Detroit, Chelian and another clinic owner developed an intricate system to move escorts to the clinics targeted for the day before antiabortion activists arrived. They successfully infiltrated the local antiabortion organizations, and their spies reported from the early-morning organizational meetings which clinic was targeted that day. At that point, Chelian would notify her escorts and the local police department, who would rush to the clinic in question to prevent a blockade that might close the clinic down. By the time the clinics were officially opened, the police had usually arrested all protestors, and the clinics had been cleared. But such efforts to keep clinics operating were extremely stressful for all involved. Detroit had about thirty abortion clinics in the late 1980s. Several of these were physician-owned, and these owners preferred to close their clinic when protestors appeared rather than participate in the clinic defense network. Chelian recalls that antiabortion protestors would frequently block those clinics because it meant they could point to a clinic closing as a result of their protest efforts.[174]

Protest activities in the late 1980s and early 1990s led to a high staff turnover in clinics across the country and contributed to a significant decline in the number of physicians willing to provide abortion services. During the two-year period of heaviest protest activity, Atlanta FWHC, which had about forty part-time and full-time staff members at any given time, employed 130 different workers. Only eleven staff members worked at Atlanta FWHC during the entire two-and-a-half-year period of protests.[175] The harassment not only made it difficult to retain staff members but frequently created problems with hiring staff as well. Regularly picketing a facility, as antiabortion activists well understood, was likely to create an environment of low morale for clinic employees and thus further hinder the smooth operation of abortion services. Between 1985 and 1988, the number of abortion providers shrank by 8 percent. In the following years—between 1988 and 1992—it fell even more dramatically, by 18 percent.[176] A 1993 survey conducted by the Alan Guttmacher Institute indicated that 30 percent of abortion providers pointed to antiabortion activity as the most important factor hindering their ability to perform services.[177] Antiabortion activists took credit, the Pro-Life Action League boasting, for instance, that it had closed down eight abortion clinics in Chicago alone and over a hundred across the country.[178]

As spectacular as OR blockades were, however, they also quickly led to the undoing of OR. By the late 1980s, public opinion was slowly turning against the clinic sit-ins, as originally favorable media coverage began to focus on the shoving, grabbing, and screaming matches in front of abortion clinics and journalists depicted OR members as the victimizers in this struggle.[179] Indeed, the chaotic events in front of clinics increased the discomfort of more moderate antiabortion activists, who disliked the emotional tone and cult-like atmosphere of many of the sit-ins. By 1990, many moderate activists had ceased participation. The militant activists who remained were pondering more severe tactics: destroying clinic equipment, dirtying sterilizers, urinating on instruments. Some of the original leaders of the sit-in movement, such as Sam Lee, who had developed their tactics with a Gandhian approach in mind, now grew silent as they realized that tactics were sliding away from the peaceful model they had advocated.[180]

Cities hit by OR blockades also tired of the increasingly aggressive antiabortion activities. Police departments, courts, and county jail systems were forced to direct law enforcement efforts away from their regular beats to monitor, control, and disperse blockades, incurring significant costs as a result. One day of protesting alone could leave a city with around $10,000 in law enforcement and vehicle charges. To discourage future protests, some cities started issuing fines against individual activists and antiabortion organizations. New York City's trial court ordered OR to pay a $50,000 contempt fine after the organization ignored a court order prohibiting the blockade of clinics in New York City. When OR refused to pay the fine, the city continued to raise it, and by 1990 OR owed New York City $450,000.[181] As jail sentences stiffened, many rank-and-file members could no longer keep up with hectic pace of blockades, arrests, and imprisonment, and they began to stay away.[182]

Antiabortion activists' experiences with police and law enforcement further contributed to the splintering of the movement and the radicalization of a smaller group of protestors. To speed up the process of arrests and minimize the chance that officers might get injured, police officers in Atlanta and other cities adopted the use of pain compliance tactics designed to force protestors to walk under their own volition to waiting police vans. Antiabortion activists complained about police brutality and charged prison officials with abuse. Stories of the alleged sexual abuse of female antiabortion activists by male officers in Pittsburgh took on legendary status in the antiabortion movement. Religious studies scholar and terrorism expert Jeffrey Kaplan notes that activists began to identify themselves as victims in the rescue activities, and by late 1989 or early 1990, rescue literature began to take on an increasingly despairing tone as it became clear that salvation would not take place through the courts and the political system. This development contributed to a decisive break between activists committed to clinic-based rescues and the larger pro-life movement that was beginning to distance itself from these maneuvers.[183]

While OR faded into background by the early 1990s, its protest activities had a lasting impact on the tactics and structure of antiabortion activism. The Siege of Atlanta put militant activists in touch with one another and solidified their commitment to incorporate violence into their protest activities. Many fringe activists who went on to commit violent acts befriended one another during the Siege of Atlanta: Shelley Shannon, who in 1993 shot Dr. George Tiller in both arms outside his Wichita Kansas clinic; John Arena, who, in the mid-1990s, was convicted of butyric acid attacks against several abortion clinics; and Father Norman Weslin, who became a leader of the violence-prone antiabortion group Lambs of Christ.[184] Other small groups, such as the Missionaries to the Pre-Born, whose members did not hesitate to turn toward more-violent tactics also emerged. By the early 1990s, as OR had receded, a group of protestors rose to prominence who combined the street-level aggression of Joan Andrews, who traveled from city to city to vandalize clinic property, with the harsh rhetoric of Joseph Scheidler.[185]

Although the Lambs of Christ, who took to the streets in the early 1990s, did not travel in groups of hundreds, their activities brought antiabortion direct action closer to its logical extreme. Led by Father Norman Weslin, the Lambs were a direct action group within a Catholic organization called Victim Souls of the Unborn Christ Child.[186] The group drew together people who dedicated themselves to full-time activism. Lambs followed a trend toward sanctified rescue, understanding their activism as acts of worship. They sold their property, stored their belongings, and left jobs and family to commit themselves to go wherever the "need seemed greatest."[187] Their vocabulary illustrated their militant approach. They referred to sit-ins as sieges, themselves as Baby Doe and Father Norman Weslin as Father Doe. Lambs distinguished themselves by initiating continuous, long-term blockades of clinics and private residences to intimidate patients and abortion providers and make their movement in and out of clinics as difficult as possible. They also adopted a long-term approach of noncooperation with legal authorities, not only refusing to give their names to authorities because, like babies, they could not speak but also refusing to walk and, at times, to use bathroom facilities if this level of noncooperation promised to increase the level of disturbance.[188] It was left to this group of extreme activists, then, to escalate protests to a level of harassment and violence that, by the early 1990s, included the killing of abortion providers and staff working at abortion clinics.

6

Truths, Lies, and Partial Truths

The Debate Surrounding Intact D&E

On a fall morning in early October 1991, Dr. Susan Wicklund woke with a start to the sound of people shouting outside her bedroom window. "Susan kills babies! Susan kills babies!" Wicklund and her husband lived in an isolated farmhouse at the end of a three-mile dirt road outside rural Cambridge, Minnesota. It was still dark, and Wicklund, who had been terrorized by antiabortion protestors for the past year, thought she was waking from a nightmare. But then she heard the chants again: "Susan kills babies!" "A cold nausea swept through me," she remembers in her autobiography. "Nausea and gut level fear."[1] Terrified, she woke her husband, asked him to call the police, crept out of bed to check on her daughter, and then hid in the only place without any windows, the shower stall. "I sat down in the stall, hugging my knees to my chest, trying to swallow the anger and fear, fighting as hard as I could to hold on to some control."[2]

Wicklund had begun to perform abortions at the Summit Women's Health Organization in Milwaukee, Wisconsin, in June 1989. By 1991, she was traveling to four abortion clinics in the Midwest. Clinic directors had warned her about the harassment she would experience. But at first, contact with the protestors was fairly uneventful. During the first weeks, demonstrators in front of Summit did not understand that she was the abortion provider. When she tried to enter the clinic, they assumed she was a patient coming for an abortion. "Mommy, don't kill your baby. Let us help you. You'll die in there!" they shouted at her as she approached the front door of the clinic. "You'll bleed to death. You'll never get pregnant again. Mommy, Mommy, don't kill me!"[3] But by the summer of 1990, protestors had figured out that Wicklund was one of the doctors. When she left an airport to go to a clinic or walked from her car to a clinic entrance, they went into a frenzy. "Murderer!" they screamed. "Baby killer!"[4]

The protestors quickly became better organized and more sophisticated. They deciphered Wicklund's irregular schedule and knew when to expect her at various clinics. They called ahead to their collaborators when she left one airport for another and followed her in cars. Within a year of her first visit to the Summit Women's Health Organization, protestors were no longer simply circling the entrance and shouting their insults. They had begun to build human barriers to block access to the clinic. Sometimes the police would arrest and remove the protestors. On other days, Wicklund would have to climb over their bodies to enter the clinic.[5] Protestors also began to physically accost her. One day, when she got to the clinic hiding in the back of a cab underneath a blanket, two protestors discovered her. As she approached the clinic's back door, one man grabbed her and slammed her against a parked van. "His face in my face, screaming at me. 'YOU KILLER! YOU KILLER!' 'YOU DESERVE TO DIE.' 'STOP KILLING BABIES, SUSAN!'" Over and over again, the screaming man slammed her against the van as she struggled to break free and alert staff inside the clinic. Eventually, staff appeared at the back door and helped her get inside. "Scared, So scared," she wrote into her journal following the incident. "Hard to write, hard to think, Heart pounding . . . Nightmare, Trying to settle down. Need to gather myself enough to see patients. Need to cry, can't stop shaking."[6] Following this incident, Wicklund began to wear disguises. She rode in the trunk of cars and made sure to arrive as early as 5:00 A.M. before clinic staff or protestors would be there. But her sense of safety was gone.[7] By late September, protestors—members of the direct action group Lambs of Christ—appeared in her hometown. They leafleted Cambridge, putting up "wanted" posters all over. "Wanted for the Murder of Children," a poster read underneath a photo of Wicklund.

When a police officer finally arrived on that October morning, Wicklund and her husband discovered that protestors had placed a bassinet on their front porch with a doll splattered with red paint and surrounded by play money. With the help of a police escort, Wicklund and her daughter were eventually able to leave their house. But the protestors stayed. Indeed, for weeks they blocked Wicklund's house day and night. Sometimes fifty to sixty demonstrators would bar her comings and goings with their bodies.[8] Although the police regularly sent a police escort to drive Wicklund's daughter to school and help Wicklund leave her property, it became difficult for Wicklund to arrive at work on time.

I often stayed alone at friends' homes so I could be sure of getting to work in the mornings. I took a different route to and from the airport each time, sometimes driving for hours feeling hunted, watching the cars behind me. Every time I went to my car, I checked the tires, looked for nails on the ground. Each time I turned the key I waited for the bomb explosion, held my breath while the engine caught. The protestors became more and more bold and self-righteous. At every airport I had to run the gauntlet. Life had turned into an awful game.[9]

More than three weeks into this ordeal, Wicklund noticed a large group of protestors with a motor home gather at her driveway on a Wednesday night and place huge cement-filled barrels to block her way out. She lost her patience. Scheduled to arrive at the Fargo Women's Health Clinic the following morning at 9:00 A.M., she took a loaded gun and escaped through the back woods under the cover of darkness. Incensed, she went public with her story. "Every shred of normalcy had been stripped from our lives," she remembered. "As long as I kept it behind a curtain, hidden from view, the protestors could remain hidden and immune to consequences."[10] In early February 1992, NBC's 60 Minutes aired an hour-long segment about Wicklund's experience of being harassed by the Lambs of Christ.[11]

During the 1990s, the escalation of antiabortion protests and protestors' increasing use of violence significantly stigmatized and isolated abortion providers and clinic staff. Providers looked for support to their professional organizations but found NAF ill equipped to meet the emotional needs of providers and staff suffering from the constant threat of violence. In addition, as antiabortion activists drew attention to the pregnancy termination procedures used after the first trimester, abortion providers and staff felt increasingly isolated and abandoned by their organization. For its part, NAF was unable to present a unified front to meet these challenges. How to best respond to antiabortion activists in the 1990s became a contentious issue within the organization. Frustrated, many clinic owners and abortion providers forged new institutional ties as they sought new conversations and answers beyond the confines of NAF.

Asking the Hard Questions: The Emergence of the November
Gang and the National Coalition of Abortion Providers

With the transition from OR protest activities to the attacks of such groups as the Lambs of Christ, the safety of individual providers was increasingly threatened. While individual clinic owners and directors tried to help abortion providers deal with these threatening situations, their ability to resolve the situation was extremely limited. Wicklund found Susan Hill, executive director of the NWHO, and clinic directors for whom she worked extremely understanding. Jane Bovard, director of the FWHO where most of the Lambs of Christ protest activity originated, "bent over backwards" to assure Wicklund's safety as she traveled to and from the clinic. Bovard sent out staff to meet Wicklund in different places, varied the cars in which Wicklund was transported from the meeting point to the clinic, and helped her come up with disguises so that protestors would not recognize her. Susan Hill sent her personal security guard to assess the situation and accompany Wicklund for part of the time. During the siege of Wicklund's residence by the Lambs of Christ, Hill herself came to stay at Wicklund's house. Hill "slept on my couch and would walk with me in the morning with the dog around the perimeter of the property to see how many protestors there were, where they were, and see about getting out. And she would call the local police and get us some help sometimes if we couldn't get out and then would travel with me up to Fargo," Wicklund remembered. Wicklund found Hill's presence helpful. "She was fearless," Wicklund reported. "And she was good at putting stuff in perspective."[12] But these were individual responses to particular moments of crisis, not strategies available to everybody all the time. Clinic owners and abortion providers became increasingly frustrated at the lack of an institutional response from NAF. As Claire Keyes recalls, when her Pittsburgh clinic was firebombed in September 1989, NAF officers responded to Keyes's call for help by promising, "I will send you some forms."[13]

Although NAF developed a range of programs to help members respond to the increase in antiabortion violence, many members felt that the organization was not responsive enough and failed to understand the pressures abortion providers were under. The program at annual meetings, planned a year in advance, frequently did not reflect the most recent developments that members urgently wanted to discuss. And while the workshops and NAF written materials offered resources and advice on how to deal with protests and clinic blockades, a discussion about the personal and emotional impact that the virulent antiabortion activism had on abortion providers, clinic staff, and their families was noticeably absent. Frustrated by the lack of acknowledgment of the devastating impact of antiabortion violence, Charlotte Taft of the Dallas Routh Street Women's Clinic brought a collection of colorful stickers to one NAF meeting: blue stickers for death threats, red stickers for vandalism, black stickers for bombs. "And I put these all out and invited people to put them on their nametags so that as we walked around during the meeting we could see what had been going on. And it was just chilling."[14] Members who experienced significant antiabortion protests at their clinics were also frustrated that until the second half of the 1980s, NAF meetings were open to antiabortion protestors. Guided by a civil libertarian approach and the feeling that the organization had nothing to hide, NAF took until 1986 or 1987 to institute security measures that excluded outsiders from meetings.[15]

The organization also sought to develop a unified public relations response, which became more urgent as the conflict surrounding abortion grew more volatile. To avoid the impression that abortion providers were giving way to antiabortion pressure, for instance, clinics were advised to stay open during blockades and to tell the press that "all scheduled patients were seen, no one was turned away."[16] Such advice overlooked the impact protestors had on clinics' ability to continue operations. In cities such as Atlanta or Buffalo, where antiabortion efforts were prolonged, the economic fallout was severe. "Clinics suffered terribly," Margaret (Peg) Johnston noted, "many of them losing leases, patients, and going out of business."[17] To add insult to injury, the national pro-choice organizations like NARAL, PPFA, and the Fund for the Feminist Majority quickly discovered that large-scale protests offered great fund-raising opportunities. At the height of the Atlanta Siege in 1988, for instance, when OR blockaded the city's clinics with massive demonstrations, NARAL reportedly raised thousands of dollars a day.[18] The resources it collected, however, were not distributed to Atlanta clinics. Beleaguered clinics, their directors, and the abortion providers who worked for them had to shoulder the skyrocketing security costs and burdens of protests on their own.

By the late 1980s, abortion providers, frustrated by an organization that seemed increasingly out of touch with their needs, began to leave NAF. While NAF membership had grown by 136 percent (from 130 clinics to a high of 307 clinics) between 1978 and 1986, by 1990 membership had dropped by 14 percent to 254 clinics. In November 1989, Charlotte Taft and Sandra Bagley from the Utah Women's Health Center in Salt Lake City invited sixty NAF members to a meeting at a Dallas airport hotel. During a year when NAF members were chafing under OR, Taft had just returned from a NAF risk management meeting devoted to opening clinics in Canada. Although OR reached the height of its protest activity that year, conducting 201 clinic blockades that seriously disrupted clinics' operations and resulted in 12,358 arrests, the risk management meeting had not addressed these debilitating protests.[19] "When I read the program," Taft recalls, "I was so freaked out because I thought: 'Do they have any idea what we are dealing with? Do they have any idea how many of us have had bomb threats and death threats and vandalism and Operation Rescue and butyric acid?'"[20] Taft's and Bagley's invitation tapped into a widespread sense of frustration. Attendees at the Dallas meeting spent the weekend talking about the emotional toll of antiabortion activism on their life and work. The meeting culminated in the formation of the November Gang—a group of counselors and clinic owners who embarked on extended conversations about the emotional issues related to abortion. "For me that was when the hard work . . . separated away from NAF," Taft recalls.[21]

NAF members who left or withdrew from the organization were frustrated that antiabortion demonstrations and attacks had put abortion providers into a defensive position, had stigmatized abortion care, and had significantly narrowed the discourse surrounding abortion. They were tired of a defensive stance that painted abortion providers as unaffected by antiabortion attacks but standing stoically against demonstrations and boycotts. In an essay titled "Opting out of the Abortion War," Peg Johnston argued that the rhetoric of an abortion war had contributed to a narrowing of the discourse surrounding abortion. In that discourse, abortion providers were depicted as—and played the role of—super heroes. But super heroes, she cautioned were not human. "Be human in the midst of a guerilla campaign against us," she urged her colleagues. "Without the super-mythic image of warriors who can fend off bullets, bombs, and blockades, we will be seen as caring people who do important work."[22] While frustrated NAF members concluded that abortion providers had to be portrayed in a more positive and honest light, they differed in the ways in which they might achieve this goal. The November Gang focused their attention inside the clinics. "The only impact I can have on the outside is what goes on inside," Chelian explained. "I have no control over those people outside. So, what can I do to make the clinics safe and make sure that my staff feels safe, my family feels safe, I feel safe, and that we're as protected as we can be? So, put those things in motion."[23]

Focusing on the inside of clinics drew the attention of clinic workers to the impact that a decade of aggressive antiabortion activism had had on women's feelings toward abortion. Patient attitude, abortion counselors noted, had changed significantly. If in the 1970s most patients had looked at abortion as a woman's right, by the late 1980s abortion had been significantly stigmatized, and many patients perceived it as a shameful, immoral, and selfish act. Noticeably more women were emotionally torn over their abortion decision. They worried that they were killing their baby or feared that God might punish them if they had an abortion. In addition, a growing number of women publicly articulated their abortion regret. After the 1987 publication of David Reardon's *Aborted Women, Silent No More*, such groups as WEBA claimed that women suffered from physical and psychological aftereffects as a result of their abortions. By the late 1980s, organizations like WEBA gave significant visibility to the notion that women would come to regret their abortions. "Every woman is right now encouraged to think that every negative thing that happens to her after an abortion is caused by the abortion," Taft commented.[24] At a November Gang meeting, she cautioned that clinics needed to guard against the creation of WEBAs. Counselors, she suggested, had to identify the small number of women who were so deeply ambivalent that they would not be able to come to terms with their abortions. Taft looked at patients' ambivalence as attitudinal contraindications to abortion that should be accorded the same weight that clinics accorded to medical contraindications. "To me the idea of doing an abortion on a woman without her owning her choice is what creates a WEBA," Taft noted. "Those women had not owned that choice."[25]

To guide women through a sometimes difficult decision-making process and offer counseling methods that might help detect potential WEBAs, members of the November Gang turned their attention to a new counseling model: head and heart counseling. Coined in the 1980s by Charlotte Taft at the Routh Street Clinic, head and heart counseling sought to connect women's decision to have an abortion—their head—with their heart—the part that had to come to terms with the decision. Taft formalized and expanded the process by generating a set of questions that could help counselors address topics with abortion patients which counselors might find difficult to discuss. "What is murder?" "Is a Fetus a person? If so, when does it become a person?" "What does your conscience say to you about abortion?" And, "Is abortion a sin? If so, what is a sin?"[26] Such questions, Taft and her colleagues recognized, were often foremost on patients' minds, and counseling staff had to be able to discuss them. Opening the possibility of such discussions meant that patients began to open up in ways they had not done before.[27]

The new counseling methods also provided clinics with a framework to screen out patients who seemed too conflicted about their abortion decision. While Taft estimated that fewer than 1 percent of all abortion patients were women who asked for, but probably should not have, an abortion, the notion that an abortion provider would send away a patient asking for a pregnancy termination—unless that patient had a medical contraindication or was too far along—seemed antithetical to a movement based on the premise that every woman should have access to abortion. But the rise of the antiabortion movement and the stigmatization of abortion had complicated these assumptions. To be sure, some abortion providers had always taken the liberty of refusing to perform an abortion if the woman was particularly hostile or displayed other behaviors that a provider might find problematic or offensive. With head and heart counseling, however, clinics gained a framework to identify and exclude women who seemed to lack a sense of resolution about their abortions. Indeed, a number of counselors and abortion providers had developed counseling techniques that allowed them to ascertain that patients "owned" their decision to have an abortion.[28] Now Taft developed a checklist of questions for clinics to ask patients at the initial check-in. Was the patient against abortion but felt she had no other choice? Was someone pressuring her into an abortion she herself did not want? Did she believe abortion was the same as murdering a born person? Did she believe that she would later regret the abortion or that it would separate her forever from her god or higher power? Women's answers to these questions indicated whether they needed additional counseling. If they did, they were asked to fill out a workbook that required them to think through some of these issues prior to a counseling session.[29] To help them clarify their feelings, patients might also be asked to write a letter saying goodbye to the fetus they were aborting. If women were unwilling to participate in the counseling process or seemed unresolved about their abortions, Taft's clinic refused to perform the abortion. For some women, she cautioned, "no amount of counseling or workbook exercises or letter writing truly gives her a sense of confidence and resolution about having an abortion."[30]

While the adoption of head and heart counseling offered abortion providers a framework for in-depth discussions about the meaning of abortion and fetal death, not all agreed that this was appropriate in a counseling session. Many found head and heart counseling invasive and manipulative. Some joked about the cumbersome nature of the counseling process, which seemed to imply that a woman was unable to get an abortion "unless she thought about it for five months and did psychoanalysis and everything else."[31] Others thought it a political mistake to engage with patients in discussions about killing.[32] Terry Beresford, who had for several years served as the director for Preterm in Washington, D.C., and spent most of her life training abortion counselors, found head and heart counseling "contrary to the basic philosophy of the women's health philosophy" in which the patient was in charge.[33] Many agreed that one did not have to "counsel women to death, that they're strong, that they know what they are doing."[34] To be sure, while the development of head and heart counseling constituted an attempt by clinics to respond to challenges brought on by the antiabortion movement, changes in reimbursements and the tighter financial situation of abortion clinics meant that most clinics moved to less rather than more counseling. Those most likely to adopt part of the head and heart counseling model were the clinics associated with the Abortion Care Network, which eventually grew out of the November Gang.[35]

If providers and clinic staff affiliated with the November Gang sought a forum in which to address the more emotionally charged issues of abortion provision, other disaffected NAF members longed for political representation. Clinic owners and operators, other than those connected with Planned Parenthood, were conspicuously absent in Washington, D.C. NAF did not engage in lobbying activities, and NARAL, which did employ a lobbyist, wanted to have as little as possible to do with the actual provision of abortion services. Indeed, even though some abortion providers were NARAL board members, the organization had a reputation of trying to distance itself from abortion clinics. "They really thought it sort of sullied them," Susan Hill recalled about her attempt to familiarize fellow NARAL board members with the work of abortion providers. Hill, who believed it might be useful for NARAL board members to see the actual operation of a clinic, repeatedly invited fellow board members to visit one of her clinics. But board members refused. "There were questions about: were we financially gaining things [making a profit from abortion]. And they didn't want that."[36] In early 1990, Hill received a phone call from Ron Fitzsimmons, a former lobbyist for NARAL. Fitzsimmons was working for a law firm in Washington, D.C., and wanted to get back to work on abortion. Did Hill have any suggestions, he wondered. Hill suggested that abortion providers get together and hire Fitzsimmons as a lobbyist. Within weeks, Fitzsimmons had contacted a number of other abortion providers, promising to be their voice in Washington, D.C., if they paid part of his salary. In July of that year, Hill invited a small number of abortion providers to Washington, D.C., to found the National Coalition of Abortion Providers (NCAP), with Fitzsimmons as the executive director.[37]

Fitzsimmons quickly became an effective spokesperson. Shortly after the founding of NCAP, he embarked on a tour of abortion clinics around the country to learn about the work and concerns of abortion providers. By the summer of 1990, he was sending out regular newsletters to NCAP members. In May, he wrote about hearings for the Freedom of Choice Act

(FOCA), first proposed in 1989 to codify in federal law that every woman had a fundamental right to terminate a pregnancy prior to fetal viability, if she so chose, or after viability when necessary to protect her life or health.[38] In June, he informed members about recent legislative efforts to protect women from antiabortion protestors and about the race between conservative Republican North Carolina senator Jesse Helms and his Democratic challenger Harvey Gantt, who had served as the first black mayor of Charlotte. And in September, he sent around a survey to poll members on their experiences getting insurance coverage for their clinics. By the following year, he had directed attention to the deceptive practices of crisis pregnancy centers. In the summer of 1991, Fitzsimmons called on NCAP members to collect patient testimony about CPCs for an upcoming hearing before the Subcommittee on Small Businesses. Together with subcommittee chair Democratic congressman Ron Wyden from Oregon, he successfully lobbied the Yellow Pages to introduce a subheading for "abortion alternatives" in its listings to differentiate ads from CPCs from those of abortion clinics.[39] Fitzsimmons interspersed his political news updates with funny anecdotes of his travels, which lent the newsletters a lighthearted note. He also organized events that connected NCAP members with Capitol Hill. At one early NCAP event, members visited the U.S. Supreme Court and stood for a formal group portrait inside the court. At another, after the election of President Bill Clinton, members met with Joycelyn Elders, who served as U.S. surgeon general during the early years of the Clinton administration.[40] Most members came from smaller towns across the United States and appreciated these events as tangible introductions to the world of politics. NCAP membership quickly grew. By 1992, the organization had 116 members, many of them small independent providers. But the membership also included a number of clinic chains.[41]

While up-to-date political information and a more direct link to Capitol Hill drew providers to NCAP, members also expressed the desire to leave defensive gestures behind. Abortion providers, Fitzsimmons emphasized, should be proud of their work, and NCAP and its members should display this pride. Fitzsimmons took this message on his clinic tours. "I need to know exactly what you do out here," he told George Tiller on a visit to Women's Health Care Services in Wichita, Kansas. "I know you do third trimester abortions. I need to know why. I need to see why. Because if I'm going to defend you on Capitol Hill, I need to know everything you do."[42] Many providers appreciated this approach as refreshingly open, and by the early 1990s, NCAP joined the November Gang in addressing some of the most sensitive questions about abortion.

To help its members respond to the emotionally powerful charges of the antiabortion movement that abortion killed babies, NCAP followed the lead of the November Gang and initiated a debate about the meaning of killing. Debating these issues, many November Gang and NCAP members felt, was unavoidable if providers wanted to counter the negative image of abortion and equip the millions of women who had had abortions, as well as their partners, relatives, and friends, with the ability to speak publicly about their choices and experiences. Taft likened antiabortion activists to ants looking for crumbs—the difficult issues surrounding abortion that those providing abortion services were loath to discuss. "If there are issues that are difficult—like abortion and disability, fetal pain, abortion and genocide—if there are things that we are unwilling to talk about, the antiabortion people will see the vacuum and swoop right in there and we have no one to blame because it just meant we were too scared to talk about it."[43] With the proliferation of ultrasound images in popular culture, abortion providers had to address antiabortion messages that abortion was murder. "We thought that the other groups were making a mistake," Chelian explained concerning the silence of abortion rights activists on the topic of fetal death. Encouraged by the opening of the conversation that came with the introduction of head and heart counseling, a small group of NCAP members began to work on a resolution that directly addressed the idea that abortion ended a human life.

These conversations and the subsequent passage of the resolution gave NCAP members the courage "to go out and speak more bluntly about abortion."[44] At a NCAP meeting in the fall of 1992, Fitzsimmons introduced the resolution to NCAP members. "Opponents of abortion believe," the resolution stated, "that human life begins at conception and that what we do is 'murder.' We disagree with that interpretation, as does the U.S. Supreme Court and religious experts around the world. While most of us do not believe that 'life' begins at conception, we do acknowledge the obvious—that abortion is the termination of a *potential* human life. And every woman who enters our clinics knows what she is doing when she decides to terminate her pregnancy."[45] "It sounds [like] nothing today," Fitzsimmons recalled, "but it was electric. . . . It was like, holy shit, we are saying it."[46] NCAP members passed the resolution without any further discussion. But not all agreed with this tactic. Although they remained silent, some NCAP members continued to feel that a public debate about killing was a tactical mistake.[47]

I Was So Scared: Escalation of Violence
and the Killing of David Gunn

On February 2, 1993, two weeks after the inauguration of President Bill Clinton, Susan Wicklund opened her own abortion clinic, Mountain Country Women's Clinic, in Bozeman, Montana. Eager to provide abortions in a setting where every step of patient care was under her control, Wicklund had taken over the office of a physician and abortion provider who was now retiring. To prevent antiabortion activists from tracing her to Bozeman, she had taken all the security precautions she could think of. In 1993, Montana had no antistalking laws, and Wicklund could be followed and approached with impunity.[48] To protect her anonymity, she kept her Minnesota driver's license, had an unlisted phone number, and made sure all accounts and bills were directed to the clinic address. Still, without friends and relatives in Bozeman, she felt exposed. And within two weeks, Wicklund received her first threatening letter from Missoula antiabortion activist Michael Ross. "Dear Susan Wicklund," Ross wrote. "Welcome to Bozeman. Those of us who value human life will never rest until we shut down your abortuary. . . . You cruel, gross, depraved person. We lay every broken, headless, legless, armless, crushed unborn baby on your doorstep. When you lift your vile hands, they run scarlet red with the blood of the innocents."[49] Ross promised to write often—and he did. His letters came two or three at a time. He would "scrawl out descriptions of how he was going to kill me," Wicklund remembered. "Tear off my arms and legs, squish my head, and watch the brains come out like Jell-O, set me on fire and listen to me scream."[50] "Dear Ethnic Cleanser," he wrote to her in early March, "You are guilty of MASS MURDER. We the people insist that you cease suffocating to death and slowly bring to death unborn Americans. How would *you* like to be slowly tortured to death by burning in saline? That's what you do, you killer. You should feel the same pain. All of it. All."[51]

On March 10, 1993, when Wicklund's clinic had barely been open for five weeks, abortion provider David Gunn was shot and killed outside Pensacola Women's Medical Services in Pensacola, Florida. Gunn, about to enter the clinic, was shot down by antiabortion activist Michael Griffin. A thirty-one-year-old factory worker, Griffin was a zealous follower of antiabortion activist John Burt who began to picket Pensacola's abortion clinics in 1983 and encouraged a small group of extremists to violent activism, including the bombing of three Pensacola clinics on Christmas Eve in 1984.[52] The news of Gunn's death shocked the abortion provider community. "I remember shaking and thinking: 'Oh my god, they really did it,'" Susan Hill recalls the moment her assistant reached her on the phone to tell her the news. "I was just begging her to tell me that he was breathing. But she said, 'No I'm telling you, they said to tell you that he's not alive.' The rest was like a blur."[53] Wicklund was on a trip in Iowa when she received the news of Gunn's death. She remembers standing in a phone booth, her knees buckling as she sank down shaking and tears flowing.[54] When she returned from her trip several nights later, Wicklund discovered that someone had broken into her Bozeman apartment and left a stack of antiabortion pamphlets on the bedside stand. "I turned and fled," she recalled.[55] That week, she received a letter from Mike Ross commenting: "Too bad about Dr. Gunn in Florida. I wonder, could it happen in Bozeman? I wonder . . ."[56] "I was real scared," Wicklund remembered.[57]

Providers across the country were devastated. Hill immediately called all NWHO clinics and doctors to inform them about the killing. "Those were really hard calls," Hill remembered.[58] "Doctors and their wives were on the phone with me at 12:00 at night, crying, all of them crying. It was horrible, it was just horrible. And I couldn't really promise them that they were safe."[59] Hill increased security at her clinics, purchased metal detectors for those clinics not yet equipped with such devices, bought bulletproof vests for her physicians, removed signs for designated physician parking spaces, and moved physician parking close to clinic doors. Worried about their own and their families' security, several physicians working for NWHO stopped providing abortion services immediately following the murder of David Gunn. Several more stopped by the summer of 1993.[60] "And then I had to figure out, can I keep running without these doctors," Hill recalled.[61]

Five days later, Hill was joined by Takey Crist, Ron Fitzsimmons, David Gunn's son David Gunn Jr., and antiabortion activist Paul Hill on the Phil Donahue Show. Lined up onstage, the five guests discussed the murder of David Gunn with a studio audience. While the show rehashed familiar arguments about abortion and a woman's right to choose, the event stood out for Paul Hill's persistent defense of the murder. Comparing Gunn to the infamous Nazi doctor Joseph Mengele, Paul Hill argued that Griffin's shooting of Dr. Gunn was "as good as Dr. Mengele being killed."[62] Indeed, Griffin's actions radicalized Paul Hill, who only sixteen months later, on July 29, 1994, shot and killed abortion provider John Britton and his bodyguard, James Barrett, at the Pensacola Ladies Center. His actions, he explained to Connie Chung in a December interview for the news show *Eye to Eye*, were "honorable."[63] Since they were intended to defend the innocent—babies that were about to be killed by their mothers—he argued he was guilty of no crime. "I have done something that I think the Lord is pleased with," he concluded in his interview.[64]

The killing of David Gunn led to an immediate escalation of harassment and violence against abortion providers personally. "Less than 24 hours after Dr. Gunn's murder," Jerry Rasmussen, who performed abortions in Minneapolis, Minnesota, recalled, "I had nails poured in my driveway, mixed with snow and ice. Two Minnesota doctors had the same thing happen. I received a telephone call at 1:10 A.M. telling me not to kill babies and sometime before 7:00 A.M. that morning, someone hurled a huge hunk of cement block through my dining room window with a note telling me not to kill babies. The force of this hurled cement sent shattered glass into my living room nearly 30 feet away."[65] On March 29 of that year, an antiabortion activist firebombed and completely destroyed the Blue Mountain Clinic in Missoula, Montana. "Isn't that just horrible how someone torched Blue Mountain Clinic in Missoula?" Michael Ross asked Wicklund in a letter the following day. "Isn't that awful? Tsk, tsk. Do you think it could happen in Bozeman?"[66] In May, someone fired shots into the playroom of the home of a Kansas City abortion provider. In August, antiabortion activist Shelley Shannon shot Wichita, Kansas, abortion provider George Tiller through both arms. In Mobile, Alabama, an assailant murdered Dr. George Wayne Patterson and shots were fired through the Mobile Center for Choice.[67] That year, antiabortion violence spiked with two murders or attempted murders; thirteen bombings, arsons, or attempted arsons; and 415 incidences of clinic invasions, assaults, vandalism, death threats, burglary, and stalking.[68] The following year, Paul Hill murdered Dr. John Britton and his bodyguard, James Barrett, and John Salvi killed two receptionists, Lee Ann Nichols and Shannon Lowney, at Planned Parenthood clinics in Brookline, Massachusetts. Seven others were wounded in the 1994 attacks.[69]

In response to the murder of David Gunn, Senator Edward Kennedy (D-Mass.) introduced the Freedom of Access to Clinic Entrances (FACE) Act on March 23, 1993. Pointing to the escalation of violence against abortion clinics and the inability of local law enforcement to meet these challenges, he noted the extensive damage that abortion clinics had suffered since the late 1970s. "Over 100 clinics have been torched or bombed in the past 15 years," he observed. "Over 300 have been invaded and over 400 have been vandalized. Already this year, clinics have sustained more than $1.3 million in damages from arson alone."[70] One week later, the Subcommittee on Crime and Criminal Justice, led by Democratic representative

Charles E. Schumer from New York, opened hearings on clinic violence. To illustrate that the federal government was finally listening, the hearings were broadcast on radio and TV, as a long list of witnesses testified to their experiences of antiabortion violence. An ob-gyn in Dallas, Texas, who provided some first trimester abortions, described antiabortion activists who had become more brazen in the months following David Gunn's murder. "I was told if I agreed not to perform abortions," he testified before the committee,

they would leave me alone. Otherwise I was to be the target of focus activity by this group similar to that directed against other physicians in the Dallas area. When I refused . . . the activities directed against me and my family began. Flyers were distributed throughout Presbyterian Hospital where I have an office; they described me as the spirit of the murderer of Presbyterian Hospital and included my photograph, home and office addresses, and telephone numbers. Wanted posters were put up all over Dallas with my photograph, home and workplaces and phone numbers labeling me as an abortionist which I am not. I am an Ob-Gyn in private practice. I became a target of focus activities, which include picketing at my hospital during the week and my home on weekends and during the week and at my church on Sundays. Even my wife has been the target of focus picketing at her office where she works for the Boy Scouts of America. I have received harassing and threatening telephone calls at my office and at my home at all hours of the day and night. My wife received similar calls at her office. Typically we receive between five to fifteen telephone calls per day. We have been receiving hate mail. We have been kept under surveillance at our home as antiabortion sympathizers sit behind our home with binoculars. We have been followed to work, to church, to the grocery store, to dinner parties, and even to the police station. The antiabortion activities that have been directed toward me have deprived us of any sense of privacy. . . . They have now reached the point where for our own safety we took vigorous security measures which include the use of bodyguards. These measures are necessary because of direct threats from antiabortion sympathizers, threats including telling my neighbors they should shoot me, threats to shoot my wife, and telephone and mail threats including a recent letter from the Ku Klux Klan. In short, I have become a prisoner in my own home because I believe a woman has the right to choose.[71]

A number of factors contributed to the gradual erosion of barriers against the use of deadly force. Religious studies and terrorism scholar

Jeffrey Kaplan describes a process of radicalization that began in the late 1980s with the arrest and prosecution of OR activists. Kaplan notes that the transformation from peaceful protest to violence took place in the aftermath of the 1988 Siege of Atlanta during which antiabortion protestors who understood themselves as rescuing American babies were for the first time exposed to police tactics involving pain compliance and to the conditions in American jails. Their experience in Atlanta radicalized some of them and contributed to the formation of a smaller militaristic network of antiabortion activists who saw the troubles of the rescue movement in apocalyptic terms, as a sign of the End Times.[72] OR, feminist scholar Carol Mason notes, employed an apocalyptic narrative that posited antiabortion activists as the light against the darkness of the abortion provider community.[73]

Debates among antiabortion activists about the use of deadly force had first emerged among imprisoned rescuers and a handful of antiabortion activists on the outside. These discussions continued in the early 1990s, when the election of President Bill Clinton and the subsequent passage of the FACE bill put the federal government in direct opposition to the activities of antiabortion activists. Having been unable to stop legal abortion during the previous twelve years of the Reagan and Bush administrations, Kaplan notes, antiabortion activists became "despairing of the efficacy of non-violent witness, convinced of their persecution by the courts and of their victimization through extraordinary violence from police and clinic guards, and facing an administration in Washington determined to protect abortion access by the criminalization of rescue activities."[74] This sense of urgency combined with a sharpened rhetoric, as some in the antiabortion movement described the work of abortion providers as satanic and those involved in abortion care as literal witches and Satanists.[75] Such rhetoric contributed to the process of dehumanization of abortion providers and clinic staff and confirmed the necessity that antiabortion activists act. Just as Paul Hill had done when he compared David Gunn to the infamous Nazi doctor Joseph Mengele, activists also drew on parallels between abortion and the Nazi Holocaust, referring to abortion care as an "American Holocaust," which justified the use of force as a form of opposition.[76] Several scholars have pointed out that there are links in ideology and tactics between the more extreme segment of the antiabortion movement, the militia movement, the Christian Identity movement, the Aryan movement, and the Ku Klux Klan and that members have migrated between antiabortion causes and white supremacist groups. In claiming that abortion is a holocaust of the unborn, or a new genocide, members of these groups expressed particular concern for the white fetus, attributing abortion with "racial genocide" fears dating back to the late nineteenth and early twentieth centuries.[77] In response to this increase in violent rhetoric, a small segment of the rescue movement began to embrace the use of lethal force. The sudden escalation of clinic violence in turn drew in marginal personalities. John Salvi, for example, who carried out the attacks in Brookline, was peripheral to the antiabortion network.[78]

For radical antiabortion activists, the move to violence was accompanied by an almost mystical identification with the unborn. Some activists maintained they could hear the cries of babies inside clinic walls. Shelley Shannon, for instance, claimed to have heard such cries and been encouraged to shoot George Tiller after listening to a taped sermon comparing abortion clinics to satanic altars. Kaplan observes that the notes and letters of other rescuers bear this out as well.[79] Others described a conscious process of total identification with the fetus as they prepared themselves for violent activities. As John Brockhoeft noted about his thoughts prior to bombing abortion clinics:

> I put myself in the baby's place, reminding myself that I had to love that baby as myself. "My arms will be torn away from my torso tomorrow! My skull will be crushed until fragments cave inward and cut into my brain!" I imagined how terrible the physical pain would be! I thought of my right arm being dismembered, and as I thought of it, I bore in mind that my arm would not be taken off cleanly with a sharp surgical instrument while under anesthesia. No, it would be brutally torn out of the shoulder socket and twisted off. It would hurt so bad. But I did not think only of the terrible physical pain. I imagined the terrible mental horror and terror of looking at my right shoulder, and my right arm is gone! And blood is gushing out of where it had been! . . . If I, like the baby, was going to suffer so much and then die tomorrow morning, and I knew I was being killed unjustly, I would not be too afraid to go to the death chamber with gasoline and destroy it tonight.[80]

The group of extremists who began to kill abortion providers and clinic staff and those who supported their violent actions articulated a theory of justifiable homicide that lent antiabortion rhetoric a new sinister tone. "Babies were not murdered on the day David Gunn was shot and a serial killer would never kill again," Donna Bray, an affiliate of the loosely connected network of antiabortion terrorists Army of God, explained in a December 1994 commentary for *Life Advocate*. "If we find it justifiable to use force to defend and save the life of our own child from a would-be killer, we had to agree that it was justifiable to use force to save the life of an unborn child too. They are as fully human as any of us."[81] While some anti-abortion activists argued that shooting providers hurt their movement, others publicly articulated their support for Griffin and Hill. Indeed, the more outrageous their rhetoric, the more attention they received.[82]

During the spring of 1993, NAF reported increased concern in Milwaukee, where on a daily talk-radio show a leader of the Missionaries to the Pre-Born compared abortion providers to man-eating tigers lusting for blood: "When a tiger in India starts attacking and killing and eating human beings, you have to go and take it out," he told listeners. "What you have in the case of an abortionist is somebody who is in the midst of a very complex medical field, and they've just gotten a taste of human blood, that's all."[83] Missionaries founder Matt Trewhella took these statements further when he urged his audience to buy weapons.[84] After David Gunn's murder, it was no longer safe to assume that these threats were merely words.

The fear for their immediate safety and lives had a tremendous impact on abortion providers. Rasmussen continued his testimony to the committee:

> I am changed. I look over my shoulder more often. I am short with my staff. I have moved my bed for safety. I am considering a gun which seems just abhorrent to me and a bulletproof vest on especially bad days. . . . I am no longer free to enjoy a nightly walk in the summer, to hear the frogs and crickets and see the fireflies on my path. I rarely walk any more. If I do, the walks have an edge to them. Did that car slow down because of the uncertainty of where to turn? Would anyone hear me with windows closed if I called out? When my phone goes dead, has someone cut the wires or is it just malfunctioning? My mother-in-law is afraid to be at my home. We never locked our doors. Now I have a sophisticated security system and keys. Air-conditioning was installed last summer because leaving the windows open presented a risk. . . . Do I fear? Does my family fear for my personal safety, my life? The answer is yes.[85]

Some providers began to wear bulletproof vests; others started to carry guns; yet others decided to quit.[86] "This is the Christian Jihad," Renee Chelian explained to an official from the Justice Department. "We had 15 butyric acid attacks in 5 days and no one local could handle it. I live with domestic terrorism. My daughter is scared. I'm scared. Are they going to take out my children?"[87]

Abortion providers increased their pleas to the White House to have the Justice Department investigate violence against abortion clinics. In October 1993, NCAP members sent a letter to President Bill Clinton asking him to launch an investigation into antiabortion harassment and violence.[88] That year, the Justice Department under Janet Reno finally created a new unit on antiabortion terrorism. And in acknowledgment that local law enforcement agencies had proven inadequate in protecting clinics from destruction and sabotage, legislators passed and Bill Clinton signed into law the 1994 FACE Act, making it a federal crime to interfere with access to any facility providing reproductive health services.

While providers were relieved at the intervention of the federal government and the passage of FACE, in particular, the immediate relief that clinic owners hoped for did not materialize. Providers complained of being ignored by the agencies that should have enforced the new laws. The Bureau of Alcohol, Tobacco, and Firearms was uncooperative when asked to investigate clinic fires. Worse, immediately after the shooting of David Gunn, abortion providers in Pensacola, Florida, and elsewhere became concerned about the behavior of Paul Hill. But attempts to have him arrested failed. When Linda Taggart of the Ladies Center called her local police after passage of the FACE law to ask for his arrest, police offices told her they had no guidelines for an arrest under FACE. "I then telephoned the ATF and was referred to the FBI. Their agent said he would 'take down the information' but could not make an arrest because he had no guidelines." Taggart finally called Janet Reno's office and was told that "this was not the time to arrest him."[89] Less than three months later, Paul Hill killed John Britton and James Barrett. Other hotspots of aggressive antiabortion activism also failed to draw federal attention and shortly after became the sites of violence. Abortion providers warned the federal government about activists at the tumultuous Wichita clinic—to no avail. Shortly after, Shelley Shannon shot George Tiller. The federal government also seemed to deem the murder investigation of Dr. Patterson the result of a robbery and hence a local matter, despite the fact that antiabortion violence was clearly perpetrated by a national network of activists.[90]

Still, by late 1994, federal intervention showed some results. While the passage of FACE was only as effective as police authorities' willingness to enforce it, in many locations it was directly responsible for the declining number of violent outbursts and blockades at clinics, actions which had now become federal crimes.[91] And when Susan Hill opened a new abortion clinic in Jackson, Mississippi, in early 1995, immediately after the devastating Brookline shootings, she received federal protection. On the day of the opening, Hill received a call from Deval Patrick, then assistant attorney general for civil rights. "He said, 'Look out your window. . . . Do you see the vans on each corner?' There were four corners, and there were vans. I said, 'Yes.' And he said, 'They're full of marshals.'"[92]

While the murder of David Gunn briefly humanized abortion providers and gave them a face, in the long run the extreme violence had the effect of further marginalizing abortion providers and their patients. To be sure, women continued to write to their providers to express their appreciation for abortion services. "I am not proud of all the facts of my life that have caused me to take extreme measures in the face of both abusive situations and economic disasters," one woman wrote to Takey Crist after seeing him on the *Donahue* show. But she also made clear that she was extremely grateful to Crist, who had performed one of her two abortions, and closed her thanks with the observation, "My present life and extended family support would not have been possible otherwise."[93] Another recounted her experience accompanying a friend to an abortion clinic. "My friend was quite fragile," she explained. "So I pretended to be the one going for the procedure as we crossed the picket lines. The experience changed my life and ever since that time I have done everything I can to support doctors such as yourself."[94]

Indeed, in light of the protests and the stigma attached to abortion, many women insisted that the abortion decision was theirs to make. "It's always hard to make this decision," one woman wrote into a comment book for patients at Susan Wicklund's clinic. "But in the end you have to know what is right for you, and what will be right for the child. Everything happens for a reason and whatever path you choose is the right one. Whatever you believe in, however your parents are, whatever people say, it's ultimately your decision to do *whatever* is best for you. Keep your head up, and just remember that there are always obstacles in our lives and it is our choice to jump over them and learn and make our lives the best they can be."[95] Many women noted that their religious beliefs gave them the strength to decide to have an abortion and follow through with it. "God is with me during this difficult decision and I see only one set of footprints," noted one woman in the book. "He is carrying me and I need his support more than anything right now! I'm in charge of me! I make my own decisions! I am loved and love! I will be okay! He is with me!"[96] Others framed their right to decide for an abortion almost defiantly. "A woman's Body is her own. Don't let any body tell you different," one patient noted.[97] "Don't let the protesters get to you," a man accompanying a woman patient wrote and continued: "Most are unemployed, and worship the bible because they were taught to, and even then only take what lessons they choose from it. Don't let the bigoted make decisions for you. Be strong, be your own, be free."[98] Women also gained comfort from reading the comments of others. "Reading this journal and all other comments made me feel at ease," one patient wrote. "There is nothing to be ashamed of. . . . Women should [be] left with their own decisions—we know what's best, we know if we can afford, or give a child enough attention. I am 21 years old and have a whole life ahead to decide to bring a child into this world. Empower your choices and never regret."[99]

But others experienced the violence and shootings as a form of personal stigmatization. A couple months after the murder of David Gunn, *Glamour* magazine published an article in which a former patient of Gunn's reflected on her experience of having had an abortion after becoming pregnant as a result of a rape when she was fifteen years old. "When I heard that Dr. Gunn had been killed," she noted, "it made me feel dirty. I saw some people on TV ranting and raving about how he deserved to die for what he did to women's babies; if what he was doing was so terrible, then maybe what I had done was terrible too, and I deserved to die as well. . . . It was easier to accept my abortion before Dr. Gunn died. Now it's tied together with his death, as if violence created this child and this child created violence."[100]

From D&E to Intact D&E: The Making of "Partial Birth Abortion"

Intact D&E entered the public discussion in 1992, just on the eve of David Gunn's murder. Dubbed "partial birth abortion" by antiabortion activists, activists depicted abortion providers who performed this variation of the D&E procedure not merely as murderers but also as killers who sought to murder their victims with particular cruelty. Now informed by an apocalyptic vision and millennial rhetoric, the language of war and killing took on a vividness. At the center of the debate again stood questions of viability and the aesthetics of an abortion procedure.

With the wide adoption of D&E in the 1980s, pregnancy terminations after the first trimester had become significantly safer and easier to perform. The number of abortions performed after the first trimester had increased only slightly from 9 percent in 1977 to 11.9 percent in 1997. Abortion rights advocates attributed this rise to the fact that access to abortion had become significantly more difficult, especially for young and poor women.[101] The development of dilation with laminaria meant that D&Es could be performed through the entire second trimester. Over the years, physicians had introduced additional medications and technologies to further improve D&E procedures, including prophylactic antibiotics, ultrasound guidance, and use of mifepristone and misoprostol to "ripen" the cervix preoperatively. Because they could be performed as outpatient procedures, D&Es also became cheaper and more accessible to women than were instillation procedures. By the 1990s, D&Es in advanced pregnancies were as safe as those at earlier gestational stages—a development that contradicted antiabortion propaganda and must have caused consternation among antiabortion activists who insisted that abortions were hazardous procedures.[102]

Despite these medical developments, D&Es were not without problems. At twenty weeks' gestation, dismemberment of the fetus became increasingly difficult, carrying the risk of perforation of the uterus and cervical tearing.[103] In the course of the 1980s, a number of physicians began to look for a technical solution to some of the problems raised by D&E. Some surgeons developed a technique allowing them to remove the fetus in one piece, without dismemberment in utero. To perform this procedure, alternately called intact D&E or D&X, the physician arranged the fetus so that it could be removed feet first. After extracting the body from the birth canal, the physician collapsed the fetal skull by inserting a cannula and extracting the fluid—a procedure that had its roots in obstetrical developments of the late nineteenth and early twentieth centuries and had in previous decades been used for the removal of hydrocephalic fetuses.[104] The method caused less trauma to the lower uterus and had an extremely low rate of complications.

But intact D&E also served compassionate purposes. Los Angeles physician James T. McMahon routinely performed pregnancy terminations for fetal abnormality at advanced gestational ages. Using intact D&E meant that he could offer women, who had wanted to keep their pregnancies, the chance to hold the fetus and grieve their loss. Finally, it permitted physicians to perform a careful autopsy and get a precise diagnosis of any fetal anomalies.[105] As physicians' ability to diagnose fetal anomalies via ultrasound improved, autopsies began to play an important role. They not only confirmed diagnoses made via ultrasound but also helped physicians and geneticists to understand the cause or mechanism leading to the anomaly, to interpret the severity of anomalies detected, to predict the probability that future pregnancies might be affected by similar problems, and to counsel parents accordingly.[106]

Like any surgical procedure, intact D&E emerged over time, as several physicians across the country experimented with different variations of

D&E, drew on a wide range of surgical techniques used in other contexts, and discussed their experiences informally with one another. As Cincinnati abortion provider Martin Haskell explained the process:

> What I saw here in my practice, because we did D&Es, was that we had patients who needed terminations at a later date. So we learned the skills. The later we did them, the more we saw patients who needed them still later. But I just kept doing D&Es because that was what I was comfortable with, up until 24 weeks. But they were very tough. Sometimes it was a 45 minute operation. I noticed that some of the later D&Es were very, very easy. So I asked myself why can't they all happen this way. You see the easy ones would have a foot length presentation, you'd reach up and grab the foot of the fetus, pull the fetus down and the head would hang up and then you would collapse the head and take it out. It was easy. At first I would reach around trying to identify a lower extremity blindly with the tip of my instrument, I'd get it right about 30–50 percent of the time. Then I said, "Well, gee, if I just put the ultrasound up there I could see it all and I wouldn't have to feel around for it." I did that and sure enough, I found it 99 percent of the time. Kind of serendipity.[107]

In the 1980s, physicians in at least four medical facilities performed intact D&Es.[108]

The procedure attracted the attention of antiabortion activists when abortion providers moved from informal discussions to formal presentations in professional settings. At a September 1992 risk management meeting of NAF, Martin Haskell presented a paper on intact D&E.[109] Antiabortion activists had successfully infiltrated the NAF mailing list, and news about Haskell's presentation reached Jenny Westberg, an Oregon activist and lay cartoonist. Westberg decided to write an article for the Oregon publication *Life Advocate* and to illustrate her comments with drawings of the procedure. In early 1993, the issues of *Life Advocate* containing Westberg's drawings were mailed to subscribers.[110] National antiabortion organizations quickly reprinted the images in newspaper advertisements and millions of widely distributed brochures.

The campaign against D&E and intact D&E emerged at a time when the tide seemed to be turning against the antiabortion activists: the abortion provider community had at last won significant legal victories against a number of leading antiabortion activists; OR, which in the late 1980s had mobilized thousands of demonstrators to block access to abortion clinics across the country, had succumbed to infighting and legal problems; and with the election of President Bill Clinton in 1992, abortion rights advocates could finally look for help from a sympathetic Justice Department. But in 1992, antiabortion activists turned to D&E and intact D&E to fight FOCA and finally to pass legislation that might outlaw at least one abortion procedure. "By depicting a procedure expected to make most readers squeamish," *American Medical News* noted, "campaign sponsors hope to convince voters and elected officials that a proposed federal abortion-rights bill is so extreme that states would have no authority to limit abortions—even on potentially viable fetuses."[111]

The centerpiece of the attack against FOCA became a four-page brochure, published in 1993 by the NRLC. The cover featured a photograph of sixteen-month-old Ana Rosa Rodriguez whose right arm had been severed during an abortion attempt when her mother was 7½ months pregnant (see ill. 6.1). The 1991 case, which had led to the indictment of New York City physician Dr. Abu Hayat, had raised significant public attention. "Everyone would agree," a caption next to the photo read, "that what happened to Ana Rosa should never happen again."[112] On the back of the brochure, readers could see Westberg's drawings (see ill. 6.2) with the commentary, "Under the radical 'Freedom of Choice Act' (FOCA), the new late-term D&X [intact D&E] abortion procedure will flourish. With the D&X procedure, which is currently being used in the United States to destroy unborn babies from the fourth to ninth months of pregnancy, abortionists work to be sure that babies like Ana Rosa do not survive."[113] Unlike the earlier gory photographs of aborted fetuses, the clean and shocking image of Ana missing an arm and the simple line drawings of intact D&E made the brochure much more palatable than any of the more gruesome handouts had ever been. By early 1993, the NRLC had distributed 4 million copies of the brochure.[114]

Pairing the drawings of intact D&E with the photograph of Ana Rosa highlighted the notion that abortion providers did, indeed, kill live babies. In fact, only 0.8 percent of pregnancy terminations took place after twenty-one weeks, and the earliest a fetus was considered viable was at twenty-three weeks' gestation. The case of Ana Rosa was a rare exception, but activists used it to give the impression that all D&Es were performed on viable fetuses. "This is an educational exercise," NRLC director Douglas Johnson commented. "We want people to be aware that abortions are being performed on unborn human beings, twenty weeks and beyond, when they look like babies and have a capacity to feel pain."[115] Indeed, the brochure presented intact D&E as a natural extension of D&E and eliminated all distinction between an intact D&E in the second trimester and

Everyone would agree that what happened to Ana Rosa should never happen again...

Ana Rosa Rodriguez, 16 months old.

Ana's right arm was severed by an abortionist during an abortion attempt when her mother was 7½ months pregnant...

Ill. 6.1. This image of Ana Rosa was reprinted in millions of antiabortion brochures. From "Everyone would agree . . . " brochure, North Carolina Right to Life, n.d., file Anti-Abortion Publicity, series Abortion, TCP.

one at term. The very use of the phrase "late-term," which conflated the second and third trimester into one period without further distinction as to gestational age, implied that any abortion after the first trimester was equivalent to a procedure at term. The phrase "late term" was not only widely used by antiabortion activists but also uncritically adopted by journalists and, occasionally, abortion rights supporters. In the following months, antiabortion materials painted Haskell as the inventor of the procedure who had "taught" the method to other providers at the NAF Risk Management Seminar. "A heinous abortion method which has recently come to light," remarked an article in the fall of 1993, "illustrates the grisly, inhumane world of the abortion industry."[116]

The impression that abortion providers brutally killed healthy babies was most powerfully asserted by nurse Brenda Shafer, who, as a temporary nurse in Haskell's Women's Medical Center, had assisted Haskell with

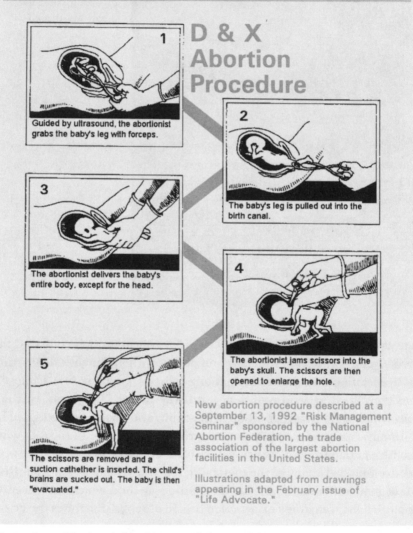

Under the radical "Freedom of Choice Act" (FOCA), the new late-term D & X abortion procedure will flourish. With the D & X procedure, which is currently being used in the United States to destroy unborn babies from the fourth to ninth months of pregnancy, abortionists work to be sure that babies like Ana Rosa do not survive.

D & X Abortion Procedure

1 Guided by ultrasound, the abortionist grabs the baby's leg with forceps.

2 The baby's leg is pulled out into the birth canal.

3 The abortionist delivers the baby's entire body, except for the head.

4 The abortionist jams scissors into the baby's skull. The scissors are then opened to enlarge the hole.

5 The scissors are removed and a suction cathether is inserted. The child's brains are sucked out. The baby is then "evacuated."

New abortion procedure described at a September 13, 1992 "Risk Management Seminar" sponsored by the National Abortion Federation, the trade association of the largest abortion facilities in the United States.

Illustrations adapted from drawings appearing in the February issue of "Life Advocate."

Ill. 6.2. Jenny Westberg's drawings provided a visual illustration of intact D&E. From "Everyone would agree . . ." brochure, North Carolina Right to Life, n.d., file Anti-Abortion Publicity, series Abortion, TCP.

three intact D&E procedures. After she left the Women's Medical Center, she volunteered her impressions to the antiabortion movement, drawing on the language and understanding of the fetus as baby that antiabortion activists had provided over previous decades.

> The baby's heartbeat was clearly visible on the ultrasound screen. The doctor delivered the baby's body and arms, everything but his little head. The baby's body was moving. His little fingers were clasping together. He was kicking his feet. The doctor took a pair of scissors and inserted them into the back of the baby's head, and the baby's arms jerked out in a flinch, a startled reaction, like a baby does when he thinks that he might fall. Then the doctor opened the scissors up. Then he stuck the high-powered suction tube into the hole and sucked the baby's brains out. Now the baby was completely limp. I never went back to the clinic. But I am still haunted by the face of that little boy. It was the most perfect, angelic face I have ever seen.[117]

Westberg's drawings and Brenda Shafer's description came to stand for all abortions. The perfect angelic face in Shafer's description implied that abortion providers killed perfect babies at term. Absent from consideration were the reasons women chose to end pregnancies and the particular hardships that led to abortions later in pregnancy. The women seeking to end their pregnancies—and their motives for doing so—disappeared from focus.

Aesthetic concerns about the death of the fetus took center stage in the public debate.[118] The fact that suctioning the fetal brain did not just collapse the skull but also killed a previously living fetus was upsetting to many on both sides of the debate.[119] Two-thirds of the fetuses, Haskell had noted, were alive at the beginning of the intact D&Es he performed. NAF received scores of calls from congressional staffers and others who had seen the ads and brochures and were now asking pointed questions about the procedure.[120] As the two abortion providers known to perform intact D&Es, McMahon and Haskell became the public face for intact D&E. Both denied that intact D&E was a cruel and inhumane procedure. Haskell explained in a sympathetic interview conducted for *Cincinnati Medicine* that he performed intact D&Es because he found it quicker, easier, and safer than a traditional D&E at or after twenty weeks' gestation. Fetal development, Haskell noted, was insufficient for a fetus to be conscious of the procedure. "Neurological pain and perception of pain are not the same [in a fetus]," he explained. "The perception of pain, the memory of pain that we fear and dread are not there."[121]

National pro-choice organizations refused to debate details of intact D&E. From the beginning, pro-choice leaders maintained that "this surgical procedure is used only in rare cases, fewer than 500 per year. It is most often performed in the case of wanted pregnancies gone tragically wrong, when a family learns late in pregnancy of severe fetal anomalies or a medical condition that threatens the pregnant woman's life or health."[122] Barbara Radford, NAF's executive director, sent a letter to NAF members outlining guidelines for the public discussion. Don't apologize, she suggested to abortion providers, reminding them that intact D&E was a legal procedure and that no abortion method was acceptable to abortion opponents. While she conceded that the language and graphics in the antiabortion ads were disturbing to some readers, she noted that this might be the case with graphic descriptions of many other surgical procedures. The real agenda, Radford concluded, was "to outlaw virtually all abortions, not just late-term ones."[123]

Pro-choice supporters chose to defend intact D&Es by arguing that abortion providers performed this particular procedure only in hardship cases. A number of articles in the mainstream press introduced readers to the truly agonizing decisions that women who chose to have an abortion later in pregnancy had to make. One woman, for instance, had had an abortion in her seventh month of pregnancy after learning that her fetus had four holes in the heart, was missing a kidney, had a defective esophagus, a cleft lip palate, and was extremely small. Another chose to terminate an advanced pregnancy because her fetus had a huge tumor on its tailbone that, if benign, would have to be removed leaving the baby with no legs or buttocks; if malignant, the baby would die. Another patient, Tammy Watts, who testified about her experience on Capitol Hill, explained:

They told me: "She has no eyes, six fingers and six toes, and enlarged kidneys which are already failing. The mass on the outside of her stomach involves her bowel and bladder, and her heart and other major organs are also affected." . . . I had a choice. I could have carried this pregnancy to term, knowing everything that was wrong. I could have gone on for two more months, doing everything that an expectant mother does but knowing my baby was going to die and would probably suffer a great deal before dying. My husband and I would have had to endure that knowledge and watch that suffering. We could never have survived that. And we made the choice together, my husband and I, to terminate this pregnancy.[124]

In cases like these, issues surrounding viability were linked to discussions about quality of life, providing a complex net of factors in which physicians and women made what were very individual decisions. Abortion providers here were positioned as moral and humanitarian medical specialists who helped women in their struggles with heartrending life-and-death decisions. Most providers, the articles noted, restricted procedures in the third trimester to women who suffered from serious health problems or whose fetuses suffered serious birth defects.[125] David Grimes, whose publications had always carefully evaluated the suitability of various abortion procedures, argued that abortions during the final trimester were only justified if the fetus was afflicted with a condition incompatible with survival for more than a few weeks or revealed an absence of cognitive function and if highly reliable diagnostic procedures were available to determine prenatally that the fetus fulfilled either of those criteria. Grimes pointed to anencephaly—a condition in which the fetal brain fails to develop—as one such qualifying condition. "I think every obstetrician struggles with this and makes his [sic] mind up what his threshold is," he commented.[126]

But from the very beginning of the debate, the conflation of intact D&E with abortions performed during the final trimester meant that sweeping statements—that intact D&Es were rare and only performed in hardship cases—were far removed from clinical practice. McMahon and Haskell laid open the complicated reasons women had abortions after the first trimester and reinforced the claim that women should be trusted with their reproductive decisions. Haskell noted that contrary to official claims, the majority of his intact D&E patients did not seek the procedure because the pregnancy significantly impaired their health or life or because the fetus suffered from severe fetal anomalies. They were typical second trimester patients between twenty and twenty-four weeks' gestation. They had abortions in their second trimester because they were either teenagers who took longer to recognize that they were pregnant and to decide what to do with an unwanted pregnancy or they were older women who had continued to menstruate during pregnancy and had thus failed to recognize that they were pregnant.

Since abortion providers did not keep official statistics about the reasons that women chose to have abortions after the first trimester—regardless of abortion procedure—it was (and indeed still is) difficult to get anything but circumstantial evidence about the reasons behind the procedure. A 1988 study by the Alan Guttmacher Institute found that only 4 percent of abortions took place after 16 weeks' gestation. Teenagers under eighteen, black women, unemployed women, and women covered by Medicaid were significantly more likely to have abortions at advanced gestational ages. Seventy-one percent explained that some time had passed before they had realized they were pregnant or had learned the actual gestation of their pregnancy. Close to half had been delayed because they had found it difficult to make arrangements for the abortion (raising money or finding an abortion provider who offered the services they needed). And one-third of all women having later abortions said they had been afraid to tell their partner or parents about the pregnancy. In a recent informal study on women's reasons for seeking late abortion care, conducted at a clinic that offers abortion services through the twenty-eighth week of pregnancy, women's reasons for seeking late abortion care ranged from experiencing "no symptoms of pregnancy" (28 percent) to "chaotic lives" (19 percent), "late diagnosis of fetal anomaly" (18 percent), "denial and denial-like processes" (14 percent) to "contraceptive failure" (7 percent). The remaining 14 percent included domestic violence victims, women who came late to the clinic because they had been held captive, women battling addiction, as well as performance athletes who did not recognize a pregnancy because their bodies were under constant strain.[127] As the recent documentary *After Tiller* further illustrates, the doctors' decisions about whether to perform an abortion for women who sought abortions under these conditions were very individual, weighing both women's reasons and their gestational age. McMahon conceded that he had mixed feelings about some of the abortions he did at later gestational stages. "I do have moral compunctions," he explained to *American Medical News* reporter Diane Gianelli. "And if I see a case that's later, like after twenty weeks where it frankly is a child to me, I really agonize over it because the potential is so imminently there. I think, 'Gee, it's too bad that this child couldn't be adopted.'" But, he argued, he had no qualms about intact D&Es, and his personal feelings should not limit women's access to the procedure. "I have another position, which I think is superior in the hierarchy of questions, and that is: 'Who owns the child?' It's got to be the mother."[128] Unwilling to "hold patients hostage to my technical skills," he concluded that he should perform the abortions.

In June 1995, Representative Charles T. Canady (R-Fla.) introduced HR 1833, the so-called Partial Birth Abortion Ban Act. Panicked representatives from NAF, NARAL, NOW, and PPFA held a phone conference to discuss strategy for defeating the bill. Susan Hill, however, suggested that they should not get involved. Both the term "partial birth abortion" and the images would make for a losing fight, she predicted. Allowing the antiabortion movement to apply the term "birth" to an abortion procedure spelled trouble. "You cannot let pictures of this on the floor of Congress," she warned. "It'll be a disaster."[129] Hill suggested that the issue should be relegated to a congressional committee that could investigate why women were having abortions after the first trimester. Should the ban pass, abortion providers could then fight it in court. Her colleagues disagreed. The national pro-choice organizations quickly agreed to defend intact D&Es as rare procedures that were only performed in the case of severe fetal anomalies or to save the life of the mother.[130]

When HR 1833 was introduced, pro-choice organizations did not merely agree on a joint line of defense but also sought to provide a unified message. Between the initial antiabortion publicity campaign against intact D&E and the 1995 introduction of the bill banning the procedure, extremists had shot thirteen people working at abortion clinics around the country, killing five of them. Two of those killed had been abortion providers. Fears about the safety of abortion providers lent the debates surrounding intact D&E a threatening character. In 1995, at this moment of pressing security concerns, NAF hired a new executive director, Vicki Saporta. Saporta continued the line of public defense on which the national pro-choice organization had embarked: intact D&Es were rare. "We only know of two physicians who do this," the *New York Times* quoted Saporta in July 1995, "and combined they do 450 a year."[131] Saporta also disputed the antiabortion claim that intact D&E was used to kill healthy babies at term. "This procedure is not taking place on live fetuses, the way it's being portrayed. The fetal demise has already occurred and most of these fetuses have severe abnormalities and were never healthy to start with."[132] Medical care and surgery, she concluded, should not become a political battleground. "Patients want to make those decisions based on their doctor's advice, not the Christian Coalition's political agenda. This legislation is dangerous because it criminalizes doctors for performing surgery and runs the risk of scaring doctors away from performing late abortions."[133]

The discussion of the procedure and its ban narrowed to a debate about fetal death. To create a scientific foundation for arguments in support of a ban, the bill's sponsor, Charles Canady, solicited expert testimony—in writing over the summer of 1995 and at a public hearing before the House Judiciary Subcommittee on the Constitution in June of that year. In September, Canady summarized the committee's findings in a report. Intact D&Es, the report argued in its opening pages, were not performed on fetuses but entailed the delivery of a baby. "The baby involved is not 'unborn,'" the report stated. "His or her life is taken during a breech delivery."[134] The report—and subsequent discussion—collapsed intact D&Es, most frequently performed between the twentieth and twenty-fourth week of pregnancy, with abortions performed later in pregnancy. Indeed, the report raised the impression that physicians performed intact D&Es after the spontaneous onset of labor of a fetus at term. "While every abortion takes a human life," the authors contended, "the partial-birth abortion method takes that life late in pregnancy as the baby emerges from the mother's womb."[135] The only difference between the partial birth abortion procedure and homicide, the authors concluded, "is a mere three inches."[136]

In addition, the report sought to dispute the claim that physicians performed intact D&Es only in rare cases of severe fetal anomalies or maternal distress. Haskell himself had noted that most of his patients were typical second trimester patients, and documents submitted by McMahon to the House Subcommittee on the Constitution listed a range of indications. McMahon categorized 1,358 abortions, all of them done on women at least twenty-four weeks pregnant. While most of them were for extremely rare fetal defects, the committee picked out the indications most likely to raise the impression that women were having abortions for frivolous reasons. Of the 1,358 cases, the report highlighted nine cases in which the fetal indication was listed as a cleft lip and—for maternal indications—pointed to 39 cases listing depression and 19 cases listing sexual assault.[137]

Just as in the Edelin trial two decades earlier, at the center of the debate stood the question of how fetal death occurred. Over and over again, committee members questioned witnesses on when and how the fetus died. Mary Campbell, medical director of Planned Parenthood of Metropolitan Washington, had authored a fact sheet on intact D&E, which stated that the fetus died while still in the womb of an overdose of anesthesia given to the mother at the beginning of the procedure.[138] But at the hearing, committee members set out to prove her wrong. After testimony by Norig Ellison, president of the American Society of Anesthesiologists, that anesthesia given to the mother prior to intact D&E did not cause a coma in the fetus, committee members questioned Campbell on her fact sheet.[139] Campbell defended herself, noting that she had based her information on McMahon's claim that the fetus was in a coma as a result of the anesthesia administered to the pregnant woman. "I do not know what causes the fetus to die," she admitted. "The fetuses are dead when delivered."[140] But witnesses for the antiabortion side concluded "that the fetus is alive until the suction device is inserted into the brain."[141] "Without question," Robert White, director of the Division of Neurosurgery and Brain Research Laboratory at Case Western Reserve School of Medicine, explained to the committee, "all of this is a dreadfully painful experience for any infant subjected to such a surgical procedure."[142] Other witnesses agreed.[143]

Those familiar with the procedure and the conditions under which it was performed described intact D&E as a compassionate procedure and the physicians who performed it as caring. In written testimony to a 1995 legislative committee debating the procedure, Dru Elaine Carlson, director of reproductive genetics and a perinatologist and geneticist at Cedars-Sinai Medical Center in Los Angeles, argued that McMahon was "caring and gentle, and ultimately life-affirming in his approach to the abortion procedure." McMahon, Carlson argued, showed tremendous compassion as he performed intact D&Es.

> When the cervix is open enough for a safe delivery of the fetus he uses ultrasound guidance to gently deliver the fetal body up to the shoulders and then very quickly and expertly performs what is called a cephalocentesis. . . . There is no struggling of the fetus; quite the contrary, from my personal observation I can tell you that the end is extremely humane and rapid. He provides dignity for all of his patients: the mothers, the fathers, the extended families and finally to the fetuses themselves. He does not "mangle" fetuses, rather they are delivered intact and that allows us (a team of physicians at Cedars) to evaluate them carefully, and for families to touch and acknowledge their baby in saying goodbye.[144]

But such testimony was lost in a debate in which most participants refused to acknowledge that women and abortion providers by necessity made life and death decisions.

Truths, Lies, and Partial Truths: The Unraveling of a Debate

Within the pro-choice community, the introduction of a bill banning intact D&E brought to light fundamental tensions around speaking the truth about abortion. What the truth was—and whether it could be spoken—became a source of contention in the abortion provider community. At the annual meeting of NAF in April 1996, several NAF members approached Director Vicki Saporta and urged her to be more honest about the estimated number of intact D&Es and the reasons the procedure was performed. "'The spin out of Washington was that it was only done for medical necessity, even though we knew it wasn't so,' said Renee Chelian, president of NCAP and a member of NAF. 'I kept waiting for NAF to clarify it and they never did it.'"[145] Pam O'Leary, whose clinic in Toledo, Ohio, performed intact D&Es in about half of its post-twenty-week cases, echoed the call for pride and honesty that members of NCAP and the November Gang had issued. "Sometimes as providers and as human beings we all have to stop and make sure that what we're doing is what we can comfortably say we're doing. I can offer intact D&E and not be ashamed of it. I believe the work we do is honorable; it's for the health of women and society in general."[146]

Disagreements about strategy within the abortion provider community rose steadily as the debate surrounding intact D&E continued through the mid-1990s. The partial birth abortion ban was passed by both Houses in 1995, and President Bill Clinton, surrounding himself with some of the women who had gone public as hardship cases—and who provided the continued backdrop to the official defense strategy—vetoed it. Toward the end of 1996 and early 1997, the media began to turn a critical eye on the debate surrounding the intact D&E ban. Reporters in the *Bergen Record* and the *Washington Post* noted that both supporters and opponents of the ban had conducted a campaign "long on rhetoric and short on accuracy."[147] While intact D&E was not used on healthy full-term fetuses, as abortion foes implied, estimates by pro-choice organizations that abortion providers performed only 450 to 600 intact D&Es annually and did so only in the most dire circumstances were similarly misleading. Both papers made clear that intact D&Es were rare—just over 1 percent (17,000 abortions) took place after twenty weeks' gestation, and only a fraction of those involved intact D&Es. But reporters also noted what Haskell had maintained all along, that the vast majority of intact D&Es were performed for elective reasons, on healthy women and healthy fetuses.[148]

The articles in both papers were based on interviews with a number of physicians who reported that they performed intact D&Es. They concurred with Haskell's 1993 characterization that the typical intact D&E patients were young, low-income women, often poorly educated or naive, whose reasons for waiting so long to end their pregnancies were rarely medical. As one New York physician explained, many of these patients, twelve to twenty years old, "are not in touch with their reproductive system as well as they should be, so they get stuck later than they want in pregnancy. They get surprised, basically."[149] Only in the small subgroup of women whose abortions are done in the last trimester, the *Washington*

Post reported, "are most of the fetuses malformed, and most of the pregnancies initially desired."[150]

The willingness of physicians who performed intact D&Es to talk with reporters from the *Record* and the *Washington Post* indicates that those who used the controversial procedure disagreed with the official strategy of defense, that intact D&Es were rare and used only in the most dire circumstances. While most of the physicians interviewed were unwilling to have their names published—hardly a surprise given the fact that by 1996 fourteen people working in abortion clinics had been shot and five of them killed—they talked freely about the second trimester abortions they performed, about their use of intact D&E, and about the patients who came to seek abortions after the first trimester. The interviews made clear that decisions whether or not to use intact D&E were based on personal preference. Providers varied on their use of techniques for later abortions—some used intact D&Es as their procedure of preference, others employed the procedure only occasionally. Noting that "the fundamental argument [of the technique's opponents] is that the fetus is alive," one physician cut the umbilical cord before performing an intact D&E to ensure that the fetus was dead.[151] Physicians also varied in the number of intact D&Es they performed. Physicians at Metropolitan Medical in Englewood, New Jersey, for instance, performed 1,500 intact D&Es, whereas another medical facility in New Jersey counted little more than 100 such procedures.

And just as providers differed in their preference for intact D&E, they differed in the indications under which they chose to perform abortions after the first trimester and in their understanding of those indications. While McMahon had reported that 20 percent of his abortions performed after the first trimester were elective procedures, physicians at UNC reported that 95 percent of their procedures were elective. It is, of course, possible that physicians at UNC had a patient population that was considerably healthier and carried healthier fetuses than those patients who consulted McMahon. Equally plausible, however, is the possibility that McMahon classified fewer procedures as elective.[152] The story of intact D&E, the articles made clear, was considerably more complicated than the official presentation of exceptional hardship cases suggested. An abortion rights bias among journalists, a reporter on *Media Matters* pointed out in early 1997, had led the press to adopt the official statements of national pro-choice organizations as proven facts and follow the five women presented by abortion rights advocates who had undergone intact D&Es for reasons of severe fetal deformity in the third trimester.[153]

By the mid-1990s, the debate over intact D&E began to tear the abortion provider community apart. The increasing number of public statements suggested that the public debate could not be controlled. Providers thought and spoke as individuals, not as a unified whole under the banner of NAF. Just as physicians' willingness to speak to reporters indicated their disagreement with the official defense strategy, other voices hinted at a larger debate over intact D&E procedures within the abortion provider community. Infighting over strategy and disagreements over other issues complicated the debate. While noting that the ban was "politically motivated," Warren Hern, who himself performed abortions at advanced gestational ages, explained to a reporter that he had "very serious reservations about this procedure."[154] Hern took issue with the position of providers who suggested intact D&E could be the safest procedure to use for women in late-term pregnancy. Turning the fetus to a breech position, he argued, was "potentially dangerous. You have to be concerned about causing amniotic fluid embolism or placental abruption if you do that."[155] Worried that abortion providers were losing credibility in light of an official defense that was increasingly challenged, NCAP's Ron Fitzsimmons suggested to members that NCAP speak more honestly about the procedure. "When we emphasize the rare, life endangerment cases, it sounds more like we're apologizing. It reminds me of when Henry Foster was saying, 'I only did 40 abortions,'" he argued.[156] But when Fitzsimmons tried to set the record straight by telling a reporter from the *American Medical News* that he had "lied through his teeth" about intact D&E in a November 1995 interview for ABC's *Nightline*, his admission seemed mostly self-aggrandizing. After all, the interview lay fifteen months in the past, and Fitzsimmons statements had never been aired. "An Abortion Rights Advocate Says He Lied about Procedure," the *New York Times* reported on February 26 and in two short columns quoted Fitzsimmons as he broke all the taboos of the pro-choice community.

> A prominent member of the abortion rights movement said today that he lied in earlier statements when he said a controversial form of late-term abortion is rare and performed primarily to save the lives or fertility of women bearing severely malformed babies. He now says the procedure is performed far more often than his colleagues have acknowledged and on healthy women bearing healthy fetuses. Ron Fitzsimmons . . . said he intentionally misled in previous remarks about the procedure . . . because he feared that the truth would damage the cause of abortion rights.[157]

The article concluded with a quote of Fitzsimmons commenting on the meaning of abortion: "One of the facts of abortion, he [Fitzsimmons] said, is that women enter abortion clinics to kill their fetuses. 'It is a form of killing,' he said. 'You're ending a life.'"[158] Fitzsimmons's comments infuriated the pro-choice community and provided additional fodder for supporters of the ban. As Renee Chelian recalls: "If Ron would have given an interview that was the same kind of conversation we had—we knew that there were doctors within the constitutionally protected time frame using this method because maybe it was safer for their patients—everything might have been different. But Ron got really arrogant. . . . He told me: 'I sat back, I crossed my feet, I put them up on the desk, and I was feeling on top of the world.' . . . And then it just took on a whole new life."[159] While some NCAP members praised Fitzsimons's honesty, many thought his choice of words ill-considered at best, and pro-choice supporters, inside and outside of NCAP, called for his immediate resignation.[160]

If those in the abortion provider community who wished for a more open conversation about intact D&E had hoped that the newspaper revelations would prompt more honesty, they were disappointed. When, two weeks later, the House and Senate Judiciary Committee held a hearing on the impending vote banning intact D&E, Fitzsimmons's words became the central issue. Witnesses and legislators used the hearing to reiterate familiar arguments, juxtaposing the plight of women in urgent need of intact D&Es with the fate of fetuses in urgent need of protection from callous abortion providers about to cruelly murder them. Seeking a representative from NCAP, the Center for Reproductive Rights summoned Chelian to testify on behalf of the organization.[161] When Chelian arrived at the NARAL offices for a preparatory meeting the day before the committee hearing, she was greeted with hostility. "They wanted Ron's head on a platter and I think I was going to be their sacrificial lamb," she recalled. "I went into this meeting where nobody talked to me."[162] Testifying on behalf of the pro-choice community were Kate Michelman of NARAL, Gloria Feldt of PPFA, Vicki Saporta of NAF, and Renee Chelian of NCAP. They were joined by Douglas Johnson from the NRLC and Helen Alvare from the National Conference of Catholic Bishops. The hearing became a stage for political posturing, taking an almost theatrical turn when Doug Johnson pulled out a baby doll and a pair of surgical scissors to pass them down to Chelian at the other end of the table.

Speaking on behalf of the abortion provider community, Chelian sought to represent independent abortion providers as deeply moral individuals who were making difficult medical decisions. Intact D&E, she explained to the committee, was one procedure in a continuity of surgical care. "Abortion providers have spent the last 24 years developing methods of abortion without the benefit of medical schools, teaching institutions or government agencies," she explained. "We have made abortion the safest surgical procedure done in this country today, and we have also managed to keep it affordable for most women. . . . Abortion surgery has been an evolution of physician-developed techniques. Each is a step in advancing the health and safety of our patients. The intact D&E and D&X were developed for precisely that reason. . . . It is a continuum of good health care."[163] NCAP, she noted, opposed the ban of intact D&E because lawmakers should not be practicing medicine. "Physicians, not politicians, must be allowed to decide which medical procedure is in the best interest of the patient."[164] But in her remarks, Chelian also tried to shift the focus away from a discussion of a particular abortion procedure to the question why women were having abortions after the first trimester in the first place. She challenged members of the committee to increase women's access to contraceptive services and early abortion if they were concerned about abortions after the first trimester. "By focusing on a *particular method of abortion*," Chelian charged, "we as a society continue to avoid the reasons why women have second trimester abortions. Why, in this age of contraception, public education and awareness are there still so many unwanted pregnancies? All of us share the responsibility for the problem of unwanted, unplanned pregnancies. The focus should not be abortion or those who provide abortion services, but rather what we can, as a country, do to solve the problem."[165] More interested in political posturing than in serious debate, however, lawmakers did not respond to her challenge.

As the 1997 vote on the ban of intact D&E approached, one organization conducted a seven-state advertising campaign comparing intact D&E to the death penalty. The ad, entitled "Death Penalty," showed a prisoner being led to his execution while an announcer noted: "What if we told you there was an execution procedure so gruesome that it started by puncturing the head with a sharp instrument?" The prisoner's leg restraints were shown tightening, followed by a close-up of the terrified prisoner. "Next the brain is sucked out. After the head collapses, the body is discarded. As hard as it is to believe, this incredibly painful procedure happens somewhere in this country on an average of ten times a day." The camera then showed the prisoner fading out of the picture, only showing the chair. "No, it's not used to execute mass murderers. That would be considered cruel and unusual punishment and therefore illegal. Instead, this procedure, called partial-birth abortion, is usually used on healthy babies of healthy mothers, in the fifth or sixth month of pregnancy."[166] The campaign captured what Nancy Roman in a *Washington Post* article called the "public revulsion with late-term abortion."[167] The strategy of going after procedures, observers concluded, was brilliant. "These are awful procedures," a chief of staff for a pro-choice Democrat in the Senate noted. "The American people cannot stomach it."[168] The issue, Roman noted, had contributed to a significant shift within the traditionally pro-choice Democratic Party where now even staunch abortion rights supporters such as California's Barbara Boxer and Dianne Feinstein were willing to discuss restrictions on access to abortion.

Physicians performing later abortions acknowledged that the procedure made some people queasy but protested the focus on the aesthetic characteristics of intact D&E. Warren Hern conceded that the technique was "emotionally disturbing."[169] But David Grimes observed that "like much of surgery, later abortion by any method is not aesthetic."[170] All held that aesthetic concerns should play no role in decisions regarding pregnancy termination. "Once you decide the uterus must be emptied," McMahon argued, "you then have to have 100% allegiance to maternal risk. There's no justification to doing more dangerous procedures because somehow this [*sic*] doesn't offend your sensibilities as much."[171] Others cautioned providers not to get sidetracked by opponents' efforts to discuss the specifics of the procedure and tried to redirect the focus to the women seeking pregnancy terminations.[172]

If individual decision making had been at the heart of the practice of pregnancy termination, the lack of uniformity in medical practice now came to haunt the abortion provider community. The diversity of practice and opinion laid open internal contradictions and disagreements among abortion providers about the use and defense of intact D&E. A lack of research on the procedure contributed to providers' inability to forcefully defend its use. Faced with the possibility of a ban, providers argued for the need of a health exception. In some cases, they maintained, intact D&E might be the safest procedure to perform, and the ultimate decision should lie with the surgeon, rather than with the legislature. But statistical evidence on the outcomes of intact D&E was unavailable. Individual practice and the recent development of the procedure severely limited statistical evidence on which providers might base their arguments; they only had informal discussion of results.[173] Both houses passed the bill in 1995 and 1997. And although President Clinton vetoed it twice, in 2003 President Bush finally signed it into law.

Gonzales v. Carhart: *The Language of Protection*

In 2007, the U.S. Supreme Court decision in the case *Gonzales v. Carhart* upheld the 2003 ban of intact D&E. Dr. LeRoy Carhart and three other physicians had filed a legal challenge in the U.S. District Court for the District of Nebraska to the federal ban against intact D&E. When the U.S. District Court struck down the law, in part, because it failed to include an exception to protect women's health, and the U.S. Court of Appeals affirmed the U.S. District Court's decision, the Department of Justice, under U.S. Attorney General Alberto Gonzales filed an appeal with the U.S. Supreme Court. On April 18, 2007, the U.S. Supreme Court upheld the ban, reversing the lower court rulings in both cases. Drawing on two decades of anti-abortion narratives that chronicled the alleged harm that abortion did to women, the justices held that the ban protected women as well as the unborn. Despite a lack of reliable data that could measure this harm, they argued, "it seems unexceptional to conclude some women come to regret their choice to abort the infant life they once created and sustained. . . . It is self-evident that a mother who comes to regret her choice to abort must struggle with grief more anguished and sorrow more profound when she learns only after the event what she once did not know: that she allowed a doctor to pierce the skull and vacuum the fast-developing brain of her unborn child, a child assuming the human form."[174] The justices rested their assertions on an amicus brief from the Justice Foundation, a conservative law center, which quoted affidavits collected by Operation Outcry—an organization that followed in the footsteps of WEBA. Like the narratives first constructed by WEBA members and put into scientific language by David Reardon, the affidavits quoted by Operation Outcry reconfirmed that women were fundamentally unable to make the abortion decision. But if, in the mid-1980s, Reardon's analysis of WEBA testimony had only suggested this lack of ability, by the early 2000s antiabortion activists and scholars officially asserted that women could not make this decision. What WEBA had started in the mid-1980s emerged into a full-scale legislative assault two decades later.

Having spent a decade since the creation of WEBA gathering narratives of women who claimed to regret their abortions, conservative lawyers first harnessed these testimonials in the mid-1990s for a lawsuit on behalf of Norma McCorvey and Sandra Cano, the two original plaintiffs in *Roe v. Wade* and *Doe v. Bolton*. Introducing evidence that abortion harmed women, activists hoped, would provide grounds for reopening and overturning the two cases that had legalized abortion. Indeed, by the late

1990s, both plaintiffs had delivered testimony or written autobiographical accounts in which they renounced any allegiance with the pro-choice movement.[175] Like the original WEBA narrators, "post-abortive" women stated in their affidavits that they had been coerced into abortion and that the procedures had caused them psychological disorders, suicidal ideations, and physical complications.[176] By the 1990s, David Reardon was no longer the only expert to lend these narratives the mantle of scientific evidence. He had now been joined by a handful of other psychologists, whose work created a body of scientific evidence that allowed for the diagnosis and categorization of women who regretted their abortions as suffering from what the psychologists called "post-abortion syndrome."[177]

The selection of these materials was highly subjective, and the narratives themselves were carefully constructed to articulate an antiabortion view that stood in stark contrast to women's actual experience of abortion. Indeed, in 2008 the American Psychological Association concluded that there was no evidence that abortion causes serious mental health problems. Given the poor quality and methodological problems of most of the studies, the association's Task Force on Mental Health and Abortion declined to offer a calculation of effect sizes or count the number of studies that showed an effect in one direction versus another.[178] Indeed, most women neither expressed regret nor felt that they had been coerced into abortion or harmed by it. "I am excited to get my body back," one woman commented about her abortion at Susan Wicklund's clinic in Livingston, Montana.[179] While many patients were anxious about the abortion experience—feelings no doubt exacerbated by negative antiabortion publicity—they also discovered that they were resilient. "As I was preparing for today," one woman explained, "all I could think about was this dark shadow that had taken over my life. I felt like I had fallen into darkness and couldn't find my way out. I kept hoping that someone would reach in and save me. Guess what—I saved myself. I made a choice to do this and it feels damn good to make a choice for myself. Everyone here made me feel so comfortable and safe. I'm not ashamed at my decision. It's the best choice for me and everyone involved. I know what's best for me."[180] Even women who had started out opposed to abortion sometimes discovered that their position changed when they themselves carried an unwanted pregnancy and received respectful counseling and care. One patient noted: "As a woman who was against abortion I find myself sitting here waiting. Never in a million years would I have imagined I would go through with this. It's a choice us women have to make. Why bring an unwanted child into this world? After today I have a different outlook. Talking to Dr. Wicklund and her staff, I feel positive, stronger, faithful to all women who are put into this position."[181] And many patients articulated a continued connection with the fetus after the abortion and an understanding that they sought abortion not because they hated the fetus or the pregnancy but because they loved the fetus and felt unable to assume responsibility for it. They imagined a fetus that might join other dead relatives, particularly children, in another world and envisioned the fetus in a better place from where it might watch over the women who had had the abortion. "Little wee one from above," wrote one woman who imagined her daughter's fetus joining a child or fetus that she herself had apparently lost, "this is your grandmother. You are safe and sound now with my wee one. We love you both more than mere words express. Hold each other tight and stay happy! All our love always!!"[182] And another one concluded: "I gave my baby back to God to watch over me! I'll be ready one day!"[183]

But narratives of determination, resilience, and resolution of women's abortion experience were purposefully excluded as antiabortion activists constructed the scientific basis for post-abortion syndrome. Supported instead by materials describing the abortion experience as a trauma, leaders of the antiabortion movement moved from the assertion that abortion harms women to the argument that women should be protected from abortion. As legal scholar Reva Siegel has noted, while the claim that abortion harmed women was aimed at discouraging women from seeking abortions, the notion that women should be protected from abortion was directed at a larger audience to garner support for political campaigns and legislative efforts in favor of prohibiting abortion. The need to protect women from abortion became the new rallying cry of the antiabortion movement and was prominently featured on antiabortion websites.[184] On the eve of *Gonzales v. Carhart*, the most comprehensive account of the arguments and evidence for protecting women from abortion came in the 2005 Report of the South Dakota Task Force to Study Abortion, issued to support legislation in South Dakota that would prohibit abortion except if the procedure would prevent the death of a pregnant woman. The report repeated claims dating back to the 1980s that abortion hurt women and that women were coerced into abortion.[185] While the report's findings included the traditional fetus-focused arguments that the fetus was a fully formed human being entitled to all protections from the moment of conception—it felt pain, etc.—more than half the ten findings and over half the report focused on women. In testimony of 1,950 women collected for the task force, virtually all stated that they thought their abortions were uninformed or coerced or both. In addition to the testimonials of women who regretted their abortions, the task force relied on evidence from CPCs to substantiate the claim that abortion harms women. Testimony from center directors sought to illustrate how abortions harm women at their very core, rendering them essentially unable to function as housewives and mothers. Nicole Osmundsen, who counseled women at a Sioux Falls crisis pregnancy center, testified to the South Dakota legislature, for instance, that women who had abortions later suffered from a range of problems: "depression, uncontrollable crying, bonding issues with subsequent children, regrets, to drug and alcohol abuse, to eating disorders . . . to suicide attempts and very, very destructive behaviors. . . . The most significant example I can give you was the woman . . . who could no longer vacuum her house because she can't hear the sound of a vacuum; it reminds her of the suction machine of her abortion procedure. . . . Do they ever fully recover? I[t] would [be] fair to say no."[186] Indeed, dating back to the 1980s, the vacuum cleaner featured repeatedly in stories of women who described their trauma resulting from abortion, paralleling the earliest antiabortion comparisons between vacuum suction machines and vacuum cleaners.[187]

Amid repeated assertions that legalized abortion had deformed the nation, the South Dakota Task Force also reiterated the notion that women did not understand that abortion terminated the life of a human being: "A mother's unique relationship with her child during pregnancy" was "one of the most intimate and important relationships," a relationship "of intrinsic beauty and benefit to both the mother and her child." Therefore, the Task Force reasoned, "it is far outside the normal conduct of a mother to implicate herself in the killing of her own child."[188] Why, then, would women seek abortions? The task force concluded that women must not understand that abortion ended a life. "The pregnant mother is not told prior to her abortion that the procedure will terminate the life of a human being," the report argued. "The psychological consequences can be devastating when that woman learns, subsequent to the abortion, that this information was withheld."[189] Given the special mother-child bond starting during pregnancy, the South Dakota Task Force concluded, "it is simply unrealistic to expect that a pregnant mother is capable of being involved in the termination of the life of her own child without risk of suffering significant psychological trauma and distress."[190] The report concluded that women who had abortions could not have knowingly and willingly chosen the procedure and must have been misled or pressured into the decision by a partner, a parent, or the clinic. "The best interests of the child and the mother are always joined," Reardon argued, "even if the mother does not initially realize it, and even if she needs a tremendous amount of love and help to see it."[191]

Supporters of an abortion ban advanced the claim that legally protected abortion exposed women to abortions they did not want and should not have.[192] The brief in *Carhart* took up the evidence collected for the 2005 South Dakota Report. It contained lengthy affidavits from "More than One Thousand Post-Abortive Women," affidavits and exhibits from post-abortion syndrome experts Theresa Burke and David Reardon, and client intake records from pregnancy crisis centers. Antiabortion activists combined arguments about public health—women must be protected from pervasive threats to their health—and women's rights—women have a right to protection from an exploitative abortion industry—with traditional notions about women's roles. As Siegel eloquently noted, the new antiabortion strategy asserts that

> abortion *must* harm women because women are *by nature* mothers. Choosing against motherhood and subverting the physiology of pregnancy will make women ill—and in all events cannot represent what women really want, because any real woman wants what is best for her child. Women who seek abortions must have been confused, misled, or coerced into the decision to abort a pregnancy—because the choice to abort a pregnancy cannot reflect a normal woman's true desires or interests. Using law to restrict abortion protects women from such pressures and confusions—and frees women to be true women.[193]

Carhart's discussion of paternalist justifications for abortion restrictions prompted passionate objection from Justice Ginsburg and three other dissenting justices, who insisted that this new rationale for restricting abortion enforced unconstitutional stereotypes about women's agency and roles.[194] Employed to restrict access to abortion with the ban of intact D&E, it is currently used to limit abortion in a growing number of states through the enactment of twenty-week abortion bans and laws imposing unnecessary restrictions on abortion clinics and providers in the name of safety and women's health. It remains to be seen how effective the women-protective antiabortion argument will be in the long run.

The *Gonzales v. Carhart* decision marked the first time that the U.S. government successfully outlawed an abortion procedure and brought to an end the long and painful debate surrounding the nature of intact D&E. What had begun in 1973, with the indictment of Kenneth Edelin for the performance of a hysterotomy, reached fruition thirty-four years later in *Gonzales v. Carhart*. Controversy about the meaning of abortion procedures lay at the heart of both the Edelin case and the debate surrounding intact D&E. The decision to shift the debate around abortion from abstract moral principles to aesthetic concerns was both tactically brilliant and has been central to the antiabortion movement. If abortion providers talked about the safety and humanity of abortion, antiabortion activists focused on the procedures' danger to women and on grisly descriptions of fetal death. Indeed, Justice Kennedy's decision in *Gonzales v. Carhart* not only included Brenda Shafer's description of intact D&E but repeated the gruesome portrayal of other abortion procedures as well.[195] The redefinition of birth, abortion, and the fetus stood at the very center of the Edelin case, was key to his conviction, and followed abortion procedures into the twenty-first century.

The explicit focus on the most unpleasant aspects of abortion procedures proved crucial to the recruitment, retention and motivation of antiabortion activists. As the conflict surrounding abortion grew increasingly violent, the description and imagery of abortion grew more and more shocking. Antiabortion activists characterized the abortion conflict as a war. On picket lines, they displayed images that featured bloody body parts and constructed narratives that told of horrifying killings. Such displays seemed to justify not only the verbal denunciation of abortion providers, clinic personnel, and patients, but with time also the bombing of clinics and the murder of physicians and staff. Abortion providers and their patients were profoundly stigmatized as a result of this discourse. Locked into a pro-choice narrative that emphasized hardship cases, providers and their staff had few defenses. The limited narrative poorly represented the realities of abortion care. Although members of the November Gang and NCAP sought to invest both abortion providers and patients with the moral agency to make life-and-death decisions and to broaden the discussion to include a consideration of the moral complexities of later abortion care, their efforts were too little and came too late. While women who chose to have an abortion asserted their ability and right to act as moral agents on their own behalf, antiabortion activists denied that women had the ability to make such moral decisions, instead asserting that women — voiceless victims yet again — needed to be protected from abortion.

Epilogue

Between the early 1970s and the end of the decade, a sense of optimism and liberation accompanied the opening of legal abortion services. The introduction of vacuum aspiration led to the establishment of outpatient services, and throughout the 1970s, physicians, feminists, and entrepreneurs established a network of freestanding clinics that made abortion cheaper and more easily accessible than ever before. The idealism of women's health activists and demands of the 1970s feminist movement set a standard for feminist abortion services that positively influenced the establishment of abortion services. In the early 1970s, the Chicago underground abortion service Jane had set out to provide abortions as acts of liberation and empowerment. And feminist collectives, such as the Emma Goldman Clinic, had emphasized the importance of women learning about their options and making their own choices. Many providers adopted these ideas as they established abortion clinics in the 1970s. Indeed, the legalization of abortion and the realization that women's health could be an appealing marketing tool led to the proliferation of a range of women's health services. To be sure, a focus on women did not necessarily mean that services were feminist in nature. A high profit margin and a lack of regulation in many places meant that some clinics offered poor services, treated patients disrespectfully, and jeopardized women's health. But such services were the exception. Feminist services put women's choices and concerns at the center. Patient education was as important as a nonjudgmental attitude that supported women in their choices.

Women seeking abortions, in turn, were relieved at their ability to have access to legal, safe abortions and felt little stigma attached to the procedure. While they were unlikely to talk openly about their legal abortions, they did discuss experiences with illegal abortion. Abortions were personal and private. "I used to ask women how they first heard the word abortion, how they learned about it," Glenna Boyd, who had started as an abortion counselor in 1974, explained. "There were always very personal stories about someone they knew, or found out had had one."[1] With legalization, abortions became an integral part of women's reproductive lives. By 1980, women were ending 30 percent of all pregnancies, up from 19.3 percent in 1973. The health benefits of legal abortion were both immediate and profound. Within a decade, the risk of death from legal abortion had fallen below one death per 100,000 abortions. Abortion had become far safer than childbirth.[2]

By the end of the decade, abortion providers had established their own professional organization, NAF, which brought together providers and clinic staff from a wide range of different backgrounds. At annual meetings, NAF members shared their experiences and discussed standards of care. While discussions at these events could become heated, NAF was crucial in bringing together providers from a broad range of philosophical backgrounds to exchange ideas and information about abortion care. And it provided a forum in which to develop clinical guidelines for abortion clinics that could stand as a model for legislators and health authorities seeking to regulate abortion clinics. By 1980, then, abortion providers had established themselves as a legitimate part of the medical profession. Largely tied to freestanding clinics at the margins of the medical profession, they nevertheless asserted their position as professionals who conducted research, published about abortion care, exchanged information at regular meetings, and developed safe and affordable abortion services. Abortion providers spent the 1980s further refining abortion procedures and improving their services. Throughout the 1980s, they collected data, presented papers, and drafted guidelines to improve abortion methods after the first trimester. By the end of the decade, they had not only demonstrated the greater safety and convenience of D&E over saline and prostaglandin instillation procedures but had also developed training and counseling protocols to integrate D&E into clinical services. As a result, women's access to outpatient abortion procedures increased to include second trimester procedures.

The election of President Ronald Reagan in 1980 brought to a close the heady period of optimism. While supporters of abortion rights spent the 1980s further increasing access to abortion, antiabortion activists spent the decade undermining their efforts by embarking on an aggressive campaign to discredit abortion providers, clinic staff, and the women who sought abortion services. They harassed and humiliated patients through sidewalk counseling, duped women into visiting CPCs where antiabortion activists scared clients away from abortion services, and created narratives that redefined the fetus as a baby and abortion as murder. Activists focused in particular on the death of the fetus in abortion. By ascribing consciousness to the fetus, these narratives emphasized the violence of abortion, severely distorted the experience of fetal death, and raised the impression that all abortions were done late in pregnancy.

By the end of the 1980s, antiabortion activists had successfully redefined the meaning of abortion. If, previously, as Glenna Boyd had noted, women had first heard about abortion through a friend or relative, "someone they knew, or found out had had one," by the end of the 1980s their first exposure to abortion was likely to be through "some ugly billboard."[3] The new narratives significantly narrowed the interpretive framework in which to understand the role of abortion providers and patients. In these antiabortion narratives, abortion providers became cold-blooded killers who lacked any sense of morality and were happy to jeopardize women's health and lives to make a profit. Women seeking abortions were depicted at best as naive and lacking in any understanding of what they were doing and at worst as colluding in the killing of their children for their own convenience. Framing abortions as acts of liberation and empowerment, as a moral choice for women, became by the late 1980s unimaginable. Indeed, a positive interpretation of abortion became unspeakable, and abortion providers, who had discussed their work in the early years, fell silent. In public discourse, women and abortion providers had lost the argument for abortion as a positive good that helped women gain control over their lives.

The antiabortion emphasis on the fetus as sensate and conscious also contributed to a significant shift in U.S. Supreme Court opinion. While, in 1977, the court had upheld states' refusal to fund abortion after the 1976 Hyde Amendment eliminated federal Medicaid funds for abortion, it had limited restrictions on abortion to the third trimester. In its 1989 decision *Webster v. Reproductive Health Services*, the Supreme Court argued for the first time since *Roe* that states could express an interest in fetal life prior to viability—before the third trimester. The notion that the state ought to be able to protect the developing fetus was further strengthened in its 1992 decision in *Planned Parenthood v. Casey*, which permitted abortion barriers the Supreme Court had previously found unconstitutional. Moreover, Supreme Court justices began to treat women, too, as a group that needed to be protected from abortion. Following *Webster* and

Casey, state legislators introduced a record number of antiabortion bills, including mandatory waiting periods, counseling laws, parental consent laws, and state-imposed restrictions on facilities that provide abortions. Abortion providers faced increasingly unnecessary and costly regulations designed to drive clinics out of business. Particularly for poor, minority, young, and rural women, access to abortion became more difficult as a result.

These changes were accompanied by growing protests in front of abortion clinics. In the course of the 1980s, antiabortion pickets and demonstrations grew in size and intensity. The rise of OR by the end of the decade drew thousands of protestors to clinics across the country, transforming the experience of performing and receiving abortion care into one of fear and intimidation. Antiabortion activists adopted increasingly aggressive tactics, terrifying patients, abortion providers, and clinic staff and attacking abortion clinics, vandalizing property, and firebombing clinics. In early 1993, the killing of abortion provider Dr. David Gunn marked the beginning of a period of terror heretofore unprecedented. Under these conditions, the number of physicians willing to provide abortions fell for the first time since abortion had become legal, from the all-time high of 2,908 in 1982 to 2,380 a decade later to 1,819 by 2000, a drop of 37 percent.[4]

By the early 1990s, the beginning of the third time period, abortion providers grew tired of a defensive stance that emphasized their resilience and professionalism but still left them feeling powerless at the hands of hostile protestors and legislators. Frustrated by a lack of support from law enforcement and a professional organization they felt was unresponsive to the growing security threats, abortion providers began to look elsewhere for representation and developed new ways to respond to antiabortion challenges. They established two new organizations—NCAP and the November Gang. While NCAP sought to improve the image of abortion providers and offer them a voice in Washington, members of the November Gang turned their attention to the implications that the increase in abortion stigma had on abortion care. Over the following decade, they developed new counseling strategies to address the shame women felt concerning their abortion and began to articulate a vision of abortion as moral care that challenged the notion that abortion providers and their patients were immoral.

When, in 1993, antiabortion activists launched a concerted campaign against intact D&E, the so-called partial birth abortion procedure, the abortion provider community found itself unable to formulate a cohesive response. Torn between a politics of respectability that dismissed the campaign against intact D&E as politically motivated and a desire to address the roots of abortion stigma, members of the abortion provider community found themselves embroiled in a heated discussion over whether and how to defend intact D&E. The debate demonstrated the need for a new kind of pro-choice discourse—one that acknowledged the violence in second trimester abortion and used honesty about D&E to strengthen abortion care.[5] If previously abortion counselors had been hesitant to engage patients in a discussion about abortion and violence, members of the November Gang now developed a counseling framework in which women and clinic staff could explore questions surrounding abortion and death. And although abortion providers lost the battle over intact D&E when the 2007 U.S. Supreme Court decision *Gonzales v. Carhart* upheld a ban of the procedure, the discussions surrounding second trimester abortions were instrumental in the creation of counseling frameworks that addressed the issue of violence inherent in abortion procedures and articulated why—despite this—abortion care is grounded in feminist values. First articulated outside NAF, these debates were eventually carried back into the organization to a larger audience of abortion providers.

More than four decades after the legalization of abortion, the abortion provider community is articulating a vision of abortion that powerfully asserts that abortion care is a moral good. Indeed, while often lost in the noise of antiabortion chants, throughout the 1990s and beyond women asserted in private that they felt good about their abortions and that the experience had strengthened their self-confidence and understanding of themselves as moral agents. As one woman wrote to Susan Wicklund in 2000, "[My abortion] was one of the most difficult experiences I've had in my 23 years, yes, but it was also somehow one of the most reassuring and affirming experiences that I have had as a woman."[6] In the past five years, the proliferation of online sites has made these voices more public and offered women and abortion providers a place to articulate their positive abortion experiences and read about the positive experiences of others. While these new voices cannot erase the stigma attached to abortion care, they offer a crucial intervention into a discourse in which women and abortion providers need to reassert their moral agency. And by doing so, they play an important role in erasing the stigma.

Still, at the moment when new interventions in counseling and training promise to revive the feminist philosophies of abortion care, the explosion of regulations makes it increasingly hard for abortion clinics to offer feminist-inspired services. Between 2011 and 2013, state lawmakers enacted more abortion restrictions than they had in the previous decade.[7]

Today, almost any aspect of abortion care is subject to regulation: from clinic buildings and the landscaping outside to the bureaucratic aspects (paperwork, patient consent forms, logs, reporting requirements); the delivery of care (including state-mandated counseling scripts that dictate what and how abortion providers and counselors are to communicate with patients); the sterilization of instruments; clinic laboratories; the disposal of fetal tissue; and the hiring, training, and professional affiliations of staff. Most of these regulations were designed to put abortion clinics out of business, and they have indeed led to the closure of many abortion clinics unable to comply with the costly regulations.

And as state regulation of abortion clinics has led to the closure of abortion clinics, the number of clinics providing substandard care has increased. Today, abortion provider LeRoy Carhart explains, there are two types of physicians performing abortions: "The doctors who are totally committed to women's health and are going to do them even if they never get another dime and the people that just want to take advantage of the situation and milk everything they can out of it."[8] Just over the past years, the cases of Dr. Kermit Gosnell and Dr. Steven Brigham illustrate that for years local and state authorities ignored complaints about the two providers who ran what sociologist Carole Joffe has termed "rogue clinics"—facilities that prey on women from low-income communities with the promise of low prices. Their clinics compared with "back alley" facilities of the pre-*Roe* era and the shoddy Chicago clinics featured in the 1978 *Chicago Sun-Times* expose, where unscrupulous and often unskilled persons provided abortions to desperate women, in substandard conditions.[9] The very existence of rogue clinics illustrates that women's reproductive health has remained a low priority in our society. Only the full acknowledgment that women are moral agents capable of making decisions about their pregnancies will lead us to a society where women can gain full reproductive control—in clinics that offer safe and respectable treatment.

Notes

Abbreviations Used in the Notes

EGC   Emma Goldman Clinic Papers, Iowa Women's Archive, University of Iowa,
Iowa City, Iowa

MHP   Merle Hoffman Papers, Duke University Libraries, Sally Bingham Center for
Women's History and Culture, Duke University, Durham, N.C.

RCP   Renee Chelian Papers, Duke University Libraries, Sally Bingham Center for
Women's History and Culture, Duke University, Durham, N.C.

SHP   Susan Hill Papers, Duke University Libraries, Sally Bingham Center for
Women's History and Culture, Duke University, Durham, N.C.

SWP   Susan Wicklund Papers, Duke University Libraries, Sally Bingham Center
for Women's History and Culture, Duke University, Durham, N.C.

TBP   Terry Beresford Papers, Duke University Libraries, Sally Bingham Center for
Women's History and Culture, Duke University, Durham, N.C.

TCP   Takey Crist Papers, Duke University Libraries, Sally Bingham Center for
Women's History and Culture, Duke University, Durham, N.C.

Introduction

1. Tape 22: UNC Infirmary—Coed requests pill, Subject Files UNC, TCP.

2. American College Health Association, [Survey], n.d. [1970], file Sex Education—College Information, Subject Files UNC, TCP.

3. This situation did not change significantly until the mid-1970s, after the 1972 Supreme Court decision *Eisenstadt v. Baird* established the right of unmarried people to possess contraception on the same basis as married couples. See Heather Munro Prescott, *Student Bodies: The Influence of Student Health Services in American Society and Medicine* (Ann Arbor: University of Michigan Press, 2007), 153.

4. Susan Hill, interview with Johanna Schoen, Raleigh, N.C., Jan. 2004.

5. See Johanna Schoen, *Choice and Coercion: Birth Control, Sterilization, and Abortion in Public Health and Welfare* (Chapel Hill: University of North Carolina Press, 2005), 179–93.

6. Anonymous, Jan. 8, 1971, file Abortion Letters UNC, Subject Files UNC, TCP.

7. No title [interview by Takey Crist with UNC student], n.d. [late 1960s/early 1970s], file Interviews Coeds, Subject Files UNC, TCP.

8. Ibid. See other interviews in ibid.

9. Anonymous to Takey Crist, Mar. 26, 1970, file Abortion Letters UNC, Subject Files UNC, TCP.

10. Student letter, Jan. 21, 1970, file Abortion Letters UNC, Subject Files UNC, TCP. See also Prescott, *Student Bodies*, 141–43.

11. Hill, interview, Jan. 2004.

12. Ibid.

13. Lawrence Lader, *Abortion* (Boston: Beacon Press, 1966), 17, 59. Even in North Carolina, where abortion reform in 1968 made hospital abortions more accessible, the increase was incremental. The number of abortions at UNC's Memorial Hospital rose from 8 in 1966, prior to reform, to 164 in 1969 to 616 in 1970. See Schoen, *Choice and Coercion*, 186.

14. Lader, *Abortion*, 42–63 (list of states on 54–55). Leslie J. Reagan, "Crossing the Border for Abortions: California Activists, Mexican Clinics, and the Creation of a Feminist Health Agency in the 1960s," *Feminist Studies* 26, no. 2 (Summer 2000): 323–48.

15. Lader, *Abortion*, 64.

16. Ibid., 2–3, 66. Other estimates of mortality rates were even higher. One study at the University of California's School of Public Health estimated 5,000 to 10,000 abortion deaths annually. Almost half of all childbearing deaths in New York City were attributed to abortion alone. See also Cynthia Gorney, *Articles of Faith: A Frontline History of the Abortion Wars* (New York: Simon and Schuster, 1998), 23, 539, and Mary Streichen Calderone, ed., *Abortion in the United States: A Conference Sponsored by the Planned Parenthood Federation of America, Inc. at Arden House and the New York Academy of Medicine* (New York: Harper and Brothers, 1958). For an assessment on the links between state interference and safety of the procedure, see Leslie J. Reagan, *When Abortion Was a Crime: Women, Medicine, and Law in the United States, 1867–1973* (Berkeley: University of California Press, 1997).

17. Reagan, *When Abortion Was a Crime*, 167.

18. Lader, *Abortion*, 3, 66.

19. Ibid., 53.

20. Hill, interview, Jan. 2004. For a discussion on finding an illegal abortion provider, see, for instance, Schoen, *Choice and Coercion*, 163–79.

21. Mary Lynn M. Luy, "Fear and Loathing in the Stirrups: What's behind Women's Wrath toward Gynecologists?," *Modern Medicine*, Oct. 14, 1974, 18.

22. Elizabeth B. Connell, "Women and Their Doctors," n.d. [early 1970s], file Women's Liberation, Subject Files Crist Clinic, TCP.

23. Kay Weiss, "Contempt for Women: What Medical Students Learn in Our Best Universities," *Off Our Backs*, Apr./May 1975, 24. See also Diana Scully and Pauline Bart, "A Funny Thing Happened on the Way to the Orifice: Women in Gynecology Textbooks," *American Journal of Sociology* 78, no. 4 (Jan. 1973): 1045–50.

24. Roxie Tullis, interview with LeAnn Erickson, undated [ca. 1993], EGC.

25. Susan Wicklund, interview with Johanna Schoen, Wilsall, Mont., Aug. 3, 2013.

26. Tullis, interview with Erickson.

27. Boston Women's Health Book Collective, 1973, p. 1, as quoted in Sandra Morgen, *Into Our Own Hands: The Women's Health Movement in the United States, 1969–1990* (New Brunswick, N.J.: Rutgers University Press, 2002), 4.

28. Wendy Kline, *Bodies of Knowledge: Sexuality, Reproduction, and Women's Health in the Second Wave* (Chicago: University of Chicago Press, 2010); Kathy Davis,

The Making of "Our Bodies, Ourselves": How Feminism Travels across Borders (Durham, N.C.: Duke University Press, 2007).

29. Laura Kaplan, *The Story of Jane: The Legendary Underground Feminist Abortion Service* (New York: Pantheon Books, 1995).

30. Reagan, "Crossing the Border for Abortions."

31. Morgen, *Into Our Own Hands*; Michelle Murphy, "Immodest Witnessing: The Epistemology of Vaginal Self-Examination in the U.S. Feminist Self-Help Movement," *Feminist Studies* 30, no. 1 (Spring 2004): 115–47; Carole E. Joffe, Tracy A. Weitz, and C. L. Staecy, "Uneasy Allies: Pro-Choice Physicians, Feminist Health Activists, and the Struggle for Abortion Rights," *Sociology of Health and Illness* 26, no. 2 (2004): 775–96.

32. Tullis, interview with Erickson.

33. Lader, *Abortion*; Bernard N. Nathanson, *Aborting America* (Garden City, N.Y.: Doubleday, 1979), 33.

34. David P. Cline, *Creating Choice: A Community Responds to the Need for Abortion and Birth Control, 1961–1973* (New York: Palgrave Macmillan, 2006), 6.

35. Prescott, *Student Bodies*, 145–48.

36. See, for instance, *Sex Information* (Raleigh: Division of Student Affairs, North Carolina State University, 1969); Richard Mier, Donald Rollins, and Thomas Blush, *Elephants and Butterflies* (Chapel Hill: University of North Carolina, EOS, 1970); Student Committee on Human Sexuality, *Sex and the Yale Student* (New Haven, Conn.: Yale University, 1970); *Venereal Disease, Abortion, Birth Control: A Guide for the Tri-Cities Area* (Schenectady, N.Y.: Union College Student Senate and Planned Parenthood Schenectady, 1971); Marian Johnson Gray and Roger W. Gray, *How to Take the Worry out of Being Close: An Egg and Sperm Handbook* (Oakland, Calif.: Son, 1971); Duke Committee on Contraception and Abortion, *A Guide to Contraception and Abortion* (Durham, N.C.: Duke University, 1971); Lynn K. Hansen, Barbara Reskin, and Diana Gray, *How to Have Intercourse . . . without Getting Screwed: A Guide to Birth Control, Abortion, and Venereal Disease* (Seattle: ASUW Women's Commission, University of Washington, 1972); Nancy Crampton, *Between Your Navel and Your Knees* (Houston: University of Houston Student Association, 1972); American University Hotline, *Sex Facts for the AU Student* (Washington, D.C.: American University, 1973).

37. Heather Munro Prescott, *A Doctor of Their Own: The History of Adolescent Medicine* (Cambridge, Mass.: Harvard University Press, 1998), 155–57.

38. William E. Easterling and Charles H. Hendricks, "Pregnancy Termination: The First Five Years at North Carolina Memorial Hospital," 1971, table 2, folder UNC Co-Ed Abortions, Subject Files UNC, TCP. For more on the reform of North Carolina's abortion law, see Schoen, *Choice and Coercion*, 179–93.

39. Anonymous to Takey Crist, Jan. 11, 1970, file Abortion Letters UNC, Subject Files UNC, TCP.

40. See, for instance, David Mastbrook to Takey Crist, Nov. 3, 1970, and enclosed returns of questionnaires on campus birth control services, folder Sex Education—College Information, Subject Files UNC, TCP.

41. Eisenstadt v. Baird, 405 U.S. 438 (1972); Prescott, *Student Bodies*, 153.

42. Prescott, *Student Bodies*, 149–50.

43. Ibid., 144.

44. Reagan, *When Abortion Was a Crime*, 216–45.

45. For a comprehensive discussion on the intersection of disability and the abortion debate in America, see Leslie J. Reagan, *Dangerous Pregnancies: Mothers, Disabilities, and Abortion in Modern America* (Berkeley: University of California Press, 2010).

46. Lader, *Abortion*, 148.

47. See, for instance, Susan Brownmiller, *In Our Time: Memoir of a Revolution* (New York: Dell, 1999); Diane Schulder and Florynce Kennedy, *Abortion Rap* (New York: McGraw-Hill, 1971); Morgen, *Into Our Own Hands*.

48. Melody Rose, *Safe, Legal, and Unavailable: Abortion Politics in the United States* (Washington, D.C.: CQPress, 2007), 6–7. See also David J. Garrow, *Liberty and Sexuality: The Right to Privacy and the Making of Roe v. Wade* (New York: Macmillan, 1994).

49. Gorney, *Articles of Faith*, 93–94; Lawrence Lader, *Abortion II: Making the Revolution* (Boston: Beacon Press, 1973). In New York City alone, 55,347 residents and 83,975 nonresidents sought legal abortions within the first year of legalization; see Gorney, *Articles of Faith*, 97.

50. Lader, *Abortion II*, 115–20.

51. Ibid., 109–15; Garrow, *Liberty and Sexuality*.

52. Rose, *Safe, Legal, and Unavailable*, 63–64.

53. Ibid., 57–85.

54. Ibid.

55. Ibid.

56. Ibid., 76.

57. Ibid., 57–85.

58. Reva B. Siegel, "The Right's Reasons: Constitutional Conflict and the Spread of Woman-Protective Antiabortion Argument," *Duke Law Journal* 57 (2008): 1641–92.

59. Willard Cates Jr. and David A. Grimes, "Morbidity and Mortality of Abortion in the United States," in *Abortion and Sterilization: Medical and Social Aspects*, ed. Jane E. Hodgson (New York: Grune and Stratton, 1981), 170.

60. Kaplan, *The Story of Jane*; Kline, *Bodies of Knowledge*; Morgen, *Into Our Own Hands*; Wendy Simonds, *Abortion at Work: Ideology and Practice in a Feminist Clinic* (New Brunswick, N.J.: Rutgers University Press, 1996).

61. Kristin Luker, *Abortion and the Politics of Motherhood* (Berkeley: University of California Press, 1984); Dallas A. Blanchard and Terry J. Prewitt, *Religious Violence and Abortion: The Gideon Project* (Gainesville: University Press of Florida, 1993); Dallas A. Blanchard, *From Polite to Fiery Protest: The Anti-Abortion Movement and the Rise of the Religious Right* (New York: Twayne Publishers, 1994); James Risen and Judy L. Thomas, *Wrath of Angels: The American Abortion War* (New York: Basic Books, 1998); Gorney, *Articles of Faith*; Carol Mason, *Killing for Life: The Apocalyptic Narrative of Pro-Life Politics* (Ithaca, N.Y.: Cornell University Press, 2002); Carol J. C. Maxwell, *Pro-Life Activists in America: Meaning, Motivation, and Direct Action* (Cambridge: Cambridge University Press, 2002). William Saletan, *Bearing Right: How Conservatives Won the Abortion War* (Berkeley: University of California Press, 2003); Alesha E. Doan, *Opposition and Intimidation: The Abortion Wars and Strategies of Political Harassment* (Ann Arbor: University of Michigan Press, 2007); Ziad W. Mun-

son, *The Making of Pro-Life Activists: How Social Movement Mobilization Works* (Chicago: University of Chicago Press, 2008); Jennifer Jefferis, *Armed for Life: The Army of God and Anti-Abortion Terror in the United States* (Santa Barbara, Calif.: Praeger, 2011); Stephen Singular, *The Wichita Divide: The Murder of Dr. George Tiller and the Battle over Abortion* (New York: St. Martin's Press, 2011).

62. Rosalind P. Petchesky, *Abortion and Woman's Choice: The State, Sexuality, and Reproductive Freedom* (Boston: Northeastern University Press, 1984); Donald Critchlow, *Intended Consequences: Birth Control, Abortion, and the Federal Government in Modern America* (New York: Oxford University Press, 1999); Garrow, *Liberty and Sexuality*; Rose, *Safe, Legal, and Unavailable?*

63. Carroll Smith-Rosenberg, *Disorderly Conduct: Visions of Gender in Victorian America* (New York: Oxford University Press, 1986), 217–44; James Mohr, *Abortion in America: The Origins and Evolution of National Policy* (New York: Oxford University Press, 1978); Janet Farrell Brodie, *Contraception and Abortion in Nineteenth-Century America* (Ithaca, N.Y.: Cornell University Press, 1994); Reagan, *When Abortion Was a Crime*; Andrea Tone, *Devices and Desires: A History of Contraceptives in America* (New York: Hill and Wang, 2001).

64. Reagan, *When Abortion Was a Crime*; Reagan, *Dangerous Pregnancies*; Schoen, *Choice and Coercion*; Patricia G. Miller, *The Worst of Times: Illegal Abortion—Survivors, Practitioners, Coroners, Cops, and Children of Women Who Died Talk about Its Horrors* (New York: Harper Collins, 1993); Rickie Solinger, *The Abortionist: A Woman against the Law* (New York: Free Press, 1994).

65. Rosalind P. Petchesky, "Foetal Images: The Power of Visual Culture in the Politics of Reproduction," in *Reproductive Technologies: Gender, Motherhood, and Medicine*, ed. Michelle Stanworth (Minneapolis: University of Minnesota Press, 1987), 57–80; Lisa M. Mitchell, *Baby's First Picture: Ultrasound and the Politics of Fetal Subjects* (Toronto: University of Toronto Press, 2001); Steven Maynard-Moody, *The Dilemma of the Fetus: Fetal Research, Medical Progress, and Moral Politics* (New York: St. Martin's Press, 1995); Lynn M. Morgan and Meredith W. Michaels, eds., *Fetal Subjects, Feminist Positions* (Philadelphia: University of Pennsylvania Press, 1999); Lynn M. Morgan, *Icons of Life: A Cultural History of Human Embryos* (Berkeley: University of California Press, 2009); Rayna Rapp, *Testing Women, Testing the Fetus: The Social Impact of Amniocentesis in America* (New York: Routledge, 2000); Sara Dubow, *Ourselves Unborn: A History of the Fetus in Modern America* (Oxford: Oxford University Press, 2011).

66. Dubow, *Ourselves Unborn*; Petchesky, "Foetal Images."

67. See Dan Healey, *Homosexual Desire in Revolutionary Russia: The Regulation of Sexual and Gender Dissent* (Chicago: University of Chicago Press, 2001), 1–18.

68. Saletan, *Bearing Right*, 2.

69. See https://www.youtube.com/user/EmilyEstherLetts. An Internet search for abortion experience yields a number of YouTube videos in which young women describe their positive abortion experiences. At the same time, Lett's video also led to postings critiquing her for glorifying the abortion procedure.

70. See, for instance, Carole Joffe, *Doctors of Conscience: The Struggle to Provide Abortion before and after Roe v. Wade* (Boston: Beacon Press, 1995); Suzanne T. Pop-

pema, *Why I Am an Abortion Doctor* (Amherst, N.Y.: Prometheus Books, 1996); Susan Wicklund and Alex Kesselheim, *This Common Secret: My Journey as an Abortion Doctor* (New York: Public Affairs, 2007); William F. Harrison, "Why I Provide Abortions," *Daily Kos*, May 31, 2007, http://www.dailykos.com/story/2007/05/31/341498/-WHY -I-PROVIDE-ABORTIONS (accessed Mar. 20, 2015); Merle Hoffman, *Intimate Wars: The Life and Times of the Woman Who Brought Abortion from the Back Alley to the Boardroom* (New York: Feminist Press, 2012). See also http://prh.org/provider-voices /why-i-provide-abortions/ (accessed Mar. 20, 2015).

71. Rickie Solinger, ed., *Abortion Wars: A Half Century of Struggle, 1950–2000* (Berkeley: University of California Press, 1998); Joffe, *Doctors of Conscience*; Eyal Press, *Absolute Convictions: My Father, a City, and the Conflict That Divided America* (New York: Henry Holt, 2006); Faye Wattleton, *Life on the Line* (New York: Ballantine Books, 1996); Gorney, *Articles of Faith*; Faye D. Ginsburg, *Contested Lives: The Abortion Debate in an American Community* (Berkeley: University of California Press, 1989); Carole Joffe, *Dispatches from the Abortion Wars: The Costs of Fanaticism to Doctors, Patients, and the Rest of Us* (Boston: Beacon Press, 2009).

72. See, for instance, http://myabortionmylife.org/; http://www.theabortiondiaries .com/; http://www.prochoiceamerica.org/womens-voices/womens-stories/; and http:// theabortiondiarypodcast.com/ (all accessed Mar. 20, 2015).

73. NAF Member Directory, 1979, and NAF Member Directory, 1982/83 (Washington, D.C.: National Abortion Federation).

74. Facts on Induced Abortion in the United States (July 2014), Guttmacher Institute, http://www.guttmacher.org/pubs/fb_induced_abortion.pdf (accessed Mar. 20, 2015).

75. David A. Grimes, "6 Things to Understand When Talking about Abortion," Huffington Post, Dec. 10, 2014, http://www.huffingtonpost.com/david-a-grimes/abortion -terminology-things-to-understand_b_6175430.html (accessed Jan. 7, 2015).

Chapter One

1. Deb Nye, interview with LeAnn Erickson, undated [ca. 1993], EGC.

2. Renee Chelian, interview with Peg Johnston, 2008.

3. Willard Cates Jr. and David A. Grimes, "Morbidity and Mortality of Abortion in the United States," in *Abortion and Sterilization: Medical and Social Aspects*, ed. Jane E. Hodgson (New York: Grune and Stratton, 1981), 170.

4. Carole E. Joffe, Tracy A. Weitz, and C. L. Staecy, "Uneasy Allies: Pro-Choice Physicians, Women's Health Activists, and the Struggle for Abortion Rights," *Sociology of Health and Illness* 26, no. 6 (2004): 775–96.

5. See, for instance, Frederick J. Taussig, *Abortion, Spontaneous and Induced: Medical and Social Aspects* (St. Louis: C. V. Mosbach, 1936); Lawrence Lader, *Abortion* (Boston: Beacon Press, 1966); Mary Streichen Calderone, ed., *Abortion in the United States: A Conference Sponsored by the Planned Parenthood Federation of America, Inc. at Arden House and the New York Academy of Medicine* (New York: Harper and Brothers, 1958); Jerome E. Bates and Edward S. Zawadzki, *Criminal Abortion: A Study in Medical Sociology* (Springfield, Ill.: Charles C. Thomas, 1964); Paul H. Gebhard, *Pregnancy,*

Birth, and Abortion (New York: Harper and Brothers, 1958); Harold Rosen, ed., *Therapeutic Abortion: Medical, Psychiatric, Legal, Anthropological, and Religious Considerations in the Prevention of Conception and the Interruption of Pregnancy* (New York: Julian Press, 1954).

6. Cates and Grimes, "Morbidity and Mortality," 155.

7. Leslie J. Reagan, *When Abortion Was a Crime: Women, Medicine, and Law in the United States, 1867–1973* (Berkeley: University of California Press, 1997), 179–80; for a discussion of hospital abortion committees, see 173–81.

8. Takey Crist, interview with Johanna Schoen, May 20, 2001 Jacksonville, N.C. Such narratives powerfully shaped physicians' approaches to abortion once the procedure became legal. See, for instance, Carole Joffe, *Doctors of Conscience: The Struggle to Provide Abortion before and after Roe v. Wade* (Boston: Beacon Press, 1995), 53–69, and Cynthia Gorney, *Articles of Faith: A Frontline History of the Abortion Wars* (New York: Simon and Schuster, 1998), 16–17, 217–18.

9. Cited in Gorney, *Articles of Faith*, 218. After legalization, this physician joined the medical staff of Reproductive Health Services, St. Louis's first abortion clinic.

10. Ibid., 25.

11. Charles deProsse, interview with Johanna Schoen, Oct. 23, 2002, Iowa City, Iowa.

12. Jane E. Hodgson, "Abortion by Vacuum Aspiration," in Hodgson, *Abortion and Sterilization*, 229.

13. Ibid., 225–26; M. Vojta, "A Critical View of Vacuum Aspiration: A New Method for the Termination of Pregnancy," *Obstetrics and Gynecology* 30, no. 1 (July 1967): 28–34; Dorothea Kerslake and Donn Casey, "Abortion Induced by Means of the Uterine Aspirator," *Obstetrics and Gynecology* 30, no. 1 (July 1967): 35–45; Franc Novak, "Experience with Suction Curettage," in *Abortion in a Changing World*, vol. 1, ed. Robert E. Hall (New York: Columbia University Press, 1970), 74–84.

14. Hodgson, "Abortion by Vacuum Aspiration," 225–26; Vojta, "A Critical View of Vacuum Aspiration"; Kerslake and Casey, "Abortion Induced by Means of the Uterine Aspirator."

15. Novak, "Experience with Suction Curettage," 77.

16. Jaroslav Hulka, interview with Johanna Schoen, Chapel Hill, N.C., May 22, 2001. Christopher Tietze and Sarah Lewit claim that the first suction machine was introduced in the United States in 1966. See Christopher Tietze and Sarah Lewit, "Joint Program for the Study of Abortion (JPSA): Early Medical Complications of Legal Abortion," *Studies in Family Planning* 3, no. 6 (June 1972): 103.

17. Hulka, interview.

18. Gorney, *Articles of Faith*, 198–99. By the summer of 1970, as New York physicians prepared for the lifting of all abortion restrictions in their state, a handful of medical equipment companies were making vacuum suction machines that promised to drastically simplify first trimester abortions.

19. Jean Pakter et al., "Surveillance of Abortion Program in New York City," *Bulletin of the New York Academy of Medicine* 47, no. 8 (Aug. 1971): 853–74. Over 65 percent of women receiving abortions in New York in the early 1970s were from outside the state.

20. Carole Joffe, "Abortion in Historical Perspective," in *A Clinician's Guide to Medical and Surgical Abortion*, ed. Maureen Paul et al. (New York: Churchill Livingstone,

1999), 3–10; Charles deProsse, interview with Johanna Schoen, Mar. 31, 2011, Iowa City, Iowa.

21. Lisa Cronin Wohl, "Would You Buy an Abortion from This Man? The Harvey Karman Controversy," *Ms. Magazine*, Sept. 1975, 60–64, 113–24; Feminist Women's Health Center, "Synopsis of the Activities of Harvey Karman," n.d., box 2, folder 2–3, "Menstrual Extraction," Detroit Feminist Women's Health Center Collection, Collections of Archives of Labor and Urban Affairs, University Archives, Wayne State University.

22. Wohl, "Would You Buy an Abortion from This Man?" See also Merle Hoffman, *Intimate Wars: The Life and Times of the Woman Who Brought Abortion from the Back Alley to the Board Room* (New York: Feminist Press, 2012).

23. Bernard N. Nathanson, "Ambulatory Abortion: Experience with 26,000 Cases (July 1, 1970, to August 1, 1971)," *New England Journal of Medicine* 286 (Feb. 24, 1972): 403–7; file Abortion Update, 1972, series Abortion, TCP; Kerslake and Casey, "Abortion Induced by Means of the Uterine Aspirator."

24. A. I. Csapo, "Termination of Pregnancy by the Intra-amniotic Injection of Hypertonic Saline," *Yearbook of Obstetrics and Gynecology*, 1966–67, ed. J. P. Greenhill (Chicago: Year Book Medical Publisher, 1966): 126–63.

25. Ibid.

26. Thomas D. Kerenyi, "Intraamniotic Techniques," in Hodgson, *Abortion and Sterilization*, 359–60; Csapo, "Termination of Pregnancy by the Intra-amniotic Injection of Hypertonic Saline."

27. In the early 1970s, one study measured case fatality ratio for 2,950 hysterotomies of 271.2 per 100,000 procedures. P. Diggory notes in an article on hysterotomy and hysterectomy as abortion techniques: "In the early days of legal abortion in the United States, when hysterotomy was still being relatively frequently performed, the mortality was approximately 100 times as great as early vaginal termination of pregnancy" (P. Diggory, "Hysterotomy and Hysterectomy as Abortion Techniques," in Hodgson, *Abortion and Sterilization*, 318). See also Gary S. Berger et al., "Maternal Mortality Associated with Legal Abortion in New York State; July 1, 1970, to June 30, 1972," *Obstetrics and Gynecology* 43, no. 3 (1974): 315.

28. Gorney, *Articles of Faith*, 294–95.

29. "When Your Patient Wants an Abortion," *Patient Care*, Aug. 1, 1974, 82–104, file Abortion Update, 1975, series Abortion, TCP.

30. M. Bygdeman, "Prostaglandins," in Hodgson, *Abortion and Sterilization*, 346–48.

31. Sixty-six institutions across the country participated in the study. See Tietze and Lewit, "Joint Program for the Study of Abortion."

32. Ibid.

33. Cates and Grimes, "Morbidity and Mortality," 155.

34. Ibid., 168–70. Between 1972 and 1977, the death-to-case rate for vacuum curettage procedures performed at twelve weeks' gestation or earlier was 1.2 per 100,000 procedures.

35. Chuck deProsse, interview with Johanna Schoen, Mar. 31, 2011, Iowa City, Iowa.

36. Ibid. Numbers for Ithaca are not available.

37. Frances Kissling, phone interview with Johanna Schoen, Nov. 21, 2011. Kissling

also worked for Eastern Women's Medical Center, which was started by Karl Fossum and functioned very much like Pelham, although Fossum's clinic was larger.

38. Chelian, interview.

39. Kissling, interview. See also Lader, *Abortion II*, 149–69. In 1970 Planned Parenthood and the Clergy Consultation Service successfully pressured for-profit hospitals to cut their cost of abortion from between $400 and $500 to between $200 and $300. See Howard Eisenberg, "The Mad Scramble for Abortion Money," *Medical Economics*, Jan. 4, 1971, 991–97.

40. Uta Landy, phone interview with Johanna Schoen, Nov. 18, 2011.

41. Kissling, interview.

42. Gorney, *Articles of Faith*, 97. Abortion services also became available in several other states. By 1970, women could travel to California and Washington, D.C., for a legal abortion. Alaska, Hawaii, and Washington offered legal abortions to their residents.

43. Kissling, interview.

44. Chelian, interview.

45. Eisenberg, "Mad Scramble for Abortion Money."

46. Byllye Y. Avery, interview with Loretta Ross, July 21–22, 2005, Provincetown, Mass., Voices of Feminism Oral History Project, 2006, Sophia Smith Collection, Smith College, Northampton, Mass.

47. The statistics differentiate only between white and nonwhite where race was known. See *CDC Abortion Surveillance Annual Report*, 1972.

48. As quoted in Eisenberg, "Mad Scramble for Abortion Money."

49. Ibid. See Joffe, *Doctors of Conscience*, for a discussion on the endurance of the negative stereotype that abortion providers were only in it for the money.

50. See, for instance, Rickie Solinger, *The Abortionist: A Woman against the Law* (New York: Free Press, 1995), for Ruth Barnett's experience working for an abortion syndicate in the early 1950s. See also Joffe, *Doctors of Conscience*.

51. As quoted in Joffe, *Doctors of Conscience*, 153.

52. Ibid., 175.

53. Bernard Nathanson, *Aborting America* (New York: Doubleday, 1979), 112–13.

54. Eisenberg, "Mad Scramble for Abortion Money," 992.

55. Quoted in ibid., 991.

56. Ibid.; Joffe, *Doctors of Conscience*, 145.

57. Quoted in Joffe, *Doctors of Conscience*, 146.

58. Ibid., 150–61. See also Lori Freedman, *Willing and Unable: Doctors' Constraints in Abortion Care* (Nashville, Tenn.: Vanderbilt University Press, 2010).

59. Eisenberg, "Mad Scramble for Abortion Money."

60. Ibid.

61. Such statistics mean that abortion is seven times safer than childbirth and carries approximately the same risk of death as receiving a shot of penicillin. See National Abortion Federation, "The Years of Legal Abortion: The Effects on Public Health," 1983, file NAF 1983; series Abortion, TCP; and Cates and Grimes, "Morbidity and Mortality."

62. Eisenberg, "Mad Scramble for Abortion Money."

63. Alan Guttmacher Institute, Table 10, Number of Abortion Providers by Provider Type by State, 1973–82, 1984–85, and 1987–88 (in author's possession).

64. DeProsse, interview, Mar. 31, 2011.

65. At Boston City Hospital, for instance, only two of the residents were willing to provide abortions immediately following legalization. As a result, the number of abortions at BCH was small compared with the demand for the procedure in a hospital that served a largely poor clientele. See Kenneth C. Edelin, *Broken Justice: A Story of Race, Sex, and Revenge in a Boston Courtroom* (Pond View Press, 2008).

66. Ann Rose, interview with Johanna Schoen, Nov. 9, 2010, Charlotte, N.C.

67. Chelian, interview.

68. In 1973, of 1,550 abortion providers who performed more than five abortions per year, 81 percent practiced in a hospital setting and 19 percent in a nonhospital setting. By 1979, of 2,734 abortion providers, 57 percent practiced in a hospital setting and 43 percent practiced in a nonhospital setting. Alan Guttmacher Institute, Table 5, Number of Providers, Abortions, and Abortions per Provider by Type of Provider and Metropolitan Status, 1977–82, 1984–85, and 1987–88 (in author's possession).

69. EPOC stood for "evacuation of the products of conception." Susan Hill, who worked in the clinic until 1975 and represented it to the outside, noted that the name was so unappealing that she suggested it be renamed "Every Person's Own Choice." Barr concurred. See Susan Hill, interview with Johanna Schoen, May 2004.

70. Ibid. Many physicians came to the Washington Preterm facility to learn abortion techniques. The Preterm model emphasized integrating abortion counseling, contraceptive services, sexual counseling, and, eventually, sterilization services with abortion care. See Joffe, *Doctors of Conscience*, 147.

71. Hill, interview.

72. Alan Guttmacher Institute, "Scarcity of Abortion Services in Rural Areas intensified by a Nineteen Percent Drop in Abortion Providers," June 28, 1990, file NAF 1990, series Abortion, TCP. See also ibid., Table 5: Number of Providers, Abortions, and Abortions per Provider.

73. Crist, interview.

74. Turner, interview; Keyes, interview with Johnston; Keyes, interview.

75. Turner, interview. See also Robert Thompson, interview with Johanna Schoen, Sept. 14, 2013, Pittsburgh, Pa., and Christopher Snowbeck, "Obituary: Robert Garland Kisner/Doctor Who Promoted Family Planning," *Pittsburgh Post-Gazette*, Apr. 1, 2004.

76. Nye, interview.

77. Deborah Nathanson, n.d., folder Correspondence—Feminists Wanting to Start Clinics, box 64, EGC. Five of the original "founders" of Emma Goldman contributed money from personal sources and bank/insurance loans. They also received a grant from RESIST and an unsolicited gift from the Clergy Council. These funds went to a down payment on a house and medical supplies and equipment. See Paula Klein to Jackie Nowell, July 12, 1976, ibid.

78. The Emma Goldman Clinic had a stipend position so that women seeking to open clinics elsewhere could work at the Emma Goldman Clinic for several months and experience a functioning clinic. FWHC regularly offered financial support for feminist clinics who joined the FWHC network. Lynn Randall, phone interview with Johanna

Schoen, Oct. 22, 2012; Sandra Morgen, *Into Our Own Hands: The Women's Health Movement in the United States, 1969–1990* (New Brunswick, N.J.: Rutgers University Press, 2002); D. Nathanson, n.d., and Paula Klein to Jackie Nowell, July 12, 1976, both in folder Correspondence—Feminists Wanting to Start Clinics, EGC; Anne Enke, *Finding the Movement: Sexuality, Contested Space, and Feminist Activism* (Durham, N.C.: Duke University Press, 2007); Wendy Simonds, *Abortion at Work: Ideology and Practice in a Feminist Clinic* (New Brunswick, N.J.: Rutgers University Press, 1996).

79. Hill, interview, May 2004.

80. Ibid.

81. Ibid.

82. Ibid.

83. Lories Caratozzolo, "Abortion Ruling—For Some Too Late," *Patterson News*, Nov. 28, 1976.

84. Hill, interview, May 2004.

85. Susan Hill, interview with Johanna Schoen, Feb. 3, 2008.

86. Lorrain Yoder and Joseph Kelly, "Wayne Target of Suit," *Patterson News*, Sept. 10, 1976; Joseph Kelly, "Abortion Center OK Near," *Patterson News*, Sept. 16, 1976; "Abortion Site Maligned," *Herald News*, Nov. 4, 1976; James J. Duggan, letter to the editor, *Wayne Today*, Dec. 1, 1976; Niles Lathem, "Abortion Foes Fail to Shut Down the Clinic," *Patterson Evening News*, Feb. 15, 1980.

87. Susan Hill, interview with Johanna Schoen, June 18, 2008, Raleigh, N.C. See *Delaware Women's Health Organ., Inc. v. Wier*, 441 F. Supp. 497 (D. Del. 1977).

88. Hill, interview, June 18, 2008.

89. Lynn Miller, Esq., "Clinic Licensing and Zoning Harassment," *NAF Quarterly*, Summer 1983, series Abortion, file NAF 1983, TCP.

90. In 1980, 459 out of a total of 2,758 providers performed 1,000 abortions or more per year. See Alan Guttmacher Institute, Table 5, Number of Providers, Abortions, and Abortions per Provider.

91. Of the 2,734 physicians who provided abortions in 1979, 56 percent were associated with a hospital, 23 percent worked in a freestanding abortion clinic, and 21 percent provided abortions from a physician's office. See Alan Guttmacher Institute, Table 5, Number of Providers, Abortions, and Abortions per Provider.

92. Pattie Pressley, interviewed by LeAnn Erickson, undated [ca. 1993], EGC.

93. Chelian, interview with Johnston.

94. *Our Bodies, Ourselves* of the Boston Women's Health Collective, first published as a newsprint pamphlet in 1970s, included chapters on anatomy and physiology, sexuality, myths about women, venereal disease, birth control, and other topics. While the very first edition in 1970 counted 130 pages, it had—by 2005—grown to an 832-page reference work. For a discussion of *Our Bodies, Ourselves*, see, for instance, Wendy Kline, *Bodies of Knowledge: Sexuality, Reproduction, and Women's Health in the Second Wave* (Chicago: University of Chicago Press, 2010), chap. 1, and Kathy Davis, *The Making of "Our Bodies, Ourselves": How Feminism Travels across Borders* (Durham, N.C.: Duke University Press, 2007). Many college campuses came up with their own publications on sexuality, reproduction, and sexual health.

95. Chelian, interview with Johnston.

96. Ibid.

97. Gayle Sand, interview with LeAnn Erickson, undated [ca. 1993], EGC.

98. Barb Yates, interview with LeAnn Erickson, undated [ca. 1993], EGC.

99. As quoted in Morgen, *Into Our Own Hands*, 7. On cervical self-exams, see also Michelle Murphy, "Immodest Witnessing: The Epistemology of Vaginal Self-Examination in the U.S. Feminist Self-Help Movement," *Feminist Studies* 30, no. 1 (Spring 2004): 115–47, and Terri Kapsalis, *Public Privates: Performing Gynecology from Both Ends of the Speculum* (Durham, N.C.: Duke University Press, 1997).

100. Charles deProsse, interview with Johanna Schoen, Iowa City, Iowa, June 3, 2004.

101. Elizabeth Fishel, "The Women's Self-Help Movement, or Is Happiness Knowing Your Own Cervix?," *Ramparts*, Nov. 1973, 29–31, 56–59, cited in Morgen, *Into Our Own Hands*, 24.

102. Hill, interview, May 2004.

103. Ibid.

104. Pressley, interview with Erickson.

105. Barb Curtin, interview with LeAnn Erickson, undated [ca. 1993], EGC.

106. Flora Cassilianos, interview with LeAnn Erickson, undated [ca. 1993], EGC.

107. Meeting with Herman, Apr. 2, 1978, box 32, file Personnel re. Hermann Falsetti, EGC.

108. Meeting to discuss the fitting of cervical caps, Jan. 12, 1979, box 36, file Minutes, Committee—Misc., Jan.–July 1979, EGC.

109. Chelian, interview with Johnston.

110. Hill, interview, May 2004.

111. Chelian, interview with Johnston.

112. DeProsse, interview, June 3, 2004. See also Doctor's Meeting, Oct. 18, 1978, box 35, file Modified Collective, Minutes, Committee—Abortion, May–Dec. 1978, EGC.

113. Abortion Committee Meeting Minutes, July 20, 1979, box 36, file Minutes, Committee—Abortion, June–Dec. 1979, EGC.

114. DeProsse, interview, June 3, 2004.

115. Ibid.; Abortion Committee Meeting Minutes, July 20, 1979, box 36, file Minutes, Committee—Abortion, June–Dec. 1979, EGC.

116. Dick Winter, the clinic's first abortion provider, regularly threatened to leave. Meeting with Herman, Apr. 2, 1978, box 32, file Personnel re. Hermann Falsetti, EGC.

117. DeProsse, interview, June 3, 2004.

118. Peter McGuinness, "Doctor at Local Abortion Center Works for Change within System," *Daily Iowan*, Nov. 14, 1973. See also Minutes from 3-19-78 Meeting with Herman, box 32, file Personnel re. Hermann Falsetti, EGC. For health activism, see John Dittmer, *The Good Doctors: The Medical Committee for Human Rights and the Struggle for Social Justice in Health Care* (New York: Bloomsbury Press, 2010), and Alondra Nelson, *Body and Soul: The Black Panther Party and the Fight against Medical Discrimination* (Minneapolis: University of Minnesota Press, 2011).

119. DeProsse, interview, June 3, 2004.

120. Susan Hill, interview with Johanna Schoen, Jan. 2004, Raleigh, N.C.

121. Ibid.

122. Hill, interview, May 2004.

123. Ibid.

124. Susan Hill, interview with Johanna Schoen, Aug. 15, 2008, Raleigh, N.C.

125. Hill, interview, May 2004.

126. Ibid.

127. Hill, interview, Jan. 2004.

128. [Minutes], Abortion Committee, Nov. 10, 1978, 4, file Modified Collective, Minutes, Committee—Abortion, May–Dec. 1978, box 35, EGC.

129. Ibid., 5.

130. Ibid.

131. Minutes, Abortion Committee, Apr. 4, 1980, box 37, file Modified Collective: Minutes, Committee—Abortion, Jan.–June, 1980, EGC.

132. Minutes, Abortion Committee, Mar. 21, 1980, box 37, file Modified Collective: Minutes, Committee—Abortion, Jan.–June, 1980, EGC.

133. Eisenberg, "Mad Scramble for Abortion Money," 996. On July 1, 1970, the New York Clergy Consultation Service, which had served as a model for other organizations in other states, was disbanded and reconstituted as Clergy and Lay Advocates for Hospital Abortion Performance. The new organization was designed to deal with local restrictions on abortions and the growth of high-priced "abortion brokers."

134. Ibid.

135. Pamela Dillett, "Inside an Abortion Clinic," *National Observer*, Feb. 15, 1975, file Abortion Update, 1975, series Abortion, TCP.

136. Alan Guttmacher Institute, Table 5, Number of Providers, Abortions, and Abortions per Provider.

137. Christopher Tietze, F. S. Jaffe, E. Weinstock, and J. G. Dryfoos, *Provisional Estimates of Abortion Need and Services in the Year following the 1973 Supreme Court Decisions* (New York: Alan Guttmacher Institute, 1975).

138. Takey Crist, interview with Johanna Schoen, Nov. 20–21, 2002, Jacksonville, N.C.

139. Paula Klein to Jackie Nowell, July 12, 1976, folder Correspondence—Feminists Wanting to Start Clinics, box 64, EGC.

140. Paula Klein, interview with LeAnn Erickson, undated [ca. 1993], EGC.

141. Roxie Tullis, interview with LeAnn Erickson, undated [ca. 1993], EGC.

142. Yates, interview.

143. Minutes Gyn, Jan. 16, 1980, Women's Health Project, Inc., box 37, folder Modified Collective, Minutes, Committee—Gyn, Jan.–July 1980, EGC.

144. Tullis, interview.

145. Stanley K. Henshaw and Kevin O'Reilly, "Characteristics of Abortion Patients in the United States, 1979 and 1980," *Family Planning Perspectives* 50, no. 1 (Jan./Feb. 1983): 13; Stanley K. Henshaw, Jacquelyn Darroch Forrest, Ellen Sullivan, and Christopher Tietze, "Abortion Services in the United States, 1979 and 1980," *Family Planning Perspectives* 14, no. 1 (Jan./Feb. 1982): 5–15.

Chapter Two

1. Massachusetts passed its first state statute regulating abortion in compliance with *Roe* in August 1974. Between January 22, 1973, when the *Roe* decision rendered all state laws regulating abortion unconstitutional, and the passage of Massachusetts's 1974 abortion statute, abortion was legal in the state. Barbara J. Culliton, "Grave-Robbing: The Charge against Four from Boston City Hospital," *Science* 186, no. 4162 (Nov. 1, 1974): 420–23; Barbara J. Culliton, "Manslaughter: The Charge against Edelin of Boston City Hospital," *Science* 186, no. 4161 (Oct. 25, 1974): 327–30; Sarah Dubow, *Ourselves Unborn: A History of the Fetus in Modern America* (New York: Oxford University Press, 2011), 67. The grave-robbing statute had originally been intended to stop the growing black market for cadavers, bought, sold, and stolen by physicians wanting to dissect them. The statute stated: "Whoever, not being lawfully authorized by the proper authorities, willfully digs up, disinters, or removes or conveys a human body or the remains thereof . . . shall be punished in the state prison for not more than three years or in jail for not more than two and one half years or by a fine of not more than two thousand dollars." The Massachusetts Grave-Robbing Statute of 1814, Massachusetts General Laws, c. 265, § 13.

2. As quoted in Kenneth C. Edelin, *Broken Justice: A True Story of Race, Sex, and Revenge in a Boston Courtroom* (Pond View Press, 2007), 241.

3. Ibid., 315.

4. William A. Henry 3rd, "Aftermath of the Edelin Trial: Lone Holdout for Acquittal Tells How He Changes His Mind," *Boston Globe*, Feb. 17, 1975, 1, 32.

5. Dubow, *Ourselves Unborn*, 84.

6. *Commonwealth of Massachusetts v. Kenneth Edelin*, Supreme Judicial Court of Massachusetts, Criminal Suffolk SS, Number S-393, Feb. 14, 1975, 111 (hereafter Edelin Trial Transcript).

7. As quoted in Barbara J. Culliton, "Edelin Trial: Jury Not Persuaded by Scientists for the Defense," *Science* 187 (Mar. 7, 1975): 816.

8. As quoted in ibid.; Henry, "Aftermath of the Edelin Trial."

9. Melva Weber, "Middlemen in the Definition of Life," *Medical World News*, Nov. 22, 1974, 61. For a brief history of fetal research, see Dubow, *Ourselves Unborn*; Conference Committee on Fetal Research and Applications, Institute of Medicine, Fetal Research and Applications: A Conference Summary (Washington, D.C.: National Academics Press, 1994); M. H. Dykes and E. E. Czapek, "Legislation and Regulation concerning Abortus Research," *JAMA* 229, no. 10 (Sept. 2, 1974): 1303–4; National Commission for the Protection of Human Subjects of Biomedical and Behavioral Research, *Report and Recommendations: Research on the Fetus*; and U.S. Department of Health, Education, and Welfare, Publication No. (OS) 76-127, 1975 (hereafter *Research on the Fetus*). See also Susan E. Lederer, *Subjected to Science: Human Experimentation in America before the Second World War* (Baltimore: Johns Hopkins University Press, 1995), 139–42.

10. Edelin, *Broken Justice*, 84–85; Culliton, "Manslaughter," 330; Edelin Trial Transcript, "A True Bill for the Indictment of Kenneth Edelin," April 11, 1975; Roy Lucas and Lynn I. Miller, "Evolution of Abortion Law in North America," in *Abortion and*

Sterilization: Medical and Social Aspects, ed. Jane E. Hodgson (New York: Grune and Stratton, 1981), 83–88.

11. Lucas and Miller, "Evolution of Abortion Law in North America," 83–88.

12. Carole Paige, *The Right to Lifers: Who They Are, How They Operate, Where They Get Their Money* (New York: Summit Books, 1983), 13.

13. Edelin, *Broken Justice*; Dubow, *Ourselves Unborn*, 69.

14. Edelin, *Broken Justice*.

15. Culliton, "Grave-Robbing."

16. Lynn Morgan, *Icons of Life: A Cultural History of Human Embryos* (Berkeley: University of California Press, 2009), 197–99. Hooker tried to slow down asphyxia and fetal death but was unsuccessful.

17. Ibid., 201. Morgan notes that Hooker and other researchers like him avoided criticism by maintaining a high standard of professionalism and integrity. Hooker was well connected professionally and was known as a conscientious researcher. His publications focused strictly on the scientific merits of the project, and he was always careful to mention that the fetuses in his study came from operations "undertaken only after the most careful consideration and after extensive consultation" (ibid.). Hooker also stressed that no member of his research team was ever involved in a decision about whether to perform a therapeutic abortion.

18. Ibid., 200–203. Monica Casper mentions a similar level of enthusiasm for images taken from live fetuses. Monica J. Casper, *The Making of the Unborn Patient: A Social Anatomy of Fetal Surgery* (New Brunswick, N.J.: Rutgers University Press, 1998), 59–67.

19. Indeed, as Morgan points out, Hooker's research was appropriated in support of pro-life causes. Antiabortion activists cited Hooker's work to make the point that "babies" are "responsive to touch" (Morgan, *Icons of Life*, 204–5). And by the 1980s, antiabortion activists had embraced the aesthetic display of fetal bodies and began to disseminate images of—this time—dead fetuses and fetal remains.

20. See Leslie J. Reagan, *Dangerous Pregnancies: Mothers, Disabilities, and Abortion in Modern America* (Berkeley: University of California Press, 2010), 181.

21. *Research on the Fetus*, 14–15.

22. Dubois, *Ourselves Unborn*, 68; Steven Maynard-Moody, *The Dilemma of the Fetus: Fetal Research, Medical Progress, and Moral Politics* (New York: St. Martin's Press, 1995), 45. Rh incompatibility develops when the mother is Rh-negative and the infant is Rh-positive. It can lead to complications for the developing infant.

23. Agneta Philipson, L. D. Sabath, and David Charles, "Transplacental Passage of Erythromycin and Clindamycin," *New England Journal of Medicine* 288, no. 23 (June 7, 1973): 1219–21. This work took place during a time of heightened interest in the transmission of potentially harmful substances from mother to fetus. See, for instance, Janet Golden's discussion of the making of fetal alcohol syndrome that also dates to the early 1970s, *Message in a Bottle: The Making of Fetal Alcohol Syndrome* (Cambridge, Mass.: Harvard University Press, 2005). See also Dubois, *Ourselves Unborn*, 68–69.

24. Maggie Scarf, "The Fetus as Guinea Pig," *New York Times*, Oct. 19, 1975, 13, 89–98, 102.

25. Ibid.; *Research on the Fetus*, 13.

26. As quoted in Scarf, "The Fetus as Guinea Pig," 92.

27. Ibid.; *Research on the Fetus*, 13–14.

28. Albert R. Jonsen, *The Birth of Bioethics* (New York: Oxford University Press, 1998), 238.

29. Martin S. Pernick, "Brain Death in a Cultural Context: The Reconstruction of Death, 1967–1981," in *The Definition of Death: Contemporary Controversies*, ed. Stuart J. Younger, Robert M. Arnold, and Renie Schapiro (Baltimore: Johns Hopkins University Press, 1999), 16.

30. Casper, *Making of the Unborn Patient*, 61.

31. Ibid., 30–72.

32. Jonsen, *Birth of Bioethics*, 133–36. The Nuremburg Code stated, among other principles, that the voluntary consent of the human subject is absolutely essential, that experiments involving human subjects should yield fruitful results for society, and that experiments should avoid all unnecessary physical and mental suffering and injury.

33. Jay Katz, "The Consent Principle of the Nuremberg Code," in *The Nazi Doctors and the Nuremberg Code: Human Rights in Human Experimentation*, ed. George J. Annas and Michael A. Grodin (New York: Oxford University Press, 1992), 228.

34. As quoted in Jonsen, *Birth of Bioethics*, 91.

35. Jonsen, *Birth of Bioethics*, 91–93; Dubow, *Ourselves Unborn*, 76.

36. Bernard Barber et al., *Research on Human Subjects: Problems of Social Control in Medical Experimentation* (New York: Russell Sage Foundation, 1973); Lederer, *Subjected to Science*; Eileen Welsome, *The Plutonium Files: America's Secret Medical Experiments in the Cold War* (New York: Delta Book, 1999); David J. Rothman, "Human Experimentation and the Origins of Bioethics in the United States," in *Social Science Perspectives on the Medical Ethics*, ed. George Weisz (Dordrecht, Netherlands: Kluwer Academic, 1990), 185–200; Henry K. Beecher, "Ethics and Clinical Research," *New England Journal of Medicine* 24, no. 274 (June 16, 1966); James H. Jones, *Bad Blood: The Tuskegee Syphilis Experiment* (New York: Free Press, 1981); Susan M. Reverby, ed., *Tuskegee's Truths: Rethinking the Tuskegee Syphilis Study* (Chapel Hill: University of North Carolina Press, 2000); David J. Rothman and Sheila M. Rothman, *The Willowbrook Wars* (New York: Harper and Row, 1984).

37. Alondra Nelson, *Body and Soul: The Black Panther Party and the Fight against Medical Discrimination* (Minneapolis: University of Minnesota Press, 2011); John Dittmer, *The Good Doctors: The Medical Committee for Human Rights and the Struggle for Social Justice in Health Care* (New York: Bloomsbury Press, 2009); Elaine Tyler May, *America and the Pill: A History of Promise, Peril, and Liberation* (New York: Basic Books, 2010), 130–36; Barbara Seaman, *The Doctors' Case against the Pill* (Alameda, Calif.: Hunter House, 1969); Ruth Rosen, *The World Split Open: How the Modern Women's Movement Changed America* (New York: Penguin Books, 2000), 175–81.

38. Harris poll cited in Peter N. Carroll, *It Seemed Like Nothing Happened: America in the 1970s* (New Brunswick, N.J.: Rutgers University Press, 1982), 235.

39. John C. Wilke and Mrs. J. C. Wilke, *Handbook on Abortion* (Cincinnati, Ohio: Hiltz, June 1972), 26–27. See also Andrew H. Merton, *Enemies of Choice: The Right-to-Life Movement and Its Threat to Abortion* (Boston: Beacon Press, 1981), 71–75, and

Cynthia Gorney, *Articles of Faith: A Frontline History of the Abortion Wars* (New York: Simon and Schuster, 1998), 100–107.

40. Wilke and Wilke, *Handbook on Abortion*, 26–27.

41. As quoted in Gorney, *Articles of Faith*, 103.

42. See, for instance, Wilke and Wilke, *Handbook on Abortion*; John C. Wilke, *How to Teach the Pro-Life Story* (Cincinnati: Hiltz and Hayes, 1973); Dr. and Mrs. J. C. Wilke, "Did You Know," 1973, file Anti-Abortion Publicity, series Abortion, TCP; and Merton, *Enemies of Choice*, 71–75. See also Gorney, *Articles of Faith*.

43. Carol Mason, *Killing for Life: The Apocalyptic Narrative of Pro-Life Politics* (Ithaca, N.Y.: Cornell University Press, 2002), 79–80, 116. See also Dorothy Roberts, *Killing the Black Body: Race, Reproduction, and the Meaning of Liberty* (New York: Random House, 1997).

44. Wilke and Wilke, *Handbook on Abortion*, 119.

45. Ibid., 118.

46. Paul Ramsey, *The Ethics of Fetal Research* (New Haven, Conn.: Yale University Press, 1975), 2.

47. Chrysso Barbara Sarkos, "The Fetal Tissue Transplant Debate in the United States: Where Is King Solomon When You Need Him," *Journal of Law and Politics* 7, no. 1 (Winter 1991): 382–87.

48. Victor Cohn, "Live-Fetus Research Debated," *Washington Post*, Apr. 10, 1973, A1, A9.

49. Ibid.

50. Ibid.

51. Victor Cohn, "Scientists and Fetus Research," *Washington Post*, Apr. 15, 1973, A1.

52. Congressional Record H3251, Apr. 24, 1974, as quoted in David W. Fisher, "Editorial: A Rampage of 'Know-Nothingism,'" *Hospital Practice* (June 1974), file Abortion Update, 1974, series Abortion, TCP.

53. Victor Cohn, "NIH Vows Not to Fund Fetus Work," *Washington Post*, Apr. 13, 1973, A1.

54. See, for instance, the pervasive appeal of the story of Frankenstein and its reinterpretation over the past century as a critique of science. Susan E. Lederer, *Frankenstein: Penetrating the Secrets of Nature* (New Brunswick, N.J.: Rutgers University Press, 2002).

55. Congressional Record H5182, June 22, 1973, as quoted in Fisher, "Editorial."

56. Congressional Record, H3428, Apr. 25, 1974, as quoted in Fisher, "Editorial."

57. Fisher, "Editorial."

58. William A. Nolen, *The Baby in the Bottle: An Investigative Review of the Edelin Case and Its Larger Meaning for the Controversy over Abortion Reform* (New York: Conrad, McCann and Geoghegan, 1978), 38.

59. Ibid., 46.

60. Ibid., 51.

61. Ibid., 70.

62. Ibid., 71.

63. Edelin, *Broken Justice*, 92.

64. Ibid., 93.

65. Nolen, *Baby in the Bottle*, 75. The record suggests that Giminez might have been an unreliable witness with an ax to grind. While Nolen describes Giminez and Edelin as close friends and Giminez torn over the fact that he had to testify against Edelin, Edelin notes in his memoirs that his relationship with Giminez was extremely difficult. In addition, at the trial a number of witnesses who had also been present at the hysterotomy challenged Giminez's recollections. Edelin, *Broken Justice*.

66. Nolen, *Baby in the Bottle*, 77–78.

67. Ibid., 78.

68. Ibid., 79–80.

69. Edelin, *Broken Justice*, 95.

70. Richard A. Knox, "BCH Trustees Reinstated Three Indicted Doctors," *Boston Globe*, Apr. 19, 1974.

71. Ibid.

72. Diane White, "Edelin Jury: Their Faces Told Nothing," *Boston Globe*, Jan. 13, 1975, 8.

73. Morris Turner, interview with Johanna Schoen, Oct. 6, 2013, Pittsburgh, Pa.

74. Robert Thompson, interview with Johanna Schoen, Sept. 14, 2013, Pittsburgh, Pa.; Turner, interview.

75. Jefferson was also the first African American woman to graduate from Harvard Medical School. See Edelin Trial Transcript, Jan. 10, 1975, 66–74; Maynard-Moody, *Dilemma of the Fetus*, 67–69; Dubow, *Ourselves Unborn*, 86; and Edelin, *Broken Justice*, 178.

76. Edelin, *Broken Justice*, 253; see also 171.

77. Ibid., 268.

78. Ibid., 212, 219.

79. Diane White, "Pathologist Says Fetus in Edelin Case Breathed," *Boston Globe*, Jan. 29, 1975, 1; Edelin Trial Transcript, Jan. 23, 1975; Diane White, "Medical Examiner Tells Court Fetus Had 'Respiratory Activity,'" *Boston Globe*, Jan. 24, 1975, 1; Dubow, *Ourselves Unborn*, 92; Edelin, *Broken Justice*, 212, 218–19, 234–35.

80. Edelin Trial Transcript, Feb. 11, 1975, 83; Diane White, "Fetus Never Breathed, Says Pathologist," *Boston Globe*, Feb. 7, 1975, 1; Edelin, *Broken Justice*, 297.

81. Edelin, *Broken Justice*, 230–31.

82. Edelin Trial Transcript, Feb. 11, 1975, 83; White, "Fetus Never Breathed"; Diane White, "Witness Says Fetus 'Very Likely' Dead before Abortion," *Boston Globe*, Feb. 12, 1975, 8; Diane White, "Survival 'Rare' at 1½ Pounds, Edelin Jury Told," *Boston Globe*, Feb. 6, 1975, 1; Diane White, "Edelin Delay in Taking Fetus Proper Practice, Expert Says," *Boston Globe*, Feb. 7, 1975, 1; Diane White, "Edelin's Judgment Sound, Say Experts," *Boston Globe*, Feb. 11, 1975, 1; Dubow, *Ourselves Unborn*, 93–94; Edelin, *Broken Justice*, 297.

83. Edelin, *Broken Justice*, 233.

84. Ibid., 232.

85. Diane White, "Edelin Colleague Supports Contention of Prosecutor," *Boston Globe*, Jan. 17, 1975, 1; Edelin Trial Transcript, Feb. 4, 1975. See also Diane White,

"2 BCH Nurses Say No Clock on Wall When Edelin Operated," *Boston Globe*, Feb. 5, 1975, 1, and Edelin, *Broken Justice*, 193, 196.

86. Edelin Trial Transcript, Feb. 3, 1975, 19–84; Edelin, *Broken Justice*, 259.

87. Julia Kagan, "The New Doubts about Abortion," *McCall's*, June 1975, 121–23. See also Lucas and Miller, "Evolution of Abortion Law in North America," 86, and David M. Alpern, "Abortion and the Law," *Newsweek*, Mar. 3, 1975, 18.

88. These included ethicist and philosopher Sissela Bok, a lecturer on medical ethics at Radcliff, Harvard, and MIT; Joseph Fletcher, visiting professor of medical ethics at the University of Virginia; Marc Lappé, an associate for biological sciences at the Institute for Society, Ethics, and the Life Sciences; Richard A. McCormick, professor of Christian ethics at the Kennedy Institute; Paul Ramsey, a Princeton religion professor; Seymour Siegel, professor of theology, ethics, and rabbinical thought; LeRoy Walters, director of the Bioethics Kennedy Institute at Georgetown University; and Richard Wasserstrom, professor of law and philosophy at the University of California at Los Angeles.

89. *Research on the Fetus*, 32.

90. National Commission for the Protection of Human Subjects of Biomedical and Behavioral Research, *Appendix: Research on the Fetus*, U.S. Department of Health, Education, and Welfare, Publication No. (OS) 76-128, 2–15.

91. Ibid., 31–39.

92. Ibid., 34–35.

93. Ibid., 44.

94. Ibid.

95. Ibid., 45.

96. Ibid.

97. Ibid., 46.

98. Floyd v. Anders, 440 F.Supp. 535 (D.S.C. 1977), vacated and remanded, 440 U.S. 445 (1979); Nebraska v. LaBenz, No. 106-31 (Neb. Dist. Ct. Douglas County, 1979); Liz Jeffries, "The Waddill Case: Abortionist Strangles Baby," *Conservative Digest*, June 1978, 16–17, file Abortion Update, 1978, series Abortion, TCP. See also Lucas and Miller, "Evolution of Abortion Law in North America," 79–88.

99. At least thirty-three of the thirty-eight infants received premature infant care. George Stroh and Alan R. Hinman, "Reported Live Births following Induced Abortion: Two and One-Half Years' Experience in Upstate New York," *American Journal of Obstetrics and Gynecology* 126, no. 1 (Sept. 1, 1976): 83, 87.

100. David A. Grimes and Willard Cates, "Complications from Legally Induced Abortion: A Review," *Obstetrical and Gynecological Survey* 34, no. 3 (1979).

101. Sissela Bok, Bernard N. Nathanson, David C. Nathan, Leroy Walters, "The Unwanted Child: Caring for the Fetus Born after an Abortion," *Hastings Center Report*, Oct. 10–15, 1976, 13.

102. Jonsen, *Birth of Bioethics*, 249–50.

103. Bok et al., "Unwanted Child," 14–15; see also ibid., 12.

104. Ibid., 11.

105. Jonsen, *Birth of Bioethics*, 158, 248–49.

106. Suzanne M. Rini, *Beyond Abortion: A Chronicle of Fetal Experimentation* (Rockford, Ill.: Tan Books and Publishers, 1988), 69.

107. Gorney, *Articles of Faith*, 98.

108. Frank Schaeffer, *Crazy for God: How I Grew Up as One of the Elect, Helped Found the Religious Right, and Lived to Take All (or Almost All) of It Back* (Cambridge, Mass.: Da Capo Press, 2008).

109. C. Everett Koop and Francis A. Schaeffer, *Whatever Happened to the Human Race? Exposing our Rapid yet Subtle Loss of Human Rights* (Old Tappan, N.J.: Fleming H. Revell, 1979), 68.

110. Ibid., 91.

111. Gorney, *Articles of Faith*, 341.

112. James Risen and Judy L. Thomas, *Wrath of Angels: The American Abortion War* (New York: Basic Books, 1998), 120–22.

Chapter Three

1. Warren Hern, interview with Johanna Schoen, Jan. 4, 2012, Boulder, Colo.

2. Ibid.

3. Ibid.

4. The paper was published as Warren M. Hern, "Laminaria in Abortion: Use in 1368 Patients in First Trimester," *Rocky Mountain Medical Journal* 72 (Sept. 1975): 390–95.

5. Hern, interview.

6. Terry Beresford, interview with Johanna Schoen, Sept. 30, 2012, Alexandria, Va.; "A History of the National Abortion Federation," n.d., file NAF History, TBP. Members of the committee, chaired by two abortion providers from Cleveland, Ohio, Penny Steenblock and Joan Crowley, included, among others, Frances Kissling, Myron Chrisman, Ignatius DeBlasi, Lynn Walker, Merle Hoffman, and Carole Dornblazer.

7. Roy Lucas and Lynn I. Miller, "Evolution of Abortion Law in North America," in *Abortion and Sterilization: Medical and Social Aspects*, ed. Jane E. Hodgson (New York: Grune and Stratton, 1981), 102–3; Cynthia Gorney, *Articles of Faith: A Frontline History of the Abortion Wars* (New York: Simon and Schuster, 1998), 280–81; Melody Rose, *Safe, Legal, and Unavailable? Abortion Politics in the United States* (Washington, D.C.: CQPress, 2007), 109–11; Ellen Frankfort, with Frances Kissling, *Rosie: The Investigation of a Wrongful Death* (New York: Dial Press, 1979). The Center for Constitutional Rights and the American Civil Liberties Union immediately challenged the Hyde Amendment's constitutionality, arguing that the amendment enforced one religious view as law, violated equal protection guarantees, and rendered the right to abortion meaningless for every woman too poor to pay for an abortion herself. In 1980, the U.S. Supreme Court upheld the Hyde Amendment in Harris v. McRae, 448 U.S. 297.

8. Pamela Zekman and Pamela Warrick, "12 Dead after Abortion in State's Walk-in Clinics," *Chicago Sun-Times*, Nov. 19, 1978, 1, 10, 44; Pamela Zekman and Pamela Warrick, "Men Who Profit from Women's Pain," *Chicago Sun-Times*, Nov. 13, 1978, 1.

9. See, for instance, attempts by the National Women's Health Organization to open a clinic in Wayne, New Jersey, NJWHO Clippings 1976–1979, SHP.

10. The committee added the Reverend Candace Adams (Women's Health Services of Knoxville); Helen Barnes, M.D. (University of Mississippi School of Medicine); Sherry Barnes (Zero Population Growth); Nancy Cleary (Provincial Hospital, Lansing); Irvin Cushner, M.D. (UCLA School of Public Health); Ilse Darling (RCAR); Betsy David (Gainesville Women's Health Center); Carol Downer (Feminist Women's Health Center, Los Angeles); Johan Eliot, M.D. (University of Michigan School of Public Health); Jimmye Kimmey (Association for the Study of Abortion); Karl Fossum, M.D. (Eastern Women's Center); Ellen Leitzer (American Civil Liberties Union); Judy Lipschutz (Women's Action Alliance); Pat Miller (Women's Health Services, Pittsburgh); Ralph Streeter, M.D. (Indianapolis Women's Center); and Christopher Tietze, M.D. (Population Council). See "History of the National Abortion Federation."

11. Ibid.

12. The group included Willard Cates, David Grimes, Jack Smith, and Ken Schultz.

13. Frances Kissling, telephone interview with Johanna Schoen, Nov. 21, 2011; Frances Kissling, interview with Rebecca Sharpless, Sept. 13–14, 2002, Washington, D.C., Sophia Smith Collection, Smith College, Northampton, Mass.; Joan Ellen Crowley, [Minutes of organizational meeting to establish National Association of Abortion Facilities], Apr. 14, 1976, Knoxville, Tenn., and Joan Ellen Crowley to All Abortion Facilities, Apr. 21, 1976, both folder Abortion: National Association of Abortion Services, series Crist Clinic, TCP; National Abortion Federation, "Celebrating 30 Years: 2007 Annual Report," National Abortion Federation, Washington, D.C., 2007.

14. Kissling, interview, Nov. 21, 2011.

15. "History of the National Abortion Federation."

16. S.1750 and S.1751, 92d Congress, 1st sess., May 3, 1971.

17. "History of the National Abortion Federation."

18. As quoted in Gorney, *Articles of Faith*, 290.

19. Renee Chilean, interview with Peg Johnston, 2008, New Mexico.

20. The meeting was organized by Warren Hern and Bonnie Andrikopoulos, a lobbyist for the Colorado National Organization for Women. The conference proceedings were published a year later by NAF, and those who attended the 1976 Denver meeting, clinic administrators, physicians, and researchers from across the country, became members of NAF and continued the discussion about standards there. See Warren M. Hern and Bonnie Andrikopoulos, eds., *Abortion in the Seventies: Proceedings of the Western Regional Conference on Abortion, Denver, Colorado, 27–29 February 1976* (New York: National Abortion Federation, 1977).

21. Jean Pakter, discussion, in ibid., 105.

22. Irvin Cushner, "Approaches to Evaluation of Abortion Services," in Hern and Andrikopoulos, *Abortion in the Seventies*, 89, 91.

23. Judy Widdicombe, "Conducting an Evaluation of an Abortion Service," in Hern and Andrikopoulos, *Abortion in the Seventies*, 102.

24. Ibid., 99.

25. Jim Armstrong, discussion, in Hern and Andrikopoulos, *Abortion in the Seventies*, 106.

26. Ibid., 104.

27. Hern, interview.

28. Stanley K. Henshaw, Jacqueline Darroch Forrest, Ellen Sullivan, and Christopher Tietze, "Abortion, 1977–1979: Need and Services in the United States, Each State and Metropolitan Area" (report of the Alan Guttmacher Institute, New York, 1981), 62–65. Medicaid cuts would have been even more drastic, had fourteen states not continued to pay for abortions from Medicaid funds.

29. Stanley K. Henshaw, ed., *Abortion Services in the United States, Each State and Metropolitan Area, 1979–80* (Alan Guttmacher Institute, 1983).

30. Merle Hoffman, *Intimate Wars: The Life and Times of the Woman Who Brought Abortion from the Back Alley to the Boardroom* (New York: Feminist Press, 2012), 106. For the debate about standards, see also Warren M. Hern, Open Letter to NAF Colleagues regarding Allegations of Treason, Mar. 25, 1997, file Abortion—National Abortion Federation, Warren Hern Dispute, 1995–1997, box CH 4, MHP.

31. Hern, interview.

32. Drs. Committee Statement, Aug. 22, 1975, folder Collective Minutes, Doctors' Committee, 1975–1978, 1980 misc., box 13, EGC; Deb Nye, interview with LeAnn Erickson, undated [ca. 1993], Emma Goldman Clinic Oral Histories, Iowa Women's Archive (IWA).

33. Martha Rosen, "New Iowa City Women's Clinic to Offer Self-Examination Courses and Abortion," *Daily Iowan*, Aug. 31, 1973, 1.

34. C/SC for meeting with Dick, Apr. 15, 1976, folder EGC Collective Minutes, Doctors' Committee, 1975–1978, 1980, box 13, EGC.

35. Ibid.

36. Ibid.

37. Adele to Abortion Committee, Mar. 20, [1980], ibid. For patient complaint, see, for instance, 1980 Summary of Follow-Up Statistics, folder Modified Collective: Minutes, Committee—Abortion, Feb.–Dec. 1981, box 38, EGC.

38. Hoffman, *Intimate Wars*, 76–77.

39. See, for instance, Leslie Reagan, "Crossing the Border for Abortions: California, Activists, Mexican Clinics, and the Creation of a Feminist Health Agency in the 1960s," *Feminist Studies* 26, no. 2 (Summer 2000): 336, and Barron H. Lerner, *The Breast Cancer Wars: Fear, Hope, and the Pursuit of a Cure in Twentieth-Century America* (New York: Oxford University Press, 2001), 89–90, 164–65. Indeed, such depictions of insensitive and sexist male physicians have made it into popular culture. See, for instance, the 1991 movie *The Doctor*, in which William Hurst plays the surgeon Dr. Jack McKee, who, while talented, is distant and arrogant. The movie is adapted from the autobiography of Dr. Edward Rosenbaum, *A Taste of My Own Medicine*, which chronicles the author's transformation into a caring and sensitive physician after he becomes a patient himself.

40. Hoffman, *Intimate Wars*, 76.

41. Ibid., 82.

42. Hern, interview.

43. Lisa Cronin Wohl, "Would You Buy an Abortion from this Man? The Harvey Karman Controversy," *Ms. Magazine*, Sept. 1975, 124. Indeed, it is possible that members of the Boulder Valley Clinic understood Hern's research with laminaria in this context. What Hern understood as crucial to a professional approach—his research

and collection of data on the use of laminaria in abortion procedures—Boulder Valley Clinic members criticized as hierarchical.

44. Paula Klein, "Lay Health Care, Midwifery, and Feminist Health Care: Reproductive Rights Issues for the 80s," n.d., folder All Clinic Minutes 7/1980–3/1981 (folder 6), box 38, EGC.

45. Emma Goldman Clinic feminists were part of a growing network of women's health activists who, in the 1970s, looked to a collective model to democratize the delivery of health information and health care services to women. The Boston Women's Health Collective researched and wrote the feminist health guide *Our Bodies, Ourselves*. The Berkeley Women's Health Collective offered a range of women's health and counseling services, although no abortions. And the Women's Community Health Center in Cambridge, Massachusetts, offered gyn services and abortion. All relied on the collective model to simultaneously empower women in health care and promote change in women and society at large. Sandra Morgan, *Into Our Own Hands: The Women's Health Movement in the United States, 1969–1990* (New Brunswick, N.J.: Rutgers University Press, 2002), 76–77.

46. EGC to Dear Sisters, n.d., folder Correspondence—Feminists Wanting to Start Clinics, box 64, EGC.

47. Ibid.

48. Ibid.

49. Gina Kaefring, interview with LeAnn Erickson, undated [ca. 1993], Emma Goldman Clinic Oral Histories, IWA. Michelle Womantree, another registered nurse who joined the Emma Goldman Clinic collective early on, reports that her acceptance as a collective member was very difficult. "The debates went on for weeks about whether or not the staff that was already there was comfortable having someone with a professional medical background. . . . They didn't need my skills and they weren't sure how my attitude would be." Michelle Womantree, interview with LeAnn Erickson, undated [ca. 1993], EGC.

50. Minutes 3:00–5:00, Nov. 21, 1980, folder All Clinic Minutes, 7/1980–3/1981 (folder 6), box 38, EGC.

51. Minutes Gyn, July 2, 1980, folder Modified Collective, Minutes, Committee—Gyn, Jan.–July 1980, box 37, EGC.

52. Minutes 2:00 PM, Feb. 23, 1980, folder Modified Collective, Minutes, Committee—2 o'clock, Jan.–June 1980, ibid.

53. Adele to Catherine, July 3, 1980, folder All Clinic Minutes, 7/1980–3/1981 (folder 5), box 38, EGC.

54. Ibid.

55. Minutes CC, Aug. 7, 1980, folder All Clinic Minutes 7/1980–3/1981 (folder 6), ibid.

56. Minutes AB Committee, Oct. 10, 1980, folder All Clinic Minutes, 7/1980–3/1981, and Workshop on Waiting Room Info, Dec. 5, 1980, folder All Clinic Minutes, 7/1980–3/1981 (folder 1), both in ibid.

57. At a very constructive meeting in May 1980, for instance, there were five physicians and ten Emma women present. This stands in contrast to other meetings between physicians and collective members in which four or five collective members might criti-

cize one doctor. Doctors and AB Committee, May 28, 1980, folder EGC, Collective Minutes, Doctors' Committee, 1975–1978, 1980, box 13, EGC.

58. Minutes Abortion, Feb. 27, 1981, folder Modified Collective, Minutes, Committee—Abortion, Feb.–Dec. 1981, box 38, EGC.

59. Minutes Abortion Committee, Mar. 6, 1981, ibid.

60. Minutes Abortion Committee, Oct. 16, 1981, ibid. Teresa McDonald voiced similar concerns about the tensions between professionalism and frequent job rotation.

61. Nye, interview.

62. Adele to EGC Collective Members, Dec. 30, 1981, folder All Committee Minutes, 12/1981–7/1982 (folder 3), box 5, EGC.

63. Morgan, *Into Our Own Hands*, 76–77.

64. Ibid., 78; Nye, interview.

65. Hoffman, *Intimate Wars*, 105.

66. Sexist behavior was not limited to the interactions between male physicians and their women patients. As noted in Chapter 1, Susan Hill remembered a pervasive level of sexual harassment that did not stop when she was no longer a young female employee. Even when she directed the network of NWHO clinics, she continued to experience sexual harassment, including at NAF meetings. Ann Rose, interview with Johanna Schoen, Nov. 9, 2010, Charlotte, N.C.

67. Carol Downer to Takey Crist, Dec. 2, 1983, file NAF 1983, series Abortion, TCP.

68. Ibid.

69. Ibid.

70. Despite diligent search, I was unable to locate a copy of the original *Standards* at the NAF office, in the archive, or in any of the papers of the abortion providers with whom I am in contact. The *Standards* do, however, articulate all the expectations proposed by NAF members in the discussions leading up to their publication: that abortion services should be safe and humanely delivered; staff should have the clinical skills; facilities should have the ability to respond to trouble; clinics should be able to provide follow-up data indicating acceptable complication rates, document evidence of patients' medical history, including appropriate laboratory tests, and offer adequate information and disclosure, including counseling.

71. Kissling, interview.

72. Uta Landy, phone interview with Johanna Schoen, Nov. 18, 2011.

73. "History of the National Abortion Federation."

74. Zekman and Warrick, "12 Dead after Abortion," 1, 10, 44; Zekman and Warrick, "Men Who Profit from Women's Pain," 1.

75. Zekman and Warrick, "The Abortion Profiteers: Making a Killing in Michigan Av. Clinics," *Chicago Sunday-Times*, Nov. 12, 1978, 4; Pamela Zekman and Pamela Warrick, "Soft Voices, Hard Sell—Twin Swindles," *Chicago Sun-Times*, Nov. 17, 1978, 4–5, 62.

76. Zekman and Warrick, "Abortion Profiteers," 4. Women needing an abortion after the twelfth week of gestation, for instance, were asked to pay $475 to $575 and sent to a dilapidated hospital in Detroit that was fighting the Michigan Department of Health to stay in business. Telephone operators failed to mention that Chicago had several hospi-

tals in excellent condition to provide second trimester abortions. Zekman and Warrick, "Soft Voices, Hard Sell," 5.

77. Zekman and Warrick, "Nurse to Aid," *Chicago Sun-Times*, Nov. 16, 1978, 4; Zekman and Warrick, "Abortion Profiteers," 5.

78. Zekman and Warrick, "12 Dead after Abortion," 1, 10, 44; Pamela Zekman and Pamela Warrick, "Probe Michigan Av. Abortion Clinic Death," *Chicago Sun-Times*, Nov. 17, 1978, 1, 4.

79. Pamela Zekman and Pamela Warrick, "The Abortion Lottery," *Chicago Sun-Times*, Nov. 14, 1978, 1, 4–5; Zekman and Warrick, "The Abortion Profiteers," 5.

80. Zekman and Warrick, "Abortion Profiteers," 5.

81. Ibid., 6; see also Pamela Zekman and Pamela Warrick, "Dr. Ming Kow Hah: Physician of Pain," *Chicago Sun-Times*, Nov. 15, 1978, 1, 4–5.

82. Zekman and Warrick, "Abortion Profiteers," 6.

83. National Abortion Federation, 1978 Membership Directory (Washington, D.C.: National Abortion Federation).

84. Zekman and Warrick, "Abortion Lottery," 1, 4–5.

85. Karen Koshner and Pamela Zekman, "Jury Subpoenas Records of Abortion Clinic," *Chicago Sun-Times*, Nov. 12, 1978, 5, 52; Zekman and Warrick, "Abortion Profiteers," 1.

86. Zekman and Warrick, "Probe Michigan Av. Abortion Clinic Death," 1, 4.

87. "The Doctor's Duty," *Chicago Sun-Times*, Nov. 13, 1978, 47.

88. G. Robert Hillman, "License All Counselors, Daley Asks," *Chicago Sun-Times*, Nov. 15, 1978, 5.

89. Karen Koshner and Sarah Snyder, "Water Tower Clinic Closes," *Chicago Sun-Times*, Nov. 18, 1978, 5. Subsequently, Scheidler took credit for the closing of several Chicago abortion clinics. See, for instance, Joseph M. Scheidler, *Closed: 99 Ways to Stop Abortion* (Rockford, Ill.: Tan Books and Publishers, 1985; rev. ed., 1993), 172–73.

90. Gorney, *Articles of Faith*, 291.

91. National Abortion Federation, Adversity, Advocacy, and Abortion Care: Annual Report, 1982, file NAF 1983, series Abortion, TCP; Landy, interview.

92. I have been unable to locate information on the amount of NAF membership dues. Dues were structured by type of facility and the number of abortions performed per facility: a) freestanding abortion providers under 3,000 procedures per annum; b) freestanding abortion providers over 3,000 procedures per annum; c) hospital or hospital-based abortion providers; d) physician's office abortion providers; e) feminist health center abortion providers; f) federal tax-exempt abortion providers; g) Planned Parenthood affiliate with abortion services; h) national organizations with a program interest in abortion; and i) management groups. NAF Membership Directory, 1980/81 (Washington, D.C.: National Abortion Federation).

93. The minutes of the Emma Goldman Clinic meetings indicate that the membership fee for the clinic would have been $500/year. Registration at the NAF conference was $70 or $45/person if more than five people from one clinic attended. See Abortion Committee Minutes, Mar. 6, 1981. The Emma Goldman Clinic finally appears as a NAF member in the 1982/83 membership directory. The inability to become a NAF member

and attend NAF meetings was especially isolating for physicians who were affiliated with an employer or hospital without an institutional membership.

94. National Abortion Federation, Policy Manual, file NAF 1983, series Abortion, TCP.

95. Hern, interview; Landy, interview; Carol Downer to Takey Crist, Dec. 2, 1983, file NAF 1983, series Abortion, TCP.

96. Minutes, Meeting of the Medical Advisory and Education Committee of the National Abortion Federation, San Diego, Calif., Dec. 9–10, 1984, file NAF 1985, series Abortion, TCP.

97. When, in 1985, George Tiller raised his gestational limits to twenty-six weeks, the board decided not to refer patients to Tiller's clinic and to inform Tiller of this decision. See Minutes, Meeting of the Medical Advisory and Education Committee of the National Abortion Federation, Mar. 16, 1985, ibid.

98. Minutes, Meeting of the Medical Advisory and Education Committee of the National Abortion Federation, San Diego, Calif., Dec. 9–10, 1984, ibid.

99. Jacqueline Darroch Forrest and Stanley K. Henshaw, "The Harassment of U.S. Abortion Providers," *Family Planning Perspectives* 19, no. 1 (Jan./Feb. 1987): 9–13.

100. Rose, *Safe, Legal, and Unavailable?*, 125–28.

101. Affidavit of Carol N. Everett, Apr. 12, 1985, Dallas, Texas, file NAF 1985, series Abortion, TCP.

102. Charlotte Taft to NAF Board Members, May 11, 1985, ibid.

103. Memo, Lewis Koplik to NAF members, Apr. 26, 1985, and Lewis Koplik, "Tissue Disposal," Jan. 1985, both in ibid.

104. As quoted in "Fetus Memorial Service Is Endorsed by Reagan," *New York Times*, May 27, 1982, B22. See also "500 Fetuses Found by Storage Company in Repossessed Crate," *New York Times*, Feb. 8, 1982, A14; Mark Gladstone, "Evidence Sought in Deaths of Fetuses," *Los Angeles Times*, Feb. 7, 1982; "Chronology of the Weisberg Incident," file Anti-Abortion Publicity, series Abortion, TCP; also file Newspaper Clippings, 1982, July–Dec., series Abortion, TCP.

105. Lewis Koplik, "Tissue Disposal," Jan. 1985, file NAF 1985, series Abortion, TCP.

106. Charlotte Taft to NAF Board Members, May 11, 1985, ibid.

107. Ibid.

Chapter Four

1. Mildred Hanson, interview with Peg Johnston, 2008, New Mexico.

2. Ibid.

3. Renee Chelian, interview with Peg Johnston, 2008.

4. Published in 1972 with Neubardt as the author, *Techniques of Abortion* was indeed coauthored by Selig Neubardt and Harold Schulman, colleagues at Albert Einstein College of Medicine. The two gynecologists wrote the book, a medical text that explains procedures for first and second trimester abortions, while working at a newly opened abortion clinic at Jacobi Medical Center in the Bronx. "We decided that we'd better write a book about abortion because we had some rather intense on-the-job training," Dr. Schulman remembered. See Jeremy Pearce, "Dr. Selig Neubardt, Early

Birth Control Proponent, Dies at 78," *New York Times*, Sept. 5, 2004. In the chapter "The Japanese Experience: A Personal Observation," Neubardt introduced readers to his experience observing abortion procedures and the use of laminaria in Japan. He concluded: "Laminaria sticks could be of value in our own approach" (Selig Neubardt, *Techniques of Abortion* [New York: Little, Brown, 1972], 151).

5. Warren Hern, e-mail to Johanna Schoen, Mar. 3, 2012.

6. The paper was published as Warren M. Hern, "Laminaria in Abortion: Use in 1,368 Patients in First Trimester," *Rocky Mountain Medical Journal* 72 (Sept. 1975): 390–95.

7. Warren M. Hern and Anna Gail Oakes, "Multiple Laminaria Treatment in Early Midtrimester Outpatient Suction Abortion: A Preliminary Report," *Advances in Planned Parenthood* 22 (1977): 93–97. Abortion providers published widely in journals ranging from the prestigious and mainstream to more specialized and local medical journals, among them *Advances in Planned Parenthood*, *American Journal of Nursing*, *American Journal of Obstetrics and Gynecology*, *American Journal of Psychiatry*, *American Journal of Public Health*, *Family Planning Perspectives*, *Fertility and Sterility*, *Journal of Nursing Administration*, *Journal of Reproductive Medicine*, *Journal of the American Medical Association*, *Lancet*, *Medical Gynecology and Sociology*, *New England Journal of Medicine*, *Obstetrics and Gynecology*, *Rocky Mountain Medical Journal*, *Social Science and Medicine*, *Studies in Family Planning*, and *Year Book of Obstetrics and Gynecology*. Prior to the establishment of the National Abortion Federation, providers were most likely to present their research at meetings of the American Public Health Association or the Association of Planned Parenthood Physicians. After the establishment of NAF, much of the specialized discussion surrounding new findings and research on abortion took place at NAF seminars and meetings.

8. Hanson, interview.

9. Warren Hern, interview with Johanna Schoen, Jan. 4, 2012, Boulder, Colo.

10. Chelian, interview.

11. Hanson, interview. This included George Tiller of Kansas City and Philip Darney of San Francisco.

12. David Grimes et al., "Mid-Trimester Abortion by Dilation and Evacuation: A Safe and Practical Alternative," *New England Journal of Medicine* 296, no. 20 (May 19, 1977): 1141–45. See also P. G. Stubblefield, "Midtrimester Abortion by Curettage Procedures: An Overview," in *Abortion and Sterilization: Medical and Social Aspects*, ed. Jane E. Hodgson (New York: Grune and Stratton, 1981), 277; Christopher Tietze and Sarah Lewit, "Joint Program for the Study of Abortion (JPSA): Early Medical Complications of Legal Abortion," *Studies in Family Planning* 3, no. 6 (June 1972): 112–17. A small number of physicians in the United States did experiment with D&E, and Warren Hern presented his results with the procedure at the 1976 meeting of the Association of Planned Parenthood Physicians. Hern and Oakes, "Multiple Laminaria Treatment."

13. Cynthia Gorney, *Articles of Faith: A Frontline History of the Abortion Wars* (New York: Simon and Schuster, 1998), 297.

14. George Stroh and Alan R. Hinman, "Reported Live Births following Induced Abortion: Two and One-Half Years' Experience in Upstate New York," *American Journal of Obstetrics and Gynecology* 126, no. 1 (Sept. 1, 1976): 83, 87.

15. Nancy B. Kaltreider, Sadja Goldsmith, and Alan J. Margolis, "The Impact of Midtrimester Abortion Techniques on Patients and Staff," *American Journal of Obstetrics and Gynecology* 135, no. 2 (Sept. 15, 1979): 237.

16. David A. Grimes and Willard Cates, "Complications from Legally Induced Abortion: A Review," *Obstetrical and Gynecological Survey* 34, no. 3 (1979).

17. W. Martin Haskell, Thomas R. Easterling, and E. Steve Lichtenberg, "Surgical Abortion after the First Trimester," in *A Clinician's Guide to Medical and Surgical Abortion*, ed. Maureen Paul et al. (Philadelphia: Churchill Livingstone, 1999), 127; Warren M. Hern, *Abortion Practice* (Philadelphia: J. B. Lippincott, 1984), 122.

18. Hern, *Abortion Practice*, 123.

19. Hanson, interview.

20. Kaltreider, Goldsmith, and Margolis, "Impact of Midtrimester Abortion Techniques," 236–37. See also Stubblefield, "Midtrimester Abortion by Curettage Procedures," 293.

21. Judith Bourne Rooks and Willard Cates, "Emotional Impact of D&E vs. Instillation," *Family Planning Perspective* 9, no. 6 (Nov./Dec. 1977): 276–77.

22. Program, "Second Trimester Abortion: Perspectives after a Decade of Experience, September 27–28, 1979"; Preliminary program, "Clinical Problems in Second Trimester Abortions, September 29, 1979." See also "Peer Support Held Important in Overcoming Stress Encountered by Abortion Providers," *Female Health Topics* 3, no. 1 (1980): 8. All in file Abortion: 2nd Trimester Abortion Conference, series Crist Clinic, TCP. Other NAF-affiliated clinics also engaged in the scientific process by sponsoring D&E seminars and participating in the scientific debate. In 1979, the Feminist Women's Health Center sponsored a D&E symposium in Los Angeles. Carol Downer to Takey Crist, Dec. 2, 1983, file NAF 1983, series Abortion, TCP.

23. "Peer Support Held Important," 8.

24. David Grimes, "Second Trimester Abortions in the United States," *Family Planning Perspectives* 16, no. 6 (Nov./Dec. 1984): 264. See also Haskell, Easterling, and Lichtenberg, "Surgical Abortion after the First Trimester," 123.

25. The data does not differentiate between vacuum aspirations and "instrumental evacuations," which include suction and sharp curettage and D&E after thirteen weeks. In 1981, abortion providers performed 152,530 abortions after the first trimester; 54,690 of those were induction procedures. In 1988, 20,760 abortion procedures out of 163,680 abortions after the first trimester were performed as induction procedures.

26. NAF amicus brief on second trimester abortion practices, counseling procedures, and standards, National Abortion Federation, Adversity, Advocacy, and Abortion Care, Annual Report, 1982, file NAF 1983, series Abortion, TCP.

27. Gorney, *Articles of Faith*, 300.

28. Ibid., 300–301.

29. Ibid., 303.

30. Ibid., 306.

31. Chelian, interview with Johnston.

32. NAF Quarterly, Summer 1983, file NAF 1983, series Abortion, TCP.

33. Ibid.

34. Ibid.

35. NAF Quarterly, Spring 1983, ibid.

36. Program, Risk Management/Quality Assurance Seminar, Jan. 30–31, 1983, National Abortion Federation files, Washington, D.C.

37. Standards for Midtrimester Abortion Services, National Abortion Federation files, Washington, D.C.

38. National Abortion Federation, Memorial Hospital, Colorado Springs, Colorado, Oct. 11–12, 1983, Workshop Evaluation Comments, file NAF Dec. 1983, Board of Directors Meeting, series Abortion, TCP.

39. Ibid. For questions about abortion at advanced gestational ages, see Evaluation Form, National Abortion Federation, Public Action Seminar, Chicago, Ill., Sept. 26, 1983, ibid.

40. Evaluation Form, National Abortion Federation, Public Action Seminar, Tampa, Florida, Mar. 13, 1983, ibid.

41. Uta Landy, phone interview with Johanna Schoen, Nov. 18, 2011.

42. Evaluation Form, National Abortion Federation Public Action Seminar, Sept. 12, 1983, Washington, D.C., file NAF Dec. 1983, Board of Directors Meeting, series Abortion, TCP.

43. Warren M Hern and B. Corrigan, "What about Us? Staff Reactions to D&E," *Advances in Planned Parenthood* 15, no. 1 (1980): 7.

44. Ibid., 5. Some health care professionals resented the seemingly casual attitudes of some of the patients who had D&E abortions. See also Gorney, *Articles of Faith*, 306.

45. Joe Scheidler's Presentation, Atlanta, Georgia, Jan. 12, 1986, Stone Mountain Community Church, file Joseph Scheidler, SHP.

46. Dena Kleiman, "When Abortion Becomes Birth," *New York Times*, Feb. 15, 1984, 14.

47. Deborah Sontag, "Doctors Say It's Just One Way," *New York Times*, Mar. 21, 1997, A1. Media coverage of these concerns contributed to the stifling of the discussion. Even journalists at such papers as the *New York Times* preferred sensational quotes over proper contextualization of the issues. While they quoted abortion providers struggling with D&Es at advanced gestational ages, for instance, they failed to discuss the serious considerations regarding viability and quality of life that neonatologists faced when confronted with extremely premature fetuses—issues that influenced the considerations of both women requesting abortions and abortion providers performing such procedures. And, in the name of objectivity, journalists also quoted antiabortion activists but failed to note how opponents of abortion misrepresented abortion providers.

48. Kleiman, "When Abortion becomes Birth."

49. Grimes, "Second Trimester Abortions in the United States," 260.

50. Quoted in Kleiman, "When Abortion becomes Birth."

51. Ibid.

52. Bernard N. Nathanson, "Deeper into Abortion," *New England Journal of Medicine* 291, no. 22 (Nov. 28, 1974): 1189–90. His resignation from the center was unconnected to emerging doubts about legal abortion. Indeed, he continued to perform abortions for his private patients for an undisclosed time after this.

53. Ibid.

54. Ibid.

55. Ibid.

56. Leslie J. Reagan, *When Abortion Was a Crime: Women, Medicine, and Law in the United States,1867–1973* (Berkeley: University of California Press, 1998), 173–79.

57. Some of the abortion providers I have interviewed also suggested that Nathanson liked to go "against the grain" and attributed his switch of position to his contrarian nature.

58. Bernard N. Nathanson, *Aborting America* (Pinnacle Books, 1981), 161, also 165.

59. Ibid., 168.

60. Magda Denes, *In Necessity and Sorrow: Life and Death in an Abortion Hospital* (New York: Basic Books, 1976), xvi.

61. Ibid., 42.

62. See, for instance, David C. Reardon, *Aborted Women: Silent No More* (Westchester Ill.: Crossway Books, 1987), and James Tunstead Burtchaell, *Rachel Weeping: The Case against Abortion* (San Francisco: Harper and Row, 1982), both of whom relied extensively on the testimonials in Denes and Francke; also see Linda Bird Francke, *The Ambivalence of Abortion* (New York: Radom House, 1978). For pre-*Roe* views on abortion patients, see Reagan, *When Abortion Was a Crime*, 58–59, 201–3.

63. Norma Rosen, "Between Guilt and Gratification: Abortion Doctors Reveal Their Feelings," *New York Times*, Apr. 17, 1977, 118.

64. Ibid.

65. Reardon, *Aborted Women*, 269. See also Burtchaell, *Rachel Weeping*, 216–17. Burtchaell uses the quote in a section in which he argues for the similarities between the Nazi Holocaust and abortion to illustrate the particular callousness of the abortion provider who continues his work despite understanding that he is taking life. The quotes sometimes differed slightly in accuracy of words and punctuation. But their meaning remained consistent throughout.

66. Deposition of Dr. Anthony Paul Levatino, Tamera Green v. Robert Lucy MD et al., District Court, County of Cass, State of North Dakota, July 27, 1991, 155, file FWHO Legal, Tamera Green v. FWHO, SHP. Six of the panel members had actually provided abortions, one illegally as a nurse. A number of them had worked for prominent physicians.

67. Andrew Scholberg, "The Ex-Abortionists Meet," *Life & Family News*, Dec. 1987, 3.

68. *Meet the Abortion Providers*, part 4 of 4, 1987, Pro-Life Action League, http://prolifeaction.org/providers/ (accessed Mar. 24, 2015).

69. Former abortionist Dr. Anthony Levatino, Pro-Life Action League, http://prolifeaction.org/providers/ (accessed Mar. 24, 2015). Beverly McMillan, the one woman physician included on the panel, noted that her experience as a resident at Cook County Hospital in the late 1960s exposed her to the grim realities of illegal abortion and convinced her to offer abortion services after the *Roe v. Wade* decision.

70. Appleton had worked at the Commonwealth Clinic in Washington, D.C. See former abortion nurse Joan Appleton, Pro-Life Action League, http://prolifeaction.org/providers/ (accessed Mar. 24, 2015).

71. *Meet the Abortion Providers*, pt. 4 of 4, 1987, Pro-Life Action League, http://prolifeaction.org/providers/ (accessed Mar. 24, 2015).

72. Ibid., pt. 3 of 4.

73. Ibid.

74. I thank several abortion providers for insight into factors leading employees to leave in a disgruntled manner. For employees disgruntled about pay and working conditions, see, for instance, Luhra Tivis, who complained about her pay as an administrator for George Tiller's clinic, and Patrick Tierno, who, after a dispute over pay and work performance with his employer Takey Crist, went to local antiabortion activists with a range of allegations against Crist and the Crist clinic. See former abortion clinic staffer Luhra Tivis, ibid., and transcript of interview with Dr. Patrick Tierno, n.d. [Nov. 1981], file Crist v. Tierno Transcript Tierno Tape, TCP. For employees who joined clinics as temporary workers and were unprepared for the work, see Luhra Tivis, who worked at George Tiller's clinic, and nurse Shafer, who worked for Martin Haskell, http://prolifeaction.org/providers/tivis.php (accessed Mar. 24, 2015).

75. In 1984, NAF had 247 clinic members, while the Alan Guttmacher Institute (AGI) counted 2,710 facilities across the country in which five or more abortions were performed.

76. Mary Meehan, "Ex-Abortion Workers: Why They Quit," *Human Life Review*, Spring/Summer 2000.

77. Appleton had worked at the Commonwealth Women's Clinic in Falls Church, Virginia, which was not a NAF member. It is safe to assume that Appleton never had the opportunity to attend a NAF meeting and hence was never able to participate in any discussion surrounding the challenges of working in an abortion clinic in a peer environment. In 1988, during Operation Rescue's National Day of Rescue, as many as 500 demonstrators showed up at the Commonwealth Women's Clinic. Two hundred and twenty-nine were arrested. National Abortion Federation, Public Affairs Notes, Nov. 4, 1988, file NAF 1988, TCP.

78. *Meet the Abortion Providers*, pt. 4 of 4.

79. Ibid. Another presumably former abortion provider confessed in an interview in the late 1980s: "I started doing D&E abortions, in which you have visible, fully formed babies and you rip them apart." See Andrew Scholberg, "The Ex-Abortionists Meet," *Life & Family News*, Dec. 1987, 3.

80. Former abortion nurse Joan Appleton, Pro-Life Action League, http://prolife action.org/providers/ (accessed Mar. 24, 2015).

81. Activists repeatedly mentioned being converted to the antiabortion movement after reading *Whatever Happened to the Human Race?* or watching the five-episode film which accompanied it. C. Everett Koop and Francis A. Schaeffer, *Whatever Happened to the Human Race? Exposing Our Rapid yet Subtle Loss of Human Rights* (Old Tappan, N.J.: Fleming H. Revell, 1979). See also John C. Wilke and Mrs. J. C. Wilke, *Handbook on Abortion* (Cincinnati, Ohio: Hiltz, 1971, 1972). For antiabortion activists' reception, see James Risen and Judy L. Thomas, *Wrath of Angels: The American Abortion War* (New York: Basic Books, 1998), 120–29; Carol J. C. Maxwell, *Pro-Life Activists in America: Meaning, Motivation, and Direct Action* (Cambridge: Cambridge University Press, 2002), esp. 90–119. For the use of the *Handbook* on picket lines, see Deposi-

tion of Joan Uebelhoer, Fort Wayne Women's Health Organization v. Nurses Concerned for Life, May 7, 1979, file FWWHO Legal Special, Nurses Concerned for Life, Joan Uebelhoer, Deposition, DU-RBMSCL, SHP; Gorney, *Articles of Faith*.

82. William F. Sayers, "Abortion: Is it Murder?," *Conservative Digest* (June 1978): 18–19, file Abortion Update, 1978, series Abortion, TCP. See also Dr. and Mrs. J. C. Wilke, "Life or Death," 1975, file Anti-Abortion Publicity, ibid.

83. Winnie Barron, "Experiences at Birthchoice Pro-Life Center," Nov. 12, 1987, file Birthchoice, ibid.

84. Ibid.

85. Susan Bolotin, "Selling Chastity: The Sly New Attack on Your Sexual Freedom," *Vogue*, Mar. 1986. This case is based on a real incident: Robert A. Munsick, "Air Embolism and Maternal Death from Therapeutic Abortion," *Obstetrics and Gynecology* 39, no. 5 (May 1972): 688–90. Thanks to Warren Hern for the tip.

86. By the 1980s, a whole industry of support groups, counselors, and lawyers had emerged to offer their services to women with negative abortion outcomes. David Reardon was part of this development. The narratives were further accompanied by warnings about negative abortion outcomes and the suggestion that women sue their abortion providers if they experienced any complications or regretted their decision. See, for instance, Reardon, *Aborted Women*. The phenomenon of psychological distress as a result of abortion is highly contested in the psychological literature. Indeed, the American Psychological Association issued a report in August 2008 concluding that no evidence existed that abortion caused negative mental health outcomes. See APA Task Force on Mental Health and Abortion, *Report of the APA Task Force on Mental Health and Abortion* (Aug. 13, 2008), accessed on Feb. 13, 2009, at http://www.apa.org /releases/abortion-report.pdf; Julia R. Steinberg, Beth Jordan, and Elisa S. Wells, "Science Prevails: Abortion and Mental Health," *Contraception* 79 (2009): 81–83.

87. Donna Turner, NC WEBA, file Meeting—1983, Oct. 27, Planned Parenthood, Charlotte, NC, subject files Crist Clinic, TCP.

88. Richard Selzer, "What I Saw at the Abortion," *Christianity Today*, Jan. 16, 1976, 11–12, file Correspondence, 1976, series Abortion, TCP (emphasis mine).

89. See, for instance, "Five Ways to Kill an Unborn Child," Sept. 1977, and Melody Green, "Children—Things We Throw Away?" (1979), 3rd ed., 1983, both in file Anti-Abortion Publicity, series Abortion, TCP; William F. Sayers, "Abortion: Is It Murder?," *Conservative Digest* (June 1978): 18–19, file Abortion Update, 1978, ibid.

90. Reardon, *Aborted Women*, xvi.

91. Monica J. Casper, *The Making of the Unborn Patient: A Social Anatomy of Fetal Surgery* (New Brunswick, N.J.: Rutgers University Press, 1998), 83–84; Susan Hill, interview with Johanna Schoen, Mar. 3, 2008, Raleigh, N.C.

92. Faye D. Ginsburg, *Contested Lives: The Abortion Debate in an American Community* (Berkeley: University of California Press, 1989), 104.

93. Wilke and Wilke, "Life or Death"; Ginsburg, *Contested Lives*, 71, 105–6. Ginsburg points out that right-to-life visual materials always juxtaposed magnified images of the fetus floating intact in the womb with gruesome, harshly lit clinical shots of mutilated and bloody fetal remains. By the mid-1980s, a popular slideshow produced by the National Right-to-Life Committee further incorporated "war pictures" into this lineup,

depicting Southeast Asian civilians burnt by napalm. Through such symbolic construc-
tions, Ginsburg holds, the pro-life campaign casts those who ignored, supported, or
participated in abortion as unwitting war criminals.

94. Gorney, *Articles of Faith*, 99, 163.

95. Bernard N. Nathanson, *The Silent Scream*, http://www.youtube.com/watch?v
=gON-8PP6zgQ (accessed July 15, 2014).

96. Ibid.

97. Louise B. Tyrer, Memo to Affiliate Executive Directors, Feb. 1985, file Abortion
Update, 1985, series Abortion, TCP. See also Rosalind Petchesky, "Foetal Images: The
Power of Visual Culture in the Politics of Reproduction," in *Reproductive Technologies:
Gender, Motherhood, and Medicine*, ed. Michelle Stanworth (Minneapolis: University
of Minnesota Press, 1987), 57–80.

98. Dan Williams argues that it was the Supreme Court's "perceived cavalier dis-
missal of questions of fetal personhood" that hardened the lines of opposition and
drew Evangelicals to join the Catholic opposition to abortion and support a constitutional amendment that would protect human life from the moment of conception.
Daniel K. Williams, "No Happy Medium: The Role of Americans' Ambivalent View of
Fetal Rights in Political Conflict over Abortion Legalization," *Journal of Policy History*
25, no. 1 (2013): 42–61. For more on the Republican strategy as it relates to antiabortion politics, see Jennifer Donnally, "The Politics of Abortion and the Rise of the New
Right" (Ph.D. diss., University of North Carolina, 2013); Sara Dubow, *Ourselves Unborn: A History of the Fetus in Modern America* (New York: Oxford University Press,
2011), 112–52. For further links between antiabortion politics and the extreme right, see
Carol Mason, *Killing for Life: The Apocalyptic Narrative of Pro-Life Politics* (Ithaca,
N.Y.: Cornell University Press, 2002); Carol Mason, "Minority Unborn," in *Fetal Subjects, Feminist Positions*, ed. Lynn M. Morgan and Meredith W. Michaels (Philadelphia: University of Pennsylvania Press, 1999), 159–174; and Dorothy Roberts, *Killing
the Black Body: Race, Reproduction, and the Meaning of Liberty* (New York: Pantheon
Books, 1997). For the roots of conservative politics and antiabortion activism, see
Gillian Frank, "The Colour of the Unborn: Anti-Abortion and Anti-Bussing in Michigan, United States, 1967–1973," *Gender and History* 26, no. 2 (Aug. 2014): 351–78, and
Rickie Solinger, "The First Welfare Case: Money, Sex, Marriage and White Supremacy
in Selma, 1966, A Reproductive Justice Analysis," *Journal of Women's History* 22, no. 3
(2010): 13–38.

99. Janelle S. Taylor, "Image of Contradiction: Obstetrical Ultrasound in American
Culture," in *Reproducing Reproduction: Kinship, Power, and Technological Innovation*,
ed. Sarah Franklin and Helena Ragone (Philadelphia: University of Pennsylvania Press,
1998), 15. For the powerful impact of *The Silent Scream* in converting individuals to
antiabortion activism, see also Maxwell, *Pro-Life Activists in America*, 90–119, and
Risen and Thomas, *Wrath of Angels*, 198.

100. Francke, *Ambivalence of Abortion*.

101. Reardon, *Aborted Women*, xxiii.

102. Ibid., 68, 254. Reardon argued that women who were "completely satisfied"
with their abortions are few and far between and that their claims must be taken with
a grain of salt because to admit otherwise was to open the door to reevaluation, doubt,

self-reproach, and despair. Some women, he held, suffered from their abortions on a subconscious level and were "walking time-bombs," waiting to explode over situations seemingly unrelated to their previous abortion. Women least likely to suffer from abortion, he concluded, were women who showed little motherliness, were aggressive rather than nurturing. They were likely to be self-centered, property oriented rather than people oriented, extremely manipulative of others. They suffered least not because they were more psychologically stable but because they were already so psychologically crippled. Ibid., 118–19, 138–39.

103. Ibid., 10–11, 14.

104. Ibid., 148.

105. Ibid., 75.

106. Ibid., xvi–xvii.

107. Ibid., xv.

108. Ibid., 157.

109. Reardon confirmed many of the characteristics of the abortion experience already familiar to readers of Magda Denes, *In Necessity and Sorrow*. Indeed, Reardon relied heavily on Rosen, Denes, and Francke as his secondary sources.

110. Reardon, *Aborted Women*, 7.

111. Ibid., 22.

112. For solicitation of such testimony, see Nancy Crow to Dear Friend, n.d., file American Rights Coalition, box 2, Susan Wicklund Papers, SWP. For the conversion of Norma McCorvey, see Norma McCorvey and Gary Thomas, *Won by Love: Norma McCorvey, Jane Roe of Roe V. Wade, Speaks Out for the Unborn as She Shares Her New Conviction for Life* (Nashville, Tenn.: Thomas Nelson, 1998). For attempts to use women's testimonials in support of abortion restriction, see *Report of the South Dakota Task Force to Study Abortion*, submitted to the Governor and Legislature of South Dakota, Dec. 2005. See also Reva B. Siegel, "The Right's Reasons: Constitutional Conflict and the Spread of Woman-Protective Antiabortion Argument," *Duke Law Journal* 57 (2008): 1641–92.

113. Reardon, *Aborted Women*, 69.

114. Ibid., xii.

115. National Organization for Women et al. v. Joseph M. Scheidler et al., U.S. District Court, Eastern Division, no. 86C788, Motion for Leave to File First Amendment Complaint, file Joseph Scheidler lawsuits, series Abortion, TCP. For more on the fetal thefts, see Hill, interview, Mar. 3, 2008.

116. *20/20* segment, Jan. 1985, SHP.

117. Takey Crist to Phillip Stubblefield, Jan. 28, 1985, file NAF 1985, series Abortion, TCP. For the conversation on the picket line, see Conversation on picket line, Crist Clinic, Oct. 21, 1984, Audio File, TCP.

118. Gina Kolata, "In Late Abortions, Decisions Are Painful and Options Few," *New York Times*, Jan. 5, 1992, 12; Kleinman, "When Abortion Becomes Birth."

119. Kleiman, "When Abortion becomes Birth."

120. Kolata, "Late Abortions," 12.

Chapter Five

1. NOW v. Scheidler, Deposition of Monica Migliorino, Oct. 11, 12, 1989, SHP.

2. Ibid., Oct. 11, 1989, 208. See also Monica Migliorino Miller, *Abandoned: The Untold Story of the Abortion Wars* (Charlotte, N.C.: St. Benedict Press, 2012), for her own memories.

3. Treva Jones, "Mass for 157 Fetuses Draws 350 Mourners," *Raleigh News and Observer*, Aug. 24, 1988, 18C.

4. Susan Hill, interview with Johanna Schoen, Feb. 3, 2008, Raleigh, N.C.

5. Deposition of Monica Migliorino, Oct. 12, 1989.

6. Ibid., 274.

7. Ibid., 277.

8. Ibid., Oct. 11 1989, 208.

9. Ibid. Oct. 12 1989, 248.

10. Ibid., 252.

11. Ibid., 257.

12. Ibid., 261–62.

13. Jones, "Mass for 157 Fetuses."

14. Ibid.; Patrick Jasperse, "500 Give Fetuses an Emotional Burial," *Milwaukee Journal*, Sept. 11, 1988.

15. Jasperse, "500 Give Fetuses an Emotional Burial."

16. In the 1990s, the decline was even more drastic as the number of abortion providers plummeted to 1,819 by 2000—a 37 percent decline from 1982. See "Abortion in the United States," http://www.guttmacher.org/media/presskits/abortion-US/graphics.html (accessed Mar. 28, 2015).

17. Hill, interview, Feb. 3, 2008.

18. Ibid.

19. Deposition of Joan Uebelhoer, 57–58, 63, FWWHO v. Nurses Concerned for Life, May 7, 1979, SHP.

20. Nurses Concerned for Life v. NWHO, Susan Hill Reply Affidavit, FWWHO Legal, Nurses Concerned for Life, Affidavit, SHP; Hill, interview, Feb. 3, 2008.

21. Hill, interview, Feb. 3, 2008.

22. Anonymous to Mary Collins, Dec. 14, 1978, FWWHO Legal RICO Case, Stipulation to Dismiss, SHP. See also Deposition of Joan Uebelhoer, and Affidavit of Terry Beresford, Ontario Court, between the Attorney General of Ontario and Joanne Dieleman et al., 93-CQ-36131, file Canada Depositions, TBP.

23. Affidavit Frederick Arnold Cravens, Feb. 1979, FWWHO Legal, Nurses Concerned for Life, Affidavit, SHP.

24. Hill, interview, Feb. 3, 2008.

25. Nurses Concerned for Life v. NWHO, Susan Hill Reply Affidavit, FWWHO Legal, Nurses Concerned for Life, Affidavit, SHP; Hill, interview, Feb. 2, 2008.

26. Lori R. Freedman and Debra B. Stulberg, "Conflicts in Care for Obstetric Complications in Catholic Hospitals," *AJOB Primary Research* 4, no. 4 (2013): 1–10.

27. Case History No. 1369, n.d., FWWHO Legal Case 1368, demonstration Aug. 11,

1979, SHP; Byron Spice, "Abortion Clinic Closes after Woman Dies," *Fort Wayne Journal Gazette*, July 20, 1979; Byron Spice, "Local Abortion Death Second of its Kind in Nation," *Journal Gazette*, July 21, 1979; "Abortion Clinic to Reopen," *News Sentinel*, July 23, 1979; Barbara Wachtman and Debby Brian, "Abortion Victim Death Accidental," n.d., FWHO Political, Mailing Received by Staff, SHP. Over the course of the following decade, hospital care for women in need of an emergency D&C or other complications related to abortions and miscarriages deteriorated further. Led by Catholic hospitals, hospitals around the country bowed to antiabortion pressure and imposed restrictions on reproductive health services, including abortion and contraceptive services that made the timely care of pregnancy-related emergencies difficult. While some physicians quietly violated hospital policies to perform what they deemed responsible medical care, they did so at risk to their careers. See Freedman and Stulberg, "Conflicts in Care"; Lori R. Freedman, Uta Landy, and J. Steinauer, "When There Is a Heartbeat: Miscarriage Management in Catholic-Owned Hospitals," *American Journal of Public Health* 98, no. 10 (Oct. 2008): 1774–78; Lori Freedman, *Willing and Unable: Doctors' Constraints in Abortion Care* (Nashville, Tenn.: Vanderbilt University Press, 2010).

28. Affidavit of Leslie D. Judd, Aug. 1979, FWWHO Legal, Nurses Concerned for Life, Affidavit, SHP.

29. Affidavit of Barbara Fageol, ibid.

30. Affidavit of Leslie D. Judd, and Affidavit of Caroline M. Budzik, Aug. 1979, both in ibid.; Byron Spice, "Clinic Forces Trade Insults," *Fort Wayne Journal Gazette*, Aug. 12, 1979.

31. Affidavit of Rosanna Herber, Aug. 1979, FWWHO Legal, Nurses Concerned for Life, Affidavit, SHP.

32. Ibid.

33. Affidavit of Caroline M. Budzik, Aug. 1979, FWWHO Legal, Nurses Concerned for Life, Affidavit, SHP.

34. Affidavit of Delores Rodgers and Affidavit of Leslie D. Judd, both in ibid.

35. Affidavit of Delores Rodgers and Affidavit of Leslie D. Judd, ibid.

36. Tapes of August [transcript of Joseph Scheidler's speech], Aug. 11, 1979, FWWHO Legal Case 1368, demonstration Aug. 11, 1979, SHP.

37. Susan Hill to Kenneth Buckmaster, Aug. 24, 1979, FWWHO Legal RICO Case, Stipulation to Dismiss, SHP.

38. Ibid.

39. Affidavit of Rosanna Herber, Aug. 1979, FWWHO Legal, Nurses Concerned for Life, Affidavit, SHP.

40. Susan Hill to Kenneth Buckmaster, Aug. 24, 1979, FWWHO Legal RICO Case, Stipulation to Dismiss, SHP.

41. For a careful analysis of this process, see Jennifer Donnally, *The Politics of Abortion and the Rise of the New Right* (Ph.D. diss., University of North Carolina, 2013).

42. Victoria Johnson, "The Strategic Determinants of a Countermovement: The Emergence and Impact of Operation Rescue Blockades," in *Waves of Protest: Social Movements Since the Sixties*, ed. Jo Freeman and Victoria Johnson (Lanham, Md.: Rowman and Littlefield, 1999), 241–66; Diane diMauro and Carole Joffe, "The Religious Right and the Reshaping of Sexual Policy: An Examination of Reproductive

Rights and Sexuality Education," *Sexuality Research and Social Policy* 4, no. 1 (Mar. 2007): 67–92.

43. *20/20* segment, Jan. 1985, SHP.

44. Faye D. Ginsburg, *Contested Lives: The Abortion Debate in an American Community* (Berkeley: University of California Press, 1989), 76–81. Bovard is identified as Kay Bellevue in *Contested Lives*.

45. Diane Minor, "Pro-Lifers React to Clinic Rumor," *Fargo-Morehead Forum*, Aug. 20, 1981, 3.

46. Ed Maixner, "Abortions Confirmed: Building Permit Suspended at New Clinic in Fargo," *Fargo-Morehead Forum*, Sept. 4, 1981, 1–2; Jim Neumann, "Lindgren Orders Clinic Permit Reissued," *Fargo-Morehead Forum*, Sept. 5, 1981, 1–2.

47. Hospital administrators pointed to community pressure to explain the absence of abortion services. The issue "just has not come up," claimed the administrator of the Dakota Hospital in Fargo. If it did, he explained, "it would have to go through proper channels for approval." Diane Minor, "Wide Variety of Abortion Services Offered in F-M Area," *Sunday Fargo-Morehead Forum*, Oct. 4, 1981, D-14.

48. Diane Minor, "Abortions Offered: Controversial Clinic Opens Thursday," file Fargo (2 of 3), box 5, SHP; Minor, "Wide Variety"; Ginsburg, *Contested Lives*, 2.

49. Peg Meier, "Abortion Clinic Opening Stirs Unflappable Fargo," *Minneapolis Tribune*, Oct. 4, 1981, 1B; Diane Minor, "Anti-abortion Group's Poll Hints at Professional Boycott," *Fargo-Morehead Forum*, Sept. 25, 1981; "'They' say . . . you've come a long way, baby," file Fargo (3 of 3), box 5, SHP; Diane Minor, "Abortion Opponents Rally against Fargo Clinic," *Fargo-Morehead Forum*, Sept. 28, 1981, 9; "Clinic Opening Uneventful," *Fargo-Morehead Forum*, Oct. 1 1981; Ginsburg, *Contested Lives*, 92.

50. Ginsburg, *Contested Lives*, 95; see also 28.

51. Partners in Vision to the City Commissioners for the City of Fargo, N.D., Oct. 1981, file Fargo (3 of 3), box 5, SHP.

52. Ibid.

53. Ibid. A number of cosmetic companies advertise that their products contain animal placenta extracts for their allegedly nourishing characteristics. The allegation that abortion clinics sell human placenta to cosmetics companies is long-standing and unsupported.

54. Diane Minor, "Injunction Sought against New Clinic," *Fargo-Morehead Forum*, Oct. 8, 1981, 1–2; Chet Gebert, "Anti-abortion Foes Fail to Close Clinic," *Fargo-Morehead Forum*, Oct. 20, 1981; Ed Maixner, "Fargo Board Rejects Clinic Hearing Request," *Fargo-Morehead Forum*, Nov. 17, 1981, 1–2.

55. Ellen Frankfort, with Frances Kissling, *Rosie: The Investigation of a Wrongful Death* (New York: Dial Press, 1979).

56. Stanley K. Henshaw, ed., "Abortion Services in the United States, East State and Metropolitan Area, 1979–1980," *Family Planning Perspectives* 14, no. 1 (Jan.–Feb. 1982): 5–8.

57. Ginsburg, *Contested Lives*, 51.

58. *Holy Terror*, 1987, SHP.

59. http://prolifeaction.org/about/news/2005v24n1/history2.htm (accessed Aug. 6, 2014).

60. *Holy Terror*, 1987, SHP.

61. Jeffrey Kaplan, "Absolute Rescue: Absolutism, Defensive Action and the Resort to Force," in *Millennialism and Violence*, ed. Michael Barkun (New York: Routledge, 1996), 129.

62. Alesha Doan, *Opposition and Intimidation: The Abortion Wars and Strategies of Political Harassment* (Ann Arbor: University of Michigan Press, 1997), 113.

63. Ginsburg, *Contested Lives*, 51.

64. National Abortion Federation, Annual Report 1983, file NAF 1984, and National Abortion Federation, Annual Report 1986, series Abortion, TCP.

65. Joseph M. Scheidler, *Closed: 99 Ways to Stop Abortion* (Rockford, Ill.: Tan Books and Publishers, 1985), 19.

66. Ibid.

67. "Pro-Life 'Abortion Clinics,'" *Harper's Magazine*, Dec. 1985, 25.

68. Ginsburg, *Contested Lives*, 97–99.

69. *Holy Terror*, 1987, SHP.

70. As quoted in Doan, *Opposition and Intimidation*, 123.

71. *Holy Terror*, 1987, SHP.

72. Testimony of Mary Bannecker before the Subcommittee on Civil and Constitutional Rights, Mar. 6, 1985, Abortion Clinic Violence: Oversight Hearings before the Subcommittee on Civil and Constitutional Rights of the Committee of the Judiciary House of Representatives, 99th Cong., 1st and 2nd sess. on Abortion Clinic Violence, Mar. 6, 12, Apr. 3, 1985, and Dec. 17, 1986, serial no. 115.

73. On at least one occasion, a picketer spit at one of the clinic volunteers. See testimony of Beverly Whipple, FWHC Yakima, WA, Mar. 6, 1985, before the Subcommittee on Civil and Constitutional Rights of the Committee of the Judiciary House of Representatives, 99th Cong., 1st and 2nd sess. on Abortion Clinic Violence, Mar. 6, 12, Apr. 3, 1985, and Dec. 17, 1986, serial no. 115.

74. Ibid.

75. Ibid.

76. Testimony of Mary Bannecker.

77. Testimony of Heather C. Green, Hillcrest Clinics, before the Subcommittee on Civil and Constitutional Rights, Mar. 6, 1985, Abortion Clinic Violence: Oversight Hearings before the Subcommittee on Civil and Constitutional Rights of the Committee of the Judiciary House of Representatives, 99th Cong., 1st and 2nd sess. on Abortion Clinic Violence, Mar. 6, 12, Apr. 3, 1985, and Dec. 17, 1986, serial no. 115.

78. Testimony of Beverly Whipple.

79. Ibid. These personal threats were commonplace. For instance, see also Susan Wicklund's experience of harassment, in *This Common Secret: My Journey as an Abortion Doctor* (New York: Public Affairs, 2007).

80. Doan, *Opposition and Intimidation*, 126–27; Catherine Cozzarelli and Brenda Major, "The Effects of Anti-Abortion Demonstrators and Pro-Choice Escorts on Women's Psychological Responses to Abortion," *Journal of Social and Clinical Psychology* 13, no. 4 (1994): 404–27; Warren Hern, "Life on the Front Lines," *Women's Health Issues* 4 (Jan./Feb. 1994): 48–54.

81. Testimony of Beverly Whipple.

82. Ibid.

83. Testimony of Heather C. Green.

84. Statement of Katherine J. Taylor, Mar. 6, 1985, before the Subcommittee on Civil and Constitutional Rights, Mar. 6, 1985. Abortion Clinic Violence: Oversight Hearings before the Subcommittee on Civil and Constitutional Rights of the Committee of the Judiciary House of Representatives, 99th Cong., 1st and 2nd sess. on Abortion Clinic Violence, Mar. 6, 12, Apr. 3, 1985, and Dec. 17, 1986, serial no. 115.

85. Deposition of Joan Uebelhoer.

86. As quoted in Wendy Simonds, *Abortion at Work: Ideology and Practice in a Feminist Clinic* (New Brunswick, N.J.: Rutgers University Press, 1996), 116.

87. Morris Turner, interview with Johanna Schoen, Oct. 6, 2013, Pittsburgh, Pa.

88. Robert Thompson, interview with Johanna Schoen, Sept. 14, 2013, Pittsburgh Pa.

89. Terry Beresford, interview with Johanna Schoen, Sept. 30, 2012, Alexandria, Va.

90. Turner, interview.

91. Ibid.

92. Ibid.

93. As quoted in Simonds, *Abortion at Work*, 119.

94. Ibid.

95. Susan Wicklund, interview with Johanna Schoen, July 15, 2013, Bozeman, Mont.

96. Renee Chelian, interview with Johanna Schoen, Nov. 4, 2011, West Bloomfield, Mich.

97. Ibid. Chelian worked with the Coalition to Defend Abortion Rights, an organization based at Wayne State University whose members, too, regularly physically intimidated antiabortion protestors.

98. Turner, interview.

99. Beresford, interview.

100. Rochelle Sharpe, "Clinics Get Little Support from Officials," *Abortion: The New Militancy*, Gannett News Service Special Report, Dec. 1985, 11, file NWHO, General Reports, Rochelle Sharp, Police Response, SHP.

101. Ibid., 11.

102. Ibid. Philadelphia police refused to enforce an injunction that would have limited picketing to six persons and required picketers to walk continuously on the public sidewalk. See Testimony of Mary Bannecker. In the early months of clinic operation, Director Beverly Whipple recalled, city officials refused to help. When antiabortion activists began to make hundreds of harassing phone calls, clinic officials filed a complaint with the police, but police officials claimed they had no record of the complaint. Clinic staff convinced General Telephone to put a trap on the phone and trace the phone harassment back to its origins—only to have General Telephone discontinue the trap after 24 hours, claiming that it did not have equipment to handle the volume of incoming calls. The clinic finally hired a private attorney to get an injunction against the antiabortion activist responsible for making the calls. Testimony of Beverly Whipple.

103. Sharpe, "Clinics Get Little Support from Officials," 12. Seeking extra security at the Yakima FWHC building in Washington, clinic director Beverly Whipple hired an

off-duty police officer. But two days later, the Yakima city attorney instructed the clinic to discontinue the use of a police officer as a security guard, arguing the police had to stay "neutral" in any situation involving the clinic. See Testimony of Beverly Whipple.

104. Testimony of Beverly Whipple.

105. Testimony of Heather C. Green.

106. Rochelle Sharpe, "Trials Make Winners out of Those Arrested," *Abortion: The New Militancy*, Gannett News Service Special Report, Dec. 1985, 13, file Joseph Scheidler, background, series Abortion, TCP.

107. Ibid.

108. Fairfield, N.J., officials, for instance, rejected Hill's request for a business permit, saying her center would generate too much traffic—even though the neighborhood allowed doctors' offices and nursing homes. Hill took the township to court, where opponents complained the clinic could trigger a herpes epidemic, she said. She won virtually every court decision in the four-year case, but her legal expenses mounted to almost $300,000, six times the clinic's annual profits. Sharpe, "Clinics Get Little Support from Officials," 12.

109. Testimony of Mary Bannecker.

110. The FWHC clinic was forced to pay $3,500 for a security and alarm system, $150 a day for a twenty-four-hour security guard for the building lobby, and $11,000 a year for a person to monitor traffic in the hallways and check everyone entering the clinic. In addition, the clinic installed double glass doors and a security wall in the corridor outside the clinic suite. Testimony of Beverly Whipple. Fort Wayne Women's Health, too, hired security guards, wired all the windows and doors, and installed bulletproof panes and a security system with buzzers throughout the facility. See FWWHO v. Nurses Concerned for Life, Hearing on Diversity, Sept. 5, 1979, SHP.

111. Testimony of Heather C. Green; Testimony of Beverly Whipple.

112. Susan Bolotin, "Selling Chastity: The Sly New Attack on Your Sexual Freedom," *Vogue*, Mar. 1986, 541; Nancy Blodgett, "Abortion Clinics That Aren't: Women Accuse Right-to-Life Clinics of Deceptive Practices," *ABA Journal*, Dec. 1, 1986, 21; Matthew Davis, "20 Fake Clinics in N.C., Pro-Choice Advocates Say," *Raleigh News and Observer*, Dec. 19, 1986, file Anti-Abortion Counseling Centers, series Abortion, TCP.

113. Davis, "20 Fake Clinics in N.C."

114. Robert J. Pearson, "How to Start and Operate Your Own Pro-Life Outreach Crisis Pregnancy Center" (1984), 5, file Pearson Manual, SWP.

115. Ginsburg refers to this growth as a "problem pregnancy industry." Ginsburg, *Contested Lives*, 100–103. Since 1983, such centers had grown from a handful to as many as 2,000 to 3,000. The pro-life group Intercessors for America estimated 2,100 such centers were in existence by the end of 1984. Bolotin, "Selling Chastity."

116. Pearson, "How to Start and Operate Your Own Pro-Life Outreach Crisis Pregnancy Center," 31.

117. Geraldo Rivera, *20/20*, Jan. 1985.

118. Ibid.

119. Jean Belfiore, [patient note], Oct. 30, 1987, file Anti-Abortion Counseling Centers, series Abortion, TCP.

120. Winnie Barron, Experiences at Birthchoice Pro-Life Center, Nov. 12, 1987, file

Birthchoice, series Abortion, TCP. Another popular visual aid in CPCs was a film called *A Matter of Choice: A Concise Report on Abortion*, which dramatized a reporter's search for the truth. The narrator, a woman reporter, took viewers to witness what was described as an actual abortion. As an article in *Vogue* reported about the film, the reporter in the film was "supposedly an observer to a late first-trimester procedure. . . . The patient, supposedly unconscious from anesthesia, supposedly screams. And the reporter, supposedly objective, explains that the operation is quick, not because of simplicity, but because the doctor is hurrying to get to his 'crowded waiting room.'" Bolotin, "Selling Chastity," 483, 540.

121. Ann Saltenberger, *Every Woman Has a Right to Know the Dangers of Legal Abortion*, 3rd ed. (American Life League, 1984); "'Every Woman Has a Right to Know the Dangers of Legal Abortion,' by Ann Saltenberger" [summary of misrepresentations], file Anti-Abortion Counseling Centers, series Abortion, TCP.

122. See, for instance, *Labour of Love* 1 (Oct. 1986), file Birthchoice, series Abortion, TCP; Voice for the Unborn, "Have You Been Told the Truth about Abortion?," n.d., file Anti-Abortion Counseling Centers, series Abortion, TCP.

123. Fargo Women's Health Organization v. Patricia Larson, Affidavit Jane Doe I, State of North Dakota, Cass County, District Court, East Central Judicial District, Jan. 3, 1985, file FWHO Legal, FWHO v. Larson, Motions, SHP. Indeed, creating doubt about the relationship a young woman had with the man who got her pregnant was a common tactic in CPCs. In another CPC, the counselors asserted to a client that her boyfriend did not really love her but saw her as a "clean towel after a shower that you use and throw away." See Jacqueline Austin, "I Went (Undercover) to an Anti-Abortion Clinic," *Cosmopolitan*, Mar. 1987, 203.

124. Fargo Women's Health Organization v. Patricia Larson, Affidavit Jane Doe I.

125. Women who could no longer obtain an abortion at Fargo Women's Health were forced to travel to Minneapolis for a second trimester abortion—a process that was not only more cumbersome but also much more expensive.

126. Fargo Women's Health Organization v. Patricia Larson, Affidavit Jane Doe IV, State of North Dakota, Cass County, District Court, East Central Judicial District, Jan. 2, 1985. File: FWHO Legal, FWHO v. Larson, Motions, SHP.

127. Ibid.

128. Geraldo Rivera, *20/20*, Jan. 1985.

129. Bolotin, "Selling Chastity," 542.

130. Takey Crist to National Abortion Federation, July 25, 1986, file NAF 1985, series Abortion, TCP.

131. Fargo Women's Health Organization, Inc. vs. Patricia Larson, State of North Dakota, Cass County, District Court East Central Judicial District, Affidavit of Jane Bovard, Feb. 21, 1985, and phone conversation, both in file Fargo Women's Health Organization v. Patricia Larson et al., 1985, series Abortion, TCP.

132. Fargo Women's Health Organization v. Patricia Larson, Motion for Temporary Restraining Order and Temporary Injunction, State of North Dakota, Cass County, District Court, East Central Judicial District, Jan. 3, 1985, file FWHO Legal, FWHO v. Larson, Motions, SHP.

133. FWHO v. Fargo Women's Help and Caring Connection, Findings of Fact, Con-

clusions of Law, and Order of Judgment, Feb. 8, 1988, file SHP-FWHO v. Larson, Order of Judgment, SHP.

134. Austin, "I Went (Undercover) to an Anti-Abortion Clinic."

135. Charlotte Taft, Approaches to Dealing with Fake Clinics, May 17, 1985, file Anti-Abortion Counseling Centers, series Abortion, TCP.

136. National Abortion Federation, "Fact Sheet: Safety of Abortion," Nov. 1985, file NAF 1985, series Abortion, TCP.

137. Dudley Clendinen, "The Abortion Conflict: What It Does to One Doctor," *New York Times*, Aug. 11, 1985, SM18.

138. Different Voices: Abortion in the US and Canada—1985 Risk Management Seminar, Oct. 27–28, 1985, NAF offices, Montreal, Canada.

139. For background on Randall Terry, see Susan Faludi, "Born out of Time," *West Magazine*, n.d., file NWHO-Operation Rescue Randall Terry, SHP.

140. James Risen and Judy L. Thomas, *Wrath of Angels: The American Abortion War* (New York: Basic Books, 1998), 175.

141. Cynthia Gorney, *Articles of Faith: A Frontline History of the Abortion Wars* (New York: Simon and Schuster, 1998), 252.

142. Ibid., 323.

143. Ibid., 323.

144. Risen and Thomas, *Wrath of Angels*, 263; Gorney, *Articles of Faith*, 462.

145. Doan, *Opposition and Intimidation*, 85–86. On Atlanta, see Risen and Thomas, *Wrath of Angels*, 278–79.

146. Gorney, *Articles of Faith*, 307.

147. John Cavanaugh-O'Keefe to Director, Delta Women's Clinic, Oct. 23, 1986, file Press Conference re. Pope, and Robert Ourlian, "Pope's Visit Won't Stop Abortions, Clinics Say," *Detroit News*, Feb. 18, 1987, file NP articles Pope's Visit, both in RCP.

148. Kathy Moriarty to Dear Clinic Personnel, n.d., file Pro-Life Action Newsletter, RCP.

149. "Please Everyone" [letter of invitation by Lynn Mills, n.d.], file Pro-Life Action Newsletter, RCP.

150. National Abortion Federation, *Public Affairs Notes*, July 10, 1987, file Judy Widdicombe CFCC meeting, RCP.

151. Coalition to Defend Abortion Rights, Mar. 15, 1989, file CDAR, RCP.

152. Important Notice and Invitation for Coordination Meeting on Pope Visit, June 24, 1987, file MOHR Meeting re. Pope Visit, RCP.

153. Chelian, interview, Nov. 4, 2011.

154. Ibid. [Renee Chelian], Plan for Pope Visit or Similar Operation, n.d. [1988], file NAF Meeting 5/88 on Pope Visit—my workshop, RCP. Chelian also sent a letter to Detroit's archbishop, Reverend Edmund C. Szoka, asking him to abandon the plan of honoring the pope's visit with protests at abortion clinics. While Szoka failed to respond to her letter, similar appeals by Planned Parenthood of Greater Miami to Archbishop Edward A. McCarthy eventually led McCarthy to issue a statement urging demonstrators in his city to avoid violence during the pope's September 10–11 visit. Five days later, local antiabortion leaders in Miami decided to cancel their official participation in all

protests organized by We Will Stand Up. Renee Chelian to Reverend Edmund C. Szoka, Aug. 18, 1987, file Press Conference re. Pope, RCP; [Renee Chelian], Plan for Pope Visit or Similar Operation, n.d. [1988], file NAF Meeting 5/88 on Pope Visit—my workshop, RCP; Aminda Marques, "Anti-abortion Groups Cancel Protests," *Miami Herald*, Aug. 26, 1987, 16A, and Planned Parenthood Association of Greater Miami, Memo, Aug. 28, 1987, both in file Judy Widdicombe CFCC meeting, RCP.

155. Rollin G. Tobin to Renee Chelian, Sept. 11, 1987, file Lawsuit, RCP.

156. Roubert Ourlian, "Abortion Clinic to be Protected from Protesters," *Detroit News*, Sept. 15, 1987, file Lawsuit Sfd, RCP.

157. Chauncey Bailey and Robert Ourlian, "Abortion Groups Face Off at Clinic," *Detroit News*, Sept. 20, 1987, file NP articles Pope's visit, RCP.

158. Bailey and Ourlian, "Abortion groups face off at clinic," and [Renee Chelian], "Plan for Pope Visit or Similar Operation" [handwritten notes for presentation at NAF panel], file NAF Meeting 5/88 on Pope Visit—my workshop, both in RCP.

159. Joanne Howes to clinic support faculty members, Apr. 29, 1988, file NAF Meeting 5/88 on Pope Visit—my workshop, RCP.

160. Schedule and Faculty: Reading the Pro-Choice Majority: A Media Skills workshop, May 22, 1988, Minneapolis, MN, and Case Study A: Operation SaveLife: Coming Soon; Case Study B: Hospital Harassment/Home Picketing, both in file NAF Meeting 5/88 on Pope Visit—my workshop, RCP.

161. "Plan for Pope Visit or Similar Operation."

162. Ibid. Pro-choice activists in Miami had also planned to screen *Holy Terror* to convince local law enforcement officials of the seriousness of antiabortion activists' threats. See Planned Parenthood Association of Greater Miami, Memo, Aug. 28, 1987, file Judy Widdicombe CFCC meeting, RCP.

163. "Plan for Pope Visit or Similar Operation."

164. Risen and Thomas, *Wrath of Angels*, 272; Simonds, *Abortion at Work*, 107–8; Lynn Randall, phone interview with Johanna Schoen, Oct. 22, 2012.

165. Simonds, *Abortion at Work*, 107.

166. Ibid., 107–8.

167. Doan, *Opposition and Intimidation*, 87.

168. Antiabortion demonstrators liked to pose in front of the sign. Indeed, Randall Terry used the sign as a backdrop when he accepted a large donation from Jerry Falwell. Randall, interview.

169. Simonds, *Abortion at Work*, 107–8; Randall, interview.

170. Simonds, *Abortion at Work*, 127.

171. As quoted in ibid., 128.

172. Randall, interview.

173. Simonds, *Abortion at Work*, 116.

174. Chelian, interview, Nov. 4, 2011.

175. Simonds, *Abortion at Work*, 108–9.

176. Doan, *Opposition and Intimidation*, 117, 120. Stanley K. Henshaw, "Factors Hindering Access to Abortion Services," *Family Planning Perspectives* 2 (Mar./Apr. 1995): 54–59, 87; Stanley K. Henshaw, "Abortion Incidence and Services in the United

States, 1995–1996," *Family Planning Perspectives* 6 (Nov. 1998): 263–70, 287. The decline continued through the 1990s, with numbers falling another 14 percent between 1992 and 1996.

177. Henshaw, "Factors Hindering Access to Abortion Services."

178. Doan, *Opposition and Intimidation*, 120.

179. Ibid., 87.

180. Gorney, *Articles of Faith*, 364–70.

181. Doan, *Opposition and Intimidation*, 87.

182. The final blow for OR came in May 1994 with passage of the Freedom of Access to Clinic Entrances (FACE) law. Ibid., 88.

183. Kaplan, "Absolute Rescue," 133–37.

184. Doan, *Opposition and Intimidation*, 88.

185. Risen and Thomas, *Wrath of Angels*, 192.

186. Carol J. C. Maxwell, *Pro-Life Activists in America: Meaning, Motivation, and Direct Action* (Cambridge: Cambridge University Press, 2002), 70–71. Missionaries to the Pre-Born arose later as a Protestant alternative to the Lambs.

187. Ibid., 72.

188. Ibid., 71.

Chapter Six

1. Susan Wicklund and Alex Kesselheim, *This Common Secret: My Journey as an Abortion Doctor* (New York: Public Affairs, 2007), 63.

2. Ibid.

3. Ibid., 45.

4. Ibid., 52.

5. Ibid., 53.

6. Ibid., 54–55.

7. Ibid., 59.

8. Ibid., 72–73.

9. Ibid., 73.

10. Ibid., 81.

11. Susan Wicklund, interview with Johanna Schoen, July 15, 2013, Bozeman, Mont.

12. Ibid., Aug. 3, 2013, Wilsall, Mont.

13. Claire Keyes, interview with Johanna Schoen, Sept. 15, 2013, Pittsburgh, Pa.

14. Charlotte Taft, phone interview with Johanna Schoen, Aug. 10, 2012.

15. I could find no written record of this change in attendance policy, and NAF members were unsure of the exact year; 1986 or 1987 is an estimate by Lynn Randall. See Lynn Randall, phone interview with Johanna Schoen, Oct. 22, 2012.

16. Margaret R. Johnston, "Opting out of the Abortion War: Thoughts on the Aftermath of Birmingham," in *Our Choices, Our Lives: Unapologetic Writings on Abortion*, ed. Krista Jacob (Lincoln, Neb.: iUniverse, 2002), 153–69.

17. Ibid.

18. Ibid. After the 1993 killing of David Gunn, Peg Johnston recalls that she and a

friend took bets on who would fund-raise off the tragedy first. David Gunn was killed on a Wednesday, and the following Monday, Planned Parenthood ran a full page ad in the *New York Times*.

19. Alesha Doan, *Opposition and Intimidation: The Abortion Wars and Strategies of Political Harassment* (Ann Arbor: University of Michigan Press, 1997), 87.

20. Taft, interview.

21. Ibid.

22. Johnston, "Opting out of the Abortion War."

23. Renee Chelian, interview with Johanna Schoen, Sept. 24, 2010, Westland, Mich.

24. Taft, interview.

25. Ibid.

26. No title, no date [list of question relating to abortion, ca. 1990], file Abortion Counseling [Charlotte Taft], SWP.

27. Carole Joffe, "The Politicization of Abortion and the Evolution of Abortion Counseling," *American Journal of Public Health* 103, no. 1 (Jan. 2013): 63. See also Chelian, interview, Sept. 24,2010.

28. Susan Wicklund reports, for instance, that she never performed an abortion on a patient before she had satisfied herself that the patient truly wanted the abortion and understood that it was her choice alone. Wicklund came to this approach through conversations with a counselor at a Wisconsin clinic. Wicklund and Kesselheim, *This Common Secret*, 51. See also Wicklund, interview, Aug. 3, 2013.

29. Margaret Johnston, *Pregnancy Options Workbook*, rev. ed. 2009, file Abortion Counseling [Charlotte Taft], SWP.

30. Charlotte Taft, "Abortion Counseling—the Full Head and Heart Process," July 30, 2010 (in author's possession).

31. Ron Fitzsimmons, phone interview with Johanna Schoen, Oct. 1, 2010.

32. Chelian, interview, Sept. 24, 2010.

33. Terry Beresford, interview with Johanna Schoen, Sept. 30, 2012, Arlington, Va.

34. Fitzsimmons, interview.

35. Joffe, "Politicization of Abortion."

36. Susan Hill, interview with Johanna Schoen, June 16, 2008, Raleigh, N.C.; Fitzsimmons, interview.

37. Ron Fitzsimmons to Takey Crist, May 14, 1990, and attachment "Summary of Issues," file NCAP 1990, series Abortion, TCP; Hill, interview, June 16, 2008; Chelian, interview, Sept. 24, 2010.

38. Antiabortion forces effectively stymied FOCA during Clinton's first term by adding such amendments to kill the bill as parental notification and waiting periods for adult women. Melody Rose notes that the closest the FOCA came to passage was in 1993, when it passed both chambers of Congress. But it died in conference committee, where the two chambers could not agree on specifics. See Melody Rose, *Safe, Legal, and Unavailable? Abortion Politics in the United States* (Washington, D.C.: CQPress, 2007), 137.

39. Fitzsimmons, interview. See also the correspondence in folders "National Coalition of Abortion Providers, 1990" and "National Coalition of Abortion Providers, 1991," both series Abortion, TCP.

40. Fitzsimmons, interview.

41. Statement of Ron Fitzsimmons, Oct. 5, 1992, file NCAP, 1992; series Abortion, TCP.

42. Fitzsimmons, interview.

43. Taft, interview.

44. Fitzsimmons, interview.

45. NCAP, Oct. 20, 1992, file NCAP 1992, series Abortion, TCP.

46. Fitzsimmons, interview.

47. Certainly, Susan Hill and Takey Crist held this opinion. Chelian, interview, Sept. 24, 2010.

48. Montana's antistalking law took effect in April 1993.

49. Mike Ross to Susan Wicklund, Feb. 16, 1993, file Anti-Abortion Michael Ross, SWP.

50. Wicklund and Kesselheim, *This Common Secret*, 113.

51. Mike Ross to Susan Wicklund, Mar. 10, 1993, file Anti-Abortion Michael Ross, SWP. When Wicklund turned for help to the Bozeman police, officers suggested that she apply for a concealed weapons permit. But doing so made her feel no safer. Wicklund, interview.

52. A former Ku Klux Klan member, Burt ran a home for wayward girls called Our Father's House. He regularly appeared on the picket line carrying dead fetuses and demonstrated on the steps of the courthouse in support for the 1984 clinic bombers while their trial unfolded inside. After their conviction, he aligned himself with Joan Andrews, who was eventually convicted of clinic arson. James Risen and Judy L. Thomas, *Wrath of Angels: The American Abortion War* (New York: Basic Books, 1998), chap. 8.

53. Susan Hill, interview with Johanna Schoen, Feb. 3, 2008, Raleigh, N.C.

54. Wicklund and Kesselheim, *This Common Secret*, 84.

55. Ibid., 119.

56. Mike Ross to Susan Wicklund, Mar. 19, 1993, file Anti-Abortion Michael Ross, SWP. Wicklund was not alone. On March 11, an antiabortion activist showed up at the Hope Clinic in Granite City, Illinois, carrying a sign that named the clinic's medical director and asked: "Dr. [name], Do you feel under the Gunn?" See Patricia Baird-Windle and Eleanor J. Bader, *Targets of Hatred: Anti-Abortion Terrorism* (New York: Palgrave, 2001), 209.

57. Wicklund, interview, July 15, 2013.

58. Hill, interview, Feb. 3, 2008.

59. Ibid.

60. Ibid.

61. Ibid.

62. *Phil Donahue Show*, Mar. 15, 1993, SHP.

63. "Paul Hill," *Eye to Eye*, Dec. 1, 1994, DVD, SHP.

64. Ibid.

65. Statement of Jeri Rasmussen, Executive Director, Midwest Health Center for Women, Minneapolis, MN, Abortion Clinic Violence, Hearings before the Subcommittee on Crime and Criminal Justice of the Committee on the Judiciary, Apr. 1, 1993, 19.

66. Michael Ross to Susan Wicklund, Mar. 30, 1993, file Anti-Abortion Michael Ross, SWP.

67. Baird-Windle and Bader, *Targets of Hatred*, 216, 218–21; Dirk Johnson, "Abortions, Bibles and Bullets, and the Making of a Militant," *New York Times*, Aug. 28, 1993, 1, 3.

68. Baird-Windle and Bader, *Targets of Hatred*, 351.

69. Ibid.

70. Ibid., 210.

71. Statement of Norman T. Tompkins, M.D., Margot Perot Center, Presbyterian Hospital, Dallas, Tex., Abortion Clinic Violence, Hearings before the Subcommittee on Crime and Criminal Justice of the Committee on the Judiciary, Apr. 1, 1993, 17–18.

72. Jeffrey Kaplan, "Absolute Rescue: Absolutism, Defensive Action and the Resort to Force," in *Millennialism and Violence*, ed. Michael Barkun (New York: Routledge, 1996), 132–41; Carol Mason, *Killing for Life: The Apocalyptic Narrative of Pro-Life Politics* (Ithaca, N.Y.: Cornell University Press, 2002).

73. Mason dates the beginning of this narrative to the 1995 publication of *Gideon's Torch*, a novel by Ellen Vaughn, a *Christianity Today* writer, and Charles Colson, who had served as special counsel to President Richard Nixon and spent seven months in federal prison on Watergate-related charges. In *Gideon's Torch*, a woman abortion provider, closely modeled on Susan Wicklund, gets shot by a young woman posing as a patient. The novel "both reflects and reproduces the millennialist sense of conflict between representatives of depravity (people with AIDS and the government that supports them) and representatives of purity (the "innocent" unborn and the Christians who defend them)" (Mason, *Killing for Life*, 111). See also Charles Colson and Ellen Vaughn, *Gideon's Torch* (Dallas: Word Publishing, 1995).

74. Kaplan, "Absolute Rescue," 145.

75. Jeffrey Kaplan "America's Last Prophetic Witness: The Literature of the Rescue Movement," *Terrorism and Political Violence* 5, no. 3 (Autumn 1993): 58–77. Kaplan attributes this language to the Lambs of Christ, for instance. "Pro-abortion Satanists" are also noted as attending Shelley Shannon's trial. See Shelley Shannon, "Shelley Shannon Trial from the Perspective of Shelley Shannon," *Prayer + Action Weekly News*, Apr. 1994, 4, as cited in Kaplan, "Absolute Rescue," 158 (n. 18).

76. On the extensive use of Nazi imaginary in the debate, see Mason, *Killing for Life*, esp. 9–45.

77. Ibid., 21–45; see also Dallas A. Blanchard and Terry J. Prewitt, *Religious Violence and Abortion: The Gideon Project* (Gainesville: University Press of Florida, 1993).

78. Mimi Swartz, "Family Secret," *New Yorker*, Nov. 17, 1997, 90–107.

79. Kaplan, "Absolute Rescue," 146–47.

80. "The Brockhoeft Report 3," *Prayer + Action Weekly News*, Dec. 1993, 31, as quoted in ibid., 147.

81. Donna Bray, "A Bitter Mercy," *Life Advocate*, Dec. 1994, 42, file NWHO Right to Lifers, Paul Hill, SHP.

82. See, for instance, Paul Hill's comparison of David Gunn with Dr. Mengele on the Phil Donahue show. It was this rhetoric that contributed to Paul Hill's rise to national prominence.

83. As quoted in Baird-Windle and Bader, *Targets of Hatred*, 211.

84. As quoted in ibid.

85. Statement of Jeri Rasmussen, 19.

86. A Wichita gynecologist resigned from his job at a family planning clinic, for instance, after finding his tires slashed and pictures of dismembered fetuses stuck on his car's windshield. Baird-Windle and Bader, *Targets of Hatred*, 209.

87. "Frustration Marks Anti-Terrorism Meeting at the Justice Department," *Networks. A Newsletter for Abortion Providers* (Spring 1994): 5.

88. NCAP, Oct. 6, 1993, file NCAP 1993, series Abortion, TCP.

89. NCAP, Sept. 29, 1994, file NCAP 1994, ibid.

90. See "Frustration Marks Anti-Terrorism Meeting at the Justice Department."

91. Rose, *Safe, Legal, and Unavailable?*, 96–97.

92. Hill, interview, June 16, 2008.

93. Anonymous to Takey Crist, Mar. 10, 1993 [Mar. 17, 1993], file David Gunn, 1993 murder, series Abortion, TCP.

94. Darolyn Hilts to Takey Crist, Mar. 16, 1993, ibid.

95. Green Notebook, Mountain Country Women's Clinic, SWP.

96. Ibid.

97. Ibid.

98. Ibid.

99. Ibid.

100. Sarah Sorenson, "They Killed the Doctor Who Saved Me," *Glamour*, May 1994, 266.

101. See, for instance, Stanley K. Henshaw, "The Accessibility of Abortion Services in the United States," *Family Planning Perspectives* 23, no. 6 (Nov./Dec. 1991): 246–53. Delay was also associated with having less education, being nonwhite, being unmarried, having had no previous abortions, and having had one or more live births.

102. David A. Grimes, "Second Trimester Abortions in the United States," *Family Planning Perspectives* 16, no. 6 (Nov./Dec. 1984): 260–66; Francis R. M. Jacot et al., "A Five-Year Experience with Second Trimester Induced Abortions," *American Journal of Obstetrics and Gynecology* 168, no. 2 (Feb. 1993): 636; W. Martin Haskell, Thomas R. Easterling, and E. Steve Lichtenberg, "Surgical Abortion after the First Trimester," in *A Clinician's Guide to Medical and Surgical Abortion*, ed. Maureen Paul et al. (Philadelphia: Churchill Livingstone, 1999), 123.

103. Martin Haskell, "Dilation and Extraction for Late Second Trimester Abortion," unpublished paper presented at the National Abortion Federation Risk Management Seminar, Sept. 13, 1992.

104. See Judith Walzer Leavitt, "The Growth of Medical Authority: Technology and Morals in Turn-of-the-Century Obstetrics," *Medical Anthropology Quarterly* 1, no. 3 (Sept. 1987): 230–55.

105. Karen Tumulty, "The Abortions of Last Resort: The Question of Ending Pregnancy in Its Later Stages May Be the Most Anguishing of the Entire Abortion Debate," *Los Angeles Times*, Jan. 7, 1990; Tamar Lewin, "Method to End 20-Week Pregnancies Stirs a Corner of the Abortion Debate," *New York Times*, July 5, 1995, A10.

106. Susan Shen-Schwartz, Carol Neish, and Lyndon M. Hill, "Antenatal Ultrasound

for Fetal Anomalies: Importance of Perinatal Autopsy," *Fetal and Pediatric Pathology* 9, no. 1 (1989): 1–9; P. A. Boyd, F. Tondi, N. R, Hicks, and P. F. Chamberlain, "Autopsy after Termination of Pregnancy for Fetal Anomaly: Retrospective Cohort Study," *BMJ* 328 (7432) (Jan. 17, 2004): 137.

107. "An Interview with W. Martin Haskell, MD," *Cincinnati Medicine*, Fall 1993, 19.

108. Diane M. Gianelli, "Bill Banning 'Partial Birth' Abortion Goes to Clinton," *American Medical News*, Apr. 15, 1996, 6; Diane M. Gianelli, "Medicine Adds to Debate on Late-Term Abortion," *American Medical News*, Mar. 3, 1997, 3, 28–29; Ruth Padawer, "The Facts on Partial Birth Abortion: Both Sides Have Misled the Public," *Bergen County (N.J.) Record*, Sept. 15, 1996.

109. Haskell, "Dilation and Extraction for Late Second Trimester Abortion"; Diane M. Gianelli, "Shock-Tactic Ads Target Late-Term Abortion Procedure: Foes Hope Campaign Will Sink Federal Abortion Rights Legislation," *American Medical News*, July 5, 1993, 3, 21–22.

110. Cynthia Gorney, "Gambling with Abortion: Why Both Sides Think They Have Everything to Lose," *Harper's Magazine*, Nov. 2004, 33–46, here 37.

111. Gianelli, "Shock-Tactic Ads," 3. Pro-choice activists first introduced FOCA after the election of President Bill Clinton, but the bill disappeared after Republicans took over Congress in 1994. See also Gorney, "Gambling with Abortion," and Risen and Thomas, *Wrath of Angels*.

112. "Everyone would agree . . . " brochure, North Carolina Right to Life, n.d., file Anti-Abortion Publicity, series Abortion, TCP. Hayat had performed abortions for mostly immigrant women. He significantly overcharged his patients and blackmailed them into paying higher fees than originally agreed upon by threatening to stop the abortion partway through. The abortion attempt for Ana's mother Rosa Rodriguez resulted in the birth of Ana two days later at thirty-two to thirty-four weeks' gestation. After his indictment, more than 30 women came forward with malpractice complaints. He was eventually convicted of assault and performing an illegal abortion—a New York law banned abortions after twenty-four weeks—and sentenced to up to twenty-nine years in prison for this and other related offenses. Gianelli, "Shock-Tactic Ads"; Richard Perez-Pena, "Prison Term for Doctor Convicted in Abortions," *New York Times*, June 15, 1993.

113. "Everyone would agree . . . " brochure.

114. Gianelli, "Shock-Tactic Ads," 3.

115. Lewin, "Method to End 20-Week Pregnancies."

116. James A. Smith, "Brutal Abortion Procedure Protected under FOCA," *Light*, Sept.–Oct. 1993, 15, file Christian Life Commission, series Abortion, TCP. See also Family Research Council, "Partial-Birth Abortions: Dispelling the Myths," *In Focus*, Aug. 21, 1996, file Abortion—pba, anti-abortion publications, 1997 and n.d., CH 5, MHP.

117. Family Research Council, "Partial-Birth Abortions," MHP.

118. Diane M. Gianelli, "Outlawing Abortion Method," *American Medical News*, Nov. 20, 1995, 27.

119. Two Pew research polls from 2007 indicate that many who usually considered themselves pro-choice were in favor of a ban. Asked whether partial birth abortion

should be legal or illegal, 75 percent responded with illegal, 17 percent with legal, and 8 percent of respondents were unsure. Asked about the legal status of abortion, 53 percent responded that abortion should be legal in all or most cases, 41 responded that abortion should be illegal in all or most cases, and 9 percent were unsure. See Pew Research Center for the People and the Press and Pew Forum on Religion and Public Life survey conducted by Schulman, Ronca and Bucuvalas, Aug. 1–18, 2007; Pew Research Center for the People and the Press survey, July 31–Aug. 10, 2008. Senators Patrick Leahy and Joe Biden had a pro-choice voting record but both supported the ban.

120. Gianelli, "Shock-Tactic Ads," 3.

121. "An Interview with W. Martin Haskell, MD."

122. Gianelli, "Shock-Tactic Ads," 3.

123. Ibid., 3, 21.

124. Partial Birth Abortion Ban of 1995, Hearing on H.R.1833/S. 939 before the Senate Committee on the Judiciary, 104th Cong. (1995) (testimony of Tammy Watts), *Congressional Record*, Nov. 8, 1995, S16769–S16770. See also Gina Kolata, "In Late Abortions, Decisions Are Painful and Options Few," *New York Times*, Jan. 5, 1992, and patient testimony in Lewin, "Method to End 20-Week Pregnancies."

125. Kolata, "Late Abortions," 12; Dena Kleiman, "When Abortion Becomes Birth," *New York Times*, Feb. 15, 1984.

126. As quoted in Kleiman, "When Abortion Becomes Birth"; Grimes, "Second Trimester Abortions in the United States," 264.

127. Aida Torres and Jacqueline Darroch Forrest, "Why Do Women Have Abortions?," *Feminist Planning Perspectives* 20, no. 4 (July/Aug. 1988): 174; personal correspondence with Glenna Boyd; chart "Reasons for Late Abortion Care," n.d. [Apr. 2013] (in author's possession). A total of 268 women were included in Glenna Boyd's study, ranging in age from twelve to forty-eight years, with a mean age of twenty-five. Further reasons listed in the chart are "other" for 4 percent, rape for 3 percent, life change for 3 percent, medical misdiagnosis for 2 percent, and took this long to decide for 2 percent.

128. Gianelli, "Shock-Tactic Ads," 22.

129. Hill, interview, June 16, 2008.

130. Press Release, "Aiming at the Right to Abortion, Congress Votes to Ban a Medical Procedure that Saves Women's Lives." PR Newswire, Nov. 1, 1995.

131. Lewin, "Method to End 20-Week Pregnancies."

132. Ibid.

133. Ibid.

134. Partial Birth Abortion Ban Act of 1995, 104th Cong., 1st sess., House of Representatives, Report 104-267, Sept. 27, 1995, 2.

135. Ibid., 3.

136. Ibid., 4.

137. This information stems from a chart that McMahon submitted to a 1995 legislative committee investigating intact D&Es. It is unclear from the record how many procedures at or after twenty-six weeks McMahon performed or what he listed as indications for the procedures. The record only cites the mention of a cleft lip as an indication for nine cases. But we do not know whether this was the only indication or whether it was one of several. Partial Birth Abortion Ban Act of 1995, 8. In August 1995, Jim

McMahon was diagnosed with brain cancer. He passed away in October of that year. As a result, his voice is missing after mid-1995. See *NAF News*, Nov.–Dec. 1995.

138. Statement of Norig Ellison, M.D., before the Committee on the Judiciary, United States Senate, Nov. 17, 1995, http://www.nrlc.org/abortion/pba/anes.html (accessed Mar. 29, 2015); Douglas Johnson, "The Partial-Birth Abortion Ban Act—Misconceptions and Realities," 5 Nov. 2003, http://www.nrlc.org/abortion/pba/pbaall110403/ (accessed Mar. 29, 2015).

139. Statement of Norig Ellison, M.D.

140. Johnson, "Partial-Birth Abortion Ban Act." For a reference to McMahon's testimony and a fact sheet issued by Mary Campbell, medical director of Planned Parenthood of Metropolitan Washington, see Watson A. Bowes to Charles Canady, July 11, 1995, 2, http://www.nrlc.org/archive/abortion/pba/Bowes%20on%20disputed%20issues%201995.pdf (accessed Mar. 29, 2015).

141. Bowes to Canady, July 11, 1995.

142. Partial Birth Abortion Ban Act of 1995, 4.

143. Bowes to Canady, July 11, 1995. See also the testimony of Pamela Smith, H.R. 1833, 104th Cong., 1st sess. (1995).

144. Dru Elaine Carlson to Patricia Schroeder, June 27, 1995, 104th Cong., 1st sess., House of Representatives, Report 104-267, Partial Birth Abortion Ban Act of 1995, Report with Dissenting Views.

145. Ruth Padawer, "Pro-Choice Advocates Admit to Deception," *Bergen County (N.J.) Record*, Feb. 27, 1997, File NCAP 1997, series Abortion, TCP.

146. Ibid.; Renee Chelian, interview with Peg Johnston, 2008, New Mexico; Renee Chelian, interview, Sept. 24, 2010.

147. Ruth Padawer, "The Facts on Partial-Birth Abortion: Both Sides Have Misled the Public," *Bergen County (N.J.) Record*, Sept. 16, 1996. See also Barbara Vobejda and David Brown, "Harsh Details Shift Tenor of Abortion Fight: Both Sides Bend Facts on Late-Term Procedure," *Washington Post*, Sept. 17, 1996, A1.

148. The continued classification of abortions as elective or nonelective, the latter describing abortions performed for medical indications, perpetuated the notion that women's reasons for seeking abortions were likely to be a matter of personal convenience and thus less defensible. While some physicians resisted classifying any abortions as elective, arguing that abortions for any reasons are needed, the medical literature continued to differentiate between elective and nonelective abortions. See, for instance, David A. Grimes, "The Continuing Need for Late Abortions," *JAMA* 280, no. 8 (Aug. 26, 1998): 747–50.

149. David Brown, "Late Term Abortions: Who Gets Them and Why," *Washington Post*, Sept. 17, 1996, Health Section, 1–2, 14, 17, 19.

150. Vobejda and Brown, "Harsh Details Shift Tenor of Abortion Fight."

151. Ibid.

152. McMahon's wide-ranging list of indications suggests, for example, that he was more concerned with listing indications for the pregnancy terminations he performed then physicians at the University of North Carolina, who considered 95 percent of their second trimester abortions elective. Brown, "Late Term Abortions."

153. Terry Eastland, "Partial Birth Abortions," *Media Matters*, PBS (Jan. 1997).

154. Gianelli, "Bill Banning 'Partial Birth' Abortion Goes to Clinton," 6.

155. Ibid.

156. Ron Fitzsimmons to NCAP Members, Feb. 18, 1997, file NCAP 1997, series Abortion, TCP.

157. David Stout, "An Abortion Rights Advocate Says He Lied about Procedure," *New York Times*, Feb. 26, 1997, A12. See also Padawer, "Pro-Choice Advocates Admit to Deception"; "Partial-Birth Betrayal: Democrats Seething, as Activist Admits Lie," *Roll Call*, Feb. 27, 1997, 8.

158. Stout, "An Abortion Rights Advocate Says He Lied about Procedure."

159. Renee Chelian, interview with Johanna Schoen, Nov. 4, 2011, Westland, Mich.

160. Renee Chelian to NCAP members, Feb. 28, 1997, NCAP 1997 series Abortion, TCP; Chelian, interview, Nov. 4, 2011; Ron Fitzsimmons to Merle Hoffman, Apr. 1, 1997, and Joy Silver to Ron Fitzsimmons, Apr. 3, 1997, both in folder Abortion—NCAP, Ron Fitzsimmons Debacle, 1997, MHP. Personality conflicts further aggravated the situation. Both Hern and Fitzsimmons were extremely outspoken and held controversial positions within the abortion provider community. In 1995, Hern found himself embroiled in an argument over his role as an expert witness. When a patient of a colleague sued the colleague after he had failed to diagnose an ectopic pregnancy, Hern provided his medical opinion that the colleague had mishandled the case. While NAF members did occasionally testify in court as expert witnesses against other NAF members, in this case an antiabortion group, Life Dynamics, had filed the case and recruited the unwitting Hern, who was faced on the other side by the Center for Reproductive Law and Policy defending the colleague. The issue became a permanent thorn in the side of many NAF members who were dissatisfied with Hern's defense that he had the right to serve as an expert witness whenever he felt the case merited it. Stover requested that NAF expel Hern from the organization. Testifying against a colleague had clearly taken on a different flavor after antiabortion activists began to kill abortion providers. See NCAP, June 26, 1995, file NCAP 1995, series Abortion, TCP.

161. Chelian, interview, Nov. 4, 2011.

162. Ibid.

163. Testimony of Renee Chelian, President, National Coalition of Abortion Providers, before the House and Senate Judiciary Committee, Mar. 11, 1997, file NCAP 1997, series Abortion, TCP.

164. Ibid.

165. Ibid.

166. "Partial Birth Abortion Ban Act" Developments, May 19, 1997, file NCAP 1997, series Abortion, TCP.

167. Nancy E. Roman, "Pro-life Forces Get Control of Debate," *Washington Post*, May 19, 1997, file NCAP 1997, series Abortion, TCP.

168. Ibid.

169. Gianelli, "Bill Banning 'Partial Birth' Abortion Goes to Clinton," 6.

170. Grimes, "Continuing Need for Late Abortions."

171. Gianelli, "Shock-Tactics Ads," 15. See similar comments by Hern and Rashbaum in Gianellli, "Bill Banning 'Partial Birth' Abortion Goes to Clinton."

172. Gianelli, "Medicine Adds to Debate on Late-Term Abortion," 29. See, for in-

stance, Grimes, "Continuing Need for Late Abortions"; Warren M. Hern, Statement before the Judiciary Committee of the United States Senate Concerning S. 939, Nov. 17, 1995 (in author's possession); Kolata, "Late Abortions."

173. Manuel Porto, "A Call for an Evidence-Based Evaluation of Late Midtrimester Abortion," *American Journal of Obstetrics and Gynecology* 190 (2004): 1175–76.

174. *Carhart*, 127 S. Ct. at 1634.

175. Norma McCorvey wrote two autobiographies, one while working at an abortion clinic in Dallas, Texas, in which she expressed her support for *Roe v. Wade* and legal abortion. In 1995, Flip Benham of Operation Rescue opened an office next to the Dallas abortion clinic and befriended McCorvey. As a result, McCorvey eventually switched to an antiabortion position, articulating her new stance. See Norma McCorvey and Andy Meisler, *I Am Roe: My Life, Roe v. Wade, and Freedom of Choice* (New York: HarperCollins, 1994), and Norma McCorvey and Gary Thomas, *Won by Love: Norma McCorvey, Jane Roe of Roe V. Wade, Speaks Out for the Unborn as She Shares Her New Conviction for Life* (Nashville, Tenn.: Thomas Nelson, Inc., 1998). Starting in 2000, Sandra Cano expressed her opposition to abortion in congressional testimony in which she argued that her attorney Margie Hames duped her in serving as a plaintiff for the *Doe v. Bolton* case. See http://www.endroe.org/media/3719/3canoaffidavit15.00.pdf and http://www.endroe.org/sandracanotestimony.aspx (accessed Aug. 13, 2014).

176. Reva Siegel, "The Right's Reasons: Constitutional Conflict and the Spread of Woman-Protective Antiabortion Argument," *Duke Law Journal* 57 (2008): 1643.

177. See, for instance, Dr. Vincent Rue, Ph.D., of the Institute of Pregnancy Loss in Jacksonville, Florida; Dr. Theresa Karminski Burke, Ph.D., who founded Rachel's Vineyard, the largest postabortion ministry in the world; and Professor Priscilla Coleman, who teaches in the College of Education and Human Development at Bowling Green State University. See also Siegel, "The Right's Reasons," 1657–64. There is a substantial body of scholarship that repudiates claims of postabortion syndrome. See, for instance, David A. Grimes and Mitchell D. Creinin, "Induced Abortion: An Overview for Internists," *Annals of Internal Medicine* 140 (2004): 620, 624, who concluded based on a review of the literature that induced abortion does not harm women's emotional health. On the contrary, the most common reaction to abortion is a profound sense of relief. See also Brenda Major, "Psychological Implications of Abortion—Highly Charged and Rife with Misleading Research," *Journal of the Canadian Medical Association* 168 (2003): 1257–58, and Siegel, "The Right's Reasons," 1653–54 n. 44, for additional references and discussion.

178. Report of the APA Task Force on Mental Health and Abortion, Executive Summary (2008), http://www.apa.org/pi/women/programs/abortion/executive-summary .pdf (accessed Nov. 30, 2014). Studies found that among adult women who have an unplanned pregnancy, the relative risk of mental health problems is no greater if they have a single elective first trimester abortion than if they deliver that pregnancy. The evidence regarding the relative mental health risks associated with multiple abortions is more equivocal. Positive associations observed between multiple abortions and poorer mental health, the association suggested, may be linked to co-occurring risks that predispose a woman to both multiple unwanted pregnancies and mental health problems.

179. Pink Notebook, Mountain Country Women's Clinic, SWP.

180. Ibid.

181. Green Notebook, Mountain Country Women's Clinic, SWP.

182. Ibid.

183. Ibid.

184. See, for instance, the website of David Reardon's Elliot Institute, which offers visitors posters and ads that spread the message of coercion and harm and claim that 64 percent of abortions are coerced and 65 percent of women who have had abortions suffer symptoms of posttraumatic stress disorder. See http://www.theunchoice.com /display.htm. Siegel notes that the creation of this line of reasoning was a political response to setbacks of the 1990s, when Clinton's election and public recoil from clinic violence motivated antiabortion activists to look for new approaches. After Clinton's election, Reardon set out to transform post abortion syndrome, a therapeutic discourse, into a political strategy framed around protecting women from abortion. See Siegel, "The Right's Reasons," 1668, 1672.

185. See Siegel, "The Right's Reasons," 1647–49, also 1646–47 n. 20; for the same claim, see also *Report of the South Dakota Task Force to Study Abortion*, submitted to the Governor and Legislature of South Dakota, Dec. 2005, 44.

186. Hearing on H.B. 1215 before the House Committee on State Affairs, 2006 Leg., 81st sess. (SD, Feb. 8, 2006) (testimony of Nicole Osmundsen), as quoted in Siegel, "The Right's Reasons," 1655.

187. See Siegel, "The Right's Reasons," 1655 nn. 47–51.

188. *Report of the South Dakota Task Force*, 55, 56.

189. Ibid., 47.

190. Ibid., 47–48.

191. David C. Reardon, *Making Abortion Rare: A Healing Strategy for a Divided Nation* (Acorn Books, 1996), 96, as quoted in Siegel, "The Right's Reasons," 1675.

192. Siegel, "The Right's Reasons," 1652; *Report of the South Dakota Task Force*.

193. Siegel, "The Right's Reasons," 1686–87.

194. Ibid., 1650.

195. Gonzales v. Carhart, 500 U.S. 124 (2007), Opinion by Justice Kennedy, Apr. 18, 2007, 4–5, 8–9.

Epilogue

1. Karen McVeigh, "'I Can't Think of a Time When It Was Worse': U.S. Abortion Doctors Speak Out," *Guardian*, Nov. 21, 2014. http://www.theguardian.com/world/2014 /nov/21/us-abortion-doctors-speak-40-years (accessed Mar. 31, 2015).

2. David A. Grimes and Linda G. Brandon, *Every Third Woman in America: How Legal Abortion Transformed Our Nation* (Carolina Beach, N.C.: Daymark Publishing, 2014).

3. McVeigh, "'I Can't Think of a Time When It Was Worse.'"

4. See http://www.guttmacher.org/tables/3500603t.html#t3 (accessed Mar. 31, 2015).

5. Lisa H. Harris, "Second Trimester Abortion Provision: Breaking the Silence and Changing the Discourse," *Reproductive Health Matters* 16 (31 Supplement) (2008): 77.

6. Anonymous to Susan Wicklund, Apr. 7, 2000, SWP.

7. McVeigh, "'I Can't Think of a Time When It Was Worse.'"

8. Eyal Press, "A Botched Operation," *New Yorker*, Feb. 3, 2014, http://www.newyorker.com/magazine/2014/02/03/a-botched-operation (accessed Mar. 31, 2015).

9. Carole Joffe, "Learning the Right Lessons from the Philadelphia Abortion Clinic Disaster," *RH Reality Check*, Apr. 16, 2013, http://rhrealitycheck.org/article/2013/04/16/learning-right-lessons-philadelphia-abortion-clinic-disaster/ (accessed Mar. 31, 2015).

Bibliography

Manuscript Collections

Duke University Libraries, Sally Bingham Center for Women's History
    and Culture, Duke University, Durham, North Carolina
    Terry Beresford Papers
    Renee Chelian Papers
    Takey Crist Papers
    Feminist Women's Health Center Records
    Susan Hill Papers
    Merle Hoffman Papers
    Claire Keyes Papers
    Susan Wicklund Papers
University Archives, Wayne State University, Detroit, Michigan
    Detroit Feminist Women's Health Center Collection, Collections of
    Archives of Labor and Urban Affairs
University of Iowa Libraries, Iowa Women's Archive, Iowa City, Iowa
    Emma Goldman Clinic Papers

Interviews

INTERVIEWS BY AUTHOR

Beresford, Terry. Sept. 30, 2012, Alexandria, Va.
Chelian, Renee. Sept. 24, 2010, Westland, Mich.
Chelian, Renee. Nov. 4, 2011, Westland, Mich.
Crist, Takey. May 20, 2001. Jacksonville, N.C.
Crist, Takey. Nov. 20–21, 2002, Jacksonville, N.C.
deProsse, Charles. Oct. 23, 2002, Iowa City, Iowa.
deProsse, Charles. June 3, 2004, Iowa City, Iowa.
deProsse, Charles. Mar. 31, 2011, Iowa City, Iowa.
Fitzsimmons, Ron. Sept. 18, 2010, phone interview.
Fitzsimmons, Ron. Oct. 1, 2010, phone interview.
Hern, Warren. Jan. 4, 2012, Boulder, Colo.
Hill, Susan. Jan. 2004, Raleigh, N.C.
Hill, Susan. May 2004, Raleigh, N.C.
Hill, Susan. Feb. 3, 2008, Raleigh, N.C.
Hill, Susan. Mar. 3, 2008, Raleigh, N.C.

Hill, Susan. June 16, 2008, Raleigh, N.C.
Hill, Susan. June 18, 2008, Raleigh, N.C.
Hill, Susan. Aug. 15, 2008, Raleigh, N.C.
Hulka, Jaroslav. May 22, 2001, Chapel Hill, N.C.
Keyes, Claire. Sept. 15, 2013, Pittsburgh, Pa.
Kissling, Frances. Nov. 21, 2011, phone interview.
Landy, Uta. Nov. 18, 2011, phone interview.
Randall, Lynn. Oct. 22, 2012, phone interview.
Rose, Ann. Nov. 9, 2010, Charlotte, N.C.
Taft, Charlotte. Aug. 10, 2012, phone interview.
Thompson, Robert. Sept. 14, 2013, Pittsburgh, Pa.
Tilley, Rosa. Nov. 1, 2010, Raleigh, N.C.
Turner, Morris. Oct. 6, 2013, Pittsburgh, Pa.
Wicklund, Susan. July 15, 2013, Bozeman, Mont.
Wicklund, Susan. Aug. 3, 2013, Wilsall, Mont.
Yeo, Elinor. Sept. 17, 2010, phone interview.

EMMA GOLDMAN CLINIC ORAL HISTORIES, LEANN ERICKSON PAPERS,
IOWA WOMEN'S ARCHIVE, UNIVERSITY OF IOWA, IOWA CITY, IOWA

Cassilianos, Flora. Interview with LeAnn Erickson, undated [ca. 1993].
Curtin, Barb. Interview with LeAnn Erickson, undated [ca. 1993].
Kaefring, Gina. Interview with LeAnn Erickson, undated [ca. 1993].
Klein, Paula. Interview with LeAnn Erickson, undated [ca. 1993].
Nye, Deb. Interview with LeAnn Erickson, undated [ca. 1993].
Pressley, Pattie. Interview with LeAnn Erickson, undated [ca. 1993].
Sand, Gayle. Interview with LeAnn Erickson, undated [ca. 1993].
Thompson, Francine. Interview with LeAnn Erickson, undated [ca. 1993].
Tullis, Roxie. Interview with LeAnn Erickson, undated [ca. 1993].
Womantree, Michelle. Interview with LeAnn Erickson, undated [ca. 1993].
Yates, Barb. Interview with LeAnn Erickson, undated [ca. 1993].

SOPHIA SMITH COLLECTION, SMITH COLLEGE, NORTHAMPTON, MASS.

Avery, Byllye Y. Interview with Loretta Ross, July 21–22, 2005, Provincetown, Mass.
    Voices of Feminism Oral History Project, 2006.
Kissling, Frances. Interview with Rebecca Sharpless, Sept. 13–14, 2002, Washington,
    D.C.

UNPUBLISHED INTERVIEWS

Chelian, Renee. Interview with Peg Johnston, 2008, New Mexico.
Hanson, Mildred. Interview with Peg Johnston, 2008, New Mexico.
Keyes, Claire. Interview with Peg Johnston, 2008, New Mexico.

Newspapers and Periodicals

American Medical News
Bergen County (N.J.) Record
Boston Globe
Chicago Sun Times
Daily Iowan
Detroit News
Fargo-Morehead (N.D.) Forum
Fort Wayne (Ind.) Journal Gazette
Fort Wayne (Ind.) News Sentinel
Los Angeles Times

Milwaukee Journal
Minneapolis Tribune
New York Times
Patterson (N.J.) Evening News
Patterson (N.J.) Herald News
Patterson (N.J.) News
Raleigh News and Observer
Science
Washington Post

Books, Articles, Dissertations, and Reports

Alpern, David M. "Abortion and the Law." *Newsweek*, Mar. 3, 1975, 18–30.

American University Hotline. *Sex Facts for the AU Student*. Washington, D.C.: American University, 1973.

Austin, Jacqueline. "I Went (Undercover) to an Anti-Abortion Clinic." *Cosmopolitan*, Mar. 1987, 200–203.

Baird-Windle, Patricia, and Eleanor J. Bader. *Targets of Hatred: Anti-Abortion Terrorism*. New York: Palgrave, 2001.

Barber, Bernard, John J. Lally, Julia Loughlin Makaraushka, and Daniel Sullivan. *Research on Human Subjects: Problems of Social Control in Medical Experimentation*. New York: Russell Sage Foundation, 1973.

Bates, Jerome E., and Edward S. Zawadzki. *Criminal Abortion: A Study in Medical Sociology*. Springfield, Ill.: Charles C. Thomas, 1964.

Beecher, Henry K. "Ethics and Clinical Research." *New England Journal of Medicine* 24, no. 274 (June 16, 1966).

Berger, Gary S., Christopher Tietze, Jean Pakter, and Selig H. Katz. "Maternal Mortality Associated with Legal Abortion in New York State; July 1, 1970, to June 30, 1972." *Obstetrics and Gynecology* 43, no. 3 (1974): 315–26.

Blanchard, Dallas A. *From Polite to Fiery Protest: The Anti-Abortion Movement and the Rise of the Religious Right*. New York: Twayne Publishers, 1994.

Blanchard, Dallas A., and Terry J. Prewitt. *Religious Violence and Abortion: The Gideon Project*. Gainesville: University Press of Florida, 1993.

Bok, Sissela, Bernard N. Nathanson, David C. Nathan, and Leroy Walters. "The Unwanted Child: Caring for the Fetus Born after an Abortion." *Hastings Center Report*, Oct. 10–15, 1976, 10–15.

Bolotin, Susan. "Selling Chastity: The Sly New Attack on Your Sexual Freedom." *Vogue*, Mar. 1986.

Boyd, P. A., F. Tondi, N. R. Hicks, and P. F. Chamberlain. "Autopsy after Termination of Pregnancy for Fetal Anomaly: Retrospective Cohort Study." *BMJ* 328 (7432) (Jan. 17, 2004): 137.

Brodie, Janet Farrell. *Contraception and Abortion in Nineteenth-Century America.* Ithaca, N.Y.: Cornell University Press, 1994.

Brownmiller, Susan. *In Our Time: Memoir of a Revolution.* New York: Dell, 1999.

Burtchaell, James Tunstead. *Rachel Weeping: The Case against Abortion.* San Francisco: Harper and Row, 1982.

Calderone, Mary Streichen, ed. *Abortion in the United States: A Conference Sponsored by the Planned Parenthood Federation of America, Inc. at Arden House and the New York Academy of Medicine.* New York: Harper and Brothers, 1958.

Crampton, Nancy. *Between Your Navel and Your Knees.* Houston: University of Houston Student Association, 1972.

Carroll, Peter N. *It Seemed Like Nothing Happened: America in the 1970s.* New Brunswick, N.J.: Rutgers University Press, 1982.

Casper, Monica J. *The Making of the Unborn Patient: A Social Anatomy of Fetal Surgery.* New Brunswick, N.J.: Rutgers University Press, 1998.

Cline, David P. *Creating Choice: A Community Responds to the Need for Abortion and Birth Control, 1961–1973.* New York: Palgrave Macmillan, 2006.

Colson, Charles, and Ellen Vaughn. *Gideon's Torch.* Dallas: Word Publishing, 1995.

Cozzarelli, Catherine, and Brenda Major. "The Effects of Anti-Abortion Demonstrators and Pro-Choice Escorts on Women's Psychological Responses to Abortion." *Journal of Social and Clinical Psychology* 13, no. 4 (1994): 404–27.

Critchlow, Donald. *Intended Consequences: Birth Control, Abortion, and the Federal Government in Modern America.* New York: Oxford University Press, 1999.

Csapo, Arpad I. "Termination of Pregnancy by the Intra-amniotic Injection of Hypertonic Saline." In *Yearbook of Obstetrics and Gynecology*, 1966–67, edited by J. P. Greenhill, 126–63. Chicago: Year Book Medical Publisher, 1966.

Davis, Kathy. *The Making of "Our Bodies, Ourselves": How Feminism Travels across Borders.* Durham, N.C.: Duke University Press, 2007.

Denes, Magda. *In Necessity and Sorrow: Life and Death in an Abortion Hospital.* New York: Basic Books, 1976.

DiIorio, Judith A., and Michael R. Nusbaumer. "Securing Our Sanity: Anger Management among Abortion Escorts." *Journal of Contemporary Ethnography* 21 (1992–93): 411–38.

diMauro, Diane, and Carole Joffe. "The Religious Right and the Reshaping of Sexual Policy: An Examination of Reproductive Rights and Sexuality Education." *Sexuality Research and Social Policy* 4, no. 1 (Mar. 2007): 67–92.

Dittmer, John. *The Good Doctors: The Medical Committee for Human Rights and the Struggle for Social Justice in Health Care.* New York: Bloomsbury Press, 2009.

Doan, Alesha. *Opposition and Intimidation: The Abortion Wars and Strategies of Political Harassment.* Ann Arbor: University of Michigan Press, 2007.

Donnally, Jennifer. "The Politics of Abortion and the Rise of the New Right." Ph.D. diss., University of North Carolina, 2013.

Dubow, Sarah. *Ourselves Unborn: A History of the Fetus in Modern America.* New York: Oxford University Press, 2011.

Duke Committee on Contraception and Abortion. *A Guide to Contraception and Abortion.* Durham, N.C.: Duke University, 1971.

Dykes, M. H., and E. E. Czapek. "Legislation and Regulation concerning Abortus Research." *JAMA* 229, no. 10 (Sept. 2, 1974): 1303–4.

Eastland, Terry. "Partial Birth Abortions." *Media Matters*, PBS (Jan. 1997).

Edelin, Kenneth C. *Broken Justice: A Story of Race, Sex, and Revenge in a Boston Courtroom*. Pond View Press, 2008.

Eisenberg, Howard. "The Mad Scramble for Abortion Money." *Medical Economics*, Jan. 4, 1971, 991–97.

Enke, Anne. *Finding the Movement: Sexuality, Contested Space, and Feminist Activism*. Durham, N.C.: Duke University Press, 2007.

Fishel, Elizabeth. "The Women's Self-Help Movement, or Is Happiness Knowing Your Own Cervix?" *Ramparts*, Nov. 1973, 29–31, 56–59.

Forrest, Jacqueline Darroch, and Stanley K. Henshaw. "The Harassment of U.S. Abortion Providers." *Family Planning Perspectives* 19, no. 1 (Jan./Feb. 1987): 9–13.

Francke, Linda Bird. *The Ambivalence of Abortion*. New York: Random House, 1978.

Frank, Gillian. "The Colour of the Unborn: Anti-Abortion and Anti-Bussing in Michigan, United States, 1967–1973." *Gender and History* 26, no. 2 (Aug. 2014): 351–78.

Frankfort, Ellen, with Frances Kissling. *Rosie: The Investigation of a Wrongful Death*. New York: Dial Press, 1979.

Freedman, Lori. *Willing and Unable: Doctors' Constraints in Abortion Care*. Nashville, Tenn.: Vanderbilt University Press, 2010.

Freedman, Lori R., and Debra B. Stulberg. "Conflicts in Care for Obstetric Complications in Catholic Hospitals." *AJOB Primary Research* 4, no. 4 (2013): 1–10.

Freedman, Lori R., Uta Landy, and J. Steinauer. "When There Is a Heartbeat: Miscarriage Management in Catholic-Owned Hospitals." *American Journal of Public Health* 98, no. 10 (Oct. 2008): 1774–78.

Garrow, David J. *Liberty and Sexuality: The Right to Privacy and the Making of Roe v. Wade*. New York: Macmillan, 1994.

Gebhard, Paul H. *Pregnancy, Birth, and Abortion*. New York: Harper and Brothers, 1958.

Ginsburg, Faye D. *Contested Lives: The Abortion Debate in an American Community*. Berkeley: University of California Press, 1989.

Golden, Janet. *Message in a Bottle: The Making of Fetal Alcohol Syndrome*. Cambridge, Mass.: Harvard University Press, 2005.

Goldstein, Michael S. "Abortion as a Medical Career Choice: Entrepreneurs, Community Physicians, and Others." *Journal of Health and Social Behavior* 25, no. 2 (June 1984): 211–29.

Gorney, Cynthia. *Articles of Faith: A Frontline History of the Abortion Wars*. New York: Simon and Schuster, 1998.

———. "Gambling with Abortion: Why Both Sides Think They Have Everything to Lose." *Harper's Magazine*, Nov. 2004, 33–46.

Gray, Marian Johnson, and Roger W. Gray. *How to Take the Worry out of Being Close: An Egg and Sperm Handbook*. Oakland, Calif.: Son, 1971.

Grimes, David A. "The Continuing Need for Late Abortions." *JAMA* 280, no. 8 (Aug. 26, 1998): 747–50.

———. "Second Trimester Abortions in the United States." *Family Planning Perspectives* 16, no. 6 (Nov./Dec. 1984): 260–66.

———. "6 Things to Understand When Talking about Abortion." *Huffington Post*, Dec. 10, 2014. http://www.huffingtonpost.com/david-a-grimes/abortion -terminology-things-to-understand_b_6175430.html. Accessed Jan. 7, 2015.

Grimes, David A., and Linda G. Brandon. *Every Third Woman in America: How Legal Abortion Transformed Our Nation.* Carolina Beach, N.C.: Daymark Publishing, 2014.

Grimes, David A., and Mitchell D. Creinin. "Induced Abortion: An Overview for Internists." *Annals of Internal Medicine* 140 (2004): 620, 624.

Grimes, David A., and Willard Cates. "Complications from Legally Induced Abortion: A Review." *Obstetrical and Gynecological Survey* 34, no. 3 (1979).

Grimes, David A., et al. "Mid-Trimester Abortion by Dilation and Evacuation: A Safe and Practical Alternative." *New England Journal of Medicine* 296, no. 20 (May 19, 1977).

Hansen, Lynn K., Barbara Reskin, and Diana Gray. *How to Have Intercourse . . . without Getting Screwed: A Guide to Birth Control, Abortion, and Venereal Disease.* Seattle: ASUW Women's Commission, University of Washington, 1972.

Harris, Lisa H. "Second Trimester Abortion Provision: Breaking the Silence and Changing the Discourse." *Reproductive Health Matters* 16 (31 Supplement) (2008): 74–81.

Harrison, William F. "Why I Provide Abortions." *Daily Kos*, May 31, 2007.

Haskell, W. Martin, Thomas R. Easterling, and E. Steven Lichtenberg. "Surgical Abortion after the First Trimester." In *A Clinician's Guide to Medical and Surgical Abortion*, edited by Maureen Paul, E. Steven Lichtenberg, Lynn Borgatta, David A. Grimes, and Phillip G. Stubblefield, 123–38. Philadelphia: Churchill Livingstone, 1999.

Healey, Dan. *Homosexual Desire in Revolutionary Russia: The Regulation of Sexual and Gender Dissent.* Chicago: University of Chicago Press, 2001.

Henshaw, Stanley K. "Abortion Incidence and Services in the United States, 1995– 1996." *Family Planning Perspectives* 6 (Nov. 1998): 263–70, 287.

———. "The Accessibility of Abortion Services in the United States." *Family Planning Perspectives* 23, no. 6 (Nov./Dec. 1991): 246–53.

———. "Factors Hindering Access to Abortion Services." *Family Planning Perspectives* 2 (Mar./Apr. 1995): 54–59, 87.

———, ed. "Abortion Services in the United States, 1979 and 1980." *Family Planning Perspectives* 14, no. 1 (Jan./Feb. 1982): 5–15.

Henshaw, Stanley K., and Kevin O'Reilly. "Characteristics of Abortion Patients in the United States, 1979 and 1980." *Family Planning Perspectives* 50, no. 1 (Jan./Feb. 1983): 5–16.

Henshaw, Stanley K., Jacqueline Darroch Forrest, Ellen Sullivan, and Christopher Tietze. "Abortion, 1977–1979: Need and Services in the United States, Each State and Metropolitan Area." Report of the Alan Guttmacher Institute, New York, 1981.

———. "Abortion Services in the United States, 1979 and 1980." *Family Planning Perspectives* 14, no. 1 (Jan./Feb. 1982): 5–15.

Hern, Warren M. *Abortion Practice*. Philadelphia: J. B. Lippincott, 1984.

———. "Laminaria in Abortion: Use in 1,368 Patients in First Trimester." *Rocky Mountain Medical Journal* 72 (Sept. 1975).

———. "Life on the Front Lines." *Women's Health Issues* 4 (Jan./Feb. 1994): 48–54.

Hern, Warren M., and Anna Gail Oakes. "Multiple Laminaria Treatment in Early Midtrimester Outpatient Suction Abortion: A Preliminary Report." *Advances in Planned Parenthood* 22 (1977).

Hern, Warren M., and B. Corrigan. "What about Us? Staff Reactions to D&E." *Advances in Planned Parenthood* 15, no. 1 (1980): 3–8.

Hern, Warren M., and Bonnie Andrikopoulos, eds. *Abortion in the Seventies: Proceedings of the Western Regional Conference on Abortion, Denver, Colorado, 27–29 February 1976*. New York: National Abortion Federation, 1977.

Hodgson, Jane E., ed. *Abortion and Sterilization: Medical and Social Aspects*. New York: Grune and Stratton, 1981.

Hoffman, Merle. *Intimate Wars: The Life and Times of the Woman Who Brought Abortion from the Back Alley to the Board Room*. New York: Feminist Press, 2012.

"An Interview with W. Martin Haskell, MD." *Cincinnati Medicine*, Fall 1993, 18–19.

Jacot, Francis R. M., Claudi Poulin, Alain P. Bilodeau, Martine Morin, Suzie Moreau, Francoise Gendron, and Dominique Mercier. "A Five-Year Experience with Second Trimester Induced Abortions." *American Journal of Obstetrics and Gynecology* 168 (Feb. 1993): 633–37.

Jefferis, Jennifer. *Armed for Life: The Army of God and Anti-Abortion Terror in the United States*. Santa Barbara, Calif.: Praeger, 2011.

Jeffries, Liz. "The Waddill Case: Abortionist Strangles Baby." *Conservative Digest*, June 1978, 16–17.

Joffe, Carole E. "Abortion in Historical Perspective." In *A Clinician's Guide to Medical and Surgical Abortion*, edited by Maureen Paul, E. Steven Lichtenberg, Lynn Borgatta, David A. Grimes, and Phillip G. Stubblefield, 3–10. New York: Churchill Livingstone, 1999.

———. *Dispatches from the Abortion Wars: The Costs of Fanaticism to Doctors, Patients, and the Rest of Us*. Boston: Beacon Press, 2009.

———. *Doctors of Conscience: The Struggle to Provide Abortion before and after Roe v. Wade*. Boston: Beacon Press, 1995.

———. "The Politicization of Abortion and the Evolution of Abortion Counseling." *American Journal of Public Health* 103, no. 1 (Jan. 2013): 57–65.

Joffe, Carole E., Tracy A. Weitz, and C. L. Staecy. "Uneasy Allies: Pro-Choice Physicians, Women's Health Activists, and the Struggle for Abortion Rights." *Sociology of Health and Illness* 26, no. 6 (2004): 775–96.

Johnson, Victoria. "The Strategic Determinants of a Countermovement: The Emergence and Impact of Operation Rescue Blockades." In *Waves of Protest: Social Movements since the Sixties*, edited by Jo Freeman and Victoria Johnson, 241–66. Lanham, Md.: Rowman and Littlefield, 1999.

Johnston, Margaret R. "Opting out of the Abortion War: Thoughts on the Aftermath of Birmingham," In Our Choices, Our Lives: Unapologetic Writings on Abortion, edited by Krista Jacob, 153–69. Lincoln, Neb.: iUniverse, 2002.

Jones, James H. Bad Blood: The Tuskegee Syphilis Experiment. New York: Free Press, 1981.

Jonsen, Albert R. The Birth of Bioethics. New York: Oxford University Press, 1998.

Kagan, Julia. "The New Doubts about Abortion." McCall's, June 1975, 121–23.

Kaltreider, Nancy B., Sadja Goldsmith, and Alan J. Margolis. "The Impact of Midtrimester Abortion Techniques on Patients and Staff." American Journal of Obstetrics and Gynecology 135, no. 2 (Sept. 15, 1979).

Kaplan, Jeffrey. "Absolute Rescue: Absolutism, Defensive Action and the Resort to Force." In Millennialism and Violence, edited by Michael Barkun, 128–63. New York: Routledge, 1996.

———. "America's Last Prophetic Witness: The Literature of the Rescue Movement." Terrorism and Political Violence 5, no. 3 (Autumn 1993): 58–77.

Kaplan, Laura. The Story of Jane: The Legendary Underground Feminist Abortion Service. New York: Pantheon Books, 1995.

Kapsalis, Terri. Public Privates: Performing Gynecology from Both Ends of the Speculum. Durham, N.C.: Duke University Press, 1997.

Katz, Jay. "The Consent Principle of the Nuremberg Code." In The Nazi Doctors and the Nuremberg Code: Human Rights in Human Experimentation, edited by George J. Annas and Michael A. Grodin, 227–39. New York: Oxford University Press, 1992.

Kerslake, Dorothea, and Donn Casey. "Abortion Induced by Means of the Uterine Aspirator." Obstetrics and Gynecology 30, no. 1 (July 1967): 35–45.

King, Charles R. "Calling Jane: The Life and Death of a Women's Illegal Abortion Service." Women and Health 20, no. 3 (1993): 75–93.

Kline, Wendy. Bodies of Knowledge: Sexuality, Reproduction, and Women's Health in the Second Wave. Chicago: University of Chicago Press, 2010.

Koop, C. Everett, and Francis A. Schaeffer. Whatever Happened to the Human Race? Exposing Our Rapid yet Subtle Loss of Human Rights. Old Tappan, N.J.: Fleming H. Revell, 1979.

Lader, Lawrence. Abortion. Boston: Beacon Press, 1966.

———. Abortion II: Making the Revolution. Boston: Beacon Press, 1973.

Leavitt, Judith Walzer. "The Growth of Medical Authority: Technology and Morals in Turn-of-the-Century Obstetrics." Medical Anthropology Quarterly 1, no. 3 (Sept. 1987): 230–55.

Leavitt, Sarah A. "'A Private Little Revolution': The Home Pregnancy Test in American Culture." Bulletin of the History of Medicine 80, no. 2 (Summer 2006): 317–45.

Lederer, Susan E. Frankenstein: Penetrating the Secrets of Nature. New Brunswick, N.J.: Rutgers University Press, 2002.

———. Subjected to Science: Human Experimentation in America before the Second World War. Baltimore: Johns Hopkins University Press, 1995.

Lerner, Barron H. The Breast Cancer Wars: Fear, Hope, and the Pursuit of a Cure in Twentieth-Century America. New York: Oxford University Press, 2001.

Luker, Kristin. *Abortion and the Politics of Motherhood*. Berkeley: University of California Press, 1984.

Luy, Mary Lynn M. "Fear and Loathing in the Stirrups: What's Behind Women's Wrath toward Gynecologists?" *Modern Medicine*, Oct. 14, 1974, 17–21.

Major, Brenda. "Psychological Implications of Abortion—Highly Charged and Rife with Misleading Research." *Journal of the Canadian Medical Association* 168 (2003): 1257–58.

Mason, Carol. *Killing for Life: The Apocalyptic Narrative of Pro-Life Politics*. Ithaca, N.Y.: Cornell University Press, 2002.

———. "Minority Unborn." In *Fetal Subjects, Feminist Positions*, edited by Lynn M. Morgan and Meredith W. Michaels, 159–74. Philadelphia: University of Pennsylvania Press, 1999.

Maxwell, Carol J. C. *Pro-Life Activists in America: Meaning, Motivation, and Direct Action*. Cambridge: Cambridge University Press, 2002.

May, Elaine Tyler. *America and the Pill: A History of Promise, Peril, and Liberation*. New York: Basic Books, 2010.

Maynard-Moody, Steven. *The Dilemma of the Fetus: Fetal Research, Medical Progress, and Moral Politics*. New York: St. Martin's Press, 1995.

McCorvey, Norma, and Andy Meisler. *I Am Roe: My Life, Roe v. Wade, and Freedom of Choice*. New York: HarperCollins, 1994.

McCorvey, Norma, and Gary L. Thomas. *Won by Love: Norma McCorvey, Jane Roe of Roe V. Wade, Speaks Out for the Unborn as She Shares Her New Conviction for Life*. Nashville, Tenn.: Thomas Nelson, 1998.

Meehan, Mary. "Ex-Abortion Workers: Why They Quit." *Human Life Review*, Spring/Summer 2000.

Mier, Richard, Donald Rollins, and Thomas Blush. *Elephants and Butterflies*. Chapel Hill: University of North Carolina, EOS, 1970.

Miller, Monica Migliorino. *Abandoned: The Untold Story of the Abortion Wars*. Charlotte, N.C.: St. Benedict Press, 2012.

Miller, Patricia G. *The Worst of Times: Illegal Abortion—Survivors, Practitioners, Coroners, Cops, and Children of Women Who Died Talk about Its Horrors*. New York: Harper Collins, 1993.

Mitchell, Lisa M. *Baby's First Picture: Ultrasound and the Politics of Fetal Subjects*. Toronto: University of Toronto Press, 2001.

Mohr, James. *Abortion in America: The Origins and Evolution of National Policy*. New York: Oxford University Press, 1978.

Morgan, Lynn M. *Icons of Life: A Cultural History of Human Embryos*. Berkeley: University of California Press, 2009.

Morgan, Lynn M., and Meredith W. Michaels, eds. *Fetal Subjects, Feminist Positions*. Philadelphia: University of Pennsylvania Press, 1999.

Morgen, Sandra. *Into Our Own Hands: The Women's Health Movement in the United States, 1969–1990*. New Brunswick, N.J.: Rutgers University Press, 2002.

Munsick, Robert A. "Air Embolism and Maternal Death from Therapeutic Abortion." *Obstetrics and Gynecology* 39, no. 5 (May 1972): 688–90.

Munson, Ziad W. *The Making of Pro-Life Activists: How Social Movement Mobilization Works*. Chicago: University of Chicago Press, 2008.

Murphy, Michelle. "Immodest Witnessing: The Epistemology of Vaginal Self-Examination in the U.S. Feminist Self-Help Movement." *Feminist Studies* 30, no. 1 (Spring 2004): 115–47.

Nathanson, Bernard N. *Aborting America*. Garden City, N.Y.: Doubleday, 1979.

———. "Ambulatory Abortion: Experience with 26,000 Cases (July 1, 1970, to August 1, 1971)." *New England Journal of Medicine* 286 (Feb. 24, 1972): 403–7.

———. "Deeper into Abortion." *New England Journal of Medicine* 291, no. 22 (Nov. 28, 1974): 1189–90.

National Commission for the Protection of Human Subjects of Biomedical and Behavioral Research. *Appendix: Research on the Fetus*. Bethesda, Md.: U.S. Department of Health, Education, and Welfare, Publication No. (OS) 76-128.

———. *Report and Recommendations: Research on the Fetus*. Bethesda, Md.: U.S. Department of Health, Education, and Welfare, Publication No. (OS) 76-127, 1975.

Nelson, Alondra. *Body and Soul: The Black Panther Party and the Fight against Medical Discrimination*. Minneapolis: University of Minnesota Press, 2011.

Nelson, Jennifer. *More Than Medicine: A History of the Feminist Women's Health Movement*. New York: New York University Press, 2015.

———. *Women of Color and the Reproductive Rights Movement*. New York: New York University Press, 2003.

Neubardt, Selig. *Techniques of Abortion*. New York: Little, Brown, 1972.

Nolen, William A. *The Baby in the Bottle: An Investigative Review of the Edelin Case and Its Larger Meaning for the Controversy over Abortion Reform*. New York: Conrad, McCann and Geoghegan, 1978.

Novak, Franc. "Experience with Suction Curettage." In *Abortion in a Changing World*, vol. 1, edited by Robert E. Hall, 74–84. New York: Columbia University Press, 1970.

Paige, Carole. *The Right to Lifers: Who They Are, How They Operate, Where They Get Their Money*. New York: Summit Books, 1983.

Pakter, Jean, David Harris, and Frieda Nelson. "Surveillance of Abortion Program in New York City." *Bulletin of the New York Academy of Medicine* 47, no. 8 (Aug. 1971): 853–74.

Paul, Maureen, E. Steven Lichtenberg, Lynn Borgatta, David A. Grimes, and Phillip G. Stubblefield, eds. *A Clinician's Guide to Medical and Surgical Abortion*. Philadelphia: Churchill Livingstone, 1999.

Pernick, Martin S. "Brain Death in a Cultural Context: The Reconstruction of Death, 1967–1981." In *The Definition of Death: Contemporary Controversies*, edited by Stuart J. Younger, Robert M. Arnold, and Renie Schapiro, 3–33. Baltimore: Johns Hopkins University Press, 1999.

Petchesky, Rosalind P. *Abortion and Woman's Choice: The State, Sexuality, and Reproductive Freedom*. Boston: Northeastern University Press, 1984.

———. "Foetal Images: The Power of Visual Culture in the Politics of Reproduction." In *Reproductive Technologies: Gender, Motherhood, and Medicine*, edited by Michelle Stanworth, 57–80. Minneapolis: University of Minnesota Press, 1987.

Philipson, Agneta, L. D. Sabath, and David Charles. "Transplacental Passage of Erythromycin and Clindamycin." *New England Journal of Medicine* 288, no. 23 (June 7, 1973): 1219–21.

Pollitt, Katha. *Pro: Reclaiming Abortion Rights*. New York: Picador, 2014.

Poppema, Suzanne T. *Why I Am an Abortion Doctor*. Amherst, N.Y.: Prometheus Books, 1996.

Porto, Manuel. "A Call for an Evidence-Based Evaluation of Late Midtrimester Abortion." *American Journal of Obstetrics and Gynecology* 190 (2004): 1175–76.

Prescott, Heather Munro. *A Doctor of Their Own: The History of Adolescent Medicine*. Cambridge, Mass.: Harvard University Press, 1998.

———. *Student Bodies: The Influence of Student Health Services in American Society and Medicine*. Ann Arbor: University of Michigan Press, 2007.

Press, Eyal. *Absolute Convictions: My Father, a City, and the Conflict That Divided America*. New York: Henry Holt, 2006.

"Pro-Life 'Abortion Clinics.'" *Harper's Magazine*, Dec. 1985, 24–25.

Ramsey, Paul. *The Ethics of Fetal Research*. New Haven, Conn.: Yale University Press, 1975.

Rapp, Rayna. *Testing Women, Testing the Fetus: The Social Impact of Amniocentesis in America*. New York: Routledge, 2000.

Reagan, Leslie J. "Crossing the Border for Abortions: California Activists, Mexican Clinics, and the Creation of a Feminist Health Agency in the 1960s." *Feminist Studies* 26, no. 2 (Summer 2000): 323–48.

———. *Dangerous Pregnancies: Mothers, Disabilities, and Abortion in Modern America*. Berkeley: University of California Press, 2010.

———. *When Abortion Was a Crime: Women, Medicine, and Law in the United States, 1867–1973*. Berkeley: University of California Press, 1997.

Reardon, David C. *Aborted Women: Silent No More*. Westchester, Ill.: Crossway Books, 1987.

———. *Making Abortion Rare: A Healing Strategy for a Divided Nation*. Acorn Books, 1996.

Report of the South Dakota Task Force to Study Abortion, submitted to the Governor and Legislature of South Dakota, Dec. 2005. http://www.lc.org/attachments/SD _abortion_rpt.pdf. Accessed Mar. 31, 2015.

Reverby, Susan M., ed. *Tuskegee's Truths: Rethinking the Tuskegee Syphilis Study*. Chapel Hill: University of North Carolina Press, 2000.

Rini, Suzanne M. *Beyond Abortion: A Chronicle of Fetal Experimentation*. Rockford Ill.: Tan Books and Publishers, 1988.

Risen, James, and Judy L. Thomas. *Wrath of Angels: The American Abortion War*. New York: Basic Books, 1998.

Roberts, Dorothy. *Killing the Black Body: Race, Reproduction, and the Meaning of Liberty*. New York: Random House, 1997.

Rooks, Judith Bourne, and Willard Cates. "Emotional Impact of D&E vs. Instillation." *Family Planning Perspective* 9, no. 6 (Nov./Dec. 1977): 276–77.

Rose, Melody. *Safe, Legal, and Unavailable? Abortion Politics in the United States*. Washington, D.C.: CQPress, 2007.

Rosen, Harold, ed. *Therapeutic Abortion: Medical, Psychiatric, Legal, Anthropological, and Religious Considerations in the Prevention of Conception and the Interruption of Pregnancy*. New York: Julian Press, 1954.

Rosen, Ruth. *The World Split Open: How the Modern Women's Movement Changed America*. New York: Penguin Books, 2000.

Rothman, David J. "Human Experimentation and the Origins of Bioethics in the United States." In *Social Science Perspectives on the Medical Ethics*, edited by George Weisz, 185–200. Dordrecht, Netherlands: Kluwer Academic, 1990.

Rothman, David J., and Sheila M. Rothman. *The Willowbrook Wars*. New York: Harper and Row, 1984.

Saletan, William. *Bearing Right: How Conservatives Won the Abortion War*. Berkeley: University of California Press, 2003.

Sarkos, Chrysso Barbara. "The Fetal Tissue Transplant Debate in the United States: Where Is King Solomon When You Need Him." *Journal of Law and Politics* 7, no. 1 (Winter 1991): 379–416.

Schaeffer, Frank. *Crazy for God: How I Grew Up as One of the Elect, Helped Found the Religious Right, and Lived to Take All (or Almost All) of It Back*. Cambridge, Mass.: Da Capo Press, 2008.

Scheidler, Joseph M. *Closed: 99 Ways to Stop Abortion*. Rockford, Ill.: Tan Books and Publishers, 1985; rev. ed., 1993.

Schoen, Johanna. *Choice and Coercion: Birth Control, Sterilization, and Abortion in Public Health and Welfare*. Chapel Hill: University of North Carolina Press, 2005.

Scholberg, Andrew. "The Ex-Abortionists Meet." *Life & Family News*, Dec. 1987, 3–4.

Schulder, Diane, and Florynce Kennedy. *Abortion Rap*. New York: McGraw-Hill, 1971.

Scully, Diana, and Pauline Bart. "A Funny Thing Happened on the Way to the Orifice: Women in Gynecology Textbooks." *American Journal of Sociology* 78, no. 4 (Jan. 1973): 1045–50.

Seaman, Barbara. *The Doctors' Case against the Pill*. Alameda, Calif.: Hunter House, 1969.

Sex Information. Raleigh: Division of Student Affairs, North Carolina State University, 1969.

Sharpe, Rochelle. "Trials Make Winners out of Those Arrested." *Abortion: The New Militancy*. Gannett News Service Special Report, Dec. 1985.

Shen-Schwartz, Susan, Carol Neish, and Lyndon M. Hill. "Antenatal Ultrasound for Fetal Anomalies: Importance of Perinatal Autopsy." *Fetal and Pediatric Pathology* 9, no. 1 (1989): 1–9.

Siegel, Reva B. "The New Politics of Abortion: An Equality Analysis of Woman-Protective Abortion Restrictions." *University of Illinois Law Review* 2007, no. 3 (2007): 991–1054.

———. "The Right's Reasons: Constitutional Conflict and the Spread of Woman-Protective Antiabortion Argument." *Duke Law Journal* 57 (2008): 1641–92.

Siegel, Reva B., and Sarah Blustain. "Mommy Dearest?" *American Prospect*, Oct. 2006, 22–26.

Simonds, Wendy. *Abortion at Work: Ideology and Practice in a Feminist Clinic.* New Brunswick, N.J.: Rutgers University Press, 1996.

———. "At an Impasse: Inside an Abortion Clinic." *Current Research on Occupations and Professions* 6 (1991): 99–115.

Singular, Stephen. *The Wichita Divide: The Murder of Dr. George Tiller and the Battle over Abortion.* New York: St. Martin's Press, 2011.

Smith-Rosenberg, Carroll. *Disorderly Conduct: Visions of Gender in Victorian America.* New York: Oxford University Press, 1986.

Snowbeck, Christopher. "Obituary: Robert Garland Kisner/Doctor Who Promoted Family Planning." *Pittsburgh Post Gazette,* Apr. 1, 2004.

Solinger, Rickie. *The Abortionist: A Woman against the Law.* New York: Free Press, 1994.

———. "The First Welfare Case: Money, Sex, Marriage and White Supremacy in Selma, 1966, a Reproductive Justice Analysis." *Journal of Women's History* 22, no. 3 (2010): 13–38.

———, ed. *Abortion Wars: A Half Century of Struggle, 1950–2000.* Berkeley: University of California Press, 1998.

Sorenson, Sarah. "They Killed the Doctor Who Saved Me." *Glamour,* May 1994, 266.

Steinberg, Julia R., Beth Jordan, and Elisa S. Wells. "Science Prevails: Abortion and Mental Health." *Contraception* 79 (2009): 81–83.

Stroh, George, and Alan R. Hinman. "Reported Live Births following Induced Abortion: Two and One-Half Years' Experience in Upstate New York." *American Journal of Obstetrics and Gynecology* 126, no. 1 (Sept. 1, 1976): 83–90.

Student Committee on Human Sexuality. *Sex and the Yale Student.* New Haven, Conn.: Yale University, 1970.

Stuhlberg, Debra B., Yael Hoffman, Irma Hasham Dahlquist, and Lori R. Freedman. "Tubal Ligation in Catholic Hospitals: A Qualitative Study of Ob-Gyns' Experiences." *Contraception* 90 (2014): 422–28.

Swartz, Mimi. "Family Secret." *New Yorker,* Nov. 17, 1997, 90–107.

Taussig, Frederick J. *Abortion, Spontaneous and Induced: Medical and Social Aspects.* St. Louis: C. V. Mosbach, 1936.

Taylor, Janelle S. "Image of Contradiction: Obstetrical Ultrasound in American Culture." In *Reproducing Reproduction: Kinship, Power, and Technological Innovation,* edited by Sarah Franklin and Helena Ragone, 15–45. Philadelphia: University of Pennsylvania Press, 1998.

Tietze, Christopher, and Sarah Lewit. "Joint Program for the Study of Abortion (JPSA): Early Medical Complications of Legal Abortion." *Studies in Family Planning* 3, no. 6 (June 1972): 97–123.

Tietze, Christopher F., S. Jaffe, E. Weinstock, and J. G. Dryfoos. *Provisional Estimates of Abortion Need and Services in the Year following the 1973 Supreme Court Decisions.* New York: Alan Guttmacher Institute, 1975.

Tone, Andrea. *Devices and Desires: A History of Contraceptives in America.* New York: Hill and Wang, 2001.

Torres, Aida, and Jacqueline Darroch Forrest. "Why Do Women Have Abortions?" *Feminist Planning Perspectives* 20, no. 4 (July/Aug. 1988): 169–76.

Venereal Disease, Abortion, Birth Control: A Guide for the Tri-Cities Area.
Schenectady, N.Y.: Union College Student Senate and Planned Parenthood
Schenectady, 1971.

Vojta, M. "A Critical View of Vacuum Aspiration: A New Method for the Termination
of Pregnancy." *Obstetrics and Gynecology* 30, no. 1 (July 1967): 28–34.

Wattleton, Faye. *Life on the Line.* New York: Ballantine, 1996.

Weber, Melva. "Middlemen in the Definition of Life." *Medical World News*, Nov. 22,
1974, 55–62.

Weiss, Kay. "Contempt for Women: What Medical Students Learn in Our Best
Universities." *Off Our Backs*, Apr./May 1975.

Welsome, Eileen. *The Plutonium Files: America's Secret Medical Experiments in the
Cold War.* New York: Delta Book, 1999.

Wicklund, Susan, and Alex Kesselheim. *This Common Secret: My Journey as an
Abortion Doctor.* New York: Public Affairs, 2007.

Wilke, John C. *How to Teach the Pro-Life Story.* Cincinnati: Hiltz and Hayes, 1973.

Wilke, John C., and Mrs. J. C. Wilke. *Handbook on Abortion.* Cincinnati: Hiltz, June
1972.

Williams, Daniel K. "No Happy Medium: The Role of Americans' Ambivalent View
of Fetal Rights in Political Conflict over Abortion Legalization." *Journal of Policy
History* 25, no. 1 (2013): 42–61.

Wohl, Lisa Cronin. "Would You Buy an Abortion from This Man? The Harvey
Karman Controversy." *Ms. Magazine*, Sept. 1975, 60–64, 113–24.

Ziegler, Mary. "Edelin: The Remaking of the Headline Abortion Trial." *Saint Louis
University Law Journal* 55 (2011): 1379–1404.

———. "The Framing of a Right to Choose: Roe v. Wade and the Changing Debate on
Abortion Law." *Law and History Review* 27, no. 2 (2009): 281–330.

Index

Abortion: access to, 11–14, 35, 43, 58, 95, 100, 110, 168, 188–89, 219, 246, 298 (n. 101); death of fetus, 62, 80–81, 83, 222–25, 229–31, 235; elective vs. nonelective, 232, 233, 301 (nn. 148, 152); fetal defects and, 9, 67, 87, 131, 152–53, 220, 226–27, 228, 229, 230, 233, 300–301 (n. 137); husband consent and, 12, 59, 95; language and, 21–22; "late-term," 22, 223, 224, 225, 227–28, 232–33, 234, 300 (n. 127); legalization of, 9–14, 23, 254 (n. 49); live birth and, 64, 79, 86–88, 122, 123, 124, 222, 269 (n. 99); maternal health and, 11, 13, 26, 64, 83, 168, 208, 226, 227, 230, 237, 240; mortality rate and, 24, 31, 38, 55, 258 (nn. 27, 34); near fetal viability, 63, 86; parental consent and, 2–3, 12, 13, 59, 95, 248; political action to protect, 207–8, 212–13, 217, 221–22, 248, 299 (n. 111); poverty and, 12, 38, 52–53, 100–101, 110, 114, 169–70, 219, 228, 248; public funding and, 11, 12, 95–96, 100–101, 166, 169, 228, 247, 272 (n. 28); race and, 18, 35, 101, 169, 170, 228; referral services and, 34–36, 41, 99, 111, 114; safety of, 14, 24, 32, 38, 55, 121, 124, 186, 246, 259 (n. 61); state laws and, 9, 10, 11–14, 59, 95, 242, 247–48, 249–50, 264 (n. 1); stigma of, 15–16, 19, 21, 34, 37, 160, 201, 204, 206, 218–19, 243, 245, 248–49; training, 28, 41, 93, 100, 102, 108, 120, 125–29, 136–37, 221, 223; woman's right to choose and, 6, 14, 15, 19, 137, 218–19, 225, 227, 239–40, 243, 247, 249, 250, 280

(n. 69). *See also* Abortion during first trimester; Abortion during second trimester; Abortion during third trimester; Abortion experience; Abortion rate; Abortion research; Antiabortion activism; Illegal abortions; "Partial birth" abortion; "Therapeutic" abortion

Abortion Care Network, 207

Abortion clinics: birth control services and, 42, 46, 47, 56, 106; death at, 164, 285–86 (n. 27); defense of, 188–89, 190–93, 194, 202, 204–5, 292–93 (n. 154); establishment of, 20, 23, 24–25, 40–45, 55–57, 93–94, 105, 245, 260 (n. 68); feminist vs. medical model, 5, 45–52, 53–54, 57–58, 100, 101–9, 245, 249–50, 273 (nn. 45, 49), 274 (n. 60); profit motive and, 24–25, 35–38, 42–43, 98–99, 111, 112, 114, 207, 245, 250, 274–75 (n. 76); opposition to, 25, 43–45, 58–59, 118, 180, 250, 290 (n. 108); rogue clinics, 96, 110–14, 116–17, 118, 245, 250, 274–75 (n. 76), 299 (n. 112); security at, 171, 180, 202, 211, 289–90 (n. 103), 290 (n. 110); standards for, 90–91, 93–95, 96–97, 99–100, 107, 109, 110, 111–12, 113–17, 246, 274 (n. 70). *See also* Abortion providers; Antiabortion activism; Feminism; Hospitals

Abortion counseling, 34, 36, 41, 53, 54, 103, 260 (n. 70); head and heart counseling, 205–7, 209, 249, 295 (n. 28); state laws and, 12, 13, 248, 250

Abortion during first trimester, 11, 21, 31, 112, 119, 121–22, 123, 125, 276–77

(n. 4), 278 (n. 25). *See also* Vacuum
aspiration abortion

Abortion during second trimester, 31, 37,
40, 119, 121–22, 123, 124, 219, 276–77
(n. 4); ethical dilemmas and, 127–28,
130; fees and, 52–53, 112, 274–75
(n. 76), 291 (n. 125); live birth and,
86–87, 88, 122; reasons for, 227–28,
232, 298 (n. 101), 300 (n. 127), 301
(nn. 148, 152); state laws and, 11, 12,
95, 124–25. *See also* Dilation and
evacuation (D&E) abortion; Hysterotomy; Intact dilation and evacuation
(intact D&E) abortion; Prostaglandins; Saline instillation abortion

Abortion during third trimester, 12, 21,
22, 208, 227, 232–33, 247, 276 (n. 97)

Abortion experience, 16, 53, 55, 57–58,
239–40, 249, 255 (n. 69), 295 (n. 28);
African Americans and, 18, 35, 41,
52, 65; in antiabortion literature,
133–36, 141–43, 146–50, 205, 238–39,
241, 282 (n. 86), 283–84 (n. 102), 284
(n. 109), 303 (n. 175), 304 (n. 184);
feminist vs. medical model and,
53–55, 57–58; illegal, 245–46; silence
and, 15–16, 21, 121, 245, 247; women
regretting, 204–6. *See also* Antiabortion activism

Abortion pill, 21

Abortion providers: African Americans
and, 19, 41, 64–65, 81–82, 163, 176–
78; ambivalence of over abortion, 130,
132, 134–40; feminism and, 98, 100,
101–4, 115, 139; intact dilation and
evacuation (D&E) abortion and, 222,
226, 227, 231–32, 233, 234, 235–36,
237; male physicians, 33, 48–51, 101–
4, 105, 272–73 (n. 43), 274 (n. 66);
murder of, 145, 197, 210–19, 229, 233,
243; number of, 17–18, 160–61, 195,
211, 248, 261 (nn. 90, 91) 285 (n. 16),
293–94 (n. 176); professionalization
of abortion and, 20, 25–26, 45, 107–8,
121, 152; women physicians, 101–2,

105–6, 107–9. *See also* Abortion clinics; Abortion experience; Antiabortion activism; Hospitals; National
Abortion Federation; National Coalition of Abortion Providers; Ob-gyn

Abortion rate, 3, 9, 34, 252 (n. 13), 254
(n. 49), 261 (n. 90); abortion techniques and, 124, 278 (n. 25); nonwhite women and, 35, 170; after *Roe*,
24, 38–39, 45, 55, 58, 64, 246; second
trimester and, 124, 219

Abortion research, 25, 104, 120–21, 123,
236, 246, 277 (nn. 7, 12); dilation and
evacuation (D&E) abortion and, 119–
21, 152; dilation by laminaria and, 94,
120, 124, 152, 272–73 (n. 43); intact
dilation and evacuation (D&E) abortion and, 220–21, 237

Abortion techniques. *See* Dilation and
curettage (D&C) abortion; Dilation
and evacuation (D&E) abortion; Hysterotomy; Intact dilation and evacuation (D&E) abortion; Prostaglandins;
Saline instillation abortion; Vacuum
aspiration abortion

Aburel, Eugen, 31

Adam, Candice, 95

African Americans, 208; abortion experience and, 18, 35, 41, 52, 65; abortion
providers and, 19, 41, 64–65, 81–82,
163, 176–78; antiabortion activism
and, 18, 176–78; medical profession
and, 71, 268 (n. 75). *See also* Edelin,
Kenneth; Thompson, Robert; Turner,
Morris

After Tiller (documentary, 2013), 228

*Akron v. Akron Center for Reproductive
Health, Inc.*, 12

Alan Guttmacher Institute, 17, 38–39, 55,
58, 97, 115, 195, 227–28, 281 (n. 75)

Albert Einstein College of Medicine, 135,
276–77 (n. 4)

American Civil Liberties Union, 43, 191

American College Health Association,
1, 9

American College of Obstetricians and Gynecologists, 110, 164
American Law Institute, 9, 10
American Medical Association, 71, 110
American Medical News, 222, 228, 234
American Psychological Association, 239, 282 (n. 86)
American Public Health Association, 94, 120, 277 (n. 7)
Amnioinfusion techniques, 120, 123, 124. *See also* Prostaglandins; Saline instillation abortion
Andrews, Joan, 187, 196, 296 (n. 52)
Antiabortion activism: abortion providers participating in, 37, 116–17, 131–33, 134–40, 145, 146, 280 (nn. 57, 65, 66, 69, 70), 281 (n. 79); African Americans and, 18, 176–78; clinic attacks and, 150, 164–67, 170–71, 186, 192, 196, 202, 204, 210, 212, 215–17, 243, 248, 296 (n. 52); clinic blockades and, 165, 170, 171, 173–75, 176–77, 187–89, 190–97, 200, 203, 217, 294 (n. 182); clinic protests and, 16, 116, 139, 151–52, 160, 161–62, 164–65, 168–69, 172, 193, 199–200, 243, 248, 281 (n. 77), 287 (n. 53), 293 (n. 168); direct action and, 151, 170–75, 186–87, 192, 195–97, 200, 201, 212–14, 215, 246–47, 248, 297 (n. 73); fetal research and, 67–68, 72, 74–75, 76–77, 78–79, 86, 89, 90, 265 (n. 19); fetal rights and, 15, 63, 89, 215–16; fetal waste and, 117, 155–60, 169, 173; harassment of abortion providers and, 199, 200, 209, 296 (n. 47); harassment of medical staff and, 22, 169, 171, 174–78, 180, 186, 199–203, 210–13, 216, 247, 288 (n. 79), 298 (n. 86); harassment of patients and, 116, 162–63, 165, 166, 171, 172–77, 178–80, 184–85, 193–94, 199, 208, 218, 247, 288 (n. 73); impact on abortion providers and, 15, 16, 20, 160–61, 195, 211, 219, 248; impact on medical staff

and, 163, 165, 175, 193–95, 202–4, 211, 216–17, 218, 248, 298 (n. 86); intact dilation and evacuation (intact D&E) abortion and, 20, 222–26, 229, 236–37; intellectual framework of, 58–59, 213–16, 219; lawsuits against, 163, 172, 179–80, 185, 188, 191, 195; movies and, 89, 90, 141, 145, 150, 151, 161, 185, 281–82 (n. 81), 290–91 (n. 120); National Abortion Federation (NAF) response and, 129, 171–72, 186, 188, 189–90, 191–92, 201, 202–4, 216, 294 (n. 15); political action and, 166, 170, 295 (n. 38); rogue abortion clinics and, 96, 113, 116–17, 275 (n. 89); second trimester abortions and, 21, 129, 130, 229, 279 (n. 47); sidewalk counseling and, 151, 172–73, 180, 181, 183, 186, 247; violence against abortion providers and, 196, 212, 215, 217, 229, 233. *See also* Abortion providers, murder of; Antiabortion literature; Army of God; Birthchoice; Birthright; Catholicism; Crisis pregnancy centers; Fetal images; Operation Rescue
Antiabortion activism, police response and, 176–77, 178–79, 202; arrests and, 180, 188, 191, 193, 195–96, 200, 203; bomb threats and, 165–66, 179; defense of abortion clinics and, 188, 190–91, 192–93, 194, 217–18, 293 (n. 162); ignoring protesters and, 178, 179, 217, 289 (n. 102), 289–90 (n. 103), 296 (n. 51). *See also* Bureau of Alcohol, Tobacco, and Firearms
Antiabortion literature, 140–43, 172–73, 222, 297 (n. 73); abortion as murder in, 59, 86, 118, 150–51, 173, 185; abortion experience and, 133–36, 141–43, 146–50, 205, 282 (n. 86), 283–84 (n. 102); abortion providers in, 130, 132, 134–40, 162, 210, 211, 214–15, 282–83 (n. 93); crisis pregnancy centers (CPCs) and, 183, 186; fetal

"experience" and, 142–44, 148, 240, 243; fetal images and, 21, 72–74, 89, 144–45, 151, 161, 162; fetal research and, 74–77; fetuses as babies and, 20, 153, 157, 158–60, 161, 171, 173, 182–83, 225, 247; *Handbook on Abortion* (Wilke and Wilke), 72–74, 75, 80, 89, 140, 162; "post-abortion syndrome" and, 239, 240, 242, 303 (n. 177), 304 (n. 184); *Whatever Happened to the Human Race?* (Koop and Schaeffer), 89–90, 140, 166–67, 281–82 (n. 81); women regretting abortions and, 146, 148, 241

Antibiotics, 65, 67, 81, 124, 164, 220

Appleton, Joan, 137, 139, 140, 280 (n. 70), 281 (n. 77)

Army of God, 171, 215–16

Association for the Study of Abortion, 9–10, 27–28

Association of Planned Parenthood Physicians, 120, 277 (nn. 7, 12)

Association to Repeal Abortion Laws, 6

Atlanta, 39, 41, 42, 97, 127, 130; Feminist Women's Health Center (FWHC), 176, 178, 192–94, 203, 204, 293 (n. 168); Siege of Atlanta, 187–89, 192–94, 196, 203, 214

Avery, Byllye, 35

Bagley, Sandra, 203, 204

Baird, William R., 7

Barr, Sam, 23, 40, 49, 51, 52, 53, 260 (n. 69)

Barrett, John, 145, 211, 212, 217

Battered women, 56

Beecher, Henry, 71

Belous, Leon, 10

Beresford, Terry, 97, 176–77, 179, 206

Bioethics: death of the fetus and, 122, 127–28, 130, 209, 296 (n. 47); and death and dying, 69–70; fetal research and, 84–85, 88–89, 269 (n. 88); human research subjects and, 70–71; neonatal care and, 87–88, 279 (n. 47); organ transplants and, 69–70, 71

Birthchoice, 141, 182

Birth control pills, 1, 2, 7, 9; abortion clinics and, 42, 46, 47, 56, 106; dangers of, 71–72, 104, 106. *See also* Contraceptives

Birth defects. *See* Fetal defects

Birthright, 181, 184

Blue Mountain Clinic (Missoula), 212

Bok, Sissela, 84, 88, 269 (n. 88)

Boston City Hospital (BCH), 19, 59, 64, 65, 67–68; abortions and, 79, 80, 82, 260 (n. 65); fetal research and, 61, 65, 78–79, 81

Boulder Abortion Clinic, 95

Boulder Valley Clinic, 93–95, 272–73 (n. 43)

Bovard, Jane, 167–68, 185, 202, 287 (n. 44)

Boxer, Barbara, 237

Boyd, Glenna, 246, 247

Bray, Donna, 215–16

Breslar, Eliot, 163

Brewter, David, 136–37, 139

Brigham, Steven, 250

Britton, John, 145, 211, 212, 217

Brockhoeft, John, 215

Bureau of Alcohol, Tobacco, and Firearms, 188, 217

Burke, Theresa, 242

Burnhill, Michael, 116

Burt, John, 210, 296 (n. 52)

Bush, George H. W., 214

Bush, George W., 237

Bykov, S. G., 27

California, 6, 28, 100, 110, 117, 123, 237; abortion clinics in, 42, 43, 188; legalizing abortion in, 10, 35, 38, 259 (n. 42); live birth during abortion in, 87, 88

Canady, Charles T., 228, 229–30

Cancer, 39, 65, 126, 149
Cano, Sandra, 238, 303 (n. 175)
Carhart, LeRoy, 238, 242, 250
Case Western Reserve University, 78, 231
Catholicism: antiabortion activism and, 77, 161, 181, 196, 294 (n. 186); antiabortion position and, 44, 81, 85, 89, 90, 235, 283 (n. 98); hospitals and, 64, 285–86 (n. 27); papal visit and, 188–89; pro-choice and, 127, 189, 190
Catholics for a Free Choice, 127, 189, 190. *See also* Kissling, Frances
Cavanaugh-O'Keefe, John, 189
Center for Reproductive and Sexual Health (CRSH), 33, 36–37, 132, 279 (n. 52)
Center for Reproductive Rights, 235
Centers for Disease Control (CDC), 17, 32, 35, 97, 120
Cervical caps, 49
Cervical self-exams, 6, 41, 47–48
Cevallos, Hector, 171
Chelian, Renee, 39, 47, 49, 52, 209; abortions in New York state and, 23, 33–34, 45–46; antiabortion activism and, 178, 216, 289 (n. 97); defense of abortion clinics and, 190–92, 194, 204, 292–93 (n. 154); dilation and evacuation (D&E) abortion and, 119, 120, 126; intact dilation and evacuation (D&E) abortion and, 232, 235–36; National Abortion Federation (NAF) and, 98–99, 109
Chicago, 6; abortion clinics in, 96, 110–11, 112–14, 195, 250, 275 (n. 89); antiabortion activism in, 136, 155, 156, 170, 172, 195, 275 (n. 89); hospitals in, 163, 274–75 (n. 76)
Choices Women's Medical Center, 30, 103
Citizens for a Pro-Life Society, 157, 158
City of Akron v. Akron Center for Reproductive Health, 170
Clergy and Lay Advocates for Hospital Abortion, 54, 263 (n. 133)

Clergy Consultation Service, 7, 8, 33, 34, 35, 38, 53, 95, 259 (n. 39), 263 (n. 133)
Clinton, Bill, 208, 210, 214, 217, 222, 232, 237, 295 (n. 38), 299 (n. 111), 304 (n. 184)
Coalition to Defend Abortion Rights, 190, 289 (n. 97)
Colorado, 10, 93–95, 99–100, 120, 122, 271 (n. 20)
Commonwealth v. Kenneth Edelin, 19, 63–64. *See also* Edelin, Kenneth
Contraceptives, 1, 5, 7–9, 236, 251 (n. 3). *See also* Birth control pills; Dalkon Shield intrauterine device; IUDs
Counseling, 54, 103; abortion clinics and, 34, 36, 41, 53, 260 (n. 70); antiabortion sidewalk counseling, 151, 172–73, 180, 181, 183, 186, 247; head and heart counseling, 205–7, 209, 249, 295 (n. 28); state laws and, 12, 13, 248, 250
Crisis pregnancy centers (CPCs), 180–86, 208, 241, 242, 247, 290 (n. 115), 290–91 (n. 120), 291 (n. 123); lawsuits against, 185
Crist, Robert, 125–26
Crist, Takey, 40, 55–56, 109–10, 296 (n. 47); antiabortion activism and, 184–85, 281 (n. 74); intact dilation and evacuation (D&E) abortion and, 151–52, 153; murders of abortion providers and, 211, 218; North Carolina legalizing abortion and, 1, 2, 7–8, 28
Crist Clinic for Women, 40, 151–52
Csapo, Arpad I., 31
Cushner, Irvin, 99–100

Dalkon Shield intrauterine device (IUD), 71–72, 104
Dallas Routh Street Women's Clinic, 202, 205
Darney, Philip, 115–16
Delaware, 43, 44, 161, 167

Del-Em kit, 6, 29–30
Denes, Magda, 134, 146, 284 (n. 109)
deProsse, Charles, 32–33, 39, 50, 51
Detroit, 23, 33, 39, 42, 189, 190–91, 194,
    274–75 (n. 76), 292–93 (n. 154)
Dilation and curettage (D&C) abortion,
    26, 27, 28, 31, 32, 72, 121, 164, 278
    (n. 25)
Dilation and evacuation (D&E) abortion,
    119, 120, 121, 124–27, 128, 152, 219–
    20, 246, 278 (nn. 22, 25); abortion
    research and, 119–21, 152; antiabor-
    tion activism and, 136, 151, 221, 222;
    ethical dilemmas and, 127–28, 129–
    30, 279 (n. 47); fetal defects and, 233;
    impact of on medical staff, 123–24,
    125, 126, 127, 129–31, 136, 152, 279
    (n. 44), 281 (n. 79); increasing use of,
    124–26, 152; introduction of, 120–21,
    277 (n. 12); laminaria and, 119, 120,
    123, 125, 127, 152, 219; safety of, 121,
    130, 152, 153, 219–20, 246; second tri-
    mester and, 119, 120, 121, 124–27, 128,
    152, 219–20, 246, 278 (n. 25). *See also*
    Intact dilation and evacuation (D&E)
    abortion
Doe v. Bolton, 10–11, 149, 150, 238–39,
    303 (n. 175)
Downer, Carol, 6, 42, 47, 101, 109–10
Dussik, Friedrich, 144

Eastern Women's Medical Center, 33,
    258–59 (n. 37)
Edelin, Kenneth: as abortion provider,
    19, 59, 61, 64–65, 79, 80, 83; impact of
    conviction, 63, 84, 86; manslaughter
    charge, 19, 59, 61, 63, 80, 81, 242; con-
    viction of, 61, 62, 63, 90, 95, 243; trial,
    62–64, 81–84, 86, 230, 268 (n. 65)
Eisenstadt v. Baird, 8, 251 (n. 3)
Emma Goldman Clinic for Women
    (EGC), 56–57, 245, 260–61 (n. 78),
    273–74 (n. 57); abortion experience
    at, 53–54; establishment of, 41–42,
    260 (n. 77); feminist vs. medical

model and, 5, 47–49, 50–51, 104–9,
    273 (nn. 45, 49), 274 (n. 60); male
    physicians and, 101–3, 104, 105, 262
    (n. 116); National Abortion Federa-
    tion (NAF) and, 114, 275–76 (n. 93);
    teaching at, 51, 56, 105, 108; woman
    physicians and, 105–6, 107–9
EPOC clinic, 40, 49, 51, 52, 53, 260
    (n. 69)
Evangelical Christians, 90, 166–67, 168,
    283 (n. 98), 294 (n. 186), 297 (n. 73)
Everett, Carol, 116–17, 118, 140

Falwell, Jerry, 168, 293 (n. 168)
Fargo, N.D., 43, 150, 151, 156, 287 (n. 47);
    antiabortion activism in, 168–69, 172,
    179. *See also* Fargo Women's Health
    Organization (FWHO)
Fargo Women's Health Organization
    (FWHO), 167–69, 172, 201, 202, 291
    (n. 125)
Fargo Women's Help Clinic, 181, 182,
    183–84, 185
Feminism: abortion clinics and, 5, 40,
    41–42, 101–9, 162, 167, 245, 249–50,
    273 (nn. 45, 49); abortion providers
    and, 98, 100, 101–4, 115, 139; abortion
    services and, 19, 24–25, 38, 45–52,
    54, 57–58, 100, 101; male physicians
    and, 15, 19, 24, 48, 49, 101–4, 109–10;
    woman's right to choose abortion
    and, 6, 14, 137; women's health and,
    5–6, 24, 47–48, 114, 133, 245
Feminist Women's Health Center
    (FWHC), 42, 100, 101, 103, 109–10,
    260–61 (n. 78), 290 (n. 110); Atlanta,
    176, 178, 192–94, 203, 204, 293
    (n. 168); Los Angeles, 29–30, 102, 278
    (n. 22); Yakima, Wash., 174, 175, 179,
    288 (n. 73), 289–90 (n. 103)
Fetal bodies, politicization of, 69
Fetal defects, 9, 67, 87, 131, 152–53, 220,
    228; abortion and, 226–27, 229, 230,
    233, 300–301 (n. 137); anencephaly,
    227; cephalosentesis, 231; Down syn-

drome, 87, 152; hydrocephaly, 220; screening of, 67; spina bifida, 152
Fetal development, 66, 83, 85, 127, 128, 132
Fetal images, 62, 66, 83; antiabortion activism and, 15, 16, 151, 155–56, 157, 158, 162, 181–83, 185, 265 (nn. 18–19), 282–83 (n. 93); antiabortion literature and, 21, 72–74, 89, 144–45, 151, 161, 162; Edelin trial and, 62–63, 83–84; ultrasounds and, 14, 142, 144–45, 209
Fetal personhood, 62, 63
Fetal research, 62, 63, 67–69, 70, 88–89, 265 (nn. 16–17, 23); aborted vs. carried-to-term fetuses and, 76, 84–85; antiabortion activism and, 67–68, 72, 74–75, 76–77, 78–79, 86, 89, 90, 265 (n. 19); Boston City Hospital (BCH) and, 61, 65, 67–68, 78–79, 81; debate surrounding, 72, 76–78, 88; fetuses showing signs of life and, 65–66, 69, 74, 76–77, 78, 79; guidelines for, 70, 75–76, 84–85; history of, 65–68; limits on, 75–76, 77–78, 84–86; purpose and extent of, 67–69
Fetal rights, 15, 63, 70, 76, 84, 89, 215–16; personhood and, 127–28, 283 (n. 98)
Fetal stories, 63, 90; in antiabortion literature, 142–44, 145
Fetal therapies, 70
Fetal viability, 22, 68, 75, 83, 84, 130, 208, 279 (n. 47); Edelin trial and, 62–64, 81, 82–83, 84, 86; intact dilation and evacuation (D&E) abortion and, 219, 222, 225, 227; live birth during abortion and, 86–88, 222, 269 (n. 99); state laws and, 11, 13, 86, 87, 88, 247; U.S. Supreme Court and, 11, 12–13, 86, 131, 247
Fetal waste, 12, 117–18, 122, 127; antiabortion activism and, 117, 155–60, 169, 173. See also Fetal research
Fetus, status of, 63, 82–83
Finkbine, Sherri, 9

Fitzsimmons, Ron, 207–8, 209, 211, 234, 235, 302 (n. 160)
Flanagan, Newman, 61, 62, 79, 80–81, 83
Florida, 35; abortion clinics and, 23, 40, 42, 43, 49, 52; antiabortion activism and, 145, 156, 170, 210–11, 217, 293 (n. 162)
Fort Wayne Women's Health Organization (FWWHO), 43, 44–45, 155, 156, 161–66, 167, 170, 176, 290 (n. 110)
Fossum, Karl, 33
Foster, Henry, 234
Francke, Linda Bird, 146, 284 (n. 109)
Frankfort, Ellen, 110
Franks, Adele, 105–6, 107–9
Free Clinic (Pittsburgh), 41
Freedom of Access to Clinic Entrances (FACE) law, 212, 214, 217, 294 (n. 182)
Freedom of Choice Act (FOCA), 207–8, 222, 224, 295 (n. 38), 299 (n. 111)
Freiman, Michael, 125, 126
Friends for Life, 113

German measles, 9, 67
Gesell, Arnold, 10
Giminez-Jimeno, Enrique, 80, 82, 83, 268 (n. 65)
Goldberg, Merle. See Hoffman, Merle
Gonzales v. Carhart, 13, 19, 20, 238–43, 249
Gorney, Cynthia, 90, 121, 125, 126, 187
Gosnell, Kermit, 250
Great Britain, 74–75
Griffin, Michael, 210, 211, 216
Grimes, David, 120, 121, 124, 227, 237
Griswold v. Connecticut, 11
Grobstein, Clifford, 127, 128
Gunn, David, 210–13, 214, 215, 216, 217, 218, 219, 248, 294–95 (n. 18), 297 (n. 82)
Gynecology. See Ob-gyn

Hachamovitch, Moshe, 33
Hanson, Millie, 107, 119, 120–21, 123, 125, 152

Harris v. McRae, 12

Harvard Medical School, 65, 71, 81, 268 (n. 75)

Haskell, Martin, 153, 221, 223, 225, 227, 230, 232

Hausknecht, Richard, 35–36

Hawaii, 10, 259 (n. 42)

Head and heart counseling, 205–7, 209, 249, 295 (n. 28)

Helms, Jesse, 208

Helms Amendment of 1976, 116

Hern, Warren, 93–95, 101, 107, 110, 125, 302 (n. 160); abortion research and, 94, 120, 152, 272–73 (n. 43); dilation and evacuation (D&E) abortion and, 122, 129–30, 277 (n. 12); intact dilation and evacuation (D&E) abortion and, 234, 237

Higuera, Gilbert, 23, 33–35, 45–46, 49

Hill, McArthur, 137, 139–40

Hill, Paul, 145, 211, 212, 214, 216, 217, 297 (n. 82)

Hill, Susan, 2, 3, 4, 23, 48, 109, 207; antiabortion activism impact and, 178, 180, 202, 211, 217, 290 (n. 108); EPOC clinic and, 49, 51, 52, 53, 260 (n. 69); Fargo Women's Health Organization (FWHO) and, 167–68, 169; Fort Wayne Women's Health Organization (FWWHO) and, 44–45, 161–63, 166; openings of clinics after *Roe* and, 42–43, 44–45; "partial birth" abortion and, 228–29, 296 (n. 47); sexual harassment and, 51, 274 (n. 66)

Hoffman, Merle, 30, 101, 103–4, 109

Holy Terror (documentary, 1987), 192, 293 (n. 162)

Hooker, Davenport, 65–66, 265 (nn. 16, 17, 19)

Hospitals: abortion after *Roe* and, 11, 25, 35–36, 39, 40, 41, 43, 45, 81, 100, 260 (nn. 65, 68), 261 (n. 91); abortion before *Roe* and, 7–8, 26–27, 28, 54, 64, 79, 252 (n. 13); cost of abortions and, 38, 259 (n. 39), 274–75 (n. 76); resis-

tance to providing abortions, 25, 168, 260 (nn. 65, 68), 285–86 (n. 27), 287 (n. 47); restrictions on abortions and, 25, 37, 43, 84, 163, 164, 263 (n. 133). *See also* Boston City Hospital

Hulka, Jaroslav, 28

Human Life Amendment, 11, 116, 127, 166, 170

Human research subjects, 70–71, 76, 85, 104, 266 (n. 32)

Hyde Amendment of 1976, 11, 59, 95–96, 100, 110, 166, 169, 247, 270 (n. 7)

Hysterectomy, 32, 51

Hysterotomy, 22, 31, 61, 68, 86; death of the fetus and, 61, 62–63, 64, 72, 80, 81, 82; Edelin trial and, 19, 61, 62–63, 64, 79, 81, 82, 242, 268 (n. 65); medical complications and, 31, 32, 258 (n. 27)

Illegal abortions, 10, 14, 18, 36, 245–46; complications from, 26–27, 38, 45, 65; deaths from, 9, 24, 41, 95–96, 169; effect of on legal abortions, 25–27, 257 (nn. 8–9); mortality rate and, 4, 24, 252 (n. 16); poverty and, 3–4, 26, 35; referral services and, 6–7, 8, 23, 24, 41, 108, 245; skilled abortionists and, 3, 6–7

Indiana, 43, 44–45, 156, 161–66, 167, 170, 176. *See also* Fort Wayne Women's Health Organization

Installation procedures, 119, 121–22, 123, 124, 125, 220. *See also* Prostaglandins; Saline instillation abortion

Intact dilation and evacuation (D&E) abortion, 222–25, 227, 230, 232, 233, 236, 249; antiabortion activism and, 19–20, 22, 153, 219, 221, 222–26, 236–37, 243, 248–49; banning of, 13, 19–20, 229–30, 235–37, 238, 242, 243, 249, 299–300 (n. 119); death of the fetus and, 225–26, 228, 229–31, 233, 235, 236–37; debate surrounding, 226–27, 229, 230, 233, 300–301

(n. 137); development of, 153, 220–21, 237; fetal viability and, 219, 222, 225, 227; frequency of, 226, 227, 229, 231–32, 233, 234–35, 249, 302 (n. 160); second trimester and, 222–25, 227, 230, 232, 233, 236, 249. *See also* Dilation and evacuation (D&E) abortion

Iowa, 6, 23, 39, 57, 102. *See also* Emma Goldman Clinic for Women

IUDs, 71–72, 104, 106

Jane (underground abortion referral service), 6, 108, 245

Japan, 27, 31, 119, 276–77 (n. 4)

Jefferson, Mildred, 82, 268 (n. 75)

Jimenez, Rosaura, 95–96, 110

Johnston, Margaret (Peg), 203, 204, 294–95 (n. 18)

Kansas, 125, 196, 208, 212, 217, 298 (n. 86)

Karman, Harvey, 29–30, 104; Karman cannula, 29

Kerenyi, Thomas, 31

Kerslake, Dorothea, 27, 28

Keyes, Claire, 178, 202

Kissling, Frances, 34, 97, 98, 110, 190, 258–59 (n. 37)

Koop, C. Everett, 89–90, 140, 166–67

Lader, Lawrence, 3, 4, 6

Lambs of Christ, 22, 196–97, 200, 201, 202, 294 (n. 186), 297 (n. 75)

Laminaria: abortion research and, 94, 120, 124, 152, 272–73 (n. 43); dilation and evacuation (D&E) abortion and, 119, 120, 123, 125, 127, 152, 219; early use of, 94, 107, 119–21, 122–23, 276–77 (n. 4)

Landy, Uta, 34, 110, 113, 127, 129

"Late-term abortion," 22, 223, 224, 226, 227–28, 232–33, 234, 300 (n. 127). *See also* "Partial birth" abortion

Lee, Samuel, 187, 195

Levatino, Anthony, 136, 137–38

Life Is For Everyone Coalition (LIFE), 168–69, 172, 181

Magee Women's Hospital (Pittsburgh), 40, 41, 81

Maher v. Roe, 12

Male physicians, 5–6, 272 (n. 39); abortion clinics and, 33, 48, 49, 101–4, 105, 272–73 (n. 43), 274 (n. 66); abortion research and, 104, 272–73 (n. 43); abortion services after *Roe* and, 24, 46, 51–52; feminists and, 15, 19, 24, 48, 49, 101–4, 109–10

Mann, Nancyjo, 143–44, 146, 148, 150

Maquire, Marjorie Reilly, 127–28

Margolis, Alan, 28

Mason, Carol, 74, 214

Massachusetts, 42, 185, 212, 215, 217; abortion law and, 61, 64, 65, 264 (n. 1). *See also* Boston

Massachusetts Citizens for Life, 79

Massachusetts Concerned for Life, 82

McCorvey, Norma, 238, 303 (n. 175)

McDonald, Teresa, 105, 274 (n. 60)

McMahon, James T., 220, 225, 227, 228, 230, 231, 233, 237, 300–301 (n. 137), 301 (n. 152)

Mecklenburg, Fred, 167

Mecklenburg, Marjorie, 167

Medicaid, 96, 100–101, 169–70, 228, 247, 272 (n. 28)

Melks, E., 27

Menstrual extraction, 6, 29–30, 48

Michelman, Kate, 235

Mifepristone, 21, 220

Migliorino, Monica, 155, 156–57, 158–59, 160

Milwaukee, 156–57, 159, 199, 216

Minnesota, 119, 120, 166, 167, 199, 210, 212

Misoprostol, 220

Missionaries to the Pre-Born, 196, 216, 294 (n. 186)

Mississippi, 217–18

Missouri, 12, 13, 31, 95, 124–25. *See also* St. Louis

Mobile Center for Choice, 212

Mondale, Walter, 70–71

Montana, 22, 210, 211, 212, 239, 296 (n. 48)

Moody, Howard, 7, 33, 54

Moral Majority, 167

Morgan, Lynn, 65, 66

Morgen, Sandra, 109

Mountain Country Women's Clinic (Montana), 210

Ms. Magazine, 104

Mulhauser, Karen, 97

Murr, William, 28

Nathanson, Bernard, 36–37, 131–33, 134, 136, 139, 145, 150, 161, 279 (n. 52), 280 (n. 57)

National Abortion Council (NAC), 97, 271 (n. 10)

National Abortion Federation (NAF), 17, 18, 19; abortion techniques and, 119–20, 121, 124, 125, 126–27, 128–29, 277 (n. 7), 278 (n. 22); antiabortion activism and, 129, 171–72, 186, 188, 189–90, 191–92, 201, 202–4, 216, 294 (n. 15); basic standards and, 99–100, 110, 111–12, 113–16, 117, 118, 127, 128, 169, 246, 276 (n. 97); dilation and evacuation (D&E) abortion and, 124, 126–27, 128–29, 153; establishment of, 97–100, 101, 271 (n. 20); ethical dilemmas and, 127–28; feminists and, 98, 100, 101, 109, 115; intact dilation and evacuation (D&E) abortion and, 153, 221, 223, 225, 226, 231–32, 234, 235, 249; male physicians and, 109–10, 274 (n. 66); membership and, 20, 114–16, 138, 203–4, 207, 275 (n. 92), 275–76 (n. 93), 281 (nn. 75, 77), 302 (n. 160); Partial Birth Abortion Ban Act (HR 1833) and, 228, 229

National Abortion Rights Action League

(NARAL), 10, 35, 97, 132, 133, 167, 189, 190, 203, 207, 228, 235

National Association of Abortion Facilities (NAAF), 95, 97, 98, 270 (n. 6)

National Coalition of Abortion Providers (NCAP), 207–9, 217, 232, 234, 235, 236, 243, 248, 302 (n. 160)

National Commission for the Protection of Human Subjects of Biomedical and Behavioral Research, 67, 88

National Conference of Catholic Bishops, 235

National Institute of Health (NIH), 75–76, 77, 84, 85–86

National Organization for Women (NOW), 137, 139, 167, 191, 228

National Right to Life Committee (NRLC), 170, 222, 235

National Science Foundation, 78

National Women's Health Organization (NWHO), 43, 44, 45, 161, 169, 180, 202, 211, 274 (n. 66)

Nazism, 70, 76, 89, 135, 158, 169, 211, 214, 280 (n. 65), 297 (n. 82)

Nebraska, 238

Neonatal care, 87, 269 (n. 99)

Neubardt, Selig, and Harold Schulman, *Techniques of Abortion*, 120, 276–77 (n. 4)

New England Journal of Medicine, 67, 132

New Jersey, 26, 43, 44, 156, 161, 167, 187, 233, 290 (n. 108)

New Jersey Supreme Court, 43

New Jersey Women's Health Organization (NJWHO), 44, 161

New Orleans, 94, 115, 120, 189

News coverage of abortion: *Boston Globe*, 81; *Chicago Sun-Times*, 96, 110–11, 113, 114, 118, 211, 219, 250; Geraldo Rivera, 150; *Media Matters*, 233; NBC, 201; *New York Times*, 130, 134, 186, 229, 234, 279 (n. 47), 294–95 (n. 18); *Nightline* (ABC) 234; *Phil*

Donahue Show, 211, 218, 197 (n. 82); *Raleigh News and Observer*, 160; *60 Minutes*, 201; *TV Guide*, 186; *20/20* news program, 150, 151, 167; *Washington Post*, 76, 77, 78, 79, 232–33, 237

New York, 30, 41, 299 (n. 112); abortion clinics in, 33–37, 43, 44, 132, 167, 187, 188, 259 (n. 39); abortion data and, 32, 34, 258 (n. 31); antiabortion activism and, 187, 188, 195; legalizing abortion in, 10, 23, 28, 32–34, 35–37, 38, 45–46, 54, 64, 99, 132, 254 (n. 49), 257 (nn. 18–19)

New York City, 34, 38, 42, 45, 97, 99, 132, 191, 195, 222, 254 (n. 49)

Nichols, Lee Ann, 212

North Carolina, 17, 208; abortion and, 1, 2, 3, 4, 7–8, 28; abortion clinics in, 40, 43, 55–56, 151–52, 156, 167, 174; abortion law and, 7–8, 10, 28, 252 (n. 13); crisis pregnancy centers (CPCs) in, 181, 182, 184–85

North Carolina Right to Life, 142

North Dakota, 43, 150, 151, 156, 167–69, 172, 179, 181, 287 (n. 47). *See also* Fargo

Novak, Franc, 28

November Gang, 204, 205, 207, 208, 209, 232, 243, 248, 249

Nuremberg Code of 1947, 70, 266 (n. 32)

Nurses Concerned for Life, 163

Nye, Deb, 41, 108

Ob-gyn (obstetrics and gynecology), 5–6, 14; abortion after *Roe* and, 39, 41, 45, 49, 99–100, 110, 120–21, 125–26, 131, 213; abortion and, 1, 7–8, 27, 28, 37–38, 61, 138; abortion clinics and, 33, 35–36; African Americans and, 59, 81–82; sexism in, 5, 101–4, 105. *See also* Edelin, Kenneth

Ohio, 95, 232

Onslow Memorial Hospital, 55, 56

Operation Rescue (OR), 195, 201, 204,
281 (n. 77), 303 (n. 175); beginnings of, 151, 187, 248; demise of, 196, 221, 294 (n. 182); Siege of Atlanta and, 187–89, 192–94, 196, 203, 214

Oregon, 175, 186, 221

Organ transplants, 69–70, 71

Our Bodies, Ourselves, 6, 261 (n. 94), 273 (n. 45)

Packwood, Robert, 98

Pakter, Jean, 99, 111

Paracervical block, 29

"Partial birth" abortion, 13, 22, 153, 219, 230, 248–49, 296 (n. 47); HR 1833 (Partial Birth Abortion Ban Act), 228–29, 232, 236–37, 299–300 (n. 119). *See also* Intact dilation and evacuation (D&E) abortion

Partners in Vision, 168, 169, 181

Pathology Lab Vital Med, 155, 156

Patrick, Deval, 218

Patterson, George Wayne, 212, 217

Pearson Foundation, 181–82

Peel Report (UK), 75

Pelham Medical Group, 33, 34, 97, 258–59 (n. 37)

Pennsylvania, 12, 13. *See also* Philadelphia; Pittsburgh

Pensacola Ladies Center, 211, 217

Pensacola Women's Medical Services, 210–11

People v. Belous, 10

Personhood, 127–28, 283 (n. 98)

Peterson, William, 101, 125

Philadelphia, 156, 173, 174, 188, 191, 289 (n. 102)

Philipson, Agneta, 65

Pittsburgh, 40–41, 81, 176–79, 196, 202

Planned Parenthood, 20, 34, 38, 97, 173, 181, 185, 191, 207, 212, 230, 259 (n. 39)

Planned Parenthood Federation (PPFA), 39, 97, 169, 189, 203, 228, 235, 294–95 (n. 18)

Planned Parenthood of Central Missouri v. Danforth, 11–12
Planned Parenthood of Southeastern Pennsylvania v. Casey, 13, 247–48
Planned Parenthood v. Ashcroft, 124–25
Planned Parenthood–World Population, 8
Polio vaccine, 66
Pope John Paul II, 188–91, 292–93 (n. 154)
"Post-abortion syndrome," 239, 240, 242, 303 (n. 177)
Pregnancy, 5, 78; antibiotics and, 65, 67, 81; free pregnancy testing, 46–47, 181; German measles and, 9, 67; Rh incompatibility and, 67, 70, 265 (n. 22); thalidomide and, 9, 67; unwanted, 1, 2–3, 4. *See also* Abortion; Abortion during first trimester; Abortion during second trimester; Crisis pregnancy centers; Fetal research; Fetal viability
Pregnancy Aid Centers, 85
President's Commission on Health Science and Society, 71
Pro-Life Action League, 113, 136, 172, 189, 191, 195
Prostaglandins, 31–32, 119, 121, 142–43, 246

Race, 18, 35, 101, 169, 170, 228
Radford, Barbara, 226
Randall, Lynn, 193, 194, 294 (n. 15)
Rape victims, 52, 56, 168, 219, 300 (n. 127)
Rashbaum, William, 135
Rasmussen, Jerry, 212, 216
Reagan, Leslie J., 4, 26
Reagan, Ronald, 89–90, 115, 116, 117, 145, 150, 151, 166–67, 170, 214, 246
Reardon, David C., 146–47, 149, 150, 205, 238, 239, 241–42, 282 (n. 86), 283–84 (n. 102), 284 (n. 109), 304 (n. 184)

Reno, Janet, 217
Report for the South Dakota Task Force to Study Abortion, 240–42
Reproductive Health Services (St. Louis), 121, 125, 126, 180, 189–90, 257 (n. 9)
Rh incompatibility, 67, 70, 265 (n. 22)
RhoGAM vaccine, 70
Rini, Suzanne, 88–89
Rockefeller, Nelson, 10
Rodriguez, Ana Rosa, 222, 223, 224, 299 (n. 112)
Roe, Alice, 61, 79, 82, 83, 84
Roe v. Wade, 63, 65, 98; abortion clinic openings and, 20, 23, 24–25, 40–45, 55–57, 93–94, 105; abortion rate after, 24, 38–39, 45, 55, 58, 64, 246; backlash against, 58–59, 81, 86, 95, 116, 150–51, 166, 170, 270 (n. 7); fetal research and, 68, 69; fetal viability and, 11, 12, 13, 131, 247; plaintiffs, 149, 238–39, 303 (n. 175); rights under, 10–11
Roncallo, Angelo D., 78
Rooks, Judith B., 124
Rosen, Norma, 134–35, 136, 284 (n. 109)
Rosoff, Jeannie, 97
Ross, Michael, 210, 211, 212
Rothman, Lorraine, 6, 29–30
Rubella. *See* German measles
Rutgers Women's Litigation Clinic, 43

Sabath, Leon, 65
St. Louis, 121, 126, 170, 173, 180, 181, 187, 189–90, 257 (n. 9)
Saline instillation abortion, 12, 30–31, 39, 95, 119, 121–22, 124, 126, 246; antiabortion activism and, 72, 142, 143–44, 148; live birth and, 79, 86, 122, 124; medical complications and, 31, 32, 121, 123, 126; state laws and, 12, 59, 95
Saltenberg, Ann, 183
Salvi, John, 212, 215

Saporta, Vicki, 229, 231, 235
Satanism, 214, 215, 297 (n. 75)
Sayles, Leah, 40–41
Schaeffer, Francis A., 89–90, 140
Schaeffer, Frank, 89
Scheidler, Joseph, 129, 130, 138, 171, 186, 187, 192, 196; Chicago antiabortion activism and, 113, 136, 156, 159, 172, 275 (n. 89); *Closed: 99 Ways to Stop Abortion* (Scheidler), 172, 186; Detroit antiabortion activism and, 178, 191; Fort Wayne antiabortion activism and, 164–65, 166, 170; Washington, D.C., antiabortion activism and, 176, 179
Schumer, Charles E., 213
Sex education, 1, 7–9, 72, 261 (n. 94); abortion clinics and, 46–49, 56
Sexual harassment, 51, 103, 196, 274 (n. 66)
Shafer, Brenda, 223, 225, 243, 281 (n. 74)
Shannon, Shelley, 196, 212, 215, 217
Siegel, Reva, 240, 242, 304 (n. 184)
Siege of Atlanta, 187–89, 192–94, 196, 203, 214
Silent Scream (movie, 1984), 145, 150, 151, 161
Simonds, Wendy, 178
Simpson, James Young, 27
Smeal, Eleanor, 191
South Carolina, 3, 4, 40, 52
South Dakota, 58, 240–42
Sterilization, 72
Stone, Norman, 173
Stubblefield, Philip, 152
Sullivan, Charles L., 80–81
Summit Clinics, 42, 191
Summit Women's Health Organization, 199, 200
Susman, Frank, 97

Taft, Charlotte, 116, 118, 186, 202–4, 205, 206, 209
Taggart, Linda, 217

Tancer, M. Leon, 38
Task Force on Mental Health and Abortion, 239
Tennessee, 65, 95
Terry, Randall, 151, 186–87, 293 (n. 168)
Texas, 116–17, 118, 140, 169, 202, 205, 206; antiabortion activism in, 140, 185, 186, 202, 205, 213
Thalidomide, 9, 66–67
"Therapeutic" abortion, 7–8, 9, 26, 27, 33, 35, 40, 43, 64, 65, 66, 133, 168
Thompson, Robert, 41, 81, 176
Thornburgh v. American College of Obstetricians and Gynecologists, 12
Tietze, Christopher, 101
Tiller, George, 196, 208, 212, 215, 217, 276 (n. 97), 281 (n. 74)
Trewhella, Matt, 216
Turner, Donna, 142
Turner, Morris, 41, 81–82, 176–77

Ultrasound, 128, 220, 221; antiabortion activism and, 142, 144–45; fetal age and, 36–37, 123, 124; images, 14, 142, 144–45, 209
U.S. Catholic Conference, 85
U.S. House and Senate Judiciary Committee, 235–36
U.S. House Judiciary Subcommittee on the Constitution, 229–30
U.S. House Subcommittee on Crime and Criminal Justice, 212–13
U.S. Supreme Court, 208, 209, 283 (n. 98); abortion law and, 10–13, 23, 170, 247–48, 249; fetal viability and, 11, 12–13, 86, 131, 247; intact dilation and evacuation (D&E) abortion and, 19–20, 238, 242, 243; medical privacy and, 8, 251 (n. 3); second trimester abortions and, 124–25. See also *Roe v. Wade*
United States v. Vuitch, 10
University of Iowa Hospital, 39, 57
University of North Carolina (UNC)

Memorial Hospital, 1, 2, 7–8, 28, 40, 55, 124, 233, 252 (n. 13), 301 (n. 152)
University of Pittsburgh, 65, 83
University of Tennessee, 95
University of Washington, 66, 67
Utah Women's Health Center, 203

Vacuum aspiration abortion, 24, 28, 30, 39, 102, 112, 121–22, 145, 148–49, 245, 257 (nn. 16, 18), 258 (n. 34); anti-abortion activism and, 72, 141, 142, 145, 148–49, 241; introduction of, 24, 27–29, 32–33, 42, 45; medical complications and, 28, 30, 141, 164, 258 (n. 34), 282 (n. 85); training, 28, 136–37, 141, 142
Vojta, M., 27
Vuitch, Milan, 10

Walters, LeRoy, 85, 88
Washington, D.C., 10, 35, 38, 41, 64, 139, 207, 259 (n. 42), 280 (n. 70)
Washington, D.C., Preterm Clinic, 10, 40, 93, 94, 176–77, 179, 206, 260 (n. 70)
Washington Hospital Center, 125
Water Tower Reproductive Clinic (Chicago), 111, 113
Watts, Tammy, 226
Webster v. Reproductive Health Services, 12–13, 247
Weslin, Norman, 196, 197
Westberg, Jenny, 221, 222, 224, 225

Whipple, Beverly, 175, 179, 289 (n. 102)
White supremacists, 214–15
Wicklund, Susan, 22, 199–201, 202, 210, 211, 212, 218, 239, 249, 295 (n. 28), 296 (n. 51)
Widdicombe, Judith, 97, 98, 100, 111, 121, 125–26, 180, 189–90
Wilke, Barbara, 72–75, 80, 89, 140, 144
Wilke, Jack, 72–75, 80, 89, 140, 144
Williams, Paul, 56
Williams' Obstetrics, 82
Willowbrook State School for the Retarded, 71
Winter, Dick, 41–42, 57, 102–3, 262 (n. 116)
Wisconsin, 171, 199, 216, 295 (n. 28)
Women Exploited by Abortion (WEBA), 142, 143, 146–50, 205, 238, 239
Women's Awareness Clinic, Fort Lauderdale, 170
Women's Health Care Services (Wichita), 208
Women's Health Services (Pittsburgh), 40–41
Wyden, Ron, 208

Yacknowitz, Joseph, 42–43, 52
Yacknowitz, Stuart, 42–43, 52
Yakima, Wash., 174, 175, 179, 288 (n. 73), 289–90 (n. 103)
Yard, Molly, 139

Nancy M. P. King, Gail E. Henderson, and Jane Stein, eds., *Beyond Regulations: Ethics in Human Subjects Research* (1999).

Laurie Zoloth, *Health Care and the Ethics of Encounter: A Jewish Discussion of Social Justice* (1999).

Susan M. Reverby, ed., *Tuskegee's Truths: Rethinking the Tuskegee Syphilis Study* (2000).

Beatrix Hoffman, *The Wages of Sickness: The Politics of Health Insurance in Progressive America* (2000).

Margarete Sandelowski, *Devices and Desires: Gender, Technology, and American Nursing* (2000).

Keith Wailoo, *Dying in the City of the Blues: Sickle Cell Anemia and the Politics of Race and Health* (2001).

Judith Andre, *Bioethics as Practice* (2002).

Chris Feudtner, *Bittersweet: Diabetes, Insulin, and the Transformation of Illness* (2003).

Ann Folwell Stanford, *Bodies in a Broken World: Women Novelists of Color and the Politics of Medicine* (2003).

Lawrence O. Gostin, *The AIDS Pandemic: Complacency, Injustice, and Unfulfilled Expectations* (2004).

Arthur A. Daemmrich, *Pharmacopolitics: Drug Regulation in the United States and Germany* (2004).

Carl Elliott and Tod Chambers, eds., *Prozac as a Way of Life* (2004).

Steven M. Stowe, *Doctoring the South: Southern Physicians and Everyday Medicine in the Mid-Nineteenth Century* (2004).

Arleen Marcia Tuchman, *Science Has No Sex: The Life of Marie Zakrzewska, M.D.* (2006).

Michael H. Cohen, *Healing at the Borderland of Medicine and Religion* (2006).

Keith Wailoo, Julie Livingston, and Peter Guarnaccia, eds., *A Death Retold: Jesica Santillan, the Bungled Transplant, and Paradoxes of Medical Citizenship* (2006).

Michelle T. Moran, *Colonizing Leprosy: Imperialism and the Politics of Public Health in the United States* (2007).

Karey Harwood, *The Infertility Treadmill: Feminist Ethics, Personal Choice, and the Use of Reproductive Technologies* (2007).

Carla Bittel, *Mary Putnam Jacobi and the Politics of Medicine in Nineteenth-Century America* (2009).

Samuel Kelton Roberts Jr., *Infectious Fear: Politics, Disease, and the Health Effects of Segregation* (2009).

Lois Shepherd, *If That Ever Happens to Me: Making Life and Death Decisions after Terri Schiavo* (2009).

Mical Raz, *What's Wrong with the Poor?: Psychiatry, Race, and the War on Poverty* (2013).

Johanna Schoen, *Abortion after* Roe (2015).